T0211852

Lecture Notes in Computer Science 13365

Founding Editors

Gerhard Goos
Karlsruhe Institute of Technology, Karlsruhe, Germany

Juris Hartmanis
Cornell University, Ithaca, NY, USA

Editorial Board Members

Elisa Bertino
Purdue University, West Lafayette, IN, USA

Wen Gao
Peking University, Beijing, China

Bernhard Steffen
TU Dortmund University, Dortmund, Germany

Moti Yung
Columbia University, New York, NY, USA

More information about this series at https://link.springer.com/bookseries/558

Patrizia Scandurra · Matthias Galster ·
Raffaela Mirandola · Danny Weyns (Eds.)

Software Architecture

15th European Conference, ECSA 2021
Tracks and Workshops; Växjö, Sweden, September 13–17, 2021
Revised Selected Papers

 Springer

Editors
Patrizia Scandurra
Università di Bergamo
Dalmine, Italy

Raffaela Mirandola
Politecnico di Milano
Milan, Italy

Matthias Galster
University of Canterbury
Christchurch, New Zealand

Danny Weyns
KU Leuven
Kortrijk, Belgium

Linnaeus University
Växjö, Sweden

ISSN 0302-9743 ISSN 1611-3349 (electronic)
Lecture Notes in Computer Science
ISBN 978-3-031-15115-6 ISBN 978-3-031-15116-3 (eBook)
https://doi.org/10.1007/978-3-031-15116-3

© The Editor(s) (if applicable) and The Author(s), under exclusive license
to Springer Nature Switzerland AG 2022
This work is subject to copyright. All rights are reserved by the Publisher, whether the whole or part of the material is concerned, specifically the rights of translation, reprinting, reuse of illustrations, recitation, broadcasting, reproduction on microfilms or in any other physical way, and transmission or information storage and retrieval, electronic adaptation, computer software, or by similar or dissimilar methodology now known or hereafter developed.
The use of general descriptive names, registered names, trademarks, service marks, etc. in this publication does not imply, even in the absence of a specific statement, that such names are exempt from the relevant protective laws and regulations and therefore free for general use.
The publisher, the authors, and the editors are safe to assume that the advice and information in this book are believed to be true and accurate at the date of publication. Neither the publisher nor the authors or the editors give a warranty, expressed or implied, with respect to the material contained herein or for any errors or omissions that may have been made. The publisher remains neutral with regard to jurisdictional claims in published maps and institutional affiliations.

This Springer imprint is published by the registered company Springer Nature Switzerland AG
The registered company address is: Gewerbestrasse 11, 6330 Cham, Switzerland

Preface

The European Conference on Software Architecture (ECSA) is the premier European conference that provides researchers and practitioners with a platform to present and discuss the most recent, innovative, and significant findings and experiences in the field of software architecture research and practice. Due to the ongoing COVID-19 pandemic, ECSA 2021 was held virtually during September 13–17, 2021, with participating researchers and practitioners from all over the world. Accepted contributions for the main research track are included in the conference proceedings, published in this Springer Lecture Notes in Computer Science volume.

In addition to the main research track, ECSA 2021 included an industry track, a Diversity, Equity and Inclusion track (DE&I), a doctoral symposium, a tools and demonstrations track, and a tutorials track. ECSA 2021 also offered six workshops on diverse topics related to the software architecture discipline:

- The 8th Workshop on Software Architecture Erosion and Architectural Consistency (SAEroCon)
- The 1st International Workshop on Software Architecture and Machine Learning (SAML)
- The 4th International Workshop on Context-aware, Autonomous and Smart Architecture (CASA)
- The 5th Workshop on Formal Approaches for Advanced Computing Systems (FAACS)
- The 2nd International Workshop on Model-Driven Engineering for Software Architecture (MDE4SA), and
- The 1st International Workshop on Mining Software Repositories for Software Architecture (MSR4SA).

This volume contains a selection of revised and extended contributions from all these satellite events of ECSA 2021. We received 17 submissions, as revised and extended versions, from a list of 23 nominated and invited articles, out of which the Program Committee accepted 15 papers for publication. Each submission was reviewed by at least three referees. We used the EasyChair conference system for managing the submission and review process.

We are grateful to the members of the Program Committee of all these tracks and the additional reviewers that helped review the revised and extended versions of papers.

We acknowledge the prompt and professional support from Springer who published these proceedings in electronic volumes as part of the Lecture Notes in Computer Science series. Finally, we would like to thank the authors of all these submissions for their contributions.

June 2022

Patrizia Scandurra
Matthias Galster
Raffaela Mirandola
Danny Weyns

Organization

General Co-chairs

Raffaela Mirandola   Politecnico di Milano, Milano, Italy
Danny Weyns   KU Leuven, Belgium, and Linnaeus University, Sweden

Workshop and Tutorial Co-chairs

Patrizia Scandurra   University of Bergamo, Italy
Matthias Galster   University of Canterbury, New Zealand

Program Committee

Michel Albonico   VU Amsterdam, The Netherlands
Aldeida Aleti   Monash University, Australia
Vasilios Andrikopoulos   University of Groningen, The Netherlands
Paolo Arcaini   National Institute of Informatics, Japan
Kousar Aslam   Vrije University Amsterdam, The Netherlands
Ajay Bandi   Northwest Missouri State University, USA
Georg Buchgeher   Software Competence Center Hagenberg, Austria
Tomas Bures   Charles University in Prague, Czech Republic
Mauro Caporuscio   Linnaeus University, Sweden
Jan Carlson   Mälardalen University, Sweden
Michel Chaudron   Eindhoven University of Technology, The Netherlands
Federico Ciccozzi   Mälardalen University, Sweden
Martina De Sanctis   Gran Sasso Science Institute, Italy
Liliana Dobrica   Politehnica University of Bucharest, Romania
Darko Durisic   Volvo Car Corporation, Sweden
Cédric Eichler   INSA Centre Val de Loire, France
Daniel Feitosa   University of Groningen, The Netherlands
Predrag Filipovikj   Scania Group, Sweden
Mariagrazia Fugini   Politecnico di Milano, Italy
Andrei Furda   Queensland University of Technology, Australia
Ilias Gerostathopoulos   Vrije Universiteit Amsterdam, The Netherlands
Fabian Gilson   University of Canterbury, New Zealand
Helena Holmström Olsson   University of Malmo, Sweden

Christoph Knieke	TU Clausthal, Germany
Heiko Koziolek	ABB Corporate Research, Germany
Stefan Kugele	Technische Hochschule Ingolstadt, Germany
Grace Lewis	Carnegie Mellon University, USA
Peng Liang	Wuhan University, China
Claudio Menghi	McMaster University, Canada
Henry Muccini	University of L'Aquila, Italy
Tobias Olsson	Linnaeus University, Sweden
Jennifer Pérez	Universidad Politécnica de Madrid, Spain
Claudia Raibulet	University of Milano-Bicocca, Italy
Marjan Sirjani	Malardalen University, Sweden
Carlos Solís	Amazon, Mexico
Catia Trubiani	Gran Sasso Science Institute, Italy
Karthik Vaidhyanathan	University of L'Aquila, Italy
Ramon Salvador Vallès	Universitat Politècnica de Catalunya, Spain
Roberto Verdecchia	Vrije Universiteit Amsterdam, The Netherlands
Thierry Villemur	LAAS-CNRS, France
Thomas Vogel	Humboldt University Berlin, Germany

Contents

Tutorial Track

Industry Track

Serving Hybrid-Cloud SQL Interactive Queries at Twitter

Chunxu Tang[(✉)], Beinan Wang, Huijun Wu, Zhenzhao Wang, Yao Li,
Vrushali Channapattan, Zhenxiao Luo, Ruchin Kabra, Mainak Ghosh,
Nikhil Kantibhai Navadiya, Prachi Mishra, Prateek Mukhedkar,
and Anneliese Lu

Twitter, Inc., San Francisco, USA
{chunxut,beinanw,huijunw,zhenzhaow,yaoli,vrushali,zluo,rkabra,
mghosh,nnavadiya,prachim,pmukhedkar,anneliesel}@twitter.com

Abstract. The demand for data analytics has been consistently increasing in the past years at Twitter. In order to fulfill the requirements and provide a highly scalable and available query experience, a large-scale in-house SQL system is heavily relied on. Recently, we evolved the SQL system into a hybrid-cloud SQL federation system, compliant with Twitter's Partly Cloudy strategy. The hybrid-cloud SQL federation system is capable of processing queries across Twitter's data centers and the public cloud, interacting with around 10PB of data per day.

In this paper, the design of the hybrid-cloud SQL federation system is presented, which consists of query, cluster, and storage federations. We identify challenges in a modern SQL system and demonstrate how our system addresses them with some important design decisions. We also conduct qualitative examinations and summarize instructive lessons learned from the development and operation of such a SQL system.

Keywords: SQL · Cloud · Query engine · Big data

1 Introduction

Twitter runs multiple large Hadoop clusters of over 300PB of data, which are among the biggest in the world [10]. Billions of events are ingested into these clusters per minute [47]. Twitter's data platform operates these clusters and exerts significant effort in pursuing system scalability and availability to fulfill the data analytics on such large volume data inventory and high throughput data flow. Data customers send tens of thousand queries for data analytics on this huge amount of data daily, usually in SQL statements.

At Twitter, a typical OLAP (Online Analytical Processing) workload mainly contains ad-hoc queries, empowering a wide range of use cases from internal tooling reporting to ads click-rate analysis. The query latencies range from seconds to minutes. There are various query types observed. As Fig. 1 indicates, *SELECT* statements dominate the distribution of SQL statements in a typical

© The Author(s), under exclusive license to Springer Nature Switzerland AG 2022
P. Scandurra et al. (Eds.): ECSA Tracks and Workshops 2021, LNCS 13365, pp. 3–21, 2022.
https://doi.org/10.1007/978-3-031-15116-3_1

Twitter's OLAP workload. Users leverage this type of SQL statements to query various datasets stored in the persistent storage. Besides *SELECT* statements, a typical Twitter's OLAP workload also contains *CREATE* statements to create temporary tables or material views, *UPDATE* statements to update records in temporary tables[1], and *OTHER* statements mainly for metadata querying.

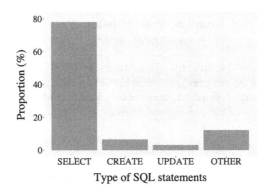

Fig. 1. Distribution of SQL statements from a typical Twitter's OLAP workload in a three-month session.

Such a SQL system needs to be capable of processing a large number of queries in parallel. Previously, we implemented an in-house SQL system in Twitter's data center (aka private cloud) with hundreds of worker nodes, accompanied by internal Twitter services such as monitoring and logging. At present, to enjoy benefits at a global scale such as faster capacity provisioning, a broader ecosystem of tools and services in the cloud, and enhanced disaster recovery capabilities, Twitter engineering is embarking on an effort to migrate ad-hoc clusters to the GCP (Google Cloud Platform), aka the "Partly Cloudy" [34]. Partly Cloudy extends Twitter's environment into the public cloud, as a first-class offering alongside on-premises platform services. Under the umbrella of Partly Cloudy, multiple large-scale data analytics jobs or systems [27,39,49,50] have been migrated to or supported in the cloud.

The hybrid-cloud environment brings challenges, leading to a fundamental architectural shift for an OLAP system. From our development and operational experience, a modern unified SQL system should handle a series of challenges:

- **Querying heterogeneous data sources in the application layer.** With the growth of the business, more use cases emerged at Twitter, leading to querying heterogeneous data sources, usually processed by different on-premises or cloud query systems with different configurations and interfaces.

---

[1] At Twitter, SQL system users cannot create or update datasets except exclusive temporary tables under personal accounts. Due to the requirements for data lineage and governance, only data pipeline system accounts have write access to public datasets. SQL individual users only have read access.

For example, data scientists from the Health team query data stored in HDFS (Hadoop Distributed File System), processed by HDFS-compatible SQL engines such as Hive [42], SparkSQL [13], and Presto [36], to analyze hate speech in the social media platform. Data engineers from the Ads team query data stored in GCS (Google Cloud Storage), processed by cloud query engines such as Presto on GCP, to validate engagement logging data existence and correctness of data schemas. Infrastructure engineers from the Tooling team gain insights from the usage data stored and processed in MySQL and create shareable dashboards. Use cases may also involve querying and joining tables from various data sources. A modern SQL system should support querying heterogeneous data sources in a unified interface.

– **Horizontal scaling in the computation layer.** We have witnessed a boost in the number of daily queries processed by Twitter's SQL system in the recent few years. From our operational experience, vertical scaling cannot handle this large number of analytical queries, which can cost a considerable amount of resources[2]. A modern SQL system usually prefers the horizontal scaling approach to serve analytical queries [37]. In addition, as an on-premises data center usually has a limited capacity, the horizontal scaling may need to cross data centers or on-premises/cloud environments. As a result, the SQL system needs to tackle the challenges brought by horizontal scaling, such as cluster orchestration, workload balancing, and fault tolerance.

– **Heterogeneous storage systems in the storage layer.** With the advent of the Big Data era, large-scale storage systems are developed to fulfill the requirements of archiving the scaling volume of data while also maintaining data availability and consistency. The variety of on-premises and cloud data storage systems also poses challenges for a modern SQL system. Operating heterogeneous storage systems is a major challenge we have faced in developing and operating Twitter's SQL system. In a modern SQL system, no matter where the dataset is stored: on-premises storage clusters and/or cloud storage systems, query engines should access the dataset through a unified interface without memorizing the concrete physical paths of target datasets.

To overcome these challenges, Twitter engineering teams implement a hybrid-cloud SQL federation system, which processes around 10PB of data daily in production. This paper presents the evolution of the SQL system at Twitter including query federation, cluster federation, and storage federation. It extends our prior work [41] from multiple perspectives. First of all, we analyze a typical Twitter's OLAP workload, whose query distribution indicates the technical design direction for the SQL federation system. Second, we discuss the rationales behind some design choices in detail such as adopting Zeppelin and Presto for query federation. Third, we explain the unified cluster provisioning strategy with some practical examples, supporting the SQL system deployment across on-premises and cloud environments. Fourth, as a SQL federation system spans

---

[2] From an analysis of a typical Twitter OLAP workload in three months, 19.2% of queries consume more than 1 TB peak memory.

a wide range of components, we discuss related work from more perspectives such as data integration and virtualization. Finally, we report some key findings during the development and operation of such a SQL system: Ad-hoc resource-consuming queries are a challenge for scaling a SQL federation system; A centralized hybrid-cloud IAM (Identity and Access Management) can help reduce the technical complexity of implementing IAM across the public and private cloud.

The remainder of this paper is organized as follows. We describe the architectural design and implementation of the hybrid-cloud SQL federation system in Sect. 2 to address the aforementioned challenges, discuss related work in Sect. 3, and reflect on lessons learned in a diverse set of contexts in Sect. 4. Section 5 concludes the paper.

2 SQL Federation System Design and Implementation

2.1 Overview

Figure 2 depicts the architectural design of the hybrid-cloud SQL federation system at Twitter. There are three components: query federation, cluster federation, and storage federation. Each federation provides a unified logical view that hides the internal implementation details. This enhances system flexibility and resilience because as long as the logical interface is consistent, any changes in a specific component will cause minimal implementation changes in other federation components.

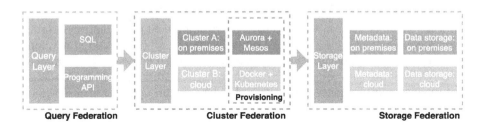

Fig. 2. Overview of the hybrid-cloud SQL federation system in three layers.

Query Federation. This exposes a unified query layer to customers such that one interface rules multiple query clusters for heterogeneous data sources. Query federation consists of a SQL component and a programming API component. At Twitter, the SQL component supports basic ANSI SQL semantics as well as some Twitter-specific features implemented into UDFs (user-defined functions). The programming API component enables auxiliary flexible programming features. User requests are eventually converted to SQL and passed to the cluster federation.

Cluster Federation. This provides a unified cluster layer to the query federation, resolving the challenge of horizontal scaling. It exposes a single entry point, a router service, and hides the cluster details, which reduces the development and operation cost. The router service acts as the coordinator of SQL engine clusters, helping to schedule queries across the clusters and balancing the workloads among the clusters. Fault tolerance is also improved by forwarding requests only to available clusters when a cluster fails and is offline.

Storage Federation. This offers a unified view of datasets stored in different archival systems. At Twitter, we are heavily leveraging HDFS as the major on-premises distributed storage platform. In a cloud environment like GCP, we use GCS as the core storage system. The unified layer provides a unique Twitter resolved path for each dataset stored in both on-premises and cloud, entirely getting rid of the burden of memorizing accurate physical locations for datasets.

2.2   Query Federation

The query federation fulfills three goals. First, as a user-facing front-end, it converts user inputs to SQL and feeds SQL to the cluster federation. Second, it defines datasets in SQL such that users can locate data from different sources with a uniform approach. Third, it provides UI for interaction and visualization. We leverage Zeppelin [4] to implement the first and third goals, while the second goal is achieved with the help of Presto in the cluster federation. Apache Zeppelin is a web-based notebook service that enables interactive data analytics. Users can fetch data results by sending SQL queries in paragraphs and easily visualize the results with multiple built-in charts or third-party libraries supported by a pluggable framework called Helium [7]. It should be noted that the SQL front-end design is not limited to Zeppelin, but can be generalized to other notebook tools such as JupyterLab [8].

Figure 3 illustrates some SQL examples of query federation in a Zeppelin notebook. In the figure, the first query and the second one are pointing to the on-premises and cloud SQL clusters respectively, identified by a prefix to flag whether the query should be processed in Twitter's data center or public cloud. No extra configuration is required. Besides explicitly setting dataset locations with prefixes, we are also implementing an automatic data recognition feature by parsing the received SQL statement, extracting target queried tables, and fetching table locality information from Twitter's unified data access layer [23]. If the dataset is located in the HDFS, the query will be sent to the on-premises SQL engine cluster; if the dataset resides in the cloud, the query will be forwarded to the cloud cluster; if the dataset locates in both HDFS and GCS, we prefer to process the query in the cloud due to more compute resources.

Besides accessing data within one data source, the third SQL statement in Fig. 3 refers to a federated query, joining two tables from HDFS and MySQL. A federated query can refer to joining tables scattered in various data sources. Thus, a query processing engine that can access various data sources should be adopted in the SQL federation system. We adopted Presto for this scenario due to several reasons. First of all, Presto separates compute and storage which allows flexible storage, fitting Twitter's scenario where hundreds of petabytes of

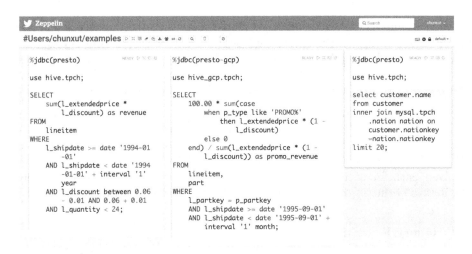

Fig. 3. Three SQL query federation examples in a Zeppelin notebook. All SQL statements are from the TPC-H benchmark [9].

data has been stored in HDFS, so it is extremely challenging to migrate data to another storage. Second, Presto is a distributed SQL query engine targeting "SQL on everything". With a Connector API communicating with external data stores, data is fetched and then converted to the unified internal Presto data types, so that further query processing, such as joining tables from different data sources, can be accomplished. Lastly, Presto supports interactive queries whose latencies range from seconds to minutes and exposes a web service endpoint, differentiating it from some other query engines such as Hive and Spark which process SQL queries as batch jobs.

2.3 Cluster Federation

Architectural Design. Figure 4 depicts the architectural design of cluster federation with the following components:

Router. The router service is the single entry point and the core of the cluster federation, which exposes a unified interface to the query tools, hides cluster details, and routes requests to concrete clusters. Meanwhile, it helps to balance the workloads among the clusters. Our prior SQL system suffered from imbalanced workloads as the clusters were exposed directly to clients. Some clients may send too many queries to a specific cluster, exhausting the compute resources of that cluster, but leaving other clusters idle. The hybrid-cloud SQL federation system harnesses multiple routing algorithms such as round-robin and random selection. We are also testing more complicated load-based scheduling algorithms with the help of a query cost predictor.

We separate SQL engine cluster endpoint information to a central storage, making the router service stateless. As a result, we can easily scale the service

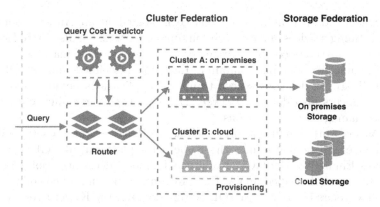

Fig. 4. Architectural design of the cluster federation.

horizontally by deploying multiple router instances. These instances share the same router endpoint and hide proxy details from users. We utilize scheduling algorithms such as the random choice to balance the load on these instances. Even when an instance fails, other router instances can still route requests to SQL engine clusters. This automatic service discovery and recovery improve the availability and avoids the single point of failure on the router.

Query Cost Predictor. This is a preditor service to forecast the CPU and memory resource usages of each SQL query. It applies machine learning techniques to train models learning from historical SQL queries. The predictor details are beyond the scope of this paper and discussed in a separate paper [40].

SQL Engine Cluster. Presto is the query engine utilized in a SQL engine cluster. Each Presto cluster consists of a coordinator node and one or more worker nodes. A SQL engine cluster may be deployed in Twitter's data center or cloud. When it is deployed in Twitter's data center, it queries data stored in on-premises services such as HDFS. By contrast, when it is in the GCP, it queries data stored in the GCS. The SQL engine clusters do not query data across data centers due to performance concerns.

With the cluster federation, users only view logical clusters. When a cluster fails and is offline, the router will remove it from the available cluster list and will not route any requests to this cluster. When the cluster recovers from the failure and is back online, the router will find the cluster through service discovery, mark it as available, and route requests to this cluster. This also improves the availability and fault tolerance, mitigating the operation pain we have faced in the prior SQL system with separate clusters.

Cluster Provisioning. In a hybrid-cloud environment, a service can be deployed in both the private cloud and public cloud. This poses challenges in the product release and deployment as we have to operate two suites of toolchains.

In Twitter's data centers, each service is hosted in an Aurora container, enabling running services and cron jobs on top of Mesos [22], a distributed system kernel. Mesos abstracts compute resources away from specific machines to treat the data center like one big computer. Each job is defined and described in Aurora DSL [1]. As developers need to upload applications before deployment, Twitter engineers also develop *Packer* [21], a package versioning and storage system, to manage the applications.

By contrast, in a cloud platform such as GCP, we wrap each service into a Docker image and deploy it into the Kubernetes platform, aka GKE (Google Kubernetes Engine) in the GCP. Kubernetes offers a declarative job specification, which can be described in YAML. For example, the simplified code snippet shown below refers to creating a SQL system demo in the Kubernetes.

```
1    apiVersion: compute.twitter.com/v1
2    kind: TwitterSetDeployment
3    metadata:
4      namespace: sqlsystem
5      name: sqlsystem-devel
6    spec:
7      replicas: 1
8      template:
9        metadata:
10         spec:
11           priorityClassName: preemptible
12           containers:
13           - name: sqlsystem
14             image: sqlsystem
15             imagePullPolicy: Always
16             command:
17             - /bin/bash
18             - -c
19             args:
20             - /usr/lib/jvm/java-1.8.0-twitter/bin/java -jar sqlsystem.jar -instance=—mesos.instance""
                 ↪   -admin.port=fl:8080fl
21             resources:
22               limits:
23                 cpu: 1000m
24                 memory: 2Gi
25                 ephemeral-storage: 2Gi
26               ports:
27               - containerPort: 8080
28                 name: http
29               - containerPort: 8080
30                 name: service
```

To fill the gaps between the two cluster provisioning strategies and resolve the challenges of provisioning in a hybrid-cloud environment, Twitter engineers implement an abstraction layer on top of Mesos and Kubernetes, only exposing the Aurora DSL to describe jobs deployed in both private and public cloud.

The following is a simplified example of describing the above GCP job in Aurora DSL, where each key-value pair in YAML is translated into Aurora DSL:

```
1    resources = Resources(cpu = 1.0, ram = 2 * GB, disk = 2 * GB)
2    port=fl8080fl
3    jobs = [
4      BasicTwitterSet(
5        cluster = flcluster1fl,
6        role = flsqlsystemfl,
7        environment = fldevelfl,
8        name = flsqlsystemfl,
9        requires = [Announcer()],
10       replicas = 1,
11       spec = PodSpec(
12         priorityClassName=flpreemptiblefl,
13         containers = [
14           KubernetesContainer(
15             name=flsqlsystemfl,
16             image=flsqlsystemfl,
17             command=JVMProcess(
18               name = flrun˙sqlsystemfl,
19               jvm = Java8,
20               arguments = fl-jar sqlsystem.jar -instance=—mesos.instance”” -admin.port=":%s"fl % port,
21               resources=resources
22             ),
23             resources = resources,
24             ports = [
25               ContainerPort(name = [flhttpfl, flservicefl], containerPort = port),]
26           )]
27         ),
28       )
29    ]
```

This unified job configuration abstraction greatly reduces the operation cost. We only devise one suite of toolchains but with different configuration details for Twitter's data center and public cloud.

Fig. 5. Unified UI for cluster federation.

Unified Interface. To ease the administration of SQL engine clusters, we build an aggregated UI, shown in Fig. 5, on top of the original Presto UI. The UI aggregates the status of all SQL engine clusters, sums the running queries, and monitors the active workers. Moreover, we can dive deeper into one specific cluster to investigate the performance metrics, collected into a unified dashboard shown in Fig. 6. This panel visualizes metrics, including query failures, cluster memory, running queries, etc., collected in the past two weeks.

2.4   Storage Federation

To fulfill both scaling data and high availability requirements, Twitter engineers maintain storage clusters in both Twitter's data center and public cloud. Figure 7 depicts the high-level design of the storage federation platform, which is backed by hundreds of thousands of data replication jobs. This platform contains an unified view for data stored in on-premises HDFS clusters and a cloud storage system (GCS in the GCP).

On-Premises HDFS. Twitter's data platform operates multiple HDFS clusters across data centers, shown as the left part in Fig. 7. Multiple namespaces are also required due to scalability and use case isolation requirements. We scale HDFS by federating these namespaces with user-friendly paths instead of long complicated URIs [14]. As shown in Fig. 7, first, the original on-premises data path is *hdfs://cluster-X-nn:8020/logs/partly-cloudy* (*nn* refers to the namenode in HDFS), indicating the data resides in Cluster X in Data Center 1, under the namespace *logs*. Second, we leverage Hadoop ViewFs [6] to provide a single view across namespaces, starting with *viewfs://*. So the original path will become *viewfs://cluster-X/logs/partly-cloudy*. Finally, we extend the ViewFs and implement Twitter's View FileSystem, offering a unified user-friendly path (*/DataCenter-1/cluster-X/logs/partly-cloudy* in Fig. 7) and enabling native HDFS access. A replicator service is also created to help access data stored in different locations.

Cloud Storage (GCS). Because of the large data volume and use case isolation, we maintain thousands of GCS buckets at Twitter. We also leverage the View FileSystem abstraction to hide GCS details behind the storage interface. The cloud storage connector is utilized to interact with GCS via Hadoop APIs. We apply the RegEx-based path resolution to resolve the GCS bucket path, by dynamically creating mountable mapping on-demand in Twitter's View FileSystem. As shown in Fig. 7, similar to HDFS, the GCS bucket *gs://logs.partly-cloudy* is finally resolved as */gcs/logs/partly-cloudy.*

As a result, the storage federation only exposes standard unique paths of datasets, no matter they reside in the on-premises HDFS clusters or GCS. In addition, Twitter engineers maintain a metadata service, connected with these storage systems, aiming to identify the closest location of the target dataset and return its standard path to query engines. For example, in Fig. 7, querying the same *partly-cloudy* dataset, if the query engine is in a Twitter's data center, the on-premises path */DataCenter-1/cluster-X/logs/partly-cloudy* will be returned. By contrast, if the query engine is in the cloud, the cloud path */gcs/logs/partly-cloudy* will be returned.

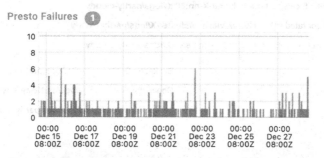

(a) SQL query failures in two weeks.

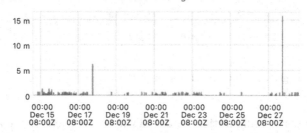

(b) The 5 minutes moving average of execution time P90 (90th percentile) in two weeks.

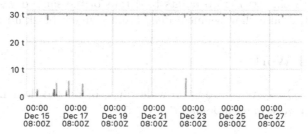

(c) Cluster memory usages in two weeks.

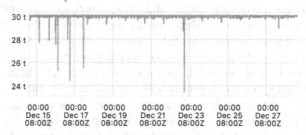

(d) SQL engine memory pool in two weeks.

Fig. 6. Monitoring and alerting of one SQL engine (Presto) cluster.

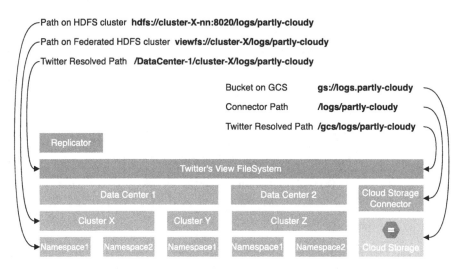

Fig. 7. Architectural design of the storage federation.

To view dataset configuration details, Twitter engineers create a unified UI, shown in Fig. 8, with segment support for files stored in various physical locations. Users can thus view different locations for the same dataset. Specifically, Fig. 8a illustrates details of the query log dataset of Presto stored in an on-premises HDFS cluster; Fig. 8b points to details of the same dataset stored in the GCS. Figures also show segment delays and segment block information.

3   Related Work

A large-scale SQL system involves a wide range of related domains. Here, we discuss related work in each domain.

3.1   Data Integration and Virtualization

Data integration involves aggregating data from heterogeneous data stores and in different formats to realize analytics on a huge amount of data. This is usually tackled by either transforming the data to a consistent data format and physically placing data in a data warehouse, or creating a virtualized middleware and offering a unified logical view of datasets, namely data virtualization.

Recently, thanks to advantages such as high scaling capability and on-the-fly processing [32], some research work emerged in the data virtualization domain, supporting ad-hoc queries on heterogeneous data stores. For example, Lawrence [25] proposed a generic standards-based architecture on top of both SQL and NoSQL systems, verified by MySQL and MongoDB. The virtualization system translates SQL queries into source-specific APIs, with minimal performance overhead reported. The author [26] later extended this work to support distributed

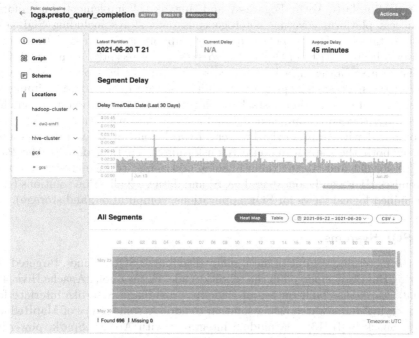

(a) Details of a dataset in on-premises HDFS.

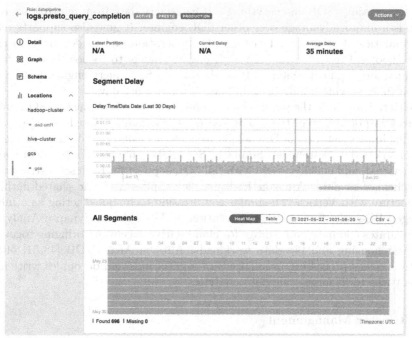

(b) Details of a dataset in GCS.

Fig. 8. Unified UI for datasets stored in HDFS and GCS.

semi-joins. Similarly, Vathy-Fogarassy and Hugyák [44] implemented a uniform data access platform covering heterogeneous data stores including SQL and NoSQL databases. Their solution does not support joins across data sources but only collects data from these data sources. More recently, Mami et al. [29] established a semantic data lake to access and process heterogeneous data at scale. Aleyasen et al. [12] proposed a context-aware query router, aiming to address the data replication obstacle in on-premises to cloud migration, similar to the router service we implemented in Twitter's data platform.

Compared with prior work, Twitter's hybrid-cloud SQL federation system relies on both the data warehouse (transforming analytical data to the Parquet [19] format and storing them in some centralized storage clusters such as on-premises HDFS and cloud-based GCS) and data virtualization solutions (creating unified logical views for SQL applications, computation, and storage).

3.2 SQL Systems

With the increasing volume of data, many distributed SQL engines, targeted for analyzing Big Data, emerged in the recent decade. For example, Apache Hive [42] is a data warehouse built on top of Hadoop, providing a SQL-like interface for data querying and a warehousing solution to address some issues of MapReduce [17,18]. Spark SQL [13] is a module integrated with Apache Spark, powering relational processing to Spark data structures, with a highly extensible optimizer, Catalyst. Presto [36], originally developed by Facebook, is a distributed SQL engine, targeting "SQL on everything". It can query data from multiple sources which is a major advantage over other SQL engines. It now also supports real-time analytics at scale [28]. Twitter's SQL federation system described in this paper chooses Presto as the core SQL engine thanks to its low latency, high flexibility, and high extensibility. Procella [15] is a SQL query engine, facilitated by YouTube, serving hundreds of billions of queries per day.

With the advent of the public cloud, some cloud-based commercial SQL products rose in popularity in the recent decade. For example, Google BigQuery [5] (a public implementation of Dremel [30,31]) offers a cloud-based, fully-managed, and serverless data warehouse. Similarly, Snowflake [16] provides a multi-tenant, transactional, and elastic system with full SQL support for both semi-structured and schema-less data. Amazon Redshift [20] applies a classic shared-nothing architecture with Vertica [24]-similar compression techniques, acting as a fully-managed PB-scale data warehouse solution in AWS. Azure Synapse Analytics [11] separates compute and storage for cloud-native execution, bringing together data warehousing and big data workloads. Alibaba AnalyticDB [48,51] offers real-time query processing in hundreds of milliseconds and decouples write and access paths to fit large-scale data analytics.

3.3 Cluster Management

The need for efficient cluster management has led to the creation of various systems in the past decade. YARN [45] is the resource management system used in

Hadoop, abstracting cluster management from computation jobs. Google developed a large-scale unified cluster management system, Borg [43,46], running hundreds of thousands of jobs. It is later open-sourced as Kubernetes. Google also created Omega [35], an offspring of Borg to improve the software engineering. Mesos [22] is a similar resource-sharing platform, used with Aurora configuration Language [1] at Twitter. Facebook established Twine [38], formerly known as Tupperware, to act as a large-scale resource-sharing infrastructure. As Twitter engineering is migrating some service to the GCP, we use both Mesos and Kubernetes for cluster deployment and management.

4   Lessons Learned

In this section, we recount some of the qualitative lessons we have learned from the development and operation of the SQL federation system at Twitter.

System monitoring and logging in a hybrid-cloud environment are vital. Although our hybrid-cloud SQL federation system almost always works well, sometimes when the system goes wrong, it can be a headache to locate the root cause. We also observed architectural differences between on-premises and cloud environments, such as cluster provisioning and security enforcement. An important design decision we have made is implementing a real-time monitoring system with metrics collection and an injectable logging system to trace execution flows. The monitoring system provides a central platform to collect predefined and user-customized metrics, serves observability dashboards/alerts, and helps developers drill down to detailed metrics. Meanwhile, the injectable logging system provides APIs to inject logging points into application source code, collects the logs, and visualizes the execution flows.

The on-premises capacity planning experience cannot be directly transferred to a hybrid-cloud environment. During the migration of parts of on-premises workload to the cloud, we discovered that the capacity planning experience cannot be easily reused and shared across data centers, due to varied technical stacks and resource provisioning strategies. For example, one of our early migrated use cases requires around 50 machines in Twitter's data center but needs around 60 to get comparable performance in the cloud, even though all these machines are sharing similar hardware configuration. Based on the lesson, we suggest additional prototypes for capacity planning and extra tuning of service in a hybrid-cloud environment.

Ad-hoc resource-consuming queries are a challenge for scaling a SQL federation system. In Twitter's data platform, we observed that more than 70% of interactive SQL queries can be completed in less than 1 min. But there is a small proportion (around 10%) of queries that cost lots of compute resources and can cost as long as a few hours to complete. This fact poses challenges in scaling our SQL system, as resource-consuming queries can rapidly exhaust a SQL engine cluster's compute resources. Furthermore, clusters across data centers with different configurations complicate the optimization. We have tried establishing a specific cluster for these resource-consuming queries, implemented multiple scheduling algorithms in the router, and are testing more complicated algorithms with forecasted query resource usages. This also implies a future research direction about more intelligent scheduling on SQL queries with high-variant resource usages across clusters under a hybrid-cloud environment.

A centralized hybrid-cloud IAM (Identity and Access Management) can help reduce the technical complexity of implementing IAM across the public and private cloud. Identity and access management is a crucial component of an enterprise-grade platform including a SQL system. IAM aims to grant the right individuals access to appropriate services. At Twitter, the on-premises SQL system utilizes LDAP (Lightweight Directory Access Protocol) and Kerberos for authorization and authentication. By contrast, GCP dramatically leverages access tokens from OAuth 2.0 for managing identity and access. During the migration, the first solution we raised is to modify codebases of all service components to support GCP IAM. However, later on, we figured out this approach would cost much more complexity in the implementation than expected as we need to explicitly support both LDAP and GSuite logins and management. Given the extreme emphasis on data privacy and security at Twitter, we finally came up with a hybrid-cloud IAM solution with a centralized IAM platform, mapping all Twitter employee LDAP accounts to GSuite accounts with corresponding credentials implicitly, hidden from end-users. This design saved us quarters of engineering effort to set up the IAM in the hybrid-cloud SQL system.

SQL is still one of the most widely used languages in data analytics. As a declarative language, SQL lets users focus on defining the data analytics tasks without worrying about the specifics on how to complete these tasks. Thanks to SQL's high expressiveness in queries and large existing customer bases, some execution engines previously without SQL support, such as Druid [3] and Beam [2], began to support SQL on top of their native query layers. In addition, some SQL variants, such as BigQuery ML [33], even introduced SQL into machine learning use cases. From our observation, SQL is still widely used in data analytics, although challenged by some competitive alternatives such as Python. Python is more like a powerful supplement for SQL in data analytics with its concise styles and extreme popularity in machine learning, instead of a complete replacement.

5 Conclusion

Understanding and identifying challenges faced within a modern SQL system are of ever-growing importance as there is a rapidly growing need for large-scale data analytics. From our development and operational experience at Twitter's data platform, we presented querying heterogeneous data sources in the application layer, horizontal scaling in the computation layer, and heterogeneous storage systems in the storage layers are three crucial challenges in a modern centralized SQL platform, focusing on interactive queries whose latencies range from seconds to minutes. We discussed the evolution of the hybrid-cloud SQL federation system in Twitter's data platform, aiming to address these challenges.

The demonstrated hybrid-cloud SQL federation system overcomes these challenges by implementing query federation, cluster federation, and storage federation, with a unified logical view in each layer.

We discussed some lessons we learned from developing, deploying, and operating the SQL system. We found some differences such as capacity planning and IAM in on-premises and cloud environments, which usually lead to extra engineering effort. Additionally, from the observation on tens of millions of interactive queries at Twitter, most queries can be completed in less than 1 min, but around 10% of queries can cost many more compute resources to complete. We saw the necessity of various solutions, such as load balancing and cluster scaling, to tackle the challenge. Finally, we observed that SQL is still one of the most widely used languages in data analytics. It has even been extended to the machine learning domain. We hope these key findings could provide some deeper insights for building a large-scale interactive query platform.

Acknowledgment. Twitter's SQL federation system is a complicated project that has evolved for years. We would like to express our gratitude to everyone who has served on Twitter's Interactive Query team, including former team members Hao Luo, Yaliang Wang, Da Cheng, Fred Dai, and Maosong Fu. We also appreciate Prateek Mukhedkar, Vrushali Channapattan, Daniel Lipkin, Derek Lyon, Srikanth Thiagarajan, Jeremy Zogg, and Sudhir Srinivas for their strategic vision, direction, and support to the team. Finally, we thank Erica Hessel, Alex Angarita Rosales, and the anonymous ECSA reviewers for their informative comments, which considerably improved our paper.

References

1. Aurora configuration (2017). http://aurora.apache.org/documentation/latest/reference/configuration-tutorial/
2. Apache Beam SQL (2021). https://beam.apache.org/documentation/dsls/sql/overview/
3. Apache Druid SQL (2021). https://druid.apache.org/docs/latest/querying/sql.html
4. Apache Zeppelin (2021). https://zeppelin.apache.org/
5. Google BigQuery (2021). https://cloud.google.com/bigquery
6. Hadoop ViewFs (2021). https://hadoop.apache.org/docs/stable/hadoop-project-dist/hadoop-hdfs/ViewFs.html
7. Helium packages (2021). https://zeppelin.apache.org/helium_packages.html
8. Jupyter project (2021). https://jupyter.org/
9. TPC-H benchmark (2021). http://www.tpc.org/tpch/
10. Agrawal, P.: A new collaboration with Google Cloud (2018). https://blog.twitter.com/engineering/en_us/topics/infrastructure/2018/a-new-collaboration-with-google-cloud.html
11. Aguilar-Saborit, J., et al.: POLARIS: the distributed SQL engine in azure synapse. Proc. VLDB Endow. **13**(12), 3204–3216 (2020)
12. Aleyasen, A., Soliman, M.A., Antova, L., Waas, F.M., Winslett, M.: High-throughput adaptive data virtualization via context-aware query routing. In: 2018 IEEE International Conference on Big Data (Big Data), pp. 1709–1718. IEEE (2018)

13. Armbrust, M., et al.: Spark SQL: relational data processing in Spark. In: Proceedings of the 2015 ACM SIGMOD International Conference on Management of Data, pp. 1383–1394 (2015)
14. Barga, R.: Hadoop filesystem at Twitter (2015). https://blog.twitter.com/engineering/en_us/a/2015/hadoop-filesystem-at-twitter
15. Chattopadhyay, B., et al.: Procella: unifying serving and analytical data at YouTube. Proc. VLDB Endow. **12**(12), 2022–2034 (2019)
16. Dageville, B., et al.: The snowflake elastic data warehouse. In: Proceedings of the 2016 International Conference on Management of Data, pp. 215–226 (2016)
17. Dean, J., Ghemawat, S.: MapReduce: simplified data processing on large clusters. Commun. ACM **51**(1), 107–113 (2008)
18. Dean, J., Ghemawat, S.: MapReduce: a flexible data processing tool. Commun. ACM **53**(1), 72–77 (2010)
19. Dem, J.L.: Graduating apache parquet (2015). https://blog.twitter.com/engineering/en_us/a/2015/graduating-apache-parquet.html
20. Gupta, A., et al.: Amazon redshift and the case for simpler data warehouses. In: Proceedings of the 2015 ACM SIGMOD International Conference on Management of Data, pp. 1917–1923 (2015)
21. Hashemi, M.: The infrastructure behind Twitter: efficiency and optimization (2016). https://blog.twitter.com/engineering/en_us/topics/infrastructure/2016/the-infrastructure-behind-twitter-efficiency-and-optimization
22. Hindman, B., et al.: Mesos: a platform for fine-grained resource sharing in the data center. In: NSDI, vol. 11, p. 22 (2011)
23. Krishnan, S.: Discovery and consumption of analytics data at Twitter (2016). https://blog.twitter.com/engineering/en_us/topics/insights/2016/discovery-and-consumption-of-analytics-data-at-twitter.html
24. Lamb, A., et al.: The vertica analytic database: C-store 7 years later. Proc. VLDB Endow. **5**(12), 1790–1801 (2012)
25. Lawrence, R.: Integration and virtualization of relational SQL and NoSQL systems including MySQL and MongoDB. In: 2014 International Conference on Computational Science and Computational Intelligence, vol. 1, pp. 285–290. IEEE (2014)
26. Lawrence, R.: Faster querying for database integration and virtualization with distributed semi-joins. In: 2017 International Conference on Computational Science and Computational Intelligence (CSCI), pp. 1406–1410. IEEE (2017)
27. Li, Y., et al.: A performance evaluation of spark graphframes for fast and scalable graph analytics at Twitter. In: 2021 IEEE International Conference on Big Data (Big Data), pp. 5959–5959. IEEE (2021)
28. Luo, Z., et al.: From batch processing to real time analytics: running presto at scale. In: 2022 IEEE 38th International Conference on Data Engineering (ICDE). IEEE (2022) (in press)
29. Mami, M.N., Graux, D., Scerri, S., Jabeen, H., Auer, S., Lehmann, J.: Uniform access to multiform data lakes using semantic technologies. In: Proceedings of the 21st International Conference on Information Integration and Web-Based Applications & Services, pp. 313–322 (2019)
30. Melnik, S., et al.: Dremel: interactive analysis of web-scale datasets. Proc. VLDB Endow. **3**(1–2), 330–339 (2010)
31. Melnik, S., et al.: Dremel: a decade of interactive SQL analysis at web scale. Proc. VLDB Endow. **13**(12), 3461–3472 (2020)
32. Mousa, A.H., Shiratuddin, N.: Data warehouse and data virtualization comparative study. In: 2015 International Conference on Developments of E-Systems Engineering (DeSE), pp. 369–372. IEEE (2015)

33. Mucchetti, M.: BigQuery ML. In: Mucchetti, M. (ed.) BigQuery for Data Ware-housing, pp. 419–468. Springer, Berkeley (2020). https://doi.org/10.1007/978-1-4842-6186-6_19

34. Rottinghuis, J.: Partly Cloudy: the start of a journey into the cloud (2019). https://blog.twitter.com/engineering/en_us/topics/infrastructure/2019/the-start-of-a-journey-into-the-cloud.html

35. Schwarzkopf, M., Konwinski, A., Abd-El-Malek, M., Wilkes, J.: Omega: flexible, scalable schedulers for large compute clusters. In: Proceedings of the 8th ACM European Conference on Computer Systems, pp. 351–364 (2013)

36. Sethi, R., et al.: Presto: SQL on everything. In: 2019 IEEE 35th International Conference on Data Engineering (ICDE), pp. 1802–1813. IEEE (2019)

37. Tan, J., et al.: Choosing a cloud DBMS: architectures and tradeoffs. Proc. VLDB Endow. **12**(12), 2170–2182 (2019)

38. Tang, C., et al.: Twine: a unified cluster management system for shared infrastructure. In: 14th USENIX Symposium on Operating Systems Design and Implementation (OSDI 2020), pp. 787–803 (2020)

39. Tang, C., et al.: Taming hybrid-cloud fast and scalable graph analytics at Twitter. arXiv preprint arXiv:2204.11338 (2022)

40. Tang, C., et al.: Forecasting SQL query cost at Twitter. In: 2021 IEEE International Conference on Cloud Engineering (IC2E), pp. 154–160. IEEE (2021)

41. Tang, C., et al.: Hybrid-cloud SQL federation system at Twitter. In: ECSA (Companion) (2021)

42. Thusoo, A., et al.: Hive: a warehousing solution over a map-reduce framework. Proc. VLDB Endow. **2**(2), 1626–1629 (2009)

43. Tirmazi, M., et al.: Borg: the next generation. In: Proceedings of the Fifteenth European Conference on Computer Systems, pp. 1–14 (2020)

44. Vathy-Fogarassy, Á., Hugyák, T.: Uniform data access platform for SQL and NoSQL database systems. Inf. Syst. **69**, 93–105 (2017)

45. Vavilapalli, V.K., et al.: Apache Hadoop YARN: yet another resource negotiator. In: Proceedings of the 4th Annual Symposium on Cloud Computing, pp. 1–16 (2013)

46. Verma, A., Pedrosa, L., Korupolu, M., Oppenheimer, D., Tune, E., Wilkes, J.: Large-scale cluster management at Google with Borg. In: Proceedings of the Tenth European Conference on Computer Systems, pp. 1–17 (2015)

47. VijayaRenu, L., Wang, Z., Rottinghuis, J.: Scaling event aggregation at Twitter to handle billions of events per minute. In: 2020 IEEE Infrastructure Conference, pp. 1–4. IEEE (2020)

48. Wei, C., et al.: AnalyticDB-V: a hybrid analytical engine towards query fusion for structured and unstructured data. Proc. VLDB Endow. **13**(12), 3152–3165 (2020)

49. Wu, H., et al.: Migrate on-premises real-time data analytics jobs into the cloud. In: 2021 IEEE 8th International Conference on Data Science and Advanced Analytics (DSAA), pp. 1–2. IEEE (2021)

50. Wu, H., et al.: Move real-time data analytics to the cloud: a case study on heron to dataflow migration. In: 2021 IEEE International Conference on Big Data (Big Data), pp. 2064–2067. IEEE (2021)

51. Zhan, C., et al.: AnalyticDB: real-time OLAP database system at Alibaba cloud. Proc. VLDB Endow. **12**(12), 2059–2070 (2019)

Blended Graphical and Textual Modelling of UML-RT State-Machines: An Industrial Experience

Malvina Latifaj[1]([ORCID]), Federico Ciccozzi[1]([ORCID]), Muhammad Waseem Anwar[1]([ORCID]), and Mattias Mohlin[2]

[1] Mälardalen University, Västerås, Sweden
{malvina.latifaj,federico.ciccozzi,muhammad.waseem.anwar}@mdh.se
[2] HCL Technologies, Malmö, Sweden
mattias.mohlin@hcl.com

Abstract. The ever increasing complexity of modern software systems requires engineers to constantly raise the level of abstraction at which they operate to suppress the excessive complex details of real systems and develop efficient architectures. Model Driven Engineering has emerged as a paradigm that enables not only abstraction but also automation. UML, an industry de-facto standard for modelling software systems, has established itself as a diagram-based modelling language. However, focusing on only one specific notation limits human communication and the pool of available engineering tools. The results of our prior experiments support this claim and promote the seamless use of multiple notations to develop and manipulate models. In this paper we detail our efforts on the provision of a fully blended (i.e., graphical and textual) modelling environment for UML-RT state-machines in an industrial context. We report on the definition of a textual syntax and advanced textual editing for UML-RT state-machines as well as the provision of synchronization mechanisms between graphical and textual editors.

Keywords: UML-RT · HCL RTist · Xtext · QVTo · Model transformation · Model synchronization · Blended modelling

1 Introduction

The complexity of software systems has been growing at an unbelievable pace for decades now. Relying merely on human efforts to develop high-quality software is presently regarded as a futile attempt. It can be argued that in the face of this complexity, without an efficient and effective architecture, software is inscrutable [8]. To tackle the architectural complexity of software development, Model Driven Engineering (MDE) has emerged as a software engineering paradigm that focuses on raising the level of abstraction when architecting software systems [2,19]. This is done by promoting modelling languages and models, which are closer to human understanding, instead of code, closer to machines,

© The Author(s), under exclusive license to Springer Nature Switzerland AG 2022
P. Scandurra et al. (Eds.): ECSA Tracks and Workshops 2021, LNCS 13365, pp. 22–44, 2022.
https://doi.org/10.1007/978-3-031-15116-3_2

as core architectural and engineering artefacts. This approach imposes limits to the problem-domain, facilitates the identification of relevant abstractions, and avoids superfluousness. Together with that, MDE pledges automation by exploiting modelling technologies that among others, enable the generation of fully fledged code from architectural models.

Domain-specific abstractions facilitating the architectural description of software systems are defined using formal specifications expressed in Domain Specific Modeling Languages (DSMLs), which capture the core aspects of a domain, thus promoting productivity, efficiency and comprehensibility of domain-specific problems.

UML is the most used architecture description language in industry [13], the de-facto modelling standard in industry [9], and an ISO/IEC (19505-1:2012) standard. It is general-purpose, but it provides powerful profiling mechanisms to constrain and extend the language to achieve UML-based DSMLS, called UML profiles; in this paper, we focus on the UML real-time profile (UML-RT) [18], as this is the profile implemented in the commercial tool HCL RTist[1] of our industrial partner. We also leverage an open-source implementation of it provided in the Eclipse Papyrus-RT[2] tool.

1.1   Problem, Motivation, and the RTist Case

Domain-specific modelling tools, like RTist, traditionally focus on one specific editing notation (such as text, diagrams, tables or forms). This limits human communication, especially across stakeholders with varying roles and expertise. Moreover, architects and engineers may have different notation preferences; not supporting multiple notations negatively affects their throughput. Besides the limits on communication, choosing one particular kind of notation has the drawback of limiting the pool of available tools to develop and manipulate models that may be needed. For example, choosing a graphical representation limits the usability of text manipulation tools such as text-based diff/merge, which is essential for team collaboration. When tools provide support for both graphical and textual modelling, it is mostly done in a mutual exclusive manner. Most off-the-shelf UML modelling tools, such as IBM Rational Software Architect[3] or Sparx Systems Enterprise Architect[4], focus on graphical editing features and do not allow seamless graphical–textual editing. This mutual exclusion suffices the needs of developing small-scale applications with only very few stakeholder types. RTist is not an exception. It provides support for modelling UML-RT architectures and applications based on graphical *composite structure diagrams*, to model structure, and *state-machine diagrams*, to model behavior. In addition, the implementation of UML-RT in RTist provides support for leveraging C/C++ action code for the description of fine-grained, algorithmic, behaviors within

---

[1] https://www.hcltechsw.com/rtist.

[2] https://www.eclipse.org/papyrus-rt/.

[3] http://www-03.ibm.com/software/products/en/ratsadesigner/.

[4] https://sparxsystems.com/.

graphical state-machines. That is needed to enable the definition of full-fledged UML-RT models from which executable code can be automatically generated. While providing means to model graphical entities and "program" algorithmic behaviours textually, the two are disjoint, since the modelling of UML-RT is graphical only and the textual C/C++ is injected in graphical models as a "foreign" entity and with almost no overlapping with graphical model elements. The aim is instead to achieve a modelling tool that is able to make different stakeholders to work on overlapping parts of the models using different modelling notations (e.g., graphical and textual) in an automated manner.

1.2 Paper Contribution

In this paper we describe our proposed solution for providing a fully blended graphical-textual modelling environment for UML-RT state-machines in an industrial setting. Our experiments in a previous study with blended graphical-textual modelling showed that the seamless use of different notations can significantly boost the architecting of software using UML profiles [1]. The results of those experiments together with the exposed wish of RTist customers of being able to design software via multiple notations led us to initiate this work towards an automated support for blended modelling of UML-RT in RTist. In a prior work [11], we describe the effort of designing, implementing and integrating a textual notation for UML-RT state machines in RTist. In this paper, we extend that work, and address the problem formulated in the previous section by providing the following additional research contributions.

C1. Definition of a textual editor for UML-RT state-machines with advanced formatting features including systematic support for hidden regions which group hidden tokens (e.g., comments, whitespaces) between two semantic tokens.

C2. Provision of synchronization mechanism between textual and graphical notations to achieve a seamless blended modelling environment and validation of the solution.

1.3 Paper Outline

The remainder of the paper is organized as follows. In Sect. 2 we describe the concept of blended modelling and in Sect. 3 we detail the design of our proposed solution. The implementation details of the solution are presented in Sect. 4, whereas the validation is discussed in Sect. 5. The related works are detailed in Sect. 6 and the paper is concluded in Sect. 7 with a brief summary and an overview of the current and upcoming enhancements to the overall blended modelling approach.

2   Blended Modelling: What and Why

We have previously defined the notion of *blended modelling* [4] as:

the activity of interacting seamlessly with a single model (i.e., abstract syntax) through multiple notations (i.e., concrete syntaxes), allowing a certain degree of temporary inconsistencies.

A seamless blended modelling environment, which allows stakeholders to freely choose and switch between graphical and textual notations, can greatly contribute to increase productivity as well as decrease costs and time to market. Such an environment is expected to support at least graphical and textual modelling notations in parallel as well as properly manage synchronisation to ensure consistency among the two. The possibility to visualise and edit the same information through a set of diverse perspectives always in sync has the potential to greatly boost communication between stakeholders, who can freely select their preferred notation or switch from one to the other at any time. Besides obvious notation-specific benefits, such as for instance, the possibility to edit textual models in any textual editor outside the modelling environment, a blended framework would disclose the following overall benefits.

Flexible Separation of Concerns and Better Communication. Providing graphical and textual modelling editors for different aspects and sub-parts (even overlapping) of a DSML like UML-RT enables the definition of concern-specific architectural views characterised by either graphical or textual modelling (or both). These views can interact with each other and are tailored to the needs of their intended stakeholders. Due to the multi-domain nature of modern software systems (e.g., cyber-physical systems, Internet-of-Things), this represents a necessary feature to allow different domain experts to describe specific parts of a system using their own domain-specific vocabulary and notation, in a so called *multi-view modelling* [3] fashion. The same information can then be rendered and visualised through other notations in other perspectives to maximise understanding and boost communication between experts from different domains as well as other stakeholders in the development process.

Faster Modelling Activities. We have experimented with blended modelling of UML profiles [1] and the seamless combination of graphical and textual modelling has shown a decreased modelling effort in terms of time thanks to the following two factors:

1. Any stakeholder can choose the notation that better fits his/her needs, personal preference, or the purpose of the current modelling task, at *any time*. For instance, while structural model details can be faster to describe by using diagrammatic notations, complex algorithmic model behaviours are usually easier and faster to describe using textual notations (e.g., Java-like action languages).
2. Text-based editing operations on graphical models[5], such as copy&paste and regex search&replace, syntax highlighting, code completion, quick fixes, cross referencing, recovery of corrupted artefacts, text-based diff and merge for

---

[5] Please note that by *graphical/textual model*, we intend a model rendered using a graphical/textual notation.

versioning and configuration, are just few of the features offered by modern textual editors. These would correspond to very complex operations if performed through graphical editors; thereby, most of them are currently not available for diagrams. Seamless blended modelling would enable the use of these features on graphically-described models through their textual editing view. These would dramatically simplify complex model changes; an example could be restructuring of a hierarchical state-machine by moving the insides of a hierarchical state. This is a demanding re-modelling task in terms of time and effort if done at graphical level, but it becomes a matter of a few clicks (copy&paste) if done at textual level.

3   Design Solution

In this section, we detail the solution design, illustrated in Fig. 1, for the provision of a blended modelling environment for UML-RT state-machines. Note that in order to maximise accessibility to our solution, we describe the solution for an open-source tool, Eclipse Papyrus-RT, which is orthogonal to the one in RTist (which also is Eclipse EMF-based).

The starting point is the already existing Ecore-based DSML formalizing the UML-RT profile (i.e., MM_G), which is utilized to instantiate graphical models (i.e., M_G) in both Papyrus-RT and RTist. Using this DSML as blueprint, we define a textual language (i.e., MM_T) in Xtext[6] that will be used to instantiate textual models (i.e., M_T) of UML-RT state-machines. Moreover, using Xtext's formatting APIs, we also customize the textual editor to preserve essential textual information, such as lines, formatting and hidden regions like comments. This provides our first contribution **C1**. Subsequently, we design and implement the synchronization mechanisms between the two notations by model-to-model (M2M) transformations [16]. These transformations are defined on the basis of implicit mappings between metaelements of the source and target metamodels and implemented in terms of the operational version of the Query/View/Transformation language (QVTo[7]) in Eclipse. QVTo supports only unidirectional transformations, thus, to achieve bidirectionality, we defined two unidirectional transformations; MM_T2MM_G, where the source metamodel is MM_T and target metamodel is MM_G, and MM_G2MM_T, where the source metamodel is MM_G and the target metamodel is MM_T. Both model transformations are horizontal as the source and target model reside in the same abstraction level, and exogenous as the models are expressed in different modelling languages. This makes for our second contribution **C2**. Further details on the definition of the textual syntax and synchronization mechanisms can be found in Sect. 3.1 and 3.2. The implementation details are included in Sect. 4, and the validation of the solution is detailed in Sect. 5.

---

[6] https://www.eclipse.org/Xtext/.
[7] https://wiki.eclipse.org/QVTo.

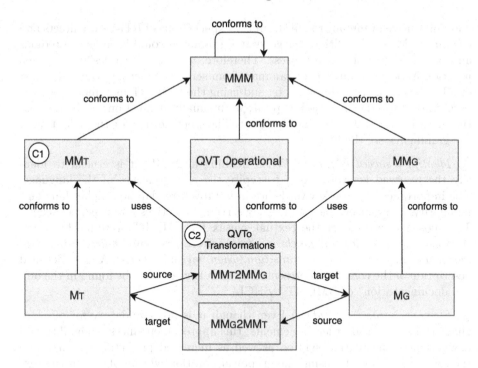

Fig. 1. Synchronization solution design

3.1   Textual Notation for UML-RT State-Machines

Textual Language Workbench. To complement the existing graphical editor in RTist with a textual notation and editor, a suitable language workbench
needs to be carefully selected. HCL RTist and Papyrus-RT are Eclipse-based
environments that leverage the Eclipse Modeling Framework (EMF)[8] as back-
bone. Thereby, by choosing an EMF-based language workbench, we could leverage EMF as a common data layer. For this reason, we chose Xtext, a framework
for the development of textual DSMLs, based on EBNF grammars. The textual editor supports an outline view, syntax highlighting, error checking, quick-
fix proposals, and many other features provided by Xtext. Furthermore, Xtext
provides code completion for keywords and cross-references by increasing the
usability of the language and decreasing the learning curve.

Textual Notation Definition. Our goal was to introduce a textual notation
(and related editor) to the already existing UML-RT profile supported by RTist.
A possible alternative was to use the underlying metamodel consumed by the
RTist's graphical editor as an input for Xtext to automatically generate a textual
editor. However, although easy to implement, this solution generates erroneous

---

[8] https://www.eclipse.org/modeling/emf/.

and unintuitive grammar, too far from the expectations of RTist's architects and customers. Manually editing this generated grammar would have been a tedious and potentially error-prone process. Therefore, we decided to design a textual notation in terms of an Xtext grammar, from scratch. Starting from a wish-list of RTist's customers and architects, and using the UML-RT metamodel portion describing state-machines as blueprint, we manually defined our UML-RT textual notation for state-machines in Xtext. The steps needed for the definition of the grammar were the following.

① *Identify reserved keywords:* When defining a DSML, it is crucial to identify the reserved keywords used to typify the core concepts of the language. The importance of these keywords lies in improved readability, higher language familiarity, and efficient parsing as they serve as directives for specific concepts. The chosen keywords for the textual syntax for UML-RT state-machines are the following: *capsule, statemachine, state, initial, junction, choice, entry, exit, entrypoint, exitpoint, history, transition, when, on* and *inherits.* A more detailed description of the concepts represented by each keyword can be found in the official documentation[9] of UML-RT by HCL.

② *Elements' ordering strategy:* Even though it is not mandatory for our language to have a fixed order of elements, this approach enhances readability and navigation of the textual syntax, as well as increased predictability on where the elements created by using the graphical notation will be placed in the textual syntax. Our grammar is based on the vertical distance approach where elements that affect each other's understandability and are closely related [14], are grouped together and have a low vertical distance. Furthermore, being that this grammar prohibits cross-references before element declaration, we take the aforementioned statement into consideration and make sure that elements that need to be cross-referenced will be declared before the cross-reference occurs.

③ *A spoonful of syntactic sugar:* The majority of programming languages, including C++, which is used as action code for behavioral state-machines, makes use of statement terminators in the form of semi-colons. Being that one of the main goals when introducing this textual syntax is for developers to use it jointly with the C++ action code, we introduced consistent use of semi-colons for indicating statement termination to make the grammar more conforming to C++ and to increase readability. For the same readability reasons and developers' preferences, we also introduce colons after transition names. Furthermore, to make the grammar more compact, we allow the declaration of multiple objects of the same type in one single line of code. Due to the combination of the textual syntax with action code, we need to handle C++ code blocks so we can "isolate" them and make them distinguishable from the rest of the grammar. For this reason, we include back-ticks in order to enclose code snippets and to make the lexer aware of where the code block begins and ends.

---

[9] https://rtist.hcldoc.com/help/topic/com.ibm.xtools.rsarte.webdoc/pdf/RTist%20C oncepts.pdf.

The overall goal during this process was to keep a fixed concrete syntax while simultaneously enhancing the abstract syntax, even though frequently we had to trade-off between ease of expression in the concrete syntax and extra complexity in the abstract syntax.

Enforcing UML-RT's Modularity. Scoping in Xtext is concerned with the visibility of elements; therefore, the scope provider computation returns the target candidates that are visible in the current context and by a given reference. In order to enforce the UML-RT's modularity, it is necessary to specify a custom scope provider. The default behavior of Xtext allows establishing a cross-reference to all the elements of a particular type that are located inside the same Eclipse resource (i.e., project). By customizing the scope provider, we restrict this behaviour, and only allow cross-references for elements declared in the same model file. The rationale behind this decision lies in the fact that multiple model files containing different capsules can be located inside the same resource, and a particular capsule should not be able to cross-reference the elements of other capsules. However, a key concept in which UML-RT relies on to reuse and extend parts of existing state-machines is the inheritance mechanism. When capsule A inherits capsule B, the state-machine of capsule A implicitly inherits the state-machine of capsule B. Therefore, to support inheritance, we need to customize the scope provider so that it allows cross-references for elements not only from the capsule itself, but also from the inherited capsule, in case there is one. Another default behavior of Xtext consists in allowing cross-references for all elements of a particular type declared in the same model file, regardless of their level of nesting. This contradicts an important UML-RT concept; compound transitions. Since transitions in UML-RT state-machines can not cross state boundaries, the concept of compound transitions is applied, consisting of multiple segments that are connected by means of pseudo-states. However, with the default behaviour of Xtext, a transition can cross state boundaries. Therefore, the scope provider is customized to restrict that and provide the desired behavior in conformance with UML-RT concepts by allowing transitions to only cross-reference pseudo states and states that are on the same level of nesting as the transition, or their immediate entry and exit points.

Advanced Textual Editing Features. The aforementioned steps provide a solid platform for developing a sophisticated editor for the specification of textual state-machines. Besides the editing features provided out-of-the-box by Xtext for textual languages, we incorporated formatting features like text indentation and syntax highlighting in the textual editor to simplify the specification of these textual models. Furthermore, the support to associate both single and multiline comments within textual specifications is provided too.

3.2   Synchronization Transformations

Model Transformation Language. For model transformations, we chose QVTo, which is an implementation of the Operational Mapping Language defined by Object Management Group's (OMG's) Meta-Object Facility (MOF) 2.0 Query/ View/Transformation (QVT[10]). The reasons behind this choice were first of all the fact that QVT is a MOF standard, and since our focus is on MOF languages, a transformation language also based on MOF is preferred. In addition, QVTo brings together benefits from both declarative and imperative QVT and it is very well-suited for both exogenous and endogenous transformations, also in-place.

Transformation Structure. The transformations are executed in Eclipse QVTo, the only actively maintained QVTo implementation, adhering to its default structure composed of the modeltype declarations, the transformation declaration, main function and mapping operations. In the following, we detail the QVTo structure.

- *Modeltype declaration*: The modeltype declaration in QVTo serves as a reference to the metamodels that will be used for the transformation. When declaring the modeltype, it is obligatory to define the name and reference. The latter can be specified either by using the package `nsURI` or file location `URI`. In our use case, we reference the metamodels via the `nsURI` which is resolved via the global package registry in the running platform instance. Optionally, the modeltype definition can include the conformance kind (i.e., strict or effective) and a set of constraint expressions (i.e., OCL expressions). In our case we do not define the conformance kind, thus by default it assumes an effective conformance. The rationale behind this decision is to allow the transformations to be applied to similar metamodels. Moreover, we do not define any constraint expressions as we have no additional restrictions over the set of the involved models. As an example, the modeltype definition that references MM_T, is detailed in the following.

> **modeltype** MM_T **uses** $MM_T\_Package\_Name$ $(MM_T\_Package\_nsURI)$

- *Transformation declaration*: The transformation declaration defines the name of the unidirectional transformation and specifies the involved metamodels. Additionally it details the direction kind of the transformation via the following values; `in`, `out`, and `inout`. As an example, the MM_T2MM_G transformation declaration has the following structure that details the name of the transformation, the involved metamodels, and the direction of the transformation.

> **transformation** MM_T2MM_G $(in\ source{:}MM_T,\ out\ target{:}MM_G)$;

- *Main function*: The main function is also referred to as the entry point of the transformation as it initiates the execution of the transformation by executing the operations defined in the body of the function. As an example,

---

[10] https://www.omg.org/spec/QVT/1.3/About-QVT/.

for the MM$_T$2MM$_G$ transformation, the defined operation selects the root metaelements (i.e., metaelements at the highest level) of MM$_T$, and filters out the **StateMachine** metaelement. Additionally, it invokes the **SM2SM()** "top-level" mapping rule that maps the **StateMachine** metaelement of MM$_T$ to the **StateMachine** metaelement of MM$_G$.

```
main() {
  src.rootObjects()[MMT::StateMachine] -> map SM2SM();
}
```

– *Mappings:* The transformations in QVTo are executed by means of mapping operations. Each mapping operation consists of a signature, an optional guard (i.e., *when* clause), a mapping body, and an optional post condition (i.e., *where* clause). The signature of the mapping operation minimally includes the following elements:

Mapping Type: A mapping operation can either be an abstract mapping or a concrete mapping (non-abstract). An abstract mapping operation is distinguished by the **abstract** keyword which indicates that the mapping can not be invoked in isolation. Such mapping operations are common when the target metaelement is abstract and are usually inherited by other mappings with concrete target types.

Metaelements: QVTo does not strictly require the fully qualified name of the metaelements that are to be mapped (i.e., metamodelName:: metaelementName), but in the presence of source and target metamodels that contain similar concepts, the fully qualified name is used to resolve possible ambiguities.

Mapping Name: Serves to identify the mapping and it is always unique.

As an example of a mapping signature, in the following we detail an abstract mapping between the concrete **State** metaelement of MM$_T$ and the abstract **State** metaelement of MM$_G$, where we use the fully qualified name to separate them from one another.

```
abstract mapping MMT::State::State2State() : MMG::State { ... }
```

Moreover, a mapping declaration can include mapping guards described with OCL expressions and distinguished by the **when** keyword. If the guard evaluates to true, it restricts the execution of the mapping operation only to a subset of elements; alternatively, the mapping operation is not invoked.

Finally, the body of the mapping operation is populated by assigning EReferences and EAttributes of the source metaelement to corresponding EReferences and EAttributes of the target metaelement. For EReferences, a type-dependent mapping operation is invoked by using the **map** keyword. When invoking the mapping on a single element, the element is followed by a dot which precedes the **map** keyword. Alternatively, when invoking the mapping on a collection of elements (i.e., Set, Bag, Sequence, or OrderedSet), the latter is followed by an arrow which precedes the **map** keyword. Moreover, the **self** and `result` variables, refer to the source and target metaelements, respectively. As an example, in the following we detail a regular mapping between `State` and `CompositeState` that is extended with a mapping condition.

---

mapping *MM_T::State::State2CMPState() : MM_G::CompositeState*
when {*not(self.states -> isEmpty() ...)*}
{
result.choicePoints := self.choice.map Choice2Choice();
result.name := self.name; }

To conclude the definition of the synchronization transformations, we detail two additional QVTo concepts that we used for this purpose: `inherits` and `disjuncts`. Inheritance enables the reuse of other mapping operations with the condition that the signature of the mapping which is inheriting must conform to the signature of the mapping that is being inherited. In short, the source and target metaelements of the inheriting mapping operation must either be the same or subtypes of the source and target metaelements of the inherited mapping, respectively. This feature allows for a more compact code and increased readability as the operations are defined once in the inherited mapping and reused in each inheriting mapping. In the following, we provide an example of these mapping operations. Mapping operation `State2SimpleState` inherits mapping operation `State2State`. The signatures are conformant as the source metaclasses are the same, while the target metaclass of the inheriting mapping (i.e., `State2SimpleState`), is a subtype of the output metaclass of the inherited mapping (i.e., `State2State`). By inheriting this mapping, in the `State2SimpleState` mapping operation, we do not need to rewrite what is already defined in the `State2State` mapping operation, as it is automatically invoked when the `State2SimpleState` mapping operation is executed.

---

mapping *MM_T::State::State2SimpleState() : MM_G::SimpleState*
inherits *MM_T::State::State2State { ... }*

Moreover, mapping operations can be defined as disjunctions of multiple other mappings, which are then extended with distinct guards. When invoking such operation, the guards of the mapping operation alternatives specified after the `disjuncts` keyword are sequentially checked. When the first guard evaluates to `true`, the corresponding mapping operation is invoked; alternatively if they all evaluate to `false` it returns `null`. The body of such mapping operations is always empty, because that part of the code is unreachable. This concept is primarily applied to operations transforming abstract types that are extended by multiple subtypes. In this case, the alternative mapping specified after the `disjunct` keyword, consists of subtypes of the original mapping.

> **mapping** *MM_T::State::StateDisjunct() : MM_G::State*
> **disjuncts** *MM_T::State::State2SimpleState,*
> *MM_T::State::State2CompositeState { }*

4   Implementation

In this section we present the implementation details of the proposed solution and show examples both of the textual syntax and model instances after applying the model transformations for synchronization.

4.1   Textual Language and Editor for UML-RT

Based on the aforementioned approach (see Sect. 3.1), in this section we detail the implementation specifics of the textual language and editor in Eclipse Xtext. We focus particularly on the customization of the scope provider in Xtext to enable inheritance and compound transitions in our textual UML-RT, as well as on the customization of the Xtext's formatter for advanced textual editing and formatting features.

Customization of the Scope Provider. Listing 1.1 provides a snippet of the customized scope provider in Xtext for supporting the concept of inheritance. The conditional `if` statement in Line 1 checks whether the current capsule inherits another capsule. If this condition evaluates to true, the `EObject` is down casted to a `Capsule` object in Line 3. Depending on the instance type of the context's container, the desired elements of the inherited capsule are added to the list of eligible candidates that the scope provider will return as detailed in Lines 4–6.

```
1  if (rootCapsule.getSuperclass() != null) {
2    parentinheritance = rootCapsule.getSuperclass();
3    Capsule inheritedCapsule = (Capsule) parentinheritance;
4    if (context.eContainer() instanceof StateMachine) {
5      transitionfrom.addAll(inheritedCapsule.getStatemachines().getStates());
6      ...
7    }
8  }
```

Listing 1.1. Inherited capsule scope provider

Listing 1.2 provides instead a snippet of the customized scope provider in Xtext for supporting the concept of compound transitions. The `eContainer()` method in Line 2 is used to return the containing object of the context object. The list of objects `T_F` in Line 3, is initialized to be used for storing all the eligible candidates that can be cross-referenced. The block of code to be executed if the specified condition of the `if` statement in Line 4 evaluates to true, down casts the `currentParent` EObject into a `StateMachine` object and uses the `addAll()` method to add all elements of a specific type that are contained in the state-machine as the context element, to the list.

```
1  else if (reference == HclScopingPackage.Literals.TRANSITION__FROM) {
2    EObject currentParent = context.eContainer();
3    List<EObject> T_F = new ArrayList<>();
4    if (currentParent instanceof StateMachine) {
5      StateMachine s = (StateMachine) currentParent;
6      T_F.addAll(s.getStates());
7      ....
8      for (State states : rootCapsule.getStatemachines().getStates()) {
9          transitionfrom.addAll(states.getEntrypoint());
10         transitionfrom.addAll(states.getExitpoint());
11     }
12   }
13 return Scopes.scopeFor(T_F, N_C, IScope.NULLSCOPE);
```

Listing 1.2. Compound transitions scope provider

Customization of the Textual Editor. Parsing and serialization are two major concepts in Xtext associated with the textual model and Abstract Syntax Tree (AST), respectively. The instance of a grammar in the editor, technically referred to as XtextResource, is represented through a textual model. The equivalent AST is generated from the textual model through the parser. On the other hand, the serializer converts the AST into the equivalent textual model. The conversions between textual model to AST and vice versa are very frequent and, therefore, Xtext supports the exploitation of built-in APIs to customize certain functionalities that may be required before or after the conversions from one to the other. We exploited the built-in APIs for customizing our textual editor.

The synchronizations targeted in our solution between the textual and graphical models lead to frequent changes in the AST related to the textual model, like deletion or addition of textual elements. In this case, the line numbers and other hidden region elements like comments need to be updated in the textual editor. Furthermore, the formatting of the text needs to be preserved in the textual editor after synchronizations since it brings along semantic information in most cases. To achieve this, we utilized Xtext's formatting infrastructure. In particular, we extended the **AbstractFormatter2** class to implement a customized state-machine formatter, composed of two core functions (i.e., *Lines* and *Hidden Regions*). The *Lines* function updates the sequence of lines in the textual editor according to the synchronized changes to the AST. *Hidden Regions* instead preserves the place of hidden regions that group all hidden tokens (e.g., whitespace, newlines, tabs and comments) between two semantic tokens upon changes to the AST.

4.2 Synchronization

Based on the aforementioned approach (see Sect. 3.2), in this section, we detail the implementation specifics of the synchronization model transformations in Eclipse QVTo. Synchronization mechanisms are provided in terms of two unidirectional M2M transformations; MM_T2MM_G and MM_G2MM_T. The majority of metaelements between the two metamodels require a one-to-one mapping, thus the mapping rules are rather straightforward. In the following, for each model transformation, we discuss the mapping operations that highlight a few interesting and less simple cases.

Textual to Graphical Synchonization – MM$_T$2MM$_G$

- The `StateMachine` metaelement behaves as a root element both in MM$_T$ and MM$_G$. Nevertheless, there is a notable difference between the two. In MM$_T$, `StateMachine` has multiple children and its containment of elements `State` has a zero-to-many (0..*) cardinality. Instead, in MM$_G$, `StateMachine` has a one-to-one (1..1) cardinality to `CompositeState`. In short, whilst in MM$_T$ `StateMachine` can contain many `States` as immediate children, in MM$_G$ the `StateMachine` can only contain one `CompositeState` as its immediate child, and in turn `CompositeState` would contain the other elements. Consequently, when transforming a `StateMachine` in MM$_T$ to a `StateMachine` in MM$_G$, two possible narratives need to be taken into account. First, if we consider a model instance of MM$_T$ (i.e., M$_T$) and the `StateMachine` of this model instance contains only one `State` and no other immediate children, `State` is transformed to a `CompositeState` in M$_G$ (i.e., model instance of MM$_G$) as detailed in Lines 4–5 in Listing 1.3. Otherwise, if the `StateMachine` in M$_T$ contains more than one immediate state, when transforming to a `StateMachine` in M$_G$, a `CompositeState` object is created (Lines 9–10) and the immediate children of the `StateMachine` in M$_T$ are assigned as immediate children (Line 11) of the `CompositeState` in M$_G$.

```
1  mapping text::StateMachine::SM2SM() : graph::StateMachine{
2  result.name:=self.name;
3
4  if (self.states -> size() = 1 and self.initialtransition -> isEmpty()
       and self.transition -> isEmpty() and self.junction -> isEmpty()
       and self.choice -> isEmpty()) {
5    result.top := self.states -> first().map State2CMPState();
6  }
7
8  else {
9    var cs := object graph::CompositeState{};
10   top :=cs;
11   cs.substates := self.states.map toState();
```

Listing 1.3. `StateMachine` to `StateMachine`

- With respect to states, MM$_T$ considers only the `State` metaclass, while MM$_G$ makes a distinction between `SimpleState` and `CompositeState`, which extend the `State` metaclass. Thus, when transforming a `State`, the mapping operations in Lines 1–9 in Listing 1.4 need to be extended with mapping guards that determine if the `State` metaclass will be transformed to a `SimpleState` or `CompositeState`. Moreover, an additional mapping operation is defined in Lines 13–14, which is a disjunction of the aforementioned mapping operations and is invoked in Line 10. Upon its execution, the guards of `State2SimpleState` and `State2CMPState` are checked in a sequential order. For a `State` to be transformed to a `SimpleState`, the `State` should have no children. To evaluate that we use the OCL expression `isEmpty()`, which evaluates whether the collection is empty or not, in Line 3. Alternatively, a `CompositeState` has children, thus in Line 8 we use the OCL expression `notEmpty()`.

```
1  mapping text::State::State2SimpleState() : graph:: SimpleState
2  inherits text::State::State2State
3  when {self.states -> isEmpty() and self.entrypoint -> isEmpty() and
         self.exitpoint -> isEmpty() and self.junction -> isEmpty() and
         self.choice -> isEmpty() }
4  {  }
5
6  mapping text::State::State2CMPState() : graph:: CompositeState
7  inherits text::State::State2State
8  when {self.states -> notEmpty() or self.entrypoint -> notEmpty() or
         self.exitpoint -> notEmpty() or self.junction -> notEmpty() or
         self.choice -> notEmpty()}
9  {
10 substates := self.states.map State2StateDisjunct();
11 ...
12 }
13 mapping text::State::State2StateDisjunct() : graph::State
14 disjuncts text::State::State2SimpleState, text::State::State2CMPState
15 {}
```

Listing 1.4. State to SimpleState and CompositeState

Graphical to Textual Synchronization – MMɢ2MMᴛ

– `SimpleState` and `CompositeState` metaelements in MMɢ both have to be transformed to `State` in MMᴛ. Hence, two corresponding mapping operations are defined in Line 1 and Line 4 in Listing 1.5. In this particular situation, a disjunctive mapping operation (i.e., `State2StateDisjunct()`) is introduced in Line 10. Contrary to the first two mapping operations where a mapping body is defined, this operation specifies a list of mapping operations (i.e., `SimpleState2State` and `CMPState2State`) which are evaluated when the mapping operation is invoked. The invocation of the operation occurs in Line 7 when trying to map `substates` to `states` as the EType for `substates` is the abstract metaclass `State` which is extended by `SimpleState` and `CompositeState`.

```
1  mapping graph::SimpleState::SimpleState2State() : text::State
2  inherits graph::State::State2State {}
3
4  mapping graph::CompositeState::CMPState2State() : text::State
5  inherits graph::State::State2State
6  {
7      result.states := self.substates -> map State2StateDisjunct();
8      ...
9  }
10 mapping graph::State::State2StateDisjunct() : text::State
11 disjuncts graph::CompositeState::CMPState2State,
12          graph::SimpleState::SimpleState2State{}
```

Listing 1.5. SimpleState and CompositeState to State

– `Transition` metaclass in MMɢ can be transformed to either `HistoryTransition`, `InitialTransition`, `InternalTransition` or `Transition` in MMᴛ, all extending the `Transitions` metaclass, depending on the source and/or target vertices it connects. First, the `T2Ts()` mapping operation is defined, which details the creation of the `TransitionBody` and the assignment operations for its children. This is then inherited by all other mapping operations that in their signature include `Transition` as source and a subtype of `Transitions` as target. Inheritance eliminates the need to rewrite the operations that are already defined in `T2Ts()` such as the creation of the `TransitionBody` and the corresponding assignments. In addition, all mapping operations that map `Transition` to subtypes of `Transitions` include a mapping guard (i.e., `when` clause) that specifies the type of vertices that the `Transition` must connect, to be transformed to a specific subtype of `Transitions`. The mapping body of these mapping operations details the assignments of the `sourceVertex` and `targetVertex` properties of the source metaelement, to `from` and `to` properties of the target metaelement, respectively as shown in Lines 18–19 in Listing 1.6. The mapping operation that is invoked on them is a disjunction of other mapping operations in which the source and target metaelements are subtypes of the source and target metaelements of the original mapping (i.e., `Vertex2VertexDisjunct`). This is because the types of the source and target metaelements of the invoked mapping (i.e., `Vertex2VertexDisjuncts`) must conform to the types of properties `from` and `to`.

```
1  mapping graph::Vertex::Vertex2VertexDisjunct() : text::Vertex
2  disjuncts graph::CompositeState::CMPState2State, graph::SimpleState::
      SimpleState2State, graph::EntryPoint::EntryPoint2EntryPoint, graph
      ::ExitPoint::ExitPoint2ExitPoint,graph::ChoicePoint::
      ChoicePoint2Choice, graph::JunctionPoint::JunctionPoint2Junction{}
3
4  mapping graph::Transition::T2Ts() : text::Transitions
5  {
6      var TransitionBodyObject := object text::TransitionBody{
       transitionguard := self.guard.map Guard2TransitionGuard();
7          ....
8      };
9      transitionbody := TransitionBodyObject;
10     result.name := self.name;
11 }
12 mapping graph::Transition::T2T() : text::Transition
13 inherits graph::Transition::T2Ts
14 when {not(self.sourceVertex.oclIsTypeOf(InitialPoint) or
15     self.targetVertex.oclIsTypeOf(DeepHistory) or
16     self.sourceVertex = null or self.targetVertex = null)}
17 {
18     result._from := self.sourceVertex.map Vertex2VertexDisjunct();
19     result.to := self.targetVertex.map Vertex2VertexDisjunct();
20 }
21
22 mapping graph::Transition::T2HT() : text::HistoryTransition
23 inherits graph::Transition::T2Ts
24 when {self.targetVertex.oclIsTypeOf(DeepHistory)} { ...}
25
26 mapping graph::Transition::T2INI_T() : text::InitialTransition
27 inherits graph::Transition::T2Ts
28 when {self.sourceVertex.oclIsTypeOf(InitialPoint)} {...}
29
30 mapping graph::Transition::T2INT_T() : text::InternalTransition
31 when {self.sourceVertex = null and self.targetVertex = null} {...}
```

Listing 1.6. Transition to Transitions

– `Trigger` metaclass in MM_G can be transformed to either `Trigger`, `PortEvent Trigger`, or `MethodParameterTrigger` in MM_T depending on which of the mapping guards (i.e., `when` clause) evaluates to true. Hence, three corresponding mapping operations are defined. The `PortEventTrigger` consists of a `Port` and `Event` separated by a dot (e.g., port.event), thus in order for a `Trigger` in MM_G to be transformed to a `PortEventTrigger` in MM_T it should match the pattern defined in Line 7 in Listing 1.7. Moreover, the `Port` and `Event` metaclasses in MM_T have no correspondence in MM_G therefore they should be created as new elements. Lines 9–17 detail the creation of `Port` and `Event` metaclasses and the assignment of the name attribute for each of them. The same procedure is applied to transform `Trigger` in MM_G to `MethodParameterTrigger` in MM_T and to create the `Method` and `Parameter` metaelements. The `MethodParameterTrigger` consists of a `Method` followed by parentheses, which may or not contain a `Parameter` (e.g., method(parameter)). In this case, the mapping condition specifies that the name of the `Trigger` in MM_G should match the pattern specified in Line 19.

```
1  mapping graph::Trigger::Trigger2Trigger() : text::Trigger
2  when {not(self.name.matches(".*\\(.*") or self.name.matches(".*\\..*"))}
3  {
4      result.name := self.name;
5  }
6  mapping graph::Trigger::Trigger2PETrigger() : text::PortEventTrigger
7  when {self.name.matches(".*\\..*")}
8  {
9      var PortObject := object text::Port{
10         name := self.name.substringBefore(".");
11     };
12     port := PortObject;
13     var EventObject := object text::Event{
14         name := self.name.substringAfter(".");
15     };
16     event := EventObject;
17 }
18 mapping graph::Trigger::Trigger2MPTrigger() : text::
       MethodParameterTrigger
19 when {self.name.matches(".*\\(.*")}
20 { ... }
```

Listing 1.7. `Trigger` to `Trigger`, `PortEventTrigger`, and `MethodParameterTrigger`

5   Validation and Discussion

The M2M transformations detailed in this paper make possible the synchronization between multiple notations. As such, the correctness of the unidirectional transformations and the consistency between them is crucial.

The validation is conducted for RTist and Papyrus-RT by applying the model transformations to instances (i.e., models) of MM_G and MM_T. The representation of the graphical instance M_G is detailed in Fig. 4, while the representation of the textual instance M_T is detailed in Fig. 5. Figure 4a details the graphical editor of M_G, whereas Fig. 4b details the Exeed editor (an extended version of the built-in tree-based reflective editor provided by EMF) of M_G. Alternatively, Fig. 5a details the Xtext editor of M$_T$, whereas Fig. 5b details the Exeed editor of M$_T$. We have included the Exeed editor for both instances, as it conveys additional structural information that is not glaring in the other editors. In the following we describe the execution of the validation process.

① The correctness of the model transformations is validated by carrying out testing of the MM$_G$2MM$_T$ and MM$_T$2MM$_G$ model transformations at the unit level [21]. To carry out this procedure, we have defined a functional decomposition diagram for each model transformation. Such diagram, can facilitate the identification of the test *subjects*, as the nodes of the diagram (i.e., mapping operations) will represent the *subjects*. Additional consideration has been given to guarantee that the test cases cover all the mapping operations of a given model transformation. The metaelements of the input metamodels will be considered as *test inputs* whereas the *expected output* will be represented by a regular expression. For a test case to *pass*, the *expected output* of a given mapping operation must match *the actual output*. The latter is the result that we get after the execution of the mapping operation. In the following we use the `CMPState2State` mapping operation defined in the MM$_G$2MM$_T$ model transformation to exemplify our manual testing process. In Fig. 2 we detail only a portion of the decomposition diagram to highlight `CMPState2State`. Then we extract the input of the `CMPState2State` mapping operation, which is the `CompositeState`. In Fig. 3 we detailed an instance of MM$_G$, which is used to test the `CMPState2State` mapping operation.

Fig. 2. Decomposition diagram portion   **Fig. 3.** Input

The *expected output* after the execution of the `CMPState2State` on the instance of MM$_G$ detailed in Fig. 3 is as follows. The `CompositeState` **Top** included in the `StateMachine` **SM** in M$_G$ must be transformed to a `CompositeState` **Top** included in the `StateMachine` **SM** in M$_T$. Lastly we execute the transformations and check whether the *actual output* is same as the *expected output*.

```
<hcl:StateMachine name=SM">
<states name=Top">
</hcl:StateMachine>
```

② The second step involves validating the consistency between the two model transformations. For achieving this, we apply the MM$_G$2MM$_T$ model transformation to M$_G$ detailed in Fig. 4. The output is M$_T$ detailed in Fig. 5. We then apply the MM$_T$2MM$_G$ model transformation to the output of the MM$_G$2MM$_T$ model

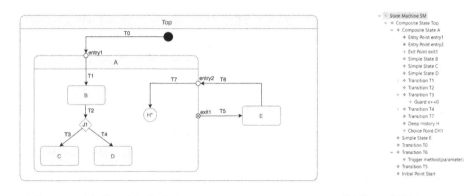

(a) Graphical editor   (b) Exeed Editor.

Fig. 4. Graphical model

transformation. The output of the MMT2MMG model transformation must be identical to the instance of MG detailed in Fig. 4 for the QVTo transformation to be considered consistent. The model transformations are revised until full consistency is achieved. In addition to the testing results, architects at HCL have assessed both the usability and usefulness of the textual notation, as well as the synchronization mechanisms between notations.

On another note, by inspecting the instances of MMG and MMT detailed in Fig. 4 and Fig. 5 respectively, we can highlight the most significant differences in terms of semantics and structure. For instance, CompositeState A and SimpleState B in MMG are transformed into State A and State B in MMT, respectively, where State A is the parent of State B. Although the structure is identical, there exist semantic differences between SimpleState B and State B, because SimpleState B cannot contain other elements, whilst State B can. For transitions, if we consider the same transformation, it is the opposite. For instance, Transition T0 in MMG is transformed into InitialTransition T0 in MMT and Transition T7 in MMG is transformed into HistoryTransition T7 in MMT. Alternatively, structural differences are prominent when creating new metaelements instead of transforming them (because of the lack of a corresponding source metaelement). This is the case of TransitionBody, Port, Event, Method, and Parameter metaelements in MMT. For instance, Transition T1 in Fig. 4 has two children, Trigger and ActionChain, whilst Transition T1 in Fig. 5 has only one child, TransitionBody, which contains the PortEventTrigger and TransitionOperation. Another interesting difference is that whilst in Fig. 4 Transition T7 and Deep History H reside on the same level (i.e., they are siblings), in Fig. 5 Deep History H is a child of Transition T7. The reason for this is to allow the user to initialize DeepHistory when writing Transition T7, and not before initializing it, and then reference it in Transition T7.

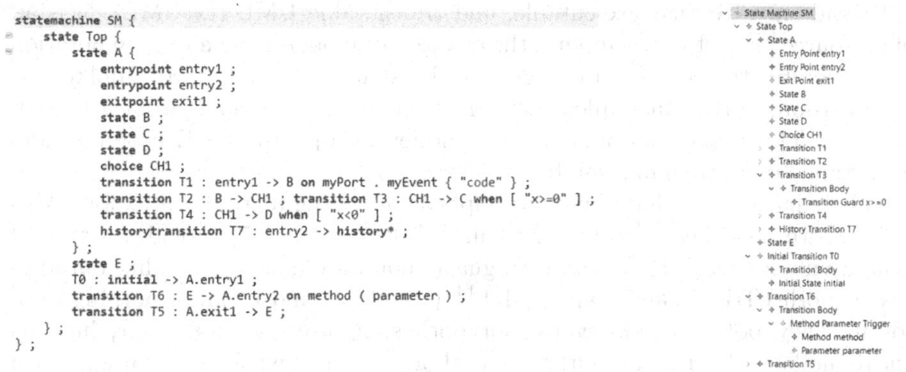

```
statemachine SM {
    state Top {
        state A {
            entrypoint entry1 ;
            entrypoint entry2 ;
            exitpoint exit1 ;
            state B ;
            state C ;
            state D ;
            choice CH1 ;
            transition T1 : entry1 -> B on myPort . myEvent { "code" } ;
            transition T2 : B -> CH1 ; transition T3 : CH1 -> C when [ "x>=0" ] ;
            transition T4 : CH1 -> D when [ "x<0" ] ;
            historytransition T7 : entry2 -> history* ;
        } ;
        state E ;
        T0 : initial -> A.entry1 ;
        transition T6 : E -> A.entry2 on method ( parameter ) ;
        transition T5 : A.exit1 -> E ;
    } ;
} ;
```

```
∨  State Machine SM
  ∨  State Top
    ∨  State A
         Entry Point entry1
         Entry Point entry2
         Exit Point exit1
         State B
         State C
         State D
         Choice CH1
       ∨  Transition T1
       ∨  Transition T2
       ∨  Transition T3
         ∨  Transition Body
              Transition Guard x>=0
         Transition T4
       ∨  History Transition T7
         State E
    ∨  Initial Transition T0
         Transition Body
         Initial State initial
    ∨  Transition T6
      ∨  Transition Body
        ∨  Method Parameter Trigger
             Method method
             Parameter parameter
       Transition T5
```

(a) Xtext editor   (b) Exeed Editor

Fig. 5. Textual model

6   Related Work

The Action Language for Foundational UML (Alf) [17] is a textual language standardized by the Object Management Group (OMG) for representing UML models. Since its underlying semantics are indicated by a limited subset of UML, named Foundational UML (fUML), the Alf syntax is restricted within its bounds and does not support state-machines as they are not available in the fUML subset. tUML is a textual language for a limited subset of the standard UML metamodel targeted at real-time embedded systems that consists of class diagrams, composite structure diagrams, and state diagrams. The implementation of tUML has been carried out to have a very close proximity to the UML metamodel. Consideration has been given to propose tUML to OMG as an extension of Alf, being that the latter lacks support for state-machines [10]. There also exists a plethora of tools and modeling languages that support textual notations for UML models. Earl Grey [15] is a textual modeling language that supports the creation of UML class and state models. MetaUML [6] is a MetaPost library for creating UML diagrams using textual notations, and it supports class diagrams, package diagrams, component diagrams, use case diagrams, activity diagrams, and state diagrams. The textual notation is not only used to define the elements and their relationships but also their layout properties. PlantUML[11] is an open-source tool that supports the generation of both UML and non-UML diagrams from a textual language. Among the most important UML diagrams they support are sequence diagrams, class diagrams, activity diagrams, state diagrams, and more. Umple [12] is an open-source modeling tool that can be used to add UML abstractions to programming languages (i.e., Java, C++, PHP, and Ruby) and create UML class and state diagrams from a textual notation. The generated graphical view for class diagrams can be edited, while for state-machines,

---

[11] http://plantuml.com/guide.

it is read-only. Textual, executable, and translatable UML (txtUML) [5] is an open-source project that supports the creation of models from a textual notation and generates the corresponding graphical visualization. TextUML Toolkit[12] is an open-source IDE that allows the creation of UML2 models from a textual notation. This toolkit is available on Cloudfier, as a plug-in for Eclipse IDE and as a standalone command-line tool.

There have been a handful of attempts at providing textual syntax for UML-RT and we have been involved in some of them. Calur [7] provides a textual syntax only for UML-RT's action language, not state-machines. Unlike our approach, both eTrice[13] and Papyrus-RT[14] provide a kind of all-or-nothing approach. They both provide syntax for both structure and behaviour, but the entire model is described as either textual or graphical, whereas in our approach the user can select only parts of the model to be represented textually. This allows the user to retain the ability to use existing RTist tooling for graphical modelling. Note also that our textual notation for UML-RT state-machines has been designed and implemented to maximise user experience of architects and engineers, as their throughput thanks to the possibility of blended modelling.

7   Outlook

In this work, we have reported on our work to provide a seamless blended graphical and textual modelling environment for UML-RT state-machines. Our proposed solution involves the provision of (i) a textual notation as complement to the existing graphical notation for UML-RT state-machines and (ii) ad hoc synchronization mechanisms between the metamodels underlying the two notations. The synchronization mechanisms have been designed as model-to-model transformations and implemented using the operational implementation of the QVT language in Eclipse. With regards to the limitations of this approach, we argue that the solution is language-agnostic (i.e., applicable to UML-RT state machines only). For any other language, the related editors and transformations have to be re-done from scratch. On a similar note, if the metamodels evolve, the model transformations would have to be manually updated.

For that reason, future work involves the definition of a mapping language that allows the definition of explicit mappings between arbitrary metamodels (MMs), and automatic generation of synchronization transformations via Higher Order Transformations (HOTs). The HOTs are transformations that take as input and/or generate as output other model transformations [20]. Given two MMs defined, a mapping model, conforming to the mapping language, would conceive the mapping rules for synchronizing models conforming to the two MMs. The mapping model together with the two MMs would be given in input to a set of HOTs that we are currently designing. The outputs of the HOTs are

---

[12] https://abstratt.github.io/textuml/.

[13] https://www.eclipse.org/etrice/.

[14] https://www.eclipse.org/papyrus-rt/.

synchronization model transformations, as the ones defined manually in Operational QVT for the solution presented in this paper. The type of generated transformations (i.e., endogenous, exogenous, out-of-place, in-place) depends on the nature of the two MMs.

In fact, this architecture and the HOTs in it would entail multiple usage scenarios, as follows. In case the MMs are two entirely disjoint (but somehow connected/dependent) languages, the generated transformations provide synchronization across different languages (either same or different notations). In case the MMs represent two notations of the same language, the generated transformations provide synchronization across different notations of the language. In addition, in case the target MM represents an evolution of the source MM, the generated transformations provide co-evolution mechanisms for models conforming to MM.

This work is run in the context of an international consortium across 4 countries within the ITEA3 BUMBLE project[15]. In that context, we will run more extensive controlled experiments and industrial case-studies too. An important element of the dissemination plan consists in leveraging the different opportunities provided in the Eclipse community, including Eclipse conferences (e.g., EclipseCon Europe) and marketing. We will also collaborate with the Eclipse Working Groups, Papyrus and Capella Industry Consortia to reach out to industrial MDE tool users. We plan to disseminate results via research forums (conferences, workshops), corporate presentations, participation to industrial events like expos, on-line community forums for Eclipse, social media, fact sheets, and wikis.

Acknowledgments. This work was supported by Vinnova through the ITEA3 BUMBLE project (rn. 18006). We would like to thank Ernesto Posse for his great support in technical discussions related to the UML-RT textual implementation in Papyrus-RT.

References

1. Addazi, L., Ciccozzi, F.: Blended graphical and textual modelling for UML profiles: a proof-of-concept implementation and experiment. J. Syst. Softw. **175**, 110912 (2021)
2. Brambilla, M., Cabot, J., Wimmer, M.: Model-driven software engineering in practice. Synth. Lect. Softw. Eng. **3**(1), 1–207 (2017)
3. Cicchetti, A., Ciccozzi, F., Pierantonio, A.: Multi-view approaches for software and system modelling: a systematic literature review. Softw. Syst. Model. **18**(6), 3207–3233 (2019). https://doi.org/10.1007/s10270-018-00713-w
4. Ciccozzi, F., Tichy, M., Vangheluwe, H., Weyns, D.: Blended Modelling - What, Why and How. In: MPM4CPS Workshop, September 2019. http://www.es.mdh.se/publications/5642-
5. Dévai, G., Kovács, G.F., An, Á.: Textual, executable, translatable UML. In: OCL@ MoDELS, pp. 3–12. Citeseer (2014)
6. Gheorghies, O.: MetaUML: tutorial, reference and test suite (2005)

---

[15] https://blended-modeling.github.io/.

7. Hili, N., Posse, E., Dingel, J.: Calur: an action language for UML-RT. In: 9th European Congress on Embedded Real Time Software and Systems (ERTS 2018) (2018)

8. Hofmeister, C., Nord, R., Soni, D.: Applied Software Architecture. Addison-Wesley Professional, Boston (2000)

9. Hutchinson, J., Whittle, J., Rouncefield, M., Kristoffersen, S.: Empirical assessment of MDE in industry. In: Proceedings of ICSE, pp. 471–480. IEEE (2011)

10. Jouault, F., Delatour, J.: Towards fixing sketchy UML models by leveraging textual notations: application to real-time embedded systems. In: OCL@ MoDELS, pp. 73–82 (2014)

11. Latifaj, M., Ciccozzi, F., Mohlin, M., Posse, E.: Towards automated support for blended modelling of UML-RT embedded software architectures. In: 15th European Conference on Software Architecture ECSA 2021, 13 September 2021, Virtual (originally Växjö), Sweden (2021)

12. Lethbridge, T.C., Abdelzad, V., Husseini Orabi, M., Husseini Orabi, A., Adesina, O.: Merging modeling and programming using Umple. In: Margaria, T., Steffen, B. (eds.) ISoLA 2016. LNCS, vol. 9953, pp. 187–197. Springer, Cham (2016). https://doi.org/10.1007/978-3-319-47169-3_14

13. Malavolta, I., Lago, P., Muccini, H., Pelliccione, P., Tang, A.: What industry needs from architectural languages: a survey. IEEE Trans. Softw. Eng. **39**(6), 869–891 (2012)

14. Martin, R.C.: Clean Code: A Handbook of Agile Software Craftsmanship. Pearson Education, London (2009)

15. Mazanec, M., Macek, O.: On general-purpose textual modeling languages. In: Dateso, vol. 12, pp. 1–12. Citeseer (2012)

16. Mens, T., Van Gorp, P.: A taxonomy of model transformation. Electron. Notes Theor. Comput. Sci. **152**, 125–142 (2006)

17. Object Management Group (OMG): Action Language for Foundational UML (Alf), Version 1.1. OMG Document Number formal/2017-07-04 (2017). http://www.omg.org/spec/ALF/1.1

18. Selic, B.: Real-time object-oriented modeling. IFAC Proc. Vol. **29**(5), 1–6 (1996)

19. Selic, B.: The pragmatics of model-driven development. IEEE Softw. **20**(5), 19–25 (2003)

20. Tisi, M., Jouault, F., Fraternali, P., Ceri, S., Bézivin, J.: On the use of higher-order model transformations. In: Paige, R.F., Hartman, A., Rensink, A. (eds.) ECMDA-FA 2009. LNCS, vol. 5562, pp. 18–33. Springer, Heidelberg (2009). https://doi.org/10.1007/978-3-642-02674-4_3

21. Tiso, A., Reggio, G., Leotta, M.: Unit testing of model to text transformations. In: AMT 2014-Analysis of Model Transformations Workshop Proceedings, p. 14 (2014)

Diversity, Equity and Inclusion Track (DE&I)

Toward Awareness Creation of Common Challenges Women are Facing in Academia: A Study from a German Perspective

Sophie Corallo[1]([✉])[iD], Manar Mazkatli[1][iD], Martina Rapp[2][iD],
Hamideh Hajiabadi[1][iD], Angelika Kaplan[1], Romina Kuehn[3][iD],
Larissa Schmid[1][iD], and Snigdha Singh[1][iD]

[1] KASTEL – Institute of Information Security and Dependability,
Karlsruhe Institute of Technology, Karlsruhe, Germany
{sophie.corallo,manar.mazkatli,hamideh.hajiabadi,angelika.kaplan,
larissa.schmid,snigdha.singh}@kit.edu
[2] FZI Research Center for Information Technology, Karlsruhe, Germany
rapp@fzi.de
[3] Technische Universität Dresden, Dresden, Germany
romina.kuehn@tu-dresden.de

Abstract. Every day, women face plenty of challenges regarding their family, taking care of the seniors, equality, and appreciation at the workplace, etc. - usually with little outside support. While these challenges are not new, the awareness level towards these challenges is still low. This research aims to create awareness towards women's difficulties by studying the challenges women in research face at German universities. We also investigate how women in research handle their challenges and whether these challenges correlate to their place of birth. We investigate how these challenges differ between the computer science community and other STEM fields. To gain data, we conducted a survey with 200 women from technical universities in Germany. The results show that parenting and family planning are the most common challenges among women in research. Many women also describe problems dealing with men. Furthermore, women in computer science solved their problems in 34% of cases, others only in 23%. Even if help from others was the most frequently described solution (29%), strategies like a workaround (27%) or changing the workplace (11%) are common. We conclude from our study, that women in research still have many problems. These problems include finding an appropriate solution to a problem.

Keywords: Inequality gap · Experiences of women in research · Women in research · Women in computer science research · Survey

1 Introduction

Women have been in science since ancient times [13]. However, the access to knowledge has been made more difficult for them over time. In the 17th century, women

© The Author(s), under exclusive license to Springer Nature Switzerland AG 2022
P. Scandurra et al. (Eds.): ECSA Tracks and Workshops 2021, LNCS 13365, pp. 47–62, 2022.
https://doi.org/10.1007/978-3-031-15116-3_3

were increasingly excluded from higher education and science [8]. A higher education and university degree was only possible for women of higher status and only at certain locations. With the beginning of the women's movement in the 19th century, first colleges and universities began to open their doors and positions for women. Some institutions even began to allow women to study and get doctoral degrees [3]. However, it took more than 50 years, until the first woman became an associate professor of mathematics [12]. From the beginning of the 20th century, increasingly more universities and colleges allowed women to study. Since then, the proportion of women at universities has risen enormously: The number of women with scientific degrees increases and in 2019 45% of doctoral degrees at German universities were given to women [6]. In the academic year 2021/22 about 1.5 million women studied at German universities and colleges – expected more than men [17].

However, women are globally still underrepresented in scientific careers. In India, only 27.3% of professorial positions in 2018–2019 were filled by women [2]. The statistics look the same in other countries – for example Canada with 28% women professors [2], USA with 34.3% [2], and Germany with 24.7% [18]. While these numbers already do not reflect the proportion of women of the whole population, for math and natural sciences (20.7%) as well as engineering (14.3%), the amount was even less [5].

Therefore, nowadays not the access to higher education and scientific degrees seems to hinder women, but socio-cultural aspects. Silim and Crosse [16] complain that only 7% of professional engineers in the UK are women. They state that many girls miss the opportunity of an engineering career because of its image. They explain that with the stereotype-view of Science, Technology, Engineering, and Mathematics (STEM), a poor understanding of engineering pathways and careers, and missing prerequisites of many girls in school (e.g. A-level in physics/mathematics). Falkner et al. [7], for example, describe in their work the perceptions of computer science from the outside and how these perceptions influenced the choice of women for a career in computer science research. Moreover, for both, industrial and academic careers, there are many publications concerning environmental factors preventing women from choosing them [10,19] and recruitment and retention strategies for students [15].

Underrepresentation and gender (in-)equality in academia is still an open issue that is constantly reported and investigated [11]. Especially, for STEM fields (science, technology, engineering, and mathematics), there is a lot of work focusing on investigating these issues. This underrepresentation is often explained with prejudices, inequality, and discrimination [9]. Beside of perception and discriminations, the underrepresentation of women in academia is often described as an effect of intertwined factors [1]. Factors can have individual, biological, social, educational, or other sources.

In this paper, we focus on problems women encounter during an academic career in a holistic view regarding personal challenges as well as challenges at work. Therefore, we restrict ourselves on STEM fields and computer science. Although the challenges and inequalities are not new, their public awareness is still insufficient. We collect solutions women found for their different problems to provide not only awareness for problems but also for their solvability. Moreover, we are interested in differences between computer science research area and other STEM fields. Therefore, we compare these groups regarding their problems and solutions.

Furthermore, we report the current situation of women in scientific careers in Germany. We study the difficulties they face at German universities and how they address their challenges (cf. RQ1–RQ2 in Sect. 2). Further, we investigate whether these problems are the same within the computer science (CS) community. Avolio et al. [1] conclude from their literature study that socio-cultural parameters influence women in academia in different stages of their lives. Therefore, we are also interested in cultural aspects: We study if cultural problems correlate with the country of birth (cf. RQ3 in Sect. 2). For this purpose, we conducted an online survey with 200 women in research working at technical German universities.

Our results show that most problems are issues in the person's environment (e.g., life planning and responsibilities) and at the workplace (e.g., equality and support). Problems referring explicitly to research, such as issues with publications and appreciation, followed. Cultural circumstances (e.g., religion) make up only 14% of the problems on average. We found no correlations between cultural problems and the country of birth. However, our results provide insights into the problems and solutions of the participants based on their free-text descriptions. In the following section, we discuss our method design and data analysis of our survey in a more detailed way.

2   Survey Design

The survey's objective is to collect problems and challenges women typically face in research and how they deal with them. Since it is common to have intercultural exchanges in science, we expect different problems for people with other cultural backgrounds. Thereby, we are interested in whether cultural problems are related to the cultural background (in our case restricted to the birth country) of women.

On this basis, we derive the following research questions:

RQ1 What problems do women face in research?
RQ2 What solutions do women find for their problems?
RQ3 Do cultural problems correlate with the country of birth?

To create a suitable survey, we needed to identify problem areas and topics we wanted to cover explicitly. Therefore, we created a mind map out of different problems and sub-problems that we knew. Based on this, we clustered the problems and identified problem areas: Cultural, personal, workplace, and research. Furthermore, we refined the areas into more specific topics. The results are provided by Table 1. More detailed information about the taxonomy can be found in our repository [4]. Based on this taxonomy, the survey is structured by the four subject areas as main question groups, each containing questions corresponding to the different topics.

Table 1. List of subject areas with corresponding topics

	Topics per area	Description/Example
Cultural	Religion	Anything concerning religion
	Clothing	E.g., wearing a hijab
	Name changing	E.g., when getting married
	Cultural Infrastructure	E.g., prayer rooms that are only for men
Personal	Hormones/Period	E.g., sick days caused by PMS have to be justified
	Life plan	E.g., the time to decide to have children
	Responsibilities	Additional responsibilities e.g., parenting or housekeeping
	Pregnancy	Problems that occur during pregnancy
Workplace	Equality	Equality issues in general
	Support	Insufficient support regarding equality
	Collaboration	Collaboration with men (e.g., not getting involved into discussions)
	Workplace Infrastructure	E.g., no toilets for women
Research	Idea sharing	Limited opportunities to share ideas (e.g., not allowed to publish)
	Appreciation	Feelings of disadvantage and discrimination
	Publications	Priority of men in author sequence of publications
	Priority	Male priority over women in research

For each topic, we asked sub-questions according to the following pattern: (1) Has the participant experienced the problem addressed by the topic during her research career? If the question was answered positively, we asked for an optional detailed description (2), the stage or possibly stages of her career (studying, doctoral student, after doctoral degree) at which the problem occurred (3), whether they solved it (4), and for an optional description of the solution (5). Additionally, we provided free text fields in every subject area to collect problems that we did not identify in our working session, called *others*.

Before sending out the survey, we asked an external experienced survey designer for feedback. We used the *Think Aloud* method [14], asking her to report what comes to her mind when seeing the questions. After that, we conducted a pretest [14] with four women. On account of the feedback, we restructured the question design. We also had some minor findings from the pretest, e.g., a technical issue. A replica of our questionnaire is available in our repository [4].

The survey is targeted towards women in different research positions and age groups. Since we restrict the survey to women who study, studied, or work in STEM fields in Germany, we decided to send out the survey to all 16 technical universities in Germany. We contacted the gender equality office of the university and asked them to forward our survey to appropriate mailing lists. We provide a list of our contacts in our repository [4]. Two of them were not able to share the survey in time; we did not receive any feedback from the other contacted universities. We decided to survey by using the online survey tool *LimeSur-vey*[1] and made the survey available for two weeks (from 05/21/2021 8 am until 06/04/2021 12 pm). For validity reasons, we as authors did not participate in the study.

3   Data Analysis

Our survey got answers from 220 women. We remove 79 partially answered sur-veys from our evaluation. In our evaluation, we want to consider only women who study, studied, or work in Germany and are currently in research. Thereby, we remove 9 data entries from our results. Finally, our validated data consists of 132 responses. The responses originate from 5 students, 61 doctoral students, 20 post-docs, 22 professors, and 46 scientific researchers. Since the question for the cur-rent position was a multiple-choice question, the sum does not correspond to the number of participants. Thereby, our study provides a good distribution across the different stages in research careers. Regarding the age, we also reached a good dis-tribution: 51 participants were 20–30 years, 50 women were 30–40 years, while the remaining 31 women were older than 40 years. Moreover, we want to capture the differences between women in computer science and other scientific fields. There-fore, we annotated data that belongs to persons from computer science accordingly (e.g., machine learning). Thereby, we have the following basic sets: 52 women in computer science (CS) and the counter group of 80 women from other scientific fields (no computer scientists) (NCS). To answer our research questions, we divide our first and second question (RQ1, RQ2) in three sub-questions:

RQ1a & RQ2a In which area did most problems/solutions occur?
RQ1b & RQ2b Which topics have most problems/solutions?
RQ1c & RQ2c What are the most frequently described problems/solutions?

3.1   RQ1a & RQ2a: Areas of Problems and Solutions

To answer the first two refined research questions, we use the mandatory responses of the questionnaire. Therefore, the raw data is based on marks, whether the sub-ject had a problem in the area/topic, and whether the subject solved it.

Figure 1 provides an overview of the problem frequency in the areas (RQ1a, RQ2a). Most women in computer science research (CS) located their problems in the personal area (32.3%) and regarding their workplace (30.9%). Research problems have a share of 23.3% of the problems. Cultural issues are only the case in 13.5%. Regarding the counter group (NCS), the proportion of problems in the personal area are 35.1% and thus higher compared to the CS group. However, the work area occurred 6 percentage points less than for women in computer science. Research (25.2%) and cultural issues (14.8%) were similarly frequent compared to the CS group.

---

[1] https://www.limesurvey.org/.

In total, women in computer science solved about 34% of their problems, while the counter group only solved about 23%. Both groups have most of their solved problems located in the personal area. However, the CS group solved more cultural, work, and personal problems, while the amount of solved research problems is almost equal.

Figure 1 shows that women have too many unsolved problems in several areas. However, problems concerning research are only at the second last rank.

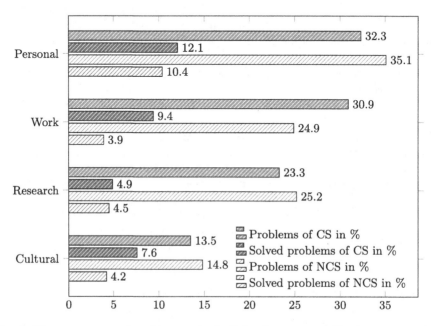

Fig. 1. The most occurred problem topics in % for the answers of both groups: women in computer science research (CS) (n = 223) and women from other scientific fields (no computer scientists) (NCS) (n = 345). Moreover, the distribution of solved problems over the topics is presented.

3.2   RQ1b & RQ2b: Topics of Problems and Solutions

Figure 2 presents a more detailed look and enables the analysis of the problem and solution frequencies between topics (RQ1b, RQ2b). The most problems of computer scientists are in the topics life plan and equality. Life planning seems to be a general problem, while equality problems are more common for computer scientists. While they also have more problems in collaborations, support, and the cultural others section, they have fewer problems in responsibilities, appreciation, and publications.

The amount of solutions for specific topics also differs greatly for some topics. In the case of collaborations, the CS group has 3.1 percentage points more solutions than the NCS group, while they only have 2.3 percentage points difference regarding the problems.

The results presented in the graph seem to indicate that there are already some good solutions for some topics (e.g., for collaborations in the CS group). However, there are overall much more open problems than solved ones.

3.3 RQ1c & RQ2c: Labeling Process

To answer RQ1c and RQ2c, we need to quantify the optionally described problems and solutions. Therefore, we labeled them. Since the descriptions were arbitrary, we had to do the labeling in an exploratory way. We decided to do the labeling per area in pairs to ensure high objectivity and consistency in each area. The pairs read the descriptions and gave them labels. We concurrently tracked the labels and their explanations in a joint table. If in any case, no existing label was fitting, they could introduce new labels. Finally, a third person reviewed the classification and discussed disagreements with the pair. It was possible to assign multiple labels to one description.

In nine cases, descriptions referred to previously given answers. In these cases, we inserted the label from the last suitable description. In total, the 193 described problems lead to 37 different problem labels. We ended up with 268 labels as each description can have multiple labels. Only 81 descriptions for solutions were submitted. We derived 8 labels from these. Finally, we assigned 100 labels to solutions. 27 of these were labeled as no real solutions. For example: "Took more painkillers than before and continued going to work with cramps and migraines". Others were described or labeled too unspecific. Moreover, we have one label (giving up) that occurs only one time. Finally, our base set contains 63 labels. The complete list of labels is found in our repository [4].

3.4 RQ1c & RQ2c: Described Problems and Solutions

Finally, we focus on the specific problems that women face in research (RQ1c, RQ2c). At the beginning of Sect. 3 we described that we assigned 268 labels to the described problems. This set includes labels referring to problems that are not exclusively related to women. Examples are equipment that is difficult to use for short people or missing children during travels. Thus, after filtering them, we derive a basic set for the following analysis containing 235 labels. The labels of the ten most often described problems are listed and explained in Table 2, the most often described solutions are labeled as in Table 3.

The most described problems are parenting and family planning (see Fig. 3). Regarding family planning, short-time contracts, and the resulting job insecurity are criticized the most. The participants write: "Family planning is complicated as there is so little job security. Taking parental leave might also be not that good for one's scientific career."; "I could not easily plan for my life because of the short contracts. It is really hard to balance work, studying[.] I search for longer contracts to support my family financially". Even during parental leave or the children's aging, the pressure in science does not seem to decrease: "As

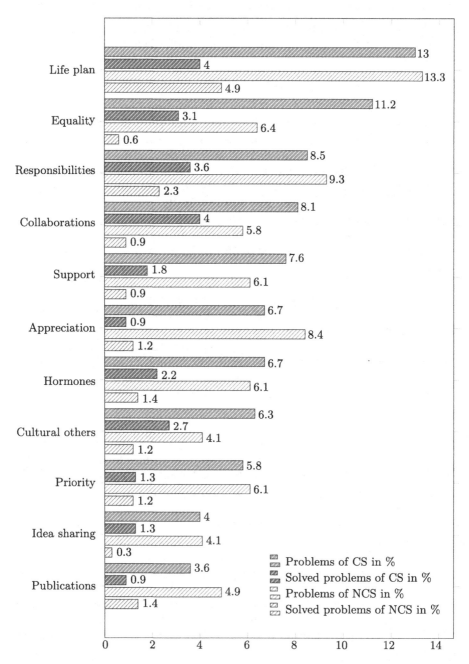

Fig. 2. The most occurred problem topics and the proportion of solved problems in it in % for the answers of both groups: women in computer science research (CS) (n = 223) and women from other scientific fields (no computer scientists) (NCS) (n = 345).

Table 2. Labels of the ten most described problems

Problem label	Description
Parenting	Parenting issues (e.g., having less time because of children, not easy to move with children (as required as a researcher), doing housekeeping)
Family planning	Issues related to family planning
Male communication	Men communicate different than women: disrespectful comments and offensive behavior; language that is men-oriented; offensive behavior, insults, sexist comments and behavior, physical, or verbal harassment
Undermining	An intentional process where men move themselves in the foreground (e.g., women are not accepted as first author or the wishes of women are intentionally ignored or being talked over)
Men promote men	Men promote men and ignore women, male networks
PMS	Physical problems during or before period
Equipment	Equipment is not suitable for women (e.g., too high) or they do not get appropriate equipment (e.g., only computer with small disk space)
Self confidence	Women have problems to be confident like men, problems during discussions or sharing their ideas etc.; afraid to discuss some topics
Expertise perception	The external perception of the person's expertise/competence
Visibility	Unintentional not seeing of women in research. Examples for visibility: Men are talking to men on conferences, or are more probably invited to talks/debates. Since people often cite more familiar authors women become invisible

Table 3. Labels of the most described solutions

Solution label	Description
No solution	Ignoring the problem
Help by others	Use help from others e.g., mentors/initiatives (esp.) for women/women networks/ask someone for help/ ...
Workaround	Creation of a workaround for the problem (e.g., schedule separate meetings)
Strengthen self-esteem	Focus on yourself, Strengthen your self-confidence, be confident of your own results and abilities, being straight forward, communicate directly
Change workplace	Change of position or workplace
Sit out	Waiting for the end of the problematic (time) period, or try to ignore it for a periodic time
Good daycare	Have a well-organized daycare
Help others	Help others with the same problem
Be role model	Be a role model for other women and/or demonstrate equality

a single mother, my colleagues considered my time with my child equivalent to their hobbies. [. . .] They expected me to "organize away" my child, but I wanted to have some hours per day with my child". These expectations seem to have a great impact on the future of young scientists: "due to familiy [sic] reasons, I gave up a professorship within the trial period, and thus could not keep the title". In general, both problems are described as time constraints that are often incompatible with work in research. This matches the results of our topics, where the life plan and responsibilities topics occurred most frequently and are therefore the most common problems of women in research.

In third and fourth place, male communication, undermining, and promotion problems are described. Male communication is sometimes related to sexist wordings or a very dominant behavior of men in discussions, talks, and lectures. For example, a participant writes: "With some men, esp. in my own lab, I find it sometimes hard to collaborate since their style of communication appears to be rather egocentric than collaborative" - another: "Then because men always speak more in public events and are less inclusive than women". However, this kind of communication does not seem to be the only obstacle. Regarding her fertility treatment, relief from stress, and traveling, a woman writes: "We are always afraid of speaking about this things [sic]. More flexibility and support will help. On the other hand, the topic is never spoken directly". Therefore, the problem seems to be not only the dominance of men in discussions but also the openness and trust.

The latter seems to be disproved regarding the comments of the undermining issues. In contrast to male communication, undermining was labeled, if women had the impression that men performed intentionally against them. An example is: "Responsibilities were taken away during/after maternity leave without discussion or warning. After making the choice to reduce working hours (to 80%!!!) my own project was taken away". Frighteningly, such impressions are not that rare as we would wish.

Promotion issues occurred in 5.96% of the labels. Here, women noted that relations between different sexes are less used in networking (e.g., for an invitation to talks or conferences): "Wheras [sic] men are supportet [sic] and invited, for example to publish with the boss and getting great recommendation letters for applying to professorships my female colleagues and I are doing the ground work, teaching for example but that doesn' [sic] count it is expected of women that they pick up the slack that some men don't like to do. The old buddy network is well alive and younger cohorts of male scientists are socialized into the old paradigm."

Other often mentioned problems (over 3.5%) are regarding PMS, the equipment at the workplace, self-confidence, the perception of the expertise, and the visibility of women. PMS is often described as a problem regarding concentration, pressure, and well-being. Regarding equipment, a woman describes that she uses the toilet for disabled people because the women toilets are not equipped well enough. In general, some women have issues regarding communication. For example: "Some male researchers [. . .] are just more confident in "selling" their work and thus get more appreciation, whereas [...] we are more critical about our own work". However, the perception of the expertise does not seem to be a confidence issue only: "I am not even seen as part of the project, although I was the key initiator. [...] I was just that one woman on the team". These topics are similar to the general visibility of women in science. A woman describes her view: "Men know men, they cite men, the propose men for awards, they chose men for their team, the mentor men, they write better letters of recommendations for men."

Other labels applied to less than 3% of the described problems.

Since the amount of described problems and solutions is too small to conclude how problems were solved, we decided to provide such an overview just for the three most frequent problems: Parenting, family planning, and male communication. Regarding parenting, 75% of the described solutions were classified as no real solution. For example: "I did not solve the problem, [...] found a permanent position after 12 years". The remaining 25% suggest a good daycare. Family planning solutions were also classified as no solutions by 66%, for example by hoping for a better moment to get children. The remaining solutions are split over workarounds, good daycares, and workplace changes. Only 50% of the solutions for the communication with men were classified as valid solutions. To strengthen the self-esteem for conversations takes 10% of the suggested solutions.

However, to get an overview of the most frequent solutions in general, we rank them by their frequency. Figure 4 shows that the described solutions depend in 28.57% on the help of others. Some women received help by talking privately to their boss, while others rely on initiatives: "Initiative of university to prefer hiring females/members of underrepresented or minority groups in case of equal qualification". Since communication and trust in men were often criticized, we also want to highlight a positive example for a solution: "In the years as professor [sic] it was more difficult as I was now competing [...]. But there were also two male mentors who helped". Frighteningly, workarounds are in the second place (26.98%) since they often lead to more effort and thus stress and time issues. For example, a woman describes that she schedules extra meetings with only some partners to avoid communication issues. The fourth place, the change of the workplace, is mostly not described since it is self-explaining. 6.35% of the described solutions are women who sit the problem out. One had problems regarding her publications and described her solution as: "I had to wait 4 years to publish my work. - but i [sic] did in the end, because i [sic] did not give up". The least labeled solutions were to find good daycare, to help others (for example when establishing rules), and to be a role model.

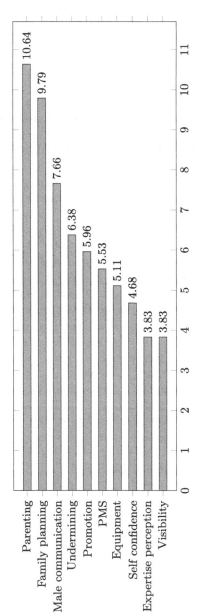

Fig. 3. Labels of described problems for both groups in % (n = 235).

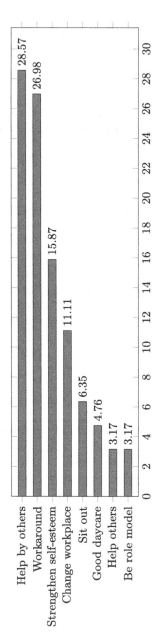

Fig. 4. Labels of described solutions for both groups in % (n = 63).

3.5   RQ3: Cultural Influences

RQ3 faces the intercultural problems of women. To find a correlation between cultural problems and the country of birth, we use a chi-square test with a significance level of 0.05. Again, we divide the third research question into several hypotheses:

$H3_{0a}$ The occurrence of cultural problems is independent of the country of birth.
$H3_{0b}$ Cultural problems do not depend on whether a woman was born in Germany.
$H3_{0c}$ Cultural problems do not depend on the difference of the place of study or work and the country the participants were born in.

Both groups are not significant for $H3_{0a}$ (CS $p = 0.31$, NCS $p = 0.18$) and $H3_{0b}$ (CS $p = 0.27$, NCS $p = 0.23$). Thus, we cannot falsify the null hypothesis, but it can be seen as an indicator: Women in computer science research tend to face less cultural problems than in other scientific fields/disciplines. The results for the last hypothesis $H3_{0c}$ (CS $p = 0.73$, NCS $p = 0.72$) are also not significant.

4   Threats to Validity

Threats to Internal Validity: Threats to internal validity are threats regarding the collected data. In our questionnaire, we tried to cover all problematic areas for women in research. Nevertheless, to miss some of them is a threat to our internal validity. Therefore, we established our taxonomy of areas and topics in a group meeting with seven women in total. However, some topics are not fully disjoint (e.g., pregnancy and hormones) and could have brought some bias in our data. The next problem concerning internal validity is that the association of a problem to a topic or area depends on the subject. Thereby, it could have happened that problems were not described because the participants forgot it or did not find a suitable topic. We counteracted these problems with the "others" topic in each area.

Threats to External Validity: Threats to external validity are threats regarding the generalization of the results. An issue regarding the external validity could be, that we conducted only technical universities. Moreover, we have 15 participants from social sciences and one who did not mention her scientific field included in the NCS group. Thereby, the NCS group may not be comparable to women in STEM fields. Moreover, our groups are not the same size. Furthermore, the problem and solution descriptions were optional. Thus, the generalization of our results based on the descriptions and labels can only be used as indicators. The reproducibility is mostly affected by the labeling process. To get a result as objective as possible, we conducted the labeling of each subject area in groups. If in any case, no existing label was fitting, groups could introduce new labels. These new labels were collected in a shared document including the name and description of the label. In this process, new labels could only be used after they were introduced, a relabeling was not done. The impact of this should be small:

New labels were only introduced when existing ones did not fit, therefore, the previous labeling should not be affected as there already were fitting labels.

Reproducibility: To enable replication of the study, we are making all of our data available. The questionnaire as well as our scripts and evaluation files can be found in our repository [4].

5   Conclusion

In this work, we report the current situation in Germany for women in research. We implemented a questionnaire and passed it to women at German universities. Our results contain data of 132 participants that we divide into two groups: Computer scientists (52) and others (80).

The average number of problems per person is almost equal between both groups. The distribution of problems across the given areas is alike. However, CS researchers solved 34% of their problems, while NCS only solved about 23%. Moreover, we found that the most important topics for problems are mostly identical for both groups. However, there are slight differences between both groups: 11.2% of problems of CS regard equality issues while this is the case for only 6.4% of problems of NCS. For collaborations as well as regarding support in research computer scientists have more problems, too. Nevertheless, they have fewer problems regarding their appreciation or publications. The most described problems in all areas are focused on parenting and family plans. These are followed by social aspects like communication with men or problems in networking. The most common solutions are to accept help from others, to make a workaround, or to strengthen self-esteem.

We could not find any evidence that cultural problems correlate with the birth country or the study/workplace history of women in research in both groups.

Future work should investigate whether the described problems and solutions can be applied in general. Additionally, it could be interesting to collect solution ideas from women in research and provide an overview about possible solutions that could be an improvement to the current state. To find out why women chose a solution could help to provide support to women in research.

Acknowledgment. This work was supported by the Competence Center for Applied Security Technology (KASTEL Projects 46.23.01 and 46.23.02). Larissa Schmid was supported by the Ministry of Science, Research and the Arts Baden-Württemberg (Az: 7712.14-0821-2).

References

1. Avolio, B., Chávez, J., Vílchez-Román, C.: Factors that contribute to the underrepresentation of women in science careers worldwide: a literature review. Soc. Psychol. Educ. **23**(3), 773–794 (2020). https://doi.org/10.1007/s11218-020-09558-y
2. Catalyst Research: Women in Academia (Quick Take). https://www.catalyst.org/research/women-in-academia/ (2020). Accessed 25 Jan 2022
3. College, W.: About wesleyan. https://web.archive.org/web/20160527072417/http://www.wesleyancollege.edu/about/index.cfm (2016). Accessed 27 Jan 2022
4. Corallo, S., et al.: Toward awareness creation of common challenges women are facing in academia: a study from a German perspective - survey results (2022). https://doi.org/10.5445/IR/1000145570
5. Destatis, S.B.: Frauenanteil in der Professorenschaft in Deutschland nach Fächergruppen 2020. https://de-statista-com.ezproxy-kit-1.redi-bw.de/statistik/daten/studie/197908/umfrage/frauenanteil-in-der-professorenschaft-nach-faechergruppen/ (2020). Accessed 7 Feb 2022
6. Destatis, S.B.: Statistik der Promovierenden (2020). https://www.destatis.de/DE/Themen/Gesellschaft-Umwelt/Bildung-Forschung-Kultur/Hochschulen/Publikationen/Downloads-Hochschulen/promovierendenstatistik-5213501197004.pdf?__blob=publicationFile. Accessed 25 Jan 2022
7. Falkner, K., Szabo, C., Michell, D., Szorenyi, A., Thyer, S.: Gender gap in academia: perceptions of female computer science academics. In: Proceedings of the 2015 ACM Conference on Innovation and Technology in Computer Science Education, pp. 111–116, ITiCSE 2015. Association for Computing Machinery, New York, NY, USA (2015). ISBN 9781450334402. https://doi.org/10.1145/2729094.2742595
8. Frize, M., Frize, P., Faulkner, N.: The Bold and the Brave: A History of Women in Science and Engineering. desLibris: Books collection, University of Ottawa Press (2009). ISBN 9780776607252. https://books.google.de/books?id=claKgik2i8AC
9. Henley, M.M.: Women's success in academic science: challenges to breaking through the ivory ceiling. Soc. Compass **9**(8), 668–680 (2015)
10. Kahn, S., Ginther, D.: Women and stem. Working Paper 23525, National Bureau of Economic Research, June 2017. https://doi.org/10.3386/w23525
11. Kearney, M.L., Lincoln, D.: Gender research: women, the academy and the workplace. Stud. Higher Educ. **41**(5), 799–800 (2016)
12. Koch, B.: Annette Vogt from the Max Planck Institute for the History of Science on Sofia Kovalevskaya, the world's first female professor of mathematics. www.mpg.de/female-pioneers-of-science/sofia-kovalevskaya#:~:text=Sofia%20Kovalevskaya%20(1850%2D1891),was%20awarded%20a%20Professorial%20Chair. Accessed 27 Jan 2022
13. Ogilvie, M.B.: Women in Science - Antiquity through the Nineteenth Century: A Biographical Dictionary with Annotated Bibliography. Massachusetts Institute of Technology (1986). ISBN 978-0262650380
14. Presser, S.: Methods for testing and evaluating survey questions. Public Opin. Q. **68**(1), 109–130 (2004)
15. Roberts, E.S., Kassianidou, M., Irani, L.: Encouraging women in computer science. SIGCSE Bull. **34**(2), 84–88 (2002), ISSN 0097–8418. https://doi.org/10.1145/543812.543837

16. Silim, A., Crosse, C.: Women in engineering fixing the talent pipeline (2014). https://dspace.ceid.org.tr/xmlui/handle/1/1579
17. Statista: Anzahl der Studierenden nach Geschlecht bis 2021/2022 (2021). https://de.statista.com/statistik/daten/studie/1083380/umfrage/anzahl-der-studenten-an-deutschen-hochschulen-nach-geschlecht/. Accessed 25 Jan 2022
18. Statista: Frauenanteile an Hochschulen in Deutschland bis 2020 (2021). https://de.statista.com/statistik/daten/studie/249318/umfrage/frauenanteile-an-hochschulen-in-deutschland/. Accessed 25 Jan 2022
19. Vitores, A., Gil-Juárez, A.: The trouble with 'women in computing': a critical examination of the deployment of research on the gender gap in computer science. J. Gender Stud. **25**(6), 666–680 (2016). https://doi.org/10.1080/09589236.2015.1087309

8th Workshop on Software Architecture Erosion and Architectural Consistency (SAEroCon)

Mapping Source Code to Modular Architectures Using Keywords

Tobias Olsson$^{(\boxtimes)}$ ⓘ, Morgan Ericsson ⓘ, and Anna Wingkvist ⓘ

Department of Computer Science and Media Technology, Linnaeus University,
Kalmar/Växjö, Sweden
{tobias.olsson,morgan.ericsson,anna.wingkvist}@lnu.se

Abstract. We implement an automatic mapper that can find the corresponding architectural module for a source code file. The mapper is based on multinomial naive Bayes, and it is trained using custom keywords for each architectural module. The mapper uses the path and file name of source code elements for prediction. We find that the needed keywords often match the module names; however, ambiguities and discrepancies exist. We evaluate the mapper using ten open-source systems with a mapping to an intended architecture and find that the mapper can successfully create a mapping with perfect precision. Still, it cannot cover all source code elements in most cases. However, other techniques can use the mapping as a foothold and automatically create further mappings. We also apply the approach to two cases where the architecture has been recovered from the implementation and find that the approach currently has limitations of applicability in such architectures.

Keywords: Orphan adoption · Software architecture · Clustering

Modular software architecture captures major design decisions regarding reuse, maintainability, changeability, and portability [8]. The source code must conform to the architecture during system evolution, or the system risks accumulating technical debt and losing the desired qualities.

Static Architecture Conformance Checking (SACC) methods, such as Reflexion modeling [14], statically analyze source code to ensure that it does not introduce architectural violations in the form of unwanted or missing dependencies [1,12]. These methods require an architecture model with modules and dependencies and a source code model with entities (e.g., source code files) and concrete dependencies (e.g., due to inheritance or method invocations). They also require a mapping from the source code model to the architecture model to detect convergent, absent, or divergent dependencies in the implementation.

Despite the importance of architecture conformance, SACC has not reached widespread use in the software industry [1,3,7,8]. Practitioners perceive the mapping from source code to architectural modules as a significant hindrance; it is often outdated or nonexistent, and it will require considerable effort to update or recreate this mapping. Many tools address this by combining manual

© The Author(s), under exclusive license to Springer Nature Switzerland AG 2022
P. Scandurra et al. (Eds.): ECSA Tracks and Workshops 2021, LNCS 13365, pp. 65–85, 2022.
https://doi.org/10.1007/978-3-031-15116-3_4

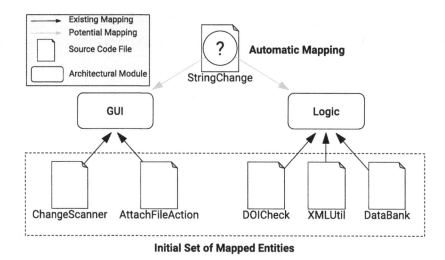

Fig. 1. An example of a mapping situation in one of the subject systems, JabRef. The entity StringChange is about to be mapped by the automatic mapper to either the GUI or Logic modules. The automatic mapper can use the information available in the initial set to aid in this. Image reworked from [21].

mapping and regular expressions to filter file, module, and package names. Still, such efforts are considered to be both time-consuming and error-prone [1,3,7,22].

Automatic mapping techniques aim to minimize the manual effort needed to create a mapping by using information available in the source code and the intended modular architecture (see Fig. 1). For example, dependencies between source code entities can be used to create a mapping. We have previously constructed an automatic mapping method, *NBAttract*, that can use different criteria (e.g., dependencies) in the source code and compute an attraction to a module [21]. Techniques such as NBAttract require an initial set to learn from, and constructing this initial set is still a manual effort. Depending on the technique and system, an initial set needs to consist of approximately 15–20% of the entities before reaching an acceptable performance [9,21]. In many cases, the physical structure of source code files is often in part or wholly reflected in the intended modular architecture [9,18,21,23]. Effective use of this information can present an attractive option for creating an initial set. However, file structure and naming are not always mapped one-to-one to a module, and there can be discrepancies, ambiguities, or simply missing information.

In contrast to methods that require an initial set to learn from, Sinkala and Herold introduces *InMap*. This mapping technique uses available architectural documentation to suggest mappings that the user will approve (or not) [22]. InMap does not require an initial set to work with but relies on good architectural documentation for each module. If an initial set can be created automatically for, e.g., NBAttract, comparing mapping performance between InMap and NBAttract becomes interesting.

Both NBAttract and InMap rely on existing architectural modules. In cases where this does not exist, architectural reconstruction can be used to find the actual, implemented architecture of a system and, as a by-product, a mapping of the source code to this recovered architecture. Garcia et al. presents a method for recovering and building ground truth architectures, including experiences from using the method to recover four different systems [11]. Recovered architectures are often different from the intended architectures, and, as such, it is interesting to investigate whether automatic mapping can be used to map a recovered architecture. This would indicate that automatic mapping could be beneficial in a reconstruction process.

We investigate how well a multinomial naive Bayes classifier trained using simple keywords derived from ground truth architectures can be used to create an initial set automatically. We pose the following questions:

1. Can the classifier construct an initial set based on a set of keywords for each module, and how complex is this set of keywords?
2. How well does NBAttract perform if using this constructed initial set as training data to learn patterns of dependencies and map the remainder of the system?
3. How well does the above combination perform compared to the NBAttract (with a random initial set) and InMap approaches?
4. Are there differences in keywords and performance between an intended architecture and a recovered implemented architecture?

We evaluate the mapper using ten open-source systems with known mappings to a specified intended modular architecture and find that the keywords are often the same as the module names. Still, more and different keywords are needed in some cases. After creating the initial set, we run NBAttract to map any remaining entities. We compare the results with NBAttract trained using a random initial set and InMap [22]. We find that the keywords-based approach can, in some cases, provide a complete mapping and that the keywords-based approach plus NBAttract performs very well on intended architectures. To test if the approach works on a reconstructed architecture, we perform the same experiments on two Hadoop subsystems that were recovered by Garcia et al. [11]. We find that we can create an initial set in this limited case, but it is suffering from poor recall. These two subsystems are significantly more complicated in their mapping, and we cannot find good support for using this simple keyword-based mapping for architectures recovered using the method described in [11].

This research is an extension of our previous work [19]. In this extension, we add three more subject systems (Jittac, Hadoop DFS, and Hadoop Mapred) (originally nine systems) with a total of 33 new modules (originally 96 modules). In addition, we double the number of data points in the experiments to cover more random combinations of the initial set. Finally, since Hadoop is a reconstructed architecture, this also adds another dimension to the analysis.

1   Background and Related Work

Tzerpos and Holt describe the general problem of mapping (or remapping) a source code entity to an architectural module [23]. They collectively call both the mapping and remapping of an entity the orphan adoption problem. They find four major criteria for solving the problem: *naming, structure, style,* and *semantics* and devise an algorithm. This algorithm is based on system-specific rules and parameters, e.g., rules for file patterns. Christl et al. later introduced the Human Guided clustering Method (HuGMe), an approach to semi-automatic mapping of source code entities to modules of the intended architecture [7]. It is an iterative approach that, at its core, uses an attraction function to compute the attraction between a source code entity and a module. The attraction is computed using an initial set of mapped entities (see Fig. 1). If the attraction is considered valid, an automatic mapping is made; if not, the attractions can be used as a suggestion for a human user. Two attraction functions based on dependencies are presented, CountAttract and MQAttract [6,7].

Bittencourt et al. present two new attraction functions based on information retrieval techniques [3]. They use semantic information in the source code, including module- and filenames. The attractions are calculated based on cosine similarity (IRAttract) and latent semantic indexing (LSIAttract). They make a quantitative comparison between the performance of their attraction functions with CountAttract and MQAttract in an evolutionary setting (where a few new files are to be assigned a mapping). They find that combining attraction functions (e.g., if CountAttract fails, try IRAttract) performs best. CountAttract usually misplaces entities on module borders, and MQAttract performs better when mapping entities with dependencies to many different modules. IRAttract and LSIAttract perform better when mapping entities in libraries or entities on module borders but worse if there are modules that share vocabulary but are not related [3].

We have created an attraction function that uses machine learning techniques and introduced the Concrete Dependency Abstraction (CDA) method [21]. In short, CDA produces textual representations of dependencies at the level of architectural modules. This allows a machine learning technique to learn the patterns of dependencies from the actual source code and combine these with information retrieval techniques that are also text-based. We implement this approach using naive Bayes as an attraction function for the HuGMe method, NBAttract. We have compared the automatic mapping performance of CountAttract, IRAttract, LSIAttract, and NBAttract over several systems using *s4rdm3x,* our open-source tool suite for automatic mapping experiments [16,17].

The main limitation for the techniques that build on HuGMe is the need for an initial set and, in some cases, the low-quality mappings in this initial set. Hence, the initial set needs to be manually created and of good quality for the attraction functions to perform well. We estimate that a randomly composed initial set needs to include approximately 15–20% of the source code entities [9,21]. Based on this, we conclude that creating the initial set is likely a significant effort.

Sinkala and Herold present InMap, which is not an automated approach to mapping per se but instead suggests mappings to the end-user, who can then choose to accept the suggested mapping (or not) [22]. It is an iterative approach that presents a suggested mapping for a fixed number of entities. The end-user accepts or rejects the suggestions, and the process is repeated. InMap uses the accepted mappings to improve the suggested mappings further in the next iteration. It also uses the negative evidence of a rejected mapping and does not suggest this mapping again. InMap produces the suggested mappings similar to Bittencourt et al., with the addition of a descriptive text for each architectural module. InMap also includes the path and filename used in the Java class and package names. It treats the source code entities as a database of documents and uses Lucene to search this database using module information as a query. Sinkala and Herold evaluate InMap using six open source systems. For the best combination (in terms of highest F1-score) of information, InMap can suggest mappings for most of a system's entities with a mean recall of 0.95, a mean precision of 0.84, and a mean F1-score of 0.89 [22].

The main limitations of InMap are its highly interactive nature and that architectural documentation needs to exist for every module. The documentation provided needs to be of good quality, i.e., as short as possible but containing good keywords. Noisy documentation will likely not help in producing high-precision suggestions. The interactiveness of InMap is in some way double-edged; the technique often seems to require more interaction (accepting or rejecting a suggested mapping) than there are entities in the source code [22]. On the other hand, if minor mapping errors can not be tolerated, a mapping validation is needed anyway.

Automatic software architecture reconstruction aims to extract architectural views from an existing system to aid developers in the further evolution of the system. Garcia et al. describes a process to obtain ground truth architectures from documentation and source code [11]. The aim is to provide better possibilities to evaluate different automatic recovery techniques. The process is based on identifying application-specific criteria to modularise the system that overrides domain and generic software engineering principles. In addition, the system documentation and context are used, and finally, the suggested architecture is validated using a system expert that can introduce changes. While any existing architectural documentation is used as input to the process, Garcia et al. notes that their recovered architectures have more modules and more dependencies between the modules compared to the conceptual architectures found in the documentation. This can be caused by architectural drift and erosion, a lower level of abstraction, difficulty in recovering certain styles of systems, and differences in architectural views. They note that both the conceptual architectures and recovered architectures were deemed valuable by the system expert validators.

In particular, Garcia et al. discuss the use of package and naming information in software architecture recovery [11]. In general, they found that their ground truth modules contained source code that often spanned or shared several packages. They could not find a correlation between modules and single package or directory names. One of their four cases presented a reasonably good correlation, and in one system, they could find a repeating pattern of packages. There is likely variation in what dimension or view of the architecture is expressed in the package structure. This variation is further supported by Buckley et al., where one out of five studied systems did not have any clear correlation between packages and modules. This presented difficulties and significant effort when performing the manual mapping [5].

Anquetil and Lethbridge propose a method for architecture recovery of legacy systems using filenames [2]. Their approach assumes that files have short names with many abbreviations and are placed in a single directory. This is due to their focus on recovering legacy systems. Nevertheless, they present some interesting findings. They identify several forces that shape a filename, i.e., what influences it. There seem to be several examples of such forces also in more modern implementations, e.g., from the subject system *Ant*, we find the feature implemented (*ant.taskdefs.SendEmail*), the algorithms or steps of algorithms (*ant.types.resources.Sort*), or data processed (*ant.taskdefs.email.Header*), as suggested in [2]. Much of the approach revolves around the problematic abbreviations found in the relatively short filenames. While this is not a technical problem in modern development, abbreviations are still common practice. For example, one of the subject systems, *ArgoUML*, defines a module *reverseEngineering*, and the corresponding directory mapping is the abbreviation *reveng*. Anquetil and Lethbridge successfully use filenames to create a clustering that corresponds well to an expert's view of a system [2].

2   Keywords and File-Based Mapping

File naming and structure seem to reflect the intended modular architectures we have studied quite well. For example, module names tend to map to the directory structure of the source code. However, the naming is often not perfect. In some cases, module names are not used, or shorter or slightly different terms are used. In other cases, several module names exist in the structure or naming of a file. A simplistic approach of just using the module name will have limited success. Instead, the file naming patterns need to be defined, e.g., fully using regular expressions or a heuristic. For regular expressions to work, there is often a need to maintain several expressions that can be conflicting and overlapping. A more attractive option would be to use machine learning and train a classifier using a good set of keywords for each module. The classifier's task is to produce a good enough initial set. An automatic mapping technique can then use this initial set for further mappings.

In this work, we implement a proof of concept mapper using a multinomial naive Bayes classifier. It is a simple, probabilistic approach that uses word frequencies to compute the probability of each class. While it is conceptually simple, naive Bayes often produce good results, especially if the training data is small. As the goal is to create a good enough mapping using a small set of predefined keywords, naive Bayes is thus a good candidate for a proof of concept study.

We base our implementation on the Weka library [24] and train the classifier using the custom keywords for each module. Note that the same keyword can be specified multiple times, increasing the importance of that particular keyword.

We derive the prediction data from the path of each source code entity, including the filename. The filename is split into words based on the common camel, kebab, and snake-case rules. In addition, we value later parts of the path more and add these words multiple times. Intuitively allowing for a deeper nested folder mapping to "override" a higher level mapping. For example, the file:

net/sf/jabref/logic/util/io/FileHistory.java

will produce the following words:

net sf jabref logic util io filehistory file history sf jabref logic util io jabref logic util io logic util io util io io

Note the six occurrences of *io* reflecting the nesting depth of the word in the path.

To generate a useful initial set, it is more important that the mappings are precise rather than complete. There needs to be a high difference between the best mapping probability and the second-best probability to achieve this. By trial and error, we found a factor of 1.99 to work well, i.e., the highest probability needs to be 1.99 times higher than the second-highest probability for mapping to occur. This ensures high precision, likely at the expense of a lower recall.

We have implemented the mapper described above in our open-source tool suite *s4rdm3x* [20].

3 Method

We study ten open-source systems with known ground truth mappings to their *intended* architectures and two major subsystems where the *implemented* architecture has been recovered from the source code. We create a keyword set for each module based on the ground truth mappings and ensure that these keywords will successfully map at least some entities to each module.

After determining the keywords, we run our keywords-based mapper and create an initial set. This initial set is then used as the input to another mapper, NBAttract, which also uses multinomial naive Bayes but instead forms training- and prediction words using dependency information in the form of concrete dependency abstractions (CDA) [17]. We compare the performance to NBAttract with random initial sets to determine whether an initial set built from keywords performs better on average. We also compare to the interactive approach InMap [22].

We collect precision, recall, and combined F1 scores for each approach. When a random initial set is used, several sets of different sizes and compositions are needed to cover an extensive range of combinations. We present the performance metrics numerically and visually as the effect of the initial set size is essential.

All systems are implemented in Java. Ant[1] is a library and command-line tool for process automation. ArgoUML[2] is a desktop application for UML modeling. Jabref[3] is a desktop application for managing bibliographical references. Jittac[4] is an eclipse plugin for just-in-time architectural conformance checking. K9[5] is an open-source email client for Android. Lucene[6] is an indexing and search library. ProM[7] is an extensible framework that supports a variety of process mining techniques. Note that we use the ProM framework and not the full ProM system. Sweet Home 3D[8] is an interior design application. TeamMates[9] is a web application for handling student peer reviews and feedback. For the recovered system, we used Hadoop[10] and the subsystems distributed file system (DFS) and MapReduce (Mapred) as described by [10]. Hadoop is a framework that allows for the distributed processing of large data sets across clusters of computers.

A documented software architecture and a mapping from the implementation to this architecture exist for each system. Jabref, TeamMates, and ProM have been the study subjects at the Software Architecture Erosion and Architectural Consistency Workshop (SAEroCon) 2016, 2017, and 2019 respectively. A systems expert has provided both the architecture and the mapping for these systems. The architecture documentation and mappings are available in the SAEroCon repository[11]. ArgoUML, Ant, and Lucene have been studied previously [4,13], and the architectures and mappings were extracted from the replication package of Brunet et al. [4]. K9 has been preliminary mapped by ourselves based on architecture documentation provided in [15][12]. We have not validated this mapping with systems experts but included it since it is an interesting case with a more complex file structure.

4   Results and Analysis

We use the existing ground truth mappings to construct a set of keywords for each system (see Tables 2, 3, and 4 in Appendix A). The keywords are tested and changed so that at least one entity for each module is mapped, and so that erroneous mappings are avoided. Tables 2 and 3 show the manually extracted keywords for the modules of the systems with intended architectures. A single keyword is sufficient for 87 of the 105 modules, and in 10 cases, a weight was

[1] https://ant.apache.org.
[2] http://argouml.tigris.org.
[3] https://jabref.org.
[4] https://git.cs.kau.se/zipasink/InMap/-/tree/master/test-systems/Jittac/sources/se.kau.cs.jittac.core.
[5] https://k9mail.app/.
[6] https://lucene.apache.org.
[7] http://www.promtools.org.
[8] http://www.sweethome3d.com.
[9] https://teammatesv4.appspot.com.
[10] https://hadoop.apache.org/.
[11] https://github.com/sebastianherold/SAEroConRepo.
[12] http://oss.models-db.com/Downloads/EASE2019_ReplicationPackage/.

needed for a keyword (i.e., repeating the same keyword). Many keywords are the same as or some variation of the module name. K9 presents an exception for the intended architectures where several keywords are needed. We relied on a high-level architectural description when creating the mapping for K9, where allowed dependencies were the most clearly defined. The keywords reflect the submodules of the high-level modules. Note that systems experts have not validated our mapping of K9. Table 1 shows each system's precision, recall, and F1 scores for the keyword mappings. The keywords can create an initial set with perfect precision and recall in Commons Imaging, ProM, and Sweet Home 3D. The keywords for these systems are straightforward and are often directly reflected in the module name. For the other systems with intended architectures, keywords can generate an initial set with perfect precision, but recall is suffering.

Table 1. Intended Architectures Precision, Recall, and F1-score for each mapping technique. For Random combined with NBAttract, the median metrics are shown. Systems marked with * are compared to InMap, and systems marked with † are based on reverse engineered architectures.

System	Keywords			Keywords and NBAttract			Random and NBAttract			InMap		
	P	R	F1	P	R	F1	P	R	F1	P	R	F1
Ant*	1.00	0.97	0.99	0.99	1.00	0.99	0.94	0.91	0.94	0.73	1.00	0.84
ArgoUML*	1.00	0.67	0.80	0.97	1.00	0.98	0.95	1.00	0.97	0.78	0.98	0.87
C Img	1.00	1.00	1.00				0.84	0.99	0.90			
JabRef*	1.00	0.95	0.98	0.98	1.00	0.99	0.91	0.98	0.94	0.96	1.00	0.98
Jittac*	1.00	0.97	0.99	0.98	0.99	0.99	0.90	1.00	0.95	0.95	0.99	0.97
K9	1.00	0.81	0.90	0.96	1.00	0.98	0.92	1.00	0.96			
Lucene	1.00	0.99	1.00	1.00	0.99	1.00	0.97	1.00	0.98			
ProM*	1.00	1.00	1.00				0.99	1.00	1.00	0.81	0.87	0.84
SH3D	1.00	1.00	1.00				0.83	1.00	0.91			
TMates*	1.00	0.60	0.75	0.97	1.00	0.99	0.97	1.00	0.98	0.95	0.97	0.96
HDFS†	0.97	0.52	0.67	0.66	0.95	0.78	0.67	0.96	0.77			
Mapred†	1.00	0.35	0.52	0.37	1.00	0.54	0.45	0.71	0.48			
*Mean**	*1.00*	*0.86*	*0.92*	*0.98*	*1.00*	*0.99*	*0.94*	*0.98*	*0.96*	*0.86*	*0.97*	*0.91*
Mean†	*0.99*	*0.43*	*0.60*	*0.51*	*0.98*	*0.66*	*0.56*	*0.83*	*0.62*			
Total Mean	1.00	0.82	0.88	0.87	0.99	0.91	0.86	0.96	0.90			

Can the classifier construct an initial set based on a set of keywords for each module, and how complex is this set of keywords? We conclude that for intended architectures, a set of keywords can be constructed that gives good precision, covers every module, and is often not different from the actual module names.

How well does NBAttract perform if using this constructed initial set as training data to learn patterns of dependencies and map the remainder of the system? We used the initial sets generated by the keywords and added the NBAttract mapper. NBAttract was configured to learn dependency patterns from the initial sets using CDA and map the remaining entities. Table 1 shows the precision, recall, and F1-scores of using keywords and NBAttract in combination. Overall, we find that this combination performs very well on systems with an intended architecture but worse on the systems with an implemented architecture (i.e., Mapred and HDFS). The lowest F1 score is 0.98 for ArgoUML and Teammates. The precision scores are over 0.95 in all cases, and the recall is almost perfect.

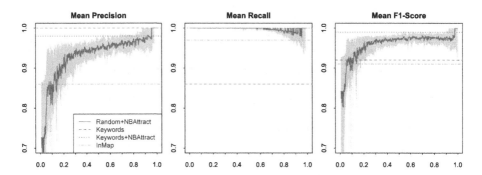

Fig. 2. Comparison of the means of the different approaches, Random + NBattract shows the running median and running quartiles over the size of the randomly composed initial sets. Note that the y-axis starts at 0.7.

How well does the above combination perform compared to the NBAttract (with a random initial set) and InMap approaches? We performed more than 3 000 experiments with random initial sets for the NBAttract mapper. NBAttract was configured to learn filename and dependency information with CDA (neither module keywords nor keywords from the code was used in the training data). We use the best-reported performance metrics for Inmap for comparison [22]. Table 1 shows the comparison of the four approaches. We aggregated 3 000 samples from Ant, ArgoUML, JabRef, Jittac, ProM, and Teammates to summarize the results. We compared these with the mean keywords, mean keywords and NBAttract, random initial sets and NBAttract, and mean InMap results. Figure 2 shows the precision, recall, and F1 scores, respectively. For random initial sets and NBAttract, the running median and the running quartiles over the size of the initial set are shown. We note that when the initial set is comparably large, we get a very high F1 score. This indicates that there is enough information in a large initial set to produce overall good mappings using only file structure information and dependencies. There is a dip a in recall that is caused by Ant, Jabref and TeamMates (cf. Fig. 4 and 5 in Appendix B). This dip indicates that there is a risk of over-fitting, and the addition of some complementary type of information, e.g., semantic information, to learn from could be beneficial in some systems. We also note that the random initial set approach performs better than the keyword approach at very high initial set sizes, i.e., mapping only a few new entities. This would indicate that in an evolutionary case, keywords are not needed to maintain the mapping.

InMap lacks precision but performs well regarding the recall. Note that InMap is a highly interactive approach to mapping. The aim is not to automate the mapping but rather to give good advice to a human user that interactively maps the source code iteratively. If there is a need to check an automatic mapping thoroughly, an interactive approach is attractive regardless of precision.

Are there differences in keywords and performance between an intended architecture and a recovered implemented architecture? For Hadoop DFS and MapReduce, we limited the analysis to modules with three or more mapped entities (cf. Table 4). There are many singleton modules in the recovered architecture, and for such modules, it would essentially mean a manual mapping of the exact entity. It also proved unfeasible to produce keywords at this low resolution. The keywords for the Hadoop subsystems are generally more complex and rely on words that are unrelated to the module. For DFS and Mapreduce, only 9 out of 24 modules could be mapped using a single keyword. These two subsystems have many modules that share the same packages, and thus, mapping based on file structure becomes cumbersome. In addition, files are often named using generic words such as *manager* or *node*, which occur in many different modules, making this approach even harder. For the implemented architectures of Hadoop subsystems DFS and Mapred, the keywords are considerably more complicated. In many cases, some particular keywords are needed that are not at all related to the module name (cf. Table 4). Particularly Mapred has several modules that are not straightforwardly mapped to a specific keyword covering many source code entities. This can be seen as a low recall in the Mapred keywords-based mapping. For DFS, we could not create a keyword-based mapping with perfect precision, as many names used in the file structure are reflected in several modules. A limitation of the current mapper is thus that recovered implemented architectures seem to have modules that correspond to naming patterns to a lesser degree. Interestingly, this would also make regular expressions much harder to implement.

Using the keywords as the initial set and then learning using dependency patterns to map the rest via NBAttract gives quite poor performance, especially when compared with the performance of the approach when mapping to an intended architecture (cf. Table 1). Mapred, in particular, has a very low performance and would likely need some additional type of information to be mapped, e.g., semantic information. This is also supported by the declining performance of Mapred as the initial set size grows for the random initial set comparison (cf. Fig. 3). So, mapping to the recovered implemented architectures of the Hadoop subsystems Mapred and HDFS seem to be considerably harder than mapping the other systems to their intended architectures. In addition, the subsystems show very different benefits of using dependencies and file structure information in the mapping. Mapping Hadoop DFS seems to benefit from this information while Mapred does not.

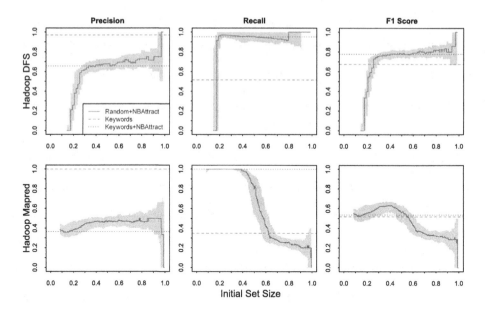

Fig. 3. F1-Score, Precision, and Recall of hadoop subsystems DFS and Mapred.

Figure 3 shows the F1-score, precision, and recall of Hadoop DFS and Mapred, respectively. The HDFS subsystem shows an overall performance similar to the systems with an intended architecture. However, the Mapred subsystem does not, and it cannot be mapped using only the file structure and dependencies. Both the precision and recall decrease as the initial set grows, so file structure and dependency information are likely not that useful for mapping purposes in Mapred. Instead, more semantic information such as identifier names from the source code might be needed. As such, Mapred provides an interesting case to study further.

5   Discussion and Validity

Keywords can be effectively used when mapping to an intended architecture and provide an excellent initial set, even a perfect mapping in some cases. It is an attractive approach compared to manually mapping an initial set. Hypothetically, it should be easier to extract the keywords and specify the corresponding module and weight of the keyword compared to mapping several tens or hundreds of files manually. The main challenge is, of course, how to find a set of keywords with high precision and low complexity. We used the already established ground truth mappings in this evaluation, but this approach is not applicable in a real case. However, analyzing the directory structure and looking for words in the module names could provide a starting point. Possibly using a deeper level in the directory hierarchy or looking for repeating patterns could be fruitful. Semantic analysis using, e.g., WordNet could be an approach to find related words in the directory structure. In addition, information from, e.g., method names and identifiers could be used.

It would arguably be easier to create and maintain a small set of keywords compared to, e.g., regular expressions, even if done entirely manually.

Using a large initial set seems to give a very high performance of NBAttract in some cases, e.g., ArgoUML, Commons Imaging, Lucene, ProM, Sweet Home 3D (cf. Fig. 4 and 5 in Appendix B). This indicates that when the mapping is established, NBAttract often performs well when only a few new source code entities are introduced (e.g., during software evolution). Still, there are cases where the F1-scores decline as the initial sets grow, e.g., JabRef, K9, and TeamMates (cf. Fig. 4 and 5 in Appendix B). Our analysis suggests that the model is over-fitted, i.e., it becomes too specific and, as a result, the recall drops (cf. Fig. 4 and 5 in Appendix B). This can be addressed by either lowering the threshold for mapping or introducing more information in the model, such as identifier names from the source code. The very high recall in ProM (cf. Fig. 5 in Appendix B) can be explained by the fact that the ProM framework has a very straightforward mapping.

In comparison, keywords for the reconstructed architectures were considerably more complex and harder to find. Also, the frequent use of singleton modules increases the complexity even further and has to be removed. This study cannot find good support for using simple keywords for neither HDFS nor Mapred. Regarding performance particularly, Mapred does not seem to benefit from using file structure and dependency information (cf. Fig. 3). Both HDFS and Mapred are subsystems of Hadoop, and this difference could indicate that different modules benefit from different information to learn from in automatic mapping. Overall Garcia et al. note that there are several differences between intended and recovered architectures [11]. Recovered architectures can be affected by architectural erosion and drift, but they are often at a lower level of abstraction and often shows a different architectural view than the intended architectures. Our findings support that intended and recovered architectures are different; the recovered Hadoop architecture is considerably more complex than the intended architectures. We find this difference interesting and challenging. More work is needed in the area of using automatic mapping techniques for recovered architectures.

We limit ourselves to systems implemented in Java, where the file structure often reflects the modular design of our subject systems well. While we could handle discrepancies and ambiguities well enough to create an initial set, this may not be the case in a system where the file structure is entirely different. However, we also show that using the file information in many cases is beneficial. Current mapping methods, e.g., NBAttract [21] and InMap [22], should likely give file information more attention.

6   Conclusions and Future Work

We have investigated the use of keywords to perform mapping of source code entities to modules in an architecture. We evaluated the approach using ten open source systems with known mappings to an intended architecture and two subsystems of Hadoop with mappings to a reconstruction of the implemented architecture.

We found that we could construct relatively simple keywords for most of the 105 modules in all ten systems. Ten modules (9.5%) required weights for keywords, and 18 (17.1%) required two or more (different) keywords. Our mapper could successfully create an initial set using the keywords, and in some cases, this resulted in a perfect mapping.

Combining the keywords-based mapping and NBAttract using CDA provided outstanding performance with a mean precision, recall, and F1 score of 0.98, 1.0, and 0.99, respectively. The performance was higher than using random initial sets, NBAttract using CDA and file information, and the interactive technique InMap (cf. Table 1).

If a mapping is already established, NBAttract with CDA and file information provides good performance in many cases. However, in some systems, the model can suffer from overfitting issues (cf. Fig. 4 and 5 in Appendix B).

Finding keywords based on file structure is significantly harder for the recovered architectures, HDFS and Mapred. 15 of 24 (62.5%) modules require two or more different keywords for these two architectures. However, there are zero weighted keywords. Modules often span several packages, file naming is usually quite generic, and the same words are used in multiple files and modules. This makes a keyword-based approach using file structure significantly harder and often pinpoints single files. This is evident from the relatively low recall of the keyword-based approach. This means that the foothold for continued mapping becomes smaller and thus more sensitive to the actual source code mapped, and in general, it has less data to learn from. HDFS seems to be more similar to the implemented architectures of the two subsystems. Mapred is quite different, and it appears that file and dependency information is not well suited to map this module.

Using keywords is an attractive approach that can significantly reduce the mapping effort. However, a central question that remains is how to extract good candidate keywords and let a human user assign weights. It is also important to realize that some mappings are not well suited to use file structure information. The keywords approach can possibly be expanded to include information from the source code, such as identifier names.

Acknowledgment. The research was supported by the Centre for Data Intensive Sciences and Applications (DISA) at Linnaeus University. We would like to thank the reviewers for their thoughtful comments and efforts towards improving our manuscript.

A   Appendix

Table 2. Ant, ArgoUML, and Commons Imaging modules and keywords.

System	Module	Keywords
Ant	compilers	2 * compiler 2 * compilers
	condition	condition
	rmic	rmic
	cvslib	cvslib
	email	email
	taskdefs	taskdefs
	listener	listener
	types	types
	ant	ant
	util	util
	zip	zip
	tar	tar
	mail	mail
	bzip2	bzip2
AUML	application	2 * application
	diagrams	2 * diagram
	notation	notation
	explorer	explorer
	codeGeneration	3 * language code generation
	javaCodeGeneration	language code generation 2 * java
	reverseEngineering	3 * reveng
	persistence	persistence
	moduleLoader	moduleloader 2 * api module modules
	gui	ui
	model	model
	internationalization	i18n
	swingExtensions	swingext
	ocl	ocl
	critics	2 * cognitive
C Img	base	imaging
	color	color
	common	common
	bmp	bmp
	dcx	dcx
	gif	gif
	icns	icns
	ico	ico
	jpeg	jpeg
	pcx	pcx
	png	png
	pnm	pnm
	psd	psd
	rgbe	rgbe
	tiff	tiff
	wbmp	wbmp
	xbm	xbm
	xpm	xpm
	icc	icc
	internal	internal
	palette	palette

Table 3. JabRef, Jittac, Lucene, K9, ProM, and TeamMates modules and keywords

System	Module	Keywords
JabRef	globals	globals
	preferences	preferences prefs
	model	model shared dbms
	logic	logic shared
	gui	gui
	cli	cli
Jittac	common.util	util
	common.exception	exception
	common.dataTransfer	datatransfer
	ui.automated	automated
	ui.controller	controller
	ui.view	ui page
	logic.core	core
	logic.api	logic api
	logic.backdoor	backdoor
Lucene	queryparser	queryparser
	search	search
	index	index
	store	store
	analysis	analysis
	util	util
	document	document
K9	business	controller service mail k9 power search migrations
	presentation	activity ui notification fragment view list widget helper crypto
	service	provider action extra
	dataaccess	mailstore util
	crosscutting	crypto autocrypt cache helper
ProM	framework	framework
	contexts	contexts
	models	models
	plugins	plugins
SH3D	sH3DModel	model
	sH3DTools	tools
	sH3DPlugin	plugin
	sH3DViewController	viewcontroller
	sH3DSwing	swing
	sH3DJava3D	j3d
	sH3DIO	io
	sH3DApplet	applet
	sH3DApplication	sweethome3d

(*continued*)

Table 3. (*continued*)

System	Module	Keywords
TMates	common.util	util
	common.exception	exception
	common.dataTransfer	datatransfer
	ui.automated	automated
	ui.controller	controller
	ui.view	ui page
	logic.core	core
	logic.api	logic api
	logic.backdoor	backdoor
	storage.entity	entity
	storage.api	storage api
	storage.search	search
	testDriver	test test
	client.remoteAPI	remoteapi
	client.scripts	scripts scripts

Table 4. Modules with keywords for DFS and Mapreduce.

Subsystem	Module	Keywords
DFS	Balancer	balancer
	Client-facing_Exceptions	namenode exception
	DataNode	datanode block metrics
	Datanode_Protocol	protocol command
	Distributed_File_System	distributed
	FS_Logging	namenode edit log
	HDFS_Upgrade_Management	upgrade
	Namenode	namenode name
	NameNode_HDFS_Protocol_Core	namenode lease
Mapred	CPP_Pipes_Job	pipes reducer
	CPP_Pipes_Protocol	pipes protocol
	DB_IO	db
	DelegatingMapper	lib delegating
	Job_History	history
	Job_Tracking	job listener
	JobClient	jobcontrol
	Join_utilities	join
	KeyFieldBasedPartitioner	lib key
	Mapred_client	lib mapper
	Mapred_utilities	task action
	Multiple_Output_File_Formatting	lib multiple output
	Sequence_File_Handling	sequence
	Task_Tracking_and_Running	task status tracker
	Value_Aggregator	aggregate

B   Appendix

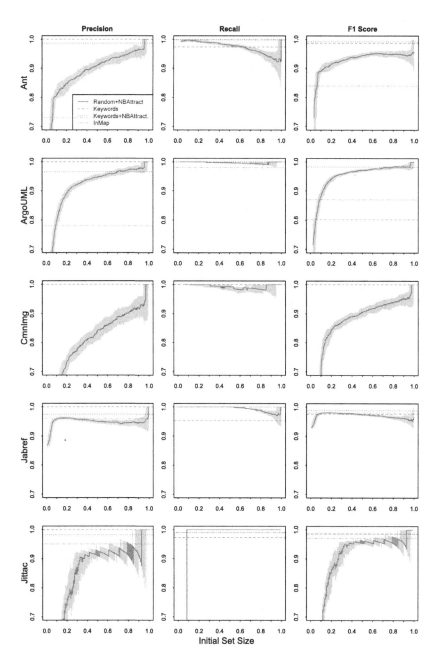

Fig. 4. The performance of each approach and system, Random+NBAttract is shown with a running median and 25th to 75th quartiles. Note that the y-axis starts at 0.7.

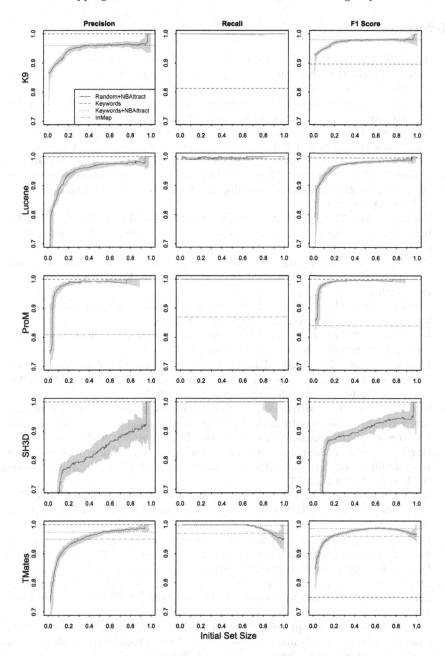

Fig. 5. The performance of each approach and system (cont.), Random+NBAttract are shown with a running median and the running 25th to 75th quartiles. Note that the y-axis starts at 0.7.

References

1. Ali, N., Baker, S., O'Crowley, R., Herold, S., Buckley, J.: Architecture consistency: state of the practice, challenges and requirements. Empir. Softw. Eng. **23**(1), 224–258 (2017). https://doi.org/10.1007/s10664-017-9515-3
2. Anquetil, N., Lethbridge, T.C.: Recovering software architecture from the names of source files. J. Softw. Maint. Res. Pract. **11**(3), 201–221 (1999)
3. Bittencourt, R.A., de Souza Santos, G.J., Guerrero, D.D.S., Murphy, G.C.: Improving automated mapping in reflexion models using information retrieval techniques. In: Working Conference on Reverse Engineering, pp. 163–172. IEEE (2010)
4. Brunet, J., Bittencourt, R.A., Serey, D., Figueiredo, J.: On the evolutionary nature of architectural violations. In: Working Conference on Reverse Engineering, pp. 257–266. IEEE (2012)
5. Buckley, J., Ali, N., English, M., Rosik, J., Herold, S.: Real-time reflexion modelling in architecture reconciliation: a multi case study. Inf. Softw. Technol. **61**, 107–123 (2015)
6. Christl, A., Koschke, R., Storey, M.A.: Equipping the reflexion method with automated clustering. In: Working Conference on Reverse Engineering, pp. 98–108. IEEE (2005)
7. Christl, A., Koschke, R., Storey, M.A.: Automated clustering to support the reflexion method. Inf. Softw. Technol. **49**(3), 255–274 (2007)
8. De Silva, L., Balasubramaniam, D.: Controlling software architecture erosion: a survey. J. Syst. Softw. **85**(1), 132–151 (2012)
9. Florean, A., Jalal, L., Sinkala, Z.T., Herold, S.: A comparison of machine learning-based text classifiers for mapping source code to architectural modules. In: 15th European Conference on Software Architecture (2021)
10. Garcia, J., Ivkovic, I., Medvidovic, N.: A comparative analysis of software architecture recovery techniques. In: 28th IEEE/ACM International Conference on Automated Software Engineering (ASE), pp. 486–496, November 2013
11. Garcia, J., Krka, I., Mattmann, C., Medvidovic, N.: Obtaining ground-truth software architectures. In: 35th International Conference on Software Engineering (ICSE), pp. 901–910 (2013)
12. Knodel, J., Popescu, D.: A comparison of static architecture compliance checking approaches. In: The IEEE/IFIP Working Conference on Software Architecture, pp. 12–21 (2007)
13. Lenhard, J., Blom, M., Herold, S.: Exploring the suitability of source code metrics for indicating architectural inconsistencies. Softw. Qual. J. **27**, 241–274 (2019). https://doi.org/10.1007/s11219-018-9404-z
14. Murphy, G.C., Notkin, D., Sullivan, K.: Software reflexion models: bridging the gap between source and high-level models. ACM SIGSOFT Softw. Eng. Notes **20**(4), 18–28 (1995)
15. Nurwidyantoro, A., Ho-Quang, T., Chaudron, M.R.V.: Automated classification of class role-stereotypes via machine learning. In: Proceedings of the Evaluation and Assessment on Software Engineering, pp. 79–88 (2019)
16. Olsson, T., Ericsson, M., Wingkvist, A.: An exploration and experiment tool suite for code to architecture mapping techniques. In: Proceedings of the 13th European Conference on Software, ECSA 2019, vol. 2, pp. 26–29 (2019)
17. Olsson, T., Ericsson, M., Wingkvist, A.: Semi-automatic mapping of source code using Naive Bayes. In: Proceedings of the 13th European Conference on Software Architecture, vol. 2, pp. 209–216 (2019)

18. Olsson, T., Ericsson, M., Wingkvist, A.: Hard cases in source code to architecture mapping using Naive Bayes. In: ECSA 2021 Companion Volume, pp. 13–17 (2021)
19. Olsson, T., Ericsson, M., Wingkvist, A.: A preliminary study on the use of keywords for source code to architecture mappings. In: CEUR Workshop Proceedings of the 15th European Conference on Software Architecture (2021)
20. Olsson, T., Ericsson, M., Wingkvist, A.: s4rdm3x: a tool suite to explore code to architecture mapping techniques. J. Open Source Softw. **6**(58), 2791 (2021)
21. Olsson, T., Ericsson, M., Wingkvist, A.: To automatically map source code entities to architectural modules with Naive Bayes. J. Syst. Softw. **183**, 111095 (2022)
22. Sinkala, Z.T., Herold, S.: InMap: automated interactive code-to-architecture mapping recommendations. In: IEEE 18th International Conference on Software Architecture (ICSA), pp. 173–183 (2021)
23. Tzerpos, V., Holt, R.C.: The orphan adoption problem in architecture maintenance. In: Working Conference on Reverse Engineering, pp. 76–82. IEEE (1997)
24. Witten, I., Frank, E., Hall, M., Pal, C.: Data Mining, Fourth Edition: Practical Machine Learning Tools and Techniques, 4th edn. Morgan Kaufmann Publishers Inc., San Francisco (2016)

Hierarchical Code-to-Architecture Mapping

Zipani Tom Sinkala$^{(\boxtimes)}$ ⬤ and Sebastian Herold ⬤

Department of Mathematics and Computer Science, Karlstad University, Karlstad, Sweden
{tom.sinkala,sebastian.herold}@kau.se

Abstract. Automating the mapping of a system's code to its architecture is important in improving the adoption of successful Software Architecture Consistency
Checking (SACC) methods like Reflexion Modelling. InMap is an interactive and
iterative code-to-architecture mapping recommendation approach that achieves a
rather decent recall and precision of 0.97 and 0.82 respectively, using minimal
architecture documentation to apply natural language techniques to a software's
codebase. Nevertheless, InMap like most other automated recommendations techniques maps to architectural modules, low-level source code units like classes.
For large complex systems, this can still hinder adoption due to the review effort
required by a software architect when accepting or rejecting the recommendations. In this paper, we present a *hierarchical package mapping technique* that
provides recommendations for higher-level source code units, i.e. packages. It utilizes InMap's information retrieval capabilities to recommend mappings between
the software's packages and its architectural modules. We show that using our proposed technique we are able to reduce the recommendation *review effort* required
by an architect, by 95% on average, for the six systems tested, and still achieve a
code coverage of 75% .

Keywords: Automated source code mapping · Software architecture
consistency · Software architecture conformance · Software maintenance

1 Introduction

A routine task in *Software Architecture Consistency Checking (SACC)* is the mapping of
a software system's *codebase* to its *architecture* [1, 11, 14, 16]. Effective SACC methods
like *Reflexion Modelling* [9, 12] encompass a code-to-architecture mapping step in order
to be able to identify if a system's codebase conforms-to or diverges-from its intended
software architectural modules [8, 9, 12, 13]. This mapping process is manual and labour-
intensive for the most part, and becomes a barrier to adoption by industry of notable
SACC techniques like Reflexion Modelling [1, 7].

There have been attempts to decrease the dreadful burden on software architects of
manually mapping code-to-architecture, especially in the case of large complex software
systems, by automating this mapping step [4–6, 11, 15, 16]. Most of these however, are
what we could call or classify as *class-* or *file-based mapping techniques* [11, 15, 16].
Classes are considered as the basic unit of source code in the case of systems developed

© The Author(s), under exclusive license to Springer Nature Switzerland AG 2022
P. Scandurra et al. (Eds.): ECSA Tracks and Workshops 2021, LNCS 13365, pp. 86–104, 2022.
https://doi.org/10.1007/978-3-031-15116-3_5

using an object oriented programming language. *Class-based mapping techniques* automate mapping at this level, i.e. class level – endeavouring to predict which architectural module, a class (or class-file) maps to. This has, for example, been done quite well with techniques like InMap [15, 16] and NBC [11]. In our paper "InMap: Automated Interactive Code-to-Architecture Mapping Recommendations" we show that InMap achieved a recall of 0.87–1.00 and precision of 0.70–0.96 for the systems tested. However, in large systems of say a 1,000 classes or more, despite a technique achieving a recall and precision of 1.00 (the perfect score), the burden still rests with an architect to review over a 1,000 recommendations (i.e. one for each class) before accepting them as correct.

In an attempt to lessen this identified *review effort* required by an architect, we consider making mapping recommendations for higher-level source code units – that is, we investigate making mapping recommendations for larger units of code at a time (packages rather than classes). In this paper, we present an automated *hierarchical package mapping technique*. It builds upon the successes of our information retrieval-based InMap approach [15, 16] that produces mapping recommendations derived from a similarity computation of an unmapped class to an architectural module using natural language. We exploit the *class-to-module similarity scores* originating from InMap to produce *package-to-module similarity scores*, which are then filtered using a well-defined set of heuristics. These are then used to produce a set of *package-to-module* mapping recommendations that are determined by a system's package hierarchy. We show that using our proposed *hierarchical package mapping technique* we are able to reduce the *review effort* required by an architect, by 95% on average, and still achieve code coverage of 75%.

Section 2 briefly discusses existing automated mapping techniques along with their hierarchical mapping capabilities. In Sect. 3, we detail our *hierarchical package mapping* approach, describing how package scores are computed and how *package-to-module mapping recommendations* are formed. Section 4 describes how we evaluate the technique and presents the results we obtained. In Sect. 5, we analyse and discuss the results and in Sect. 6, we conclude on our findings and present opportunities for further research.

This paper is an extended version of our pre-proceedings paper [17]. Our contributions are, an enhancement to the approach of our hierarchical mapping technique by making it iterative; an inclusion of all six systems in the analysis and discussion of our results on *effort required* by an architect in reviewing mapping recommendations; and an expansion on the limitation and validity of the study.

2   Related Work

Christl et al. propose HuGME as a *dependency analysis (DA) based mapping recommendation* technique. HuGME clusters source code using an architect's knowledge about its intended architecture [4, 5]. By means of a *dependency-based attraction function*, which minimizes coupling and maximizes cohesion, it produces a matrix of attraction scores for unmapped entities [18]. The score is calculated using the dependency between unmapped entities and mapped entities. The greater the score, the higher the possibility that an unmapped entity belongs to a given module. All unmapped entities that result in only one candidate having an attraction score higher than the arithmetic mean of all scores result in a single recommendation for these entities. All unmapped entities for which two or more candidates exist are presented to the user in ranked order, from highest to lowest, as recommendations. HuGME presents the recommendations to the user to let cluster decisions to be made entirely by the architect. HuGME does not attempt to map all source code entities in one complete step; rather it maps a subset at a time until no more mapping is possible. This classifies it as an *incremental mapping technique*. HuGME's automated mapping approach is *non-hierarchical* since it views this task from a clustering perspective in which source code entities that are mapped to the same hypothesized architectural module form a cluster [4].

HuGME is shown to have on average about 0.90 recall and 0.80–0.90 precision [5]. The technique is also shown to need about 20% of a system's codebase to be manually *pre-mapped* before proceeding with automated-mapping in order to get these results. It is important to note that because this mapping technique is *dependency-based*, for it to give meaningful results, the required 20% pre-mapped codebase needs to be spread out evenly across the various architectural modules of the system under investigation. In addition, the mapped source entities *must have* dependencies to unmapped entities of the system. This drawback entails that in order to benefit from this technique an architect needs to not only devote some time for pre-mapping but must also spend time ensuring that mappings chosen are evenly spread across the modules. Additionally, one must also ensure that the selected pre-mapped source code entities have dependencies to the unmapped entities otherwise, entity relationship discovery is poor. This all becomes a highly labour-intensive and cognitively demanding exercise especially for large complex software systems where 20% of codebase is still sufficiently large. Furthermore, because HuGME uses clustering algorithms based on high cohesion and low coupling, if the developers of a software system do not follow this principle in its implementation then the mapping recommendations produced by HuGME will be skewed negatively [2].

Bittencourt et al. conceived an *information retrieval (IR) based mapping technique* that uses the same automated mapping recommendations approach as HuGME. The difference being that Bittencourt et al. replace HuGME's *DA-attraction functions* with an *IR-based similarity function* [3]. They calculate the similarity of an unmapped source entity to an architectural module by searching for specific terms within the source code of an unmapped class. Specifically, they search an architectural module's name and names of its mapped classes, class methods and class fields. Just like HuGME, Bittencourt et al.'s technique requires some manual pre-mapping before it can automate mapping, hence it suffers from the same pre-mapping drawbacks as HuGME.

Olsson et al. combine IR & DA methods in their automated mapping technique called Naive Bayes Classification (NBC) [11]. They uses Bayes' theorem to construct a probabilistic model of classifications using words taken from the source code entities of a software system. The model gives the probability of words (or tokens) belonging to a source file entity. This is then enhanced with syntactical information of the incoming and outgoing dependencies of a source entity, a method they call *Concrete Dependency Abstraction* [11]. Similar to HuGME, Olsson et al.'s proposed technique requires a pre-mapped set in order to perform well and inadvertently suffers from the downsides that come with pre-mapping requirements. The results of both Bittencourt et al.'s and Olsson et al.'s automated mapping techniques showed that when there was a smaller pre-mapped set there was a decreasing trend in the f_1-score of their techniques [3, 11]. Additionally, both automated mapping techniques do not address *hierarchical mapping* in their approaches.

Naim et al. propose a technique called *Coordinated Clustering of Heterogeneous Datasets (CCHD)* that uses both *DA* and *IR* methods to compute a *similarity score* for source code files [10]. CCHD benefits from an architect's feedback on a recovered architecture to iteratively modify the results until there are no more recommendations for change. These adjusted results train a classifier that automatically places new code added to a codebase in the "right" architectural module. However, the technique is not necessarily meant for automated mapping in SACC but rather for *software architecture recovery* tasks. Moreover, the approach too does not directly address *hierarchical mapping*.

Commonly used in industry tools is the use of *naming patterns* (or *regular expressions*). For example, the expressions ***/gui/*** or **.gui.* or net.java.gui.** can be used to map source code entities (whether classes or packages) to an architecture module named *GUI*. This approach is used by both **Sonargraph Architect** and **Structure101 Studio** in addition to their *drag & drop* capability. Nonetheless, the limitation of using naming patterns and/or drag & drop functionality is that they do not solve the problem of decreasing the tediousness of the mapping exercise because they are both manual tasks. At the risk of repetition, in large software systems that have complex mapping configurations this is a burden on the architect to say the least.

In summary, in spite of improvements made to mapping, available techniques that are designed to automate this task have shortfalls. Some require an initial set of the codebase to be pre-mapped manually [3–5, 11], while others like the standard industry tools that do not require pre-mapping offer manual methods. Furthermore, the automated mapping techniques that require pre-mapping demand that in order to properly "jump-start" automated mapping (so that one gets worthwhile results), as it were, an architect needs to manually pre-map about 20% of the codebase [4–6, 15].

InMap [15, 16] addresses the limitations of these techniques in that it is able to automate mapping without needing manual pre-mapping. Using simple concise natural language descriptions of a software system's architecture modules, InMap is able to automate mapping of a completely unmapped system with a rather decent recall and precision of 0.97 and 0.82 respectively. However, its limitation is that the mapping recommendations provided are for low-level source code units, namely, classes. Even if InMap achieved a perfect score of 1.00 for recall and precision, in a large system with a high number of classes, an architect would need to review a set of recommendations equal to the size of the system (in terms of number of classes). This results in considerable work for an architect in such an instance.

In an attempt to lessen the *effort required* by an architect *to review a high number of recommendations*, we consider making mapping recommendations for higher-level source code units – that is, we investigate making mapping recommendations for larger units of code at a time, i.e. recommending packages rather than classes. We therefore aim to answer the following research question in this paper:

How can we exploit InMap's class-to-module mapping recommendations to produce package-to-module mapping recommendations, thereby reducing the effort needed by an architect in accepting and/or rejecting mapping recommendations?

In the following section, we describe our approach to answering the above research question.

3   Approach

We begin by describing, in brief, InMap's approach to *class-to-module mapping*. We then describe a technique for *hierarchical package-to-module mapping* that builds on top of InMap.

3.1   InMap Class Mapping

InMap is an interactive and iterative automated mapping technique that uses concepts from information retrieval to produce *class-to-module mapping* recommendations. It does not require a manually pre-mapped set before automating mapping; rather it is able to compute mapping recommendations from scratch with no pre-mapping requirement. InMap achieves this by using natural language architectural descriptions of a software system's architectural modules as input to kick-start the mapping technique. InMap presents its best *class-to-module mapping* recommendations a page/set at a time to an architect who accepts and/or rejects them. As recommendations from each page/set are accepted or rejected by an architect, InMap updates the state of the mapping but also learns what are bad recommendations. It uses this knowledge to ideally improve its next page/set of recommendations. This approach to mapping works quite well giving an average recall of 97% and an average precision of 82% for the systems evaluated [16].

Class-to-Module Similarity. The InMap mapping technique is composed of seven steps [16]. *Firstly*, a software system's source code files are filtered to omit any third-party package libraries or system classes that the architect does not want to include in the mapping exercise. *Secondly*, the contents of the filtered source code files are stripped of any special characters and programming language keywords. *Third*, the pre-processed source files are indexed, using Lucene, as an inverted index.

In steps *four* InMap formulates a query for each architectural module. In step *five*, it uses the formed queries to search the indexed source code files for the similarity of every unmapped class to each module. The query is derived from four items namely: (1) the name of a module; (2) the module's natural language architectural description (stripped of any special characters and stop words); (3) the names of classes mapped to a module; and (4) the names of methods contained within classes mapped to a module. In its first iteration, when there are no mapped classes, InMap uses only information from items (1) and (2) to build the queries as this is the only information it has at the time. However, once the first set of classes are mapped, InMap then adds to the query items (3) and (4). Items (3) and (4) 'enrich' the query used to search for the similarity of an unmapped class to a module. Therefore, after each iteration of newly mapped classes the query to produce the next set of recommendations is enriched with new information. The searches performed in step five return a set of scores for every *class-module pair* based on the similarity information retrieval function, *tf-idf*. The *tf-idf* scores are called *class-to-module similarity scores (SS_{cm})*, where, c and m are a class-module pair in the system. Details of how *tf-idf* is calculated can be found in [16]. Step five results in a matrix of *class-to-module similarity scores (SS_{cm})* for every class against every module.

Class-to-Module Mapping Recommendations. In step *six*, InMap derives the highest scoring class-to-module pairs, from the *class-to-module similarity scores (SS_{cm})* matrix, and gives them as *class-to-module mapping recommendations*. In step *seven*, the architect accepts or rejects the recommendations. That said, it is important to note that InMap presents as recommendations either: only those above the arithmetic mean of all highest scoring class-module pairs; or the best 30 recommendations (if those above the mean is greater than 30). Thirty was found to give the most optimal results based on the systems tested. After an architect gives feedback on the recommendations given as either an approval or rejection, InMap returns to step four and iterates steps four through to seven until no more recommendations can be given.

Our proposed *hierarchical package-to-module mapping* technique picks up right after InMap's fifth step, that is, once InMap produces the matrix of *class-to-module similarity scores (SS_{cm})*.

3.2   Hierarchical Package Mapping

As pointed out in Sect. 2, in as much as InMap is able to attain fairly decent results (an average f_1-score of 0.89), with the method described in Sect. 3.1 because it produces *class-to-module mapping recommendations*, the effort required by architects to review the recommendations could still be considered a significant amount of work for large and complex systems. However, if we could map larger units of a software system's codebase at a time e.g. entire packages then we could essentially lessen the effort needed by an architect to review recommendations given by InMap. To illustrate, a package that has 50 classes that all map to the same architectural module could be (or should be) given as a single *package-to-module mapping recommendation*. Moreover, because packages are hierarchal in nature, this offers further opportunity to lessen the number of "necessary" mapping recommendations to present to an architect. For example, if packages A_p and B_p are both sub-packages of C_p; and if A_p and B_p have 50 classes each which all map to the same architectural module D_m; then mapping the package C_p to the module D_m would be the only recommendation needed and would save an architect from having to review 99 other *class-level mapping recommendations*. Figure 1 shows an example of package hierarchy that our technique (and certainly others) can benefit from to lessen the number of mapping recommendations needed.

Package-to-Module Similarity. Our package-to-module mapping technique picks up from step 5 in the InMap algorithm, which is the point when it produces a matrix of class-to-module similarity scores (SS_{cm}). We group these class-level scores according to the packages they belong to. This implies that for each package we have a cluster of classes

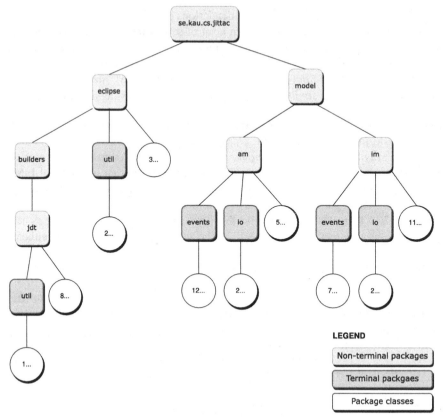

Fig. 1. Example of a package hierarchy. It shows some of the packages contained in Jittac - one of the systems we used to evaluate our *hierarchical package-to-module mapping* technique.

with scores to each identified module. From this cluster of class-to-module similarity scores that have a given package as their parent we calculate the interquartile mean (IQM_{pm}), where, p and m are a package-module pair in the system under consideration. That is, the range of class-to-module similarity scores between the first quartile and third quartile (the interquartile range, IQR) are used to calculate the arithmetic mean of a package. Module IQRs for a package taken from Jittac are demonstrated in Fig. 2. The lowest and highest 25%, that is class-to-module similarity scores existing outside the module's IQR, are ignored. The IQR, and hence the IQM, of a non-terminal package is derived from the classes that belong to the package as well as the classes of its child packages (whether terminal or non-terminal). For example, *se.kau.cs.jittac.eclipse.b-uilders.jdt* shown in the package tree in Fig. 1 has its IQR calculated using the 8 classes that belong to it but also the single class in *se.kau.cs.jittac.eclipse.buil-ders.jdt.util.*

Formally, we define IQM_{pm} as,

$$IQM_{pm} = \frac{2}{n} \sum_{i=\frac{n}{4}+1}^{\frac{3}{4}n} SS_{cm_i} \tag{1}$$

where, p and m are a package-module pair in the software system under consideration, c has p as its parent package, n is the number of classes that make up the package p and i is the position of SS_{cm} in the ordered set of *class-to-module similarity scores* for the package p.

We opt to use the *class-to-module similarity scores* within the *IQR* of a module as opposed to its full set of similarity scores in order to ensure the *package-to-module similarity* we define, is unaffected by the existence of outlier *class-to-module similarity scores*. *Figure 2* shows some outlier classes. In a box plot of the cluster of classes that have similarity scores for a chosen module, outlier classes are those with *class-to-module similarity scores* that are either lower than the *first quartile (Q1) or* higher than the *third quartile (Q3)*. The result of this step is a matrix of *IQMs* for each *package-module pair*.

We follow this by applying feature scaling to normalize the matrix of *IQM* module scores for each package. We use *z-score normalization* (also known as *standardization*) which ensures the scores for each *package-module pair* have a zero-mean. In our hierarchical package mapping technique, we call these resulting z-scores *package-to-module similarity scores (SS_{pm})*. Formally, we define SS_{pm} as,

$$SS_{pm} = \frac{IQM_{pm} - average(IQM_{pm})}{\sigma} \tag{2}$$

where, p and m are a package-module pair in the software system under consideration, IQM_{pm} is the original *package-to-module similarity score*, $average(IQM_{pm})$ is the mean of the IQM_{pm} scores for a specific package to the range of given modules, and σ is the standard deviation of IQM_{pm}. Using this method on all package module pairs, we obtain a matrix of *package-to-module similarity scores (SS_{pm})* for the entire system. *Table 1* shows an extract of these scores.

Package Mapping Filtering. Using the matrix of *package-to-module similarity scores (SS_{pm})* we traverse a software system's package-tree bottom-up starting with the terminal packages and working our way up to the root package. At each level of the package tree-depth, we get two sets of mappings for each package. We obtain *good mappings*, which are mappings in which a package and all its sub-packages have a *package-to-module similarity score* above a specified good threshold. We also obtain *outstanding mappings*, which are mappings of a package that have a *package-to-module similarity score* above a specified *outstanding threshold* and all its sub-packages have a *package-to-module similarity score* above a specified *good threshold*. We formally define this notion with the following two rules,

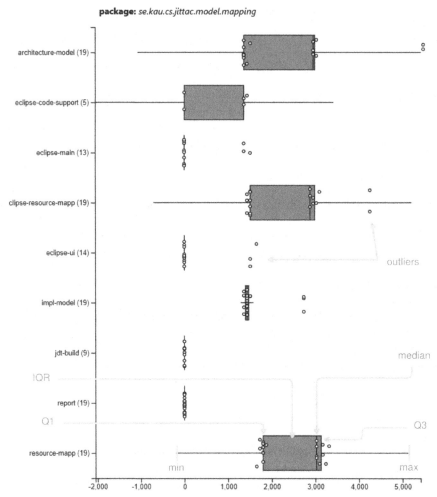

Fig. 2. Box plots for a package taken from Jittac showing the IQRs of class scores for its modules as well as their distribution. The x-axis shows the class SS_{cm} scores and the y-axis shows the architectural modules of the system. The number in brackets beside a module indicates the total number of classes for the given package that have an SS_{cm} score to that module.

Table 1. Extract of SS_{pm} scores taken from Jittac. A value ≥ 0.6 (highlighted blue) implies it is a *good package-to-module similarity score*; a score ≥ 1.5 (highlighted red) implies it is an *outstanding package-to-module similarity score.*

Packages	Modules		
	architecture-model	eclipse-ui	impl-model
se.kau.cs.jittac.model	2.3	-0.6	1.0
se.kau.cs.jittac.model.am	2.6	-0.4	0.4
se.kau.cs.jittac.model.am.events	2.4	-0.4	0.3
se.kau.cs.jittac.model.am.io	2.3	-0.5	0.6
se.kau.cs.jittac.model.im	1.0	-0.5	2.3
se.kau.cs.jittac.model.im.events	0.9	-0.6	1.6
se.kau.cs.jittac.model.im.io	0.5	-	1.6

Given:
> Package **p**
> Module **m**
> Package-to-module score SS_{pm}
> Good score threshold **GSt**
> Outstanding score threshold **OSt**

Rule 1: A mapping (p₁m) is called good iff

$$SS_{pm} >= GSt$$

and for all sub-packages p₁ of **p**, p₁m is a good mapping.

Rule 2: A mapping (p₁m) is called outstanding iff

$$SS_{pm} >= OSt$$

and for all sub-packages p₁ of **p**, p₁m is a good mapping.

Figure 3 illustrates the rules with an example using SS_{pm} scores shown in *Table 1*. Note that in spite of the package *se.kau.cs.jittac.model* having good and outstanding scores for the modules *impl-model* and *architecture-model* respectively in *Table 1*, *Fig. 3* shows that the package has no good or outstanding mappings as a result of the two rules we just defined for identifying what *package-to-module mappings* to recommend. This is because *se.kau.cs.jittac.model* fails to satisfy the second part of *Rule 2*, that is, that all its sub-packages must have good mappings to the same module. Though, one of *se.kau.cs.jittac.model* sub-packages has a good mapping to the same

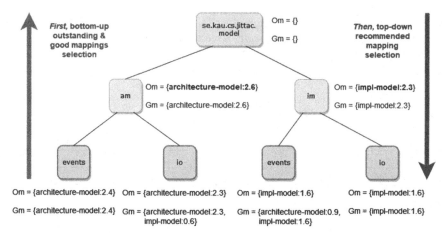

Fig. 3. Illustration of package tree traversal in order to produce package-to-module mappings recommendations.

module the other does not therefore there are no good or outstanding mappings for the *se.kau.cs.jittac.model* package.

The two package mapping filtering rules are applied from the bottom of the package tree starting with the deepest terminal packages then to their parent packages, then to their grandparent packages working our way upwards until we reach the root package. This is necessitated by the fact that packages higher up in the package tree depend on recommendations of packages lower in the package tree.

3.3 Package-to-Module Mapping Recommendation Selection

Once both sets of good and outstanding mappings for each package are obtained from the ground up, we then traverse the package tree in the opposite direction i.e. top-down. At each tree-level we check if a package has outstanding mappings and pick the highest scoring mapping to recommend it as the most plausible *package-to-module mapping*. As we traverse the package tree if a package returns an empty set, then we go one-step lower in the package tree and check its outstanding mappings. However, if a package is recommended we terminate continuing downwards along that path, we instead proceed to check its siblings. *Figure 3* illustrates this; it shows two *package-to-module mapping recommendations* (in bold). Observe that *architecture-model* is recommended as the module to which *se.kau.cs.jittac.model.am* should map to and *impl-model* as the module to which *se.kau.cs.jittac.model.im* should map to. Their sub-packages are skipped since they are already considered as a result of *Rule 2* and *se.kau.cs.jittac.model* has no mapping recommendations since it retained no mappings after the package mapping score filtering step.

Interactive and Iterative Mapping Recommendations. Similar to InMap, our proposed *hierarchical package mapping technique* is interactive. This means that the *package-to-module mapping recommendations* the technique produces for a system under consideration are presented to an architect for him to accept and/or reject.

Our technique is also iterative in that once the architect accepts or rejects the recommendations it acquires new knowledge to ideally improve its next set of recommendations. Thus, it returns to generating new package-to-module similarity scores as described in Sect. 3.2, under "Package-to-Module Similarity". When a package is mapped this implies all classes belonging to it as well as those belonging to its sub-packages all get mapped. As a result, InMap can produce new *class-to-module similarity scores* for all the unmapped classes, which our *hierarchical package mapping technique* uses to produce new *package-to-module mapping recommendations* for all unmapped packages. Our *hierarchical package mapping technique* continues iterating through this process until no more mapping recommendations can be produced. In an earlier prototypical version of this technique, recommendations were given once after a single pass on the test systems [17]. However, the enhanced and refined version presented in this paper iterates until no more recommendations can be produced.

4 Evaluation

4.1 Test Cases

We evaluated our *hierarchical package mapping technique* on six Java-based systems that were used in the evaluation of InMap's *class-to-module mapping* approach. These are *Ant*, a command line and API-based tool for automating processes; *ArgoUML*, a desktop-based application for modelling in UML; *JabRef* a desktop-based bibliographic application for managing references; *Jittac* an eclipse plugin for applying reflexion modelling to Java-based systems; *ProM* a desktop-based tool for mining processes; and *TeamMates* a web-based application for peer reviews and feedback. *Table 2* shows the characteristics of these systems. The architectural module descriptions, in natural language, used as input by InMap to generate *class-module similarity scores* were obtained from the previous study of InMap. In that study the oracle class mappings, that is the ground truth *code-to-module mappings*, were obtained from experts involved in developing each respective open-source software system. The oracle *package-to-module mappings* used in this study were derived from these. We retained in the package mappings oracle only packages that had a direct 1-1 mapping with a module, and excluded packages that had child entities that map to more than one module.

From the oracle mappings, we only extracted *package-to-module mappings*, leaving out the *class-to-module mappings* to allow us to evaluate the performance of our proposed *hierarchical package mapping technique* strictly at a package-level. *Table 2* shows the number of packages in the oracle package mapping of each system. This determines the number of packages our *hierarchical package mapping technique* should predict mappings for, in other words, the packages that are of concern. For example, if *se.kau.cs.jittac.eclipse* is part of the oracle mapping and our proposed technique provides *se.kau.cs.jittac.eclipse.builders* as a recommended mapping we count this as a false positive even though the latter is a child package of the former. The reason is our technique is meant to lessen the review effort needed by an architect; therefore, it must be penalized for recommending sub-packages of a parent package that is part of the oracle mappings. In other words, in line with the aim of reducing review effort, sub-packages of packages in the oracle package mappings should preferably, not be put forth as recommendations by the *hierarchical package mapping technique.*

Table 2. System cases

System attributes	Ant	Argo UML	JabRef	Jittac	ProM	Team mates
Version #	r584500	r13713	3.7	0.1 (…)	6.9	5.11
# of source files(/classes)	778	1,429	843	124	700	467
# of source files after filtering	724	763	840	110	699	293
# of source files in oracle package mapping	558	692	812	98	675	293
# of packages	64	60	118	27	162	18
# of packages in oracle mapping	14	21	11	9	30	11
# of modules	15	17	6	9	11	11

Table 3. Results showing the optimal thresholds for each system tested.

Test system	Good thresh.	Oustand thresh.	# of recomm.	Package recall	Package precision	Class coverage
Ant	1.9	2.3	10	0.64	0.90	276/558 (49%)
ArgoU	0.1–1.6	3.0	16	0.48	0.63	436/692 (63%)
JabRef	0.1–1.4	2.0	6	0.55	1.00	794/812 (98%)
Jittac	1.0–1.4	1.8	7	0.67	0.86	88/98 (90%)
ProM	1.4	1.8–1.9	40	0.53	0.36	275/675 (41%)
TeamM	1.3–1.4	0.1–1.4	11	1.00	1.00	293/293 (100%)

4.2 Investigation and Data Collection

To test our *hierarchical package mapping technique* we extended the InMap evaluator tool developed in our previous studies to accommodate the evaluation of *package-based mappings* with various good and outstanding threshold combinations. The evaluator

Table 4. Effort comparison of class vs package mappings.

Test system	Class mapping		Package mapping		Effort saved
	Class coverage after ...	# of recomm.	Class coverage after completion	# of recomm.	(*effort reduced*)
Ant	*12 passes, 49%*	360	49%	10	350 (–97%)
ArgoU	*19 passes, 63%*	570	63%	16	554 (–97%)
JabRef	*31 passes, 98%*	848	98%	6	842 (–99%)
Jittac	*7 passes, 90%*	123	90%	7	116 (–94%)
ProM	*11 passes, 41%*	330	41%	40	290 (–88%)
TeamM	*14 passes, 97%*	275	100%	11	264 (–96%)

automatically simulated a "human architect" accepting and rejecting the recommendations produced using the oracle package mappings for each system. For all possible single decimal combinations within the range −5.0 to 5.0 for the good and outstanding thresholds we collected the package mapping recall and precision of our technique. The selection of the test range was derived from the lowest and highest *package-to-module similarity scores (SS_{cm})* obtained across all six test systems. We also recorded the number of recommendations it took to get whatever recall and/or precision was achieved by the technique. Finally, we also collected the class coverage (or code reach), that is, the number of classes that were mapped as a result of their parent packages being correctly mapped by our *hierarchical package mapping technique* and compared this with results from InMap's *class-level mapping* approach.

4.3 Results

Table 3 gives the results obtained for the optimal good and outstanding thresholds for each system tested. These values gave the best results for the range of values tested. We got two systems, *JabRef* and *TeamMates*, with perfect package mapping precision with *TeamMates* getting the same for its class coverage. We found six out of *JabRef's* eleven package mappings and ten of *Ant's* fourteen, which resulted in a class coverage of 98% and 49% respectively for the two systems. For *Jittac*, 90% of its classes were mapped by finding six of its nine package mappings with a recommendation precision of 0.86. *ArgoUML* had low package mapping precision (0.63), relative to the results obtained for the other five systems, and a class coverage of 63%. *ProM*, appeared to be an outlier obtaining poor package mapping precision (0.36) and the lowest class coverage from the six systems tested, 41%.

In *Table 4*, we compare the effort required by an architect to review the recommendations produced by our *hierarchical mapping technique* with the effort required to review recommendations produced by InMap. We do this by looking at the number of recommendations an architect has to review for a similar class coverage obtained for each respective technique. We express our findings as *effort saved (ES)* and *effort reduced (ER)* as shown in *Table 4* for the six system under study. *ES* and *ER* are defined as follows,

$$ES = |R^p - R^c| \tag{3}$$

$$ER = -100 \times \frac{ES}{R^c} \tag{4}$$

where R^c is the number of *class-to-module recommendations* needed by the InMap class-based technique and R^p is the number of *package-to-module recommendations* needed by our *hierarchical package mapping technique*. As an example, *Table 4* shows that in the case of a relatively large system like JabRef that has 840 classes an architect would have to review 848 class recommendations to map 98% of JabRef's classes using InMap's *class-based mapping approach*. Whereas an architect would only have to review only 6 package recommendations to map 98% of JabReft's classes using our *hierarchical package mapping technique*. This results in an *effort saved (ES)* of 842 recommendations and *effort reduced (ER)* of 99% on the part of the architect. You will also notice from *Table 4* that the *effort saved (ES)* for all six systems is 88% or higher.

5   Discussion

5.1   Findings

For four out of the six systems under study *Table 3* shows that our *hierarchical package mapping technique* has a package mapping precision of 0.86 or higher – excluding ArgoUML and ProM. This is likely due to the fact that our *hierarchal package mapping technique* profits from InMap's *class-to-module similarity function*. Using simple natural language descriptions of a system's architecture modules the InMap algorithm, which has the *class-to-module similarity score* SS_{cm} function at its core, was shown to obtain a precision of 0.82 and f_1-score of 0.89 [16]. Our *hierarchical package mapping technique* builds on InMap's success by using the information retrieval based *class-to-module similarity scores* SS_{cm} to generate is own *package-to-module similarity scores* SS_{pm}.

The package mapping recall of our technique averages around 0.65 for the six systems tested. This tells us that our *hierarchical package mapping technique* is able to find correct recommendations for about 65% of the packages in the systems it was evaluated on. What is interesting however is that this translates to a class coverage averaging 75% for all six systems. The class coverage is of more importance to our study than the package mapping recall because we are more interested in reducing the number of recommendations an architect has to review than the number of packages we get right. To illustrate, if we have a hypothetical system with 1000 classes split as 600 classes in package *A*, 300 classes in package *B* and 100 classes in package *C*. We are more interested in finding a high number of classes in the system than its packages. So even if we correctly find packages B and C (i.e. a package recall of 0.67) this would only represent a class coverage of 0.40. However, if we correctly find package A only (and fail to find B and C), even though our package mapping recall would be 0.33, the result only seems poor at face value because our code coverage is 0.60 meaning we save more effort for the architect in the latter case compared to the former. In other words, we are more interested in finding packages that represent the most classes in a system compared to getting a high recall with low coverage. Finding packages with only one class in them (and they do exist) is of no benefit as the effort saved and effort reduced respective to that package is zero.

We observe in *Table 4* an average reduction of recommendation review effort of 95% for all test systems. Three of the six system achieved a reduction in effort of 97% or greater and the lowest *effort reduction* observed was 88%. We can attribute these promising results of our *hierarchical package mapping technique* to two things possibly. Firstly, the technique takes advantage of the premise that it is likely that developers of a system may structure or organize their code with package names similar to the architectural module names defined by an architect. To illustrate this effect consider an architect names an architectural module *GUI* and the developers create a package called *se.jittac.gui.* If the *se.jittac.gui.* package maps entirely onto the *GUI* architectural module then recommending the mapping *se.jittac.gui.* to *GUI* saves us the headache of having to recommend all classes belonging to *se.jittac.gui.* and its sub-packages. That said, there are many cases including in some of the systems we tested, were sub-packages of *se.jittac.gui.* could be mapped to other architectural modules but because our technique profits from the natural language similarity function in InMap it is able to easily identify cases where packages map to modules in a 1-1 fashion.

The other reason we believe our *hierarchical package mapping technique* gets such decent *effort reduction* results is its method of filtering which packages to recommend. Recall from Sect. 3.3, which describes how our technique selects which *package-to-module mappings* to recommend, that despite our technique finding a number of possible packages mappings it selects the packages with least depth in the package tree which meets the threshold requirements. By traversing the tree top-down, we avoid having to recommend child packages that also meet the threshold requirements. A recommendation of a parent package subsumes all child package recommendations which subsume its grandchild package recommendations and so on and so forth. This allows us to reduce the *review effort* exponentially. The deeper a system's package tree the more effort we save if a recommendation is found much closer to the root package as we traverse the tree top-down.

Table 3 shows the threshold values that give the optimal results for each system evaluated. However, we observed some similarities across the six systems in our threshold values experiments. The optimal *outstanding score threshold* is very close to or the same as the arithmetic mean of the max *package-to-module similarity scores* SS_{pm} for each module of the system. In addition, the optimal *good score threshold* was usually 0.5 less than the optimal *outstanding score threshold*. This establishes a basis for developing an automated approach for deriving threshold values that will give optimal results across different systems.

Something to point out is the flexibility of our *hierarchical package mapping* app-roach. Although it uses *similarity scores* generated by InMap's *class-to-module similar-ity function* this can be replaced by any class-based *similarity* or *attraction function*. For example, the *CountAttract* and *MQAttract* used in the HuGME [4, 5] or *IRAttract* and *LSIAttract* used by Bittencourt et al. [3]. The fact that our *hierarchical package mapping* technique can use similarity scores produced by any class-based similarity or attraction function makes it easier to port and adopt by other mapping techniques.

5.2   Limitations and Validity

The *hierarchical package mapping technique* presented in this paper is a purely *package-based mapping approach,* meaning if a system has a package with class members that map to different architectural models then the technique is not appropriate. This is because many systems, including the ones we tested against, have *many-to-many* class-to-module mappings. This is not to say that our *hierarchical package mapping technique* is not practical. It is more likely the case that a software system's code-to-architecture mappings is a combination of both package and class mappings. They are likely to have complex mapping configurations that combine both *many-to-many* class-module mapping as well as *many-to-one*. Our aim was to reduce the effort in mapping the *many-to-one* class-to-module mappings, which we did and hope we have successfully demon-strated. Cases where a package's class members are spread across multiple modules (*many-to-many*) require a class-based technique. Therefore, an approach that combines *class-based* with *package-based* mapping would cater for all mapping cases while still reducing the recommendation review effort required by architects compared to a purely class-based approach.

Our *package-based mapping technique* builds on top of InMap's *class-to-module similarity score* SS_{cm} function, therefore the same factors that affect the external validity of InMap's results are inherited by our *hierarchical package mapping technique*. That is to say, factors such as the number of classes, packages and modules; the code commenting quality and style; and the length and quality of the architecture description quality could likely affect the external validity of the results of our *hierarchical package mapping technique*. Therefore, more case study systems with varying attributes would add to the validity of the results. That said, the results of the six test systems used, along with their varying characteristics as shown in *Table 2,* provide a compelling case for the reduction in recommendation review effort that *hierarchical package mapping technique* provides.

With regard to construct validity, the effort required by an architect using our tech-nique needs to be evaluated against other package-based mapping methods provided by industry tools like drag & drop, naming patterns or regular expressions. For example, how does our hierarchical package-based technique compare with manually mapping packages by dragging? What requires the least effort dragging & dropping, defining regular expression or reviewing a list of recommendations presented by our *hierarchi-cal package mapping technique*? Evaluations such as these would require enhanced user studies with the involvement of software architects in appropriately planned and controlled experiments.

6   Conclusion and Future Work

In this paper, we have presented a solution to reducing the review effort required by an architect in *interactive* mapping recommendation techniques by means of our *hierarchical package-based mapping* approach. It extends or builds on InMap, an information retrieval *class-based mapping technique* that uses simple and concise natural language architectural descriptions of modules. Our *hierarchical package-based mapping technique* reduces recommendation review effort by about 95% on average compared to interactive *class-based mapping techniques* such as InMap. It provides far much less mapping recommendations and still achieves a code coverage of about 75%.

Despite the gains made in reducing the *review effort* required, the drawback of using a purely package-based technique is that it may not handle the *many-to-many* class-module mapping cases that exist in combination with *many-to-one* mappings in the majority of systems. It is more likely the case that a software system's code-to-architecture mapping has a combination of both package and class mappings. Cases where package members are spread across multiple modules (*many-to-many*) require a class-based technique. Therefore, we plan as future work, to investigate an approach where we combine InMap's *class-based technique* with the *hierarchical package mapping technique* presented in this paper. The goal would be to combine class and package mapping recommendations in a way that gains the benefits, and negates the weaknesses, of both mapping techniques. Nonetheless, the *hierarchical package-based mapping technique* presented in this paper remains useful in cases where it is appropriate to map entire packages.

References

1. Ali, N., Baker, S., O'Crowley, R., Herold, S., Buckley, J.: Architecture consistency: state of the practice, challenges and requirements. Empir. Softw. Eng. **23**(1), 224–258 (2018). https://doi.org/10.1007/s10664-017-9515-3
2. Bauer, M., Trifu, M.: Architecture-aware adaptive clustering of OO systems. In: Proceedings - 8th European Conference on Software Maintenance and Reengineering, pp. 3–14 (2004)
3. Bittencourt, R.A., et al.: Improving automated mapping in reflexion models using information retrieval techniques. In: Proceedings - Working Conference on Reverse Engineering, WCRE, pp. 63–172 (2010)
4. Christl, A., et al.: Automated clustering to support the reflexion method. Inf. Softw. Technol. **49**(3), 255–274 (2007)
5. Christl, A., et al.: Equipping the reflexion method with automated clustering. In: 12th Working Conference on Reverse Engineering (2005)
6. Fontana, F.A., et al.: Tool support for evaluating architectural debt of an existing system: an experience report. In: Proceedings of the 31st Annual ACM Symposium on Applied Computing, pp. 1347–1349 (2016)
7. Knodel, J.: Sustainable Structures in Software Implementations by Live Compliance Checking. Fraunhofer-Verl, Stuttgart (2011)
8. Knodel, J., Popescu, D.: A comparison of static architecture compliance checking approaches. In: Proceedings of the 6th Working IEEE/IFIP Conference on Software Architecture (2007)
9. Murphy, G.C., et al.: Software reflexion models: bridging the gap between source and high-level models. IEEE Trans. Softw. Eng. **27**(4), 364–380 (2001)

10. Naim, S.M., Kostadin Damevski, M., Hossain, S.: Reconstructing and evolving software architectures using a coordinated clustering framework. Autom. Softw. Eng. **24**(3), 543–572 (2017). https://doi.org/10.1007/s10515-017-0211-8
11. Olsson, T., et al.: Semi-automatic mapping of source code using Naive Bayes. In: Proceedings of the 13th European Conference on Software Architecture, pp. 209–216 (2019)
12. Passos, L., et al.: Static architecture-conformance checking: an illustrative overview. IEEE Softw. **27**(5), 82–89 (2010)
13. Rosik, J., et al.: Assessing architectural drift in commercial software development: a case study. Softw. Pract. Exp. **41**, 63–86 (2011)
14. de Silva, L., Balasubramaniam, D.: Controlling software architecture erosion: a survey. J. Syst. Softw. **85**(1), 132–151 (2012)
15. Sinkala, Z.T., Herold, S.: InMap: automated interactive code-to-architecture mapping. In: Proceedings of the ACM Symposium on Applied Computing, pp. 1439–1442 (2021)
16. Sinkala, Z.T., Herold, S.: InMap: automated interactive code-to-architecture mapping recommendations. In: Proceedings - IEEE 18th International Conference on Software Architecture, pp. 173–183 (2021)
17. Sinkala, Z.T., Herold, S.: Towards hierarchical code-to-architecture mapping using information retrieval. In: Companion Proceedings - IEEE 15th European Conference on Software Architecture (2021)
18. Wiggerts, T.A.: Using clustering algorithms in legacy systems remodularization. In: Proceedings of the 4th Working Conference on Reverse Engineering, pp. 33–43 (1997)

1st International Workshop on Mining Software Repositories for Software Architecture (MSR4SA)

Building the MSR Tool Kaiaulu: Design Principles and Experiences

Carlos Paradis$^{(\boxtimes)}$ and Rick Kazman

University of Hawaii at Manoa, Honolulu, HI 96822, USA
{cvas,kazman}@hawaii.edu

Abstract. Background: Since Alitheia Core was proposed and subsequently retired, tools that support empirical studies of software projects continue to be proposed, such as Codeface, Codeface4Smells, Grimoire-Lab and SmartSHARK, but they all make different design choices and provide overlapping functionality. Aims: We seek to understand the design decisions adopted by these tools–the good and the bad–along with their consequences, to understand why their authors reinvented functionality already present in other tools, and to help inform the design of future tools. Method: We used action research to evaluate the tools, and to determine a set of principles and anti-patterns to motivate a new tool design. Results: We identified 7 major design choices among the tools: 1) Abstraction Debt, 2) the use of Project Configuration Files, 3) the choice of Batch or Interactive Mode, 4) Minimal Paths to Data, 5) Familiar Software Abstractions, 6) Licensing and 7) the Perils of Code Reuse. Building on the observed good and bad design decisions, we created our own tool architecture and implemented it as an R package. Conclusions: Tools should not require onerous setup for users to obtain data. Authors should consider the conventions and abstractions used by their chosen language and build upon these instead of redefining them. Tools should encourage best practices in experiment reproducibility by leveraging self-contained and readable schemas that are used for tool automation, and reuse must be done with care to avoid depending on dead code.

Keywords: Mining software repositories · Design choices · Action research

1 Introduction

Research into quality dimensions of software project requires the analysis of large quantities of data. For researchers this typically means mining data from multiple open source software projects. Pre-processing data, calculating metrics and flaws, and synthesizing composite results from a large corpus of project artefacts is a tedious and error prone task lacking immediate scientific value [13]—it is seen merely as a means to an end. This was the motivation for the Alitheia Core [13], which was made available in 2009 for the software engineering community. It provided features for data collection, integration and analysis services and

© The Author(s), under exclusive license to Springer Nature Switzerland AG 2022
P. Scandurra et al. (Eds.): ECSA Tracks and Workshops 2021, LNCS 13365, pp. 107–129, 2022.
https://doi.org/10.1007/978-3-031-15116-3_6

emphasized an easy to use extension mechanism. Yet, as of today, Alitheia Core is a dormant (read-only) project in GitHub[1] and several other tools replicate at least some of its functionality.

What went wrong? Why have many tools re-implemented the same "tedious and error prone" tasks the Alitheia Core? And do the current tools live up to the promise of Alitheia Core? In this work, we revisit lessons learned by the Alitheia Core authors and the design choices made by the other more recent tools using an action research [11] approach. We extend our prior work [7] in Sect. 4, where we detail how the design principles are applied to Kaiaulu, and showcase the tool's various features.

Our contributions in this paper are twofold: first, we present a set of key design decisions derived from an analysis of the aforementioned tools which either facilitated or hindered reusability, reproducibility, interoperability and extension of functionality. Second, we present our tool, Kaiaulu[2], which builds upon the design decisions made from these prior tools, and which we believe fills a gap in the existing mining software repositories ecosystem. Kaiaulu implements and expands on a familiar package abstraction for the R language, provides a minimal path to data, flexibility in usage with both API, CLIs and Notebooks, and granular customization and clarity of assumptions made in the analysis by utilizing project configuration files. The tool is intended to take as input common software development infrastructure logs (e.g. git logs, mailing lists, issue trackers), and provides both commonly adopted software engineering metrics (e.g. churn, bug count, LOC), and socio-technical metrics and network representation within these data sources (e.g. communication, collaboration, and socio-technical debt [6]). Kaiaulu has already been used in three theses [7,9,21] and one published research study [1].

2   Studied Tools and Lessons Learned

We employed an action research methodology in studying these tools. An action research methodology consists of iterating across four major steps—Plan, Act, Observe, and Reflect—with the potential for minor iterations within a step and among the steps. In the remainder of Sect. 2 we describe our "Plan" step, its motivations and the lessons we drew from it. In Sects. 3 and 4 we discuss how we "Acted", designing and implementing Kaiaulu with frequent small reflection activities. In the introduction, we briefly cited some of the uses that we have already found for Kaiaulu, the "Observe" step. And finally in Sect. 5 we sketch our final reflections.

The tools that we studied in our planning activity were Codeface [14], Codeface4Smells [29], GrimoireLab [10,24] SmartSHARK, [30,31] and PyDriller [28]. We now present our observations regarding the strengths and weaknesses of these tools in terms of their design choices and we note the lessons learned by

---

[1] https://github.com/istlab/Alitheia-Core.

[2] The documentation for the tool can be found at https://github.com/sailuh/kaiaulu.

the authors of Alitheia Core [13] presented in [22]. These lessons are applicable to new tools with similar intents.

2.1 Abstraction Debt

We have observed different levels of abstraction employed in the surveyed tools, ranging from applications that are built as monoliths to those built from smaller components. This is consistent with what has been noted in machine learning systems as abstraction debt [27], i.e. a lack of key abstractions to support the functions and growth of MSR tools.

Codeface was created as a monolithic application, in which an entire project's Git log or mailing list is analyzed. It abstracts a complete end-to-end pipeline, implemented by a command line interface (CLI), and outputs a database dump of a project. It is therefore difficult for other applications to build on some of its unique features, for example, using its Git log parser that parses at function (rather than file) granularity.

Both GrimoireLab and SmartSHARK define several components, each with its own CLI, but the component abstractions they employ are not the same. To provide a point of comparison, Grimoire's Lab Perceval provides a CLI to obtain data from many data sources (e.g. GitHub, Git, Bugzilla, Jira, mailing lists, etc.), serving as a single interface for data collection. In contrast, SmartSHARK defines its abstraction per data source type and, in the case of data acquisition, at a more fine-grained level than Perceval. For example, consider issueShark and vcsShark, two components of SmartShark. IssueShark defines abstractions for different types of issues tracker sources, and vcsShark for different types of version control systems. SmartSHARK's abstractions facilitate defining additional features specific to a data source type, such as separating static vs. dynamic data in issue trackers (e.g. creation time of the issue vs. comments), regardless of its underlying implementation (e.g. Jira or Bugzilla)[3].

Pydriller is a single component and is smaller in scope as it only abstracts Git repositories. However it is different from the other tools in that it provides an API instead of a CLI. Its motivation is also different: it wraps around PythonGit, which in itself provides a Pythonic API to nearly all features of Git, to provide an API catered towards mining software repositories only. In providing just a subset of Git functionality, it exposes functionality catering specifically to the needs of mining repositories.

The decision between choosing a CLI or API has tradeoffs. An issue with command line only interfaces occurs when an end-user may be interested in a different abstraction of the data not preconceived by the authors. However an API requires the user to be familiar with the programming language the tool was built on top of, whereas a CLI does not.

From the above we derive the following lessons learned: End-to-end pipelines such as Codeface's limit the ability of researchers to build on top of them. Defining more specific abstractions per data type, whether via CLI or API, as issueShark

---

[3] https://github.com/smartshark/issueSHARK#introduction.

and PyDriller do, facilitates adding functionality specific to a particular data type, or audience. Moreover, CLIs can be built on top of a well-defined API, providing the benefit of both interfaces, as we do in Kaiaulu.

2.2 Tool Configuration Files vs Project Configuration Files

In [30], the authors of SmartSHARK noted that one of their goals was to support replication through the storage of data in a single harmonized schema. Replication, it is argued, is supported by a common dataset. However, we have observed that replication is also being done within configuration files in Codeface.

Codeface uses a concept we named project configuration files. These files provide a single compact source where parameters associated with the acquisition and manipulation of a dataset can be stored. Project configuration file parameters are required for tool execution, and they are a pragmatic, lightweight and human-readable way to specify reproducible results. Project configuration files also save time when a project is re-analyzed in other studies, as some project-specific information may not be obvious from the dataset alone.

Of all the tools we have reviewed, only Codeface provides users with a means to specify project configuration files. This led to a large collection of project configurations that have been versioned in Codeface over time[4]. This information, which supports repeatability, may otherwise not have been possible (or at least easy) to reconstruct if all that was shared was the data.

We note that externalizing parameter choices in data acquisition and manipulation tasks has been more prominent in machine learning frameworks, for example to define experiments in configuration files[5], which include machine learning model selection and choice of model hyper-parameters [25].

From the above, we derive the following lessons: integrating configuration files that are human-readable and leveraged by the tool can enable reproducibility, without the hurdles of sharing large quantities of primary data. Kaiaulu implements and extends project configuration files, as discussed in Sect. 4.

2.3 Batch Mode, Interactive Mode, and Literate Programming

As we noted before, with the exception of PyDriller, every tool defines a CLI, but not an API. This means the only way to interact with these tools is batch mode. Meanwhile, PyDriller does not offer a CLI, only an API, which confers its users the ability to leverage Python's interactive mode to *explore* the data. However, it does not include a CLI for batch mode processing, for out-of-the-box data acquisition, processing or data analysis. What we observe then is that existing tools decide on either CLI or API, but not both. We believe, however, that the mining of software repositories requires a tool capable of both, supporting an

---

[4] See https://github.com/siemens/codeface/tree/master/conf and https://github.com/maelstromdat/codeface4smells_TR/tree/master/Configurations for Codeface and Codeface4Smells respectively.

[5] https://xnmt.readthedocs.io/en/latest/experiment_config_files.html.

iterative process of data exploration, and when concluded, a way to enact batch processing to scale up.

To illustrate our claim—as no existing tool provides both capabilities—we provide a few examples: in a recent socio-technical study, identity matching was needed. This required applying heuristics that have been published by other authors (e.g. [4,33]) to assign identities to developers who use different names and e-mails in version control systems and mailing lists. Consider the case where we chose the simplest method, where developers whose name or e-mail match are assigned the same id. At first glance, this seems like a reasonable assumption. However, it was due to experimenting interactively with the identity matching API that we discovered that all core developers, due to the use of an issue tracking system, ended up sharing the same e-mail address. We then saved the observed parameters in a project configuration file, and used it to deploy a batch process to collect various computationally intensive architectural metrics.

We have had similar experience in determining and testing heuristics to filter files in a repository, or determining the method that developers adopt to annotate issue numbers in commit messages. Because each project may apply its own conventions, tools that offer an experimentation capability, and then defer mass data processing to batch more efficiently support the full workflow of a researcher in mining software repositories.

The described interactive data explorations could certainly have been done in a Python or R session, but it is better to leverage literate programming using, for example, Python or R Notebooks, so that the rationale of the design experiment is not lost. However, care must be taken to not extensively rely on notebooks without further refactoring functionality into the code base, leading to dead experimental code paths [27].

Our learned lessons here were: existing tools choose either APIs or CLIs (supporting batch or interactive modes). However, making both interfaces available will better support users in their various research efforts in mining software repositories. The use of Notebooks to illustrate and explain the API complements the API, provided functionality is not entirely written in Notebooks. In Kaiaulu, we leverage both APIs and Notebooks, which is a common practice in R packages, therefore avoiding abstraction debt.

2.4   Minimal Paths to Data

According to [22, p. 233], the effort required to learn how infrastructure code works has to be proportional to the gains and account for deprecation. We agree with this observation. Let us look at how existing tools manage this concern.

When using GrimoireLab components (in particular Perceval) the minimal path to data is surprisingly short. Provided with a Git repository URL, or a local copy, it will output a JSON file to stdout. Likewise, provided with a URL to a website mbox or local file, it will also provide a JSON file to stdout. A developer can easily integrate wrappers to its CLI, and users can easily obtain data for a project of interest. In this ecosystem, a database is available, but it is optional: users need not to concern themselves with learning GrimoireLab's Elastic Search database to obtain data.

This is in contrast to Codeface and SmartSHARK, both of which require user familiarity with MySQL and MongoDB respectively, along with their data model schemas to obtain the equivalent version control system and mailing list data. The minimal path to data in these cases is much longer, including the setup overhead and integration with other tools.

When data integration is sought in the database, GrimoireLab retains its approach of keeping the data closest to source, and not harmonizing it in a schema that facilitates integration [30]. Codeface's MySQL and SmartSHARK's MongoDB provide a harmonized schema, which makes it easier for users to store the various types of data.

In the case of PyDriller, which provides an API, the minimal path to data requires familiarity with the Python programming language. This offers the convenience of reshaping the data to the user's final need, but adds an overhead to the user for familiarization with the API, instead of just the raw data schema from the source of interest (which the user is likely already familiar with for their research purposes). One researcher [12, p. 39] who extended Codeface4Smells identified a problem of Pipeline Jungles [27], due to heavy reliance on a folder hierarchy and file name conventions.

Our lessons learned here were: databases need not be a requirement to provide users with various data sources. This also simplifies component reuse by other tools and decreases the likelihood of reinventing the wheel. Providing a minimal path does not exclude providing a database for researchers, as Perceval shows. However providing a harmonized schema can save researchers from having to re-implement code to integrate the same kinds of infrastructure repeatedly. Lastly, providing an API gives some flexibility to users to reshape the data with the tool. However, user familiarity with the programming language and API is also an overhead, as the data could be ideally provided directly via a CLI. As such, we believe having available a CLI that outputs the data as Perceval does, and a harmonized schema as in Codeface and SmartSHARK, provides the best combination. We therefore provide a CLI, an API, and a standardized nomenclature for the different data sources, making it easier to perform different data transformations in Kaiaulu.

2.5   Other Design Decisions

We briefly mention here other (more minor) design decisions that we believe may cause difficulties in adoption.

Familiar Software Abstractions. Both Perceval and PyDriller leverage a common interface for end-users. They are both Python libraries, and provide the expected interactions for CLI and API respectively. In Perceval's CLI, provided with a list of parameters and flags, data is output to stdout. PyDriller exposes an API, an extension to a programmer's familiar programming paradigm. This is in contrast to ecosystems that define a different abstraction, such as SmartSHARK, where detailed instructions must be followed to extend its functionality[6]. Extension instructions are also not available for Perceval or Codeface.

Licensing. Another important consideration in reusing a code component is how permissive its license is. For example, stringr, an R package to manipulate strings used by XGBoost, a popular machine learning algorithm, was replaced by stringi, another R package to manipulate strings, solely based on the difference in licenses.[7] Similar reasoning also led an R package that represents data tables efficiently to adopt a different license because the existing license "could be interpreted as preventing closed-source products from using data.table"[8]. Lack of clarity on interactions of open source licenses has been reported by [2]. Among the tools we studied, we have observed the following licenses: Codeface adopts GPL 2.0, PyDriller Apache 2.0, SmartSHARK Apache 2.0, and Grimoire's Lab GPL 3.0 and LGPL 3.0. Kaiaulu uses MPL 2.0, as it serves as a middle ground between both the GPL and Apache licenses, which we found more flexible to accommodate external libraries.

Perils of Code Reuse. With the availability of package managers such as CRAN and PyPi which greatly facilitate code reuse, one can declare dependencies on others' code instead of copying it into your own project, taking advantage of their functionality without assuming the burden of maintenance. However code interdependence also poses risks [32], such as dependencies going extinct [8]. Hence, care has to be taken to avoid dependencies to non-maintained third-party code.

An interesting example occurs in mecoSHARK[9] through a chain of dependencies which exemplifies the concern posed here. mecoSHARK is a component that serves as a wrapper for OpenStaticAnalyzer[10], with a last commit date of July 13, 2018. In turn, OpenStaticAnalyzer also wraps several other dependencies, including FindBugs[11], last released in March 15, 2015. In its bug tracker[12], FindBugs requests for bugs to no longer be reported, noting that SpotBugs[13], FindBugs' successor, should be used instead. This confirms that the mecoSHARK wrapper, which provides OpenStaticAnalyzer functionality to SmartSHARK, is now dependent on dead code, further increasing the burden of the SmartSHARK ecosystem maintainers. Nonetheless, SmartSHARK's approach to wrap black-box packages into common APIs is considered good practice [27].

As a means to mitigate this risk, relying on and contributing work to open source communities that more carefully assess the health of projects and try to maintain them, such as the Apache Software Foundation, ROpenSci[14], and CHAOSS[15] may be an important consideration. For example, ROpenSci

---

[6] https://smartshark.github.io/plugin/tutorial/python.

[7] https://github.com/dmlc/xgboost/issues/1338.

[8] https://github.com/Rdatatable/data.table/pull/2456.

[9] https://github.com/smartshark/mecoSHARK.

[10] https://github.com/sed-inf-u-szeged/OpenStaticAnalyzer.

[11] http://findbugs.sourceforge.net/.

[12] https://sourceforge.net/p/findbugs/bugs/1487/.

[13] https://github.com/spotbugs/spotbugs.

[14] https://ropensci.org/about/.

[15] https://chaoss.community/.

accepts R packages via a streamlined peer review process and, for accepted packages, provides community support, package promotion, and fast-track publication to journals[16].

3 Design Principles in Kaiaulu

In this section, we discuss how our design principles are translated into Kaiaulu's specific design decisions. In the following section, we detail Kaiaulu's modules and features.

Batch Mode, Interactive Mode, and Literate Programming in Kaiaulu. We chose to use the R language[17], due to the familiarity of the authors with the language and a preference for its package architecture.

Minimally, the structure of an R package consists of the package metadata and its API. In addition, the R ecosystem encourages and promotes best practices to include vignettes for package documentation, which leads R users to expect an API and R Notebooks when installing packages from CRAN (The Comprehensive R Archive Network).[18] CRAN treats R Notebooks as first class citizens in an R package[19] showing on each package's website any R Notebooks available. Because of R package structure, complying with familiar software abstractions (see Sect. 2.5) automatically brings the benefits of literate programming (see Sect. 2.3).

Abstraction Debt in Kaiaulu. R natively supports tables and vectors as data types, which is a familiar abstraction for data analysts. To capitalize on this, Kaiaulu's *parse_* functions map most data sources (Git logs, mailing lists, file dependencies, software vulnerability feeds, metrics, etc.) as tables with standardized column naming, which allows for quick identification of what data can be combined. Kaiaulu also offers various *transform_to_network_* functions to represent and interactively visualize these data sources as networks[20] which in turn enables more complex socio-technical analyses at different granularities: functions, files, classes, etc.

Tool Configuration Files vs Project Configuration Files in Kaiaulu. Following the design choice of Codeface (see Sect. 2.2), and building on best practices for machine learning configuration files [27] we implemented project configuration files using YAML. Because we externalize all parameters in project configuration files, an important concern is that the file does not grow overly complex, requiring documentation of its own. That is, we do not wish the minimal path to data to increase as new features are added, as we discuss next.

---

[16] https://devguide.ropensci.org/softwarereviewintro.html#whysubmit.

[17] https://www.r-project.org/.

[18] https://cran.r-project.org/web/packages/.

[19] See for example under Vignettes: https://cran.r-project.org/web/packages/ggplot2/index.html.

[20] https://github.com/sailuh/kaiaulu/blob/master/R/network.R.

Minimal Path to Data in Kaiaulu. As discussed in Sect. 2.4, it is important that the path to data remains as simple and short as possible. We again build upon familiar concepts, specifically with the intent of applying the rule of least surprise [26, Ch. 11][21] i.e. 'do the least surprising thing'. In an R package, it is expected that R Notebooks provide examples of how to leverage the API to accomplish a task by combining multiple functions, while individual functions provide self-contained examples, which can be obtained in the R environment at any time by preceding a function name with a question mark, e.g. '*?parse_gitlog*'.

To build upon this we: 1) *Do not create* any dependency between configuration files and the API: functions take, as input, parameters which are familiar to any programmer (e.g. file paths or TRUE/FALSE flags); 2) *Use* project configuration files only in the first code block in R Notebooks to load the variables required to use the functions of the API, similar to how best practices in static programming languages encourage variable definitions at the beginning of a program; 3) *Create* a dependency between the CLI and the project configuration files, to facilitate batch processing and reproducibility.

Our intent is that users will first observe the R Notebooks to get a better understanding of the API for a particular task of interest, and in doing so will familiarize themselves with both the relevant portion of the API and the project configuration file. If the interest is only, for example, to understand how to parse Git logs, using for example the Git log R notebook, then users should not be concerned with specifying the mailing list. When comfortable, users can then use their newfound understanding to scale the analysis to the entire project using the configuration file for the CLI, build their own analyses as vignettes, or define new CLI interfaces. This design is consistent with a mining software repositories workflow, in which a researcher should first explore the data qualitatively to assess threats to validity, before scaling up data processing in batch mode without clarity of what assumptions the tool is making using default parameters or arbitrary thresholds.

Kaiaulu also further decreases the minimal path to data in terms of how it handles third party dependencies. Users need only concern themselves with installing dependencies for their task of interest. For example, if the interest is only to parse Git logs, they need only set up Perceval, and provide its binary path as a parameter to Kaiaulu's *parse_gitlog* to obtain the parsed data. More generally, the *parse_* API minimizes effort to researchers by transforming various tool-specific data formats, if the researcher so desires, into tables, and performing minimal processing on potentially inconsistent fields, such as file paths, to make them internally consistent. An example of a minimal path to data is shown in the Parse Gitlog Notebook[22] where the project configuration file parameters are loaded first into variables, and only them used on the R package API.

---

[21] Also publicly available at: http://www.catb.org/~esr/writings/taoup/html/ch11s01.html.

[22] https://github.com/sailuh/kaiaulu/blob/master/vignettes/gitlog_showcase.Rmd.

4   The Kaiaulu R Package

Based on the above observations and lessons learned, we now describe the realized modules and features resulting from the design decisions behind the Kaiaulu R package.

Mining software repositories often requires the handling of multiple data sources to analyze a project's ecosystem. Minimally, a researcher is required to understand the data source in its native form, acquire it (typically using an API), parse and save it (e.g. as a table of data). Overhead is incurred if a tool needs to be purpose-built to accomplish these steps. In the best case, the acquisition and parsing steps can be accomplished by using an existing tool. When designing Kaiaulu, we asked ourselves how to emphasize the minimal path to data (as discussed in Sect. 2.4). To illustrate our rationale, Fig. 1 revisits some of the tools' design decisions we discussed earlier.

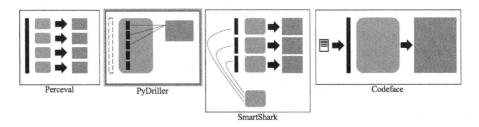

Fig. 1. Conceptual diagram of interface, input, and output of tools showcasing differences in design.

In Fig. 1, Perceval (left) provides a single CLI interface for acquisition of various data sources. For example, a project's issues can be fetched by using the 'jira' endpoint, while 'git' may be used to parse repositories. Pydriller (center-left), provides functions via a Python API. Users of these tools gain flexibility in parsing the data, at the cost of a higher learning curve and familiarity with the language. SmartShark (center-right) provides similar functionality to Perceval, but endpoints such as 'jira' and 'git' are now realized as entirely separate tools, orchestrated by another tool. Finally, Codeface (right) provides a single CLI interface, like Perceval. But most of its functionality is executed in batch mode and output into a single database dump, offering the least flexibility in terms of what analyses to execute. Unique to these tools, Codeface stores project parameters in reusable configuration files.

Using Fig. 1 as a basis for comparison, Kaiaulu's design is shown in Fig. 2, separated into parts 1) through 4). Kaiaulu borrows from the design of PyDriller by defining an API and a set of functions (2). The use of configuration files, inspired by Codeface (3), is done at the R Notebook level (rather than at the function level). That is, project configuration parameters are read into an R Notebook, and appropriate parameters are then passed to functions. This allows us to decouple configurations from function signatures, to tell best practice stories (interspersed with code) of how parameters are used in various analyses [4,5,17], and offer a reusable end-to-end pipeline for specific exploratory analysis. For example, the social smells notebook[23] emphasizes care in assessing project's communication, which are often fragmented over multiple archives. More importantly, R notebooks enable easy manual inspection of intermediate data, such as the use of identity match heuristics. We found this use of 'reusable data stories' particularly useful to familiarize undergraduate and graduate research assistants to common pitfalls.

We borrowed the use of CLIs (4) from Perceval and Smartshark. The CLI serves to accommodate users who are unfamiliar with R; it also supports scaling analyses defined and prototyped in Notebooks, so that they can be run in batch mode. To build upon (2), the CLI simply utilizes the defined API behind the scenes, which simplifies code maintenance. As with the Notebooks (3), the CLI parses project configuration files, which also facilitate server-side reuse.

Kaiaulu was designed by combining these concepts from (1–4). It was implemented as an R package, building upon familiar software abstractions. Typically R packages are defined as an API of functions as found in PyDriller and R Notebooks. By showcasing project configuration files where users are expected to learn about the package, users can familiarize themselves with project configuration files and the command line interface, which is less commonly found in R packages, and entirely optional. In the following subsections, Kaiaulu's major processing elements are discussed.

4.1 Parsers

In the *Parsers* module, our goal was to minimize a user's effort, in terms of acquiring and parsing project source code. These functions were combined into a single interface with consistent nomenclature.

Each of Kaiaulu's parsers is defined as a function (e.g. *parse_mbox*, *parse_gitlog*), which are also accessible via a CLI. We wanted parsers in Kaiaulu to reflect Perceval's philosophy of minimal paths to data, with a small learning curve. That is, given a data source, we would like users to quickly be able to see the data without spending excessive time on setup. As such, each parser function is given a single responsibility: to display a data source as a table with a standardized column nomenclature (in case multiple sources referred to the same data with different names). Unlike Perceval, since an API option is also available, users can interactively prototype and analyze the data in the R environment. Having tables as the default output option minimizes the time spent learning what fields are available in the source. The standardized nomenclature allows for intuitive joining operations across the outputs of different parsers.

To account for *the perils of code reuse*, Kaiaulu limits its interface only to third party software that have CLI interfaces. Parsers with third party dependencies simply contain in their signatures an additional parameter for path to

---

[23] https://github.com/sailuh/kaiaulu/blob/master/vignettes/social_smell_showcase. Rmd.

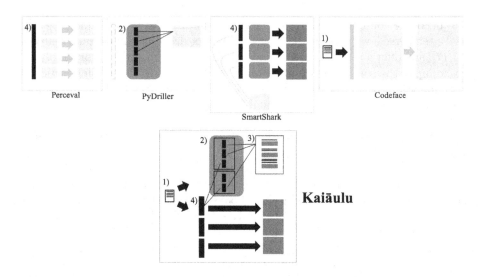

Fig. 2. Conceptual diagram of interface, input, and output of tools showcasing how Kaiaulu compares to the tools.

the required binary. This dependency mechanism allows users to bypass setting up third party tools which they do not directly need to use. Additionally, users benefit from using the Kaiaulu function to obtain a tabulated and standardized data input. For example, the *parse_gitlog(git_repo_path,perceval_path)* function requires, as input, Perceval's binary to tabulate its JSON output. In this way parsers can build upon third party functionality to implement new features. For example, *parse_gitlog_entity(git_repo_path,utags_path,project_git_log,kinds)* implements a git log parser capable of tabulating developer changes from git logs at the granularity of functions rather than files (inspired by Joblin et al. [15]). In addition, the assumptions and threats to validity in the cited work are provided in the Notebook[24].

While simple in concept, we note that existing tools do not offer this functionality. For instance, Codeface [15] offers an implementation of a function-based git log parser, but since it has an 'all-in-all-out' interface, this function can not be reused elsewhere. The same is true for SmartShark. Perceval, while containing a shorter path to data, still requires tabulation and standardization of the collected results. Lastly, PyDriller does not adopt the philosophy used here for extending functionality based on third party software, as it limits its scope to Git.

Kaiaulu currently employs a variety of parsers, providing the ability to parse git logs, mailing list archives (e.g. pipermail, Apache's mod_mbox), issue trackers (e.g. Jira, GitHub), static parsers (file and function dependencies), evolutionary parsers (file and function changes), commit hashes (e.g. to identify issue ids from commit messages), and software vulnerability feeds. Parsers which contain

---

[24] https://github.com/sailuh/kaiaulu/blob/master/vignettes/blamed_line_types_show case.Rmd.

filepaths also contain optional regular expression filters to whitelist or blacklist files based on their extensions or naming conventions. For example, we use this to remove test files from analyses as these files could compromise code metrics.

4.2   Transformers, Graphs and Networks

Kaiaulu's Transformer, Graph, and Network modules are grounded on the observation that most software and social metrics are graph-based (e.g. co-change, fan-in, fan-out, communication). These modules *transform* the data provided by various kinds of parsers that parse the raw project data. Transformers reformat the data provided by parsers into lists of nodes and edges which are then represented as networks, using *graph* data structures. In this way we can more easily visualize and explore the *networks* of relationships among a software project's elements.

Kaiaulu represents the socio-technical network for each snapshot as a graph $G_{st} = (V, E)$, where the set of nodes $V = V_a \cup V_f \cup V_t$ comprises authors V_a, source files V_f and e-mail threads V_t. The set of edges $E = E_{comm} \cup E_{chg}$ models communication and collaboration between authors, where communication is done via $E_{comm} \subseteq V_a \times V_t$, and file changes via $E_{chg} \subseteq V_a \times V_f$. Observe by this construction, the socio-technical network is in fact two bi-modal bipartite networks $G_{st} = G_{chg} \cup G_{comm}$. Both G_{chg} and G_{comm} are also weighted (representing an author's count of changes to a file within a user specified time window (e.g. 3 months), and the number of replies submitted to an e-mail thread respectively), and undirected (the direction is irrelevant in this case because it could only go in one direction in each bipartite network). Likewise, the CVE and File Networks are weighted, undirected, bipartite graphs. The definition of various transformations are encapsulated separately in functions, consistent to the overall architecture.

Projection Transformations. Familiar software engineering metrics can be derived from graph projections. Consider a bipartite graph as containing nodes of two colors, black and blue. Intuitively, a graph projection operation eliminates one set of the 'colored', e.g. the blue nodes, and connects the adjacent black nodes together, where the resulting edge weight is the sum of the eliminated edges. In a bipartite network represented by file and commit nodes, eliminating the commit nodes would result in a file's co-change metric, revealing *indirect collaboration*. For example, if five authors modified the same file within a given time period, then the projection operation shows that *all five authors indirectly collaborated*, irrespective of the order of their changes (note that the derived uni-modal networks are undirected). We define this as the projection transformation to go from bi-modal to uni-modal networks.

Temporal Transformations. Let us now consider a second approach to obtain uni-modal networks. In [15], the authors define one method to construct uni-modal networks from the same data by defining indirect collaboration using the notion of incremental contributions through the timestamps on commits. For example, if author A modifies a file, and the very next change to the same file is performed by author B, then B is said to have *indirectly collaborated with A*. A similar intuition and transformation could be used to categorize e-mail replies. We define this method, to go from the bipartite network to the uni-modal network, a *temporal* transformation (as it relies on the timestamps). Observe in this case that the derived uni-modal networks will be directed graphs (which indicate the flow of time). The edge's weight is defined as the sum of lines of code added by both developers in their respective file changes (Fig. 3).

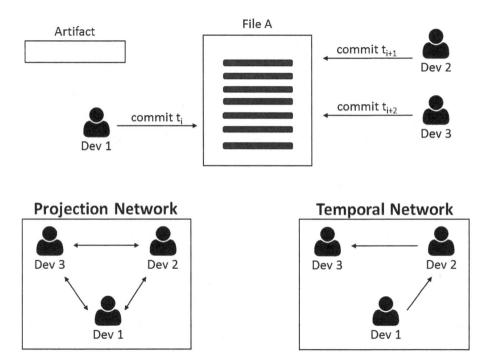

Fig. 3. Temporal vs projection networks, format adapted from [16].

Which method to derive uni-modal networks should we choose? This decision is encapsulated in Kaiaulu by the choice of functions. By swapping projection and temporal transformation functions, users can experiment with, and visualize, their various implications.

An example of both projection and temporal networks is shown in Fig. 4 (the name of each node's developer has been blurred). In the projection network, developers are connected if in a given time window they modified any file in common. In the temporal network, the direction displays which developers changed files after which in the given time window. For example, a bidirectional arrow means two developers change the same file together. A uni-directional arrow suggests another developer may have "taken over" during that time window. In both cases, we could derive hypothesis of the nature of collaboration, and derive hypothesis to be tested in the exploratory analysis.

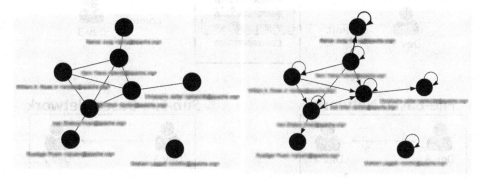

(a) CVE and File Network.   (b) Projection Network. Nodes indicate developers. Edges represent common changed files.

Fig. 4. Temporal network. Nodes indicate developers. Edges represent common changed files. The edge direction indicates the temporal order of change. Names are blurred for author privacy. Kaiaulu can also replace names by IDs for privacy in visualizations.

File, Functions, and Entities. Another consideration encapsulated in Kaiaulu's functions is which entities are analyzed to derive indirect collaboration. For example, consider Fig. 5. As we can see, the choice of granularity will also affect the number of edges generated, where a file granularity generates more edges than function granularity. A larger number of edges, in turn, may impact the social smell metrics, as the existence of connections between developers in one network, and the absence of edges in another network, may inflate the count of metrics, such as social smells (which we define in the next section). The authors in [15] used a combination of temporal transformation and function granularity. In Kaiaulu, we implemented both the file granularity, and generalized the function granularity to *entities*, where a sub-file unit can be any source code block region of interest (e.g. functions, classes, or language specific features like structs in C).

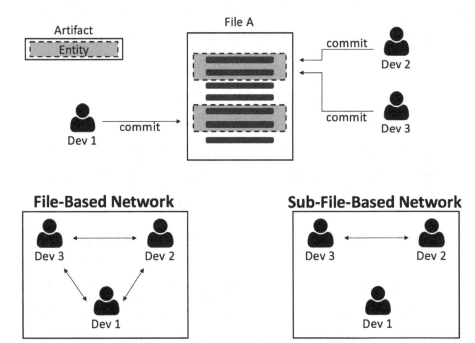

Fig. 5. File vs sub-file (e.g. function) networks, adapted from [16].

4.3   Identity

A critical component of conducting socio-technical analysis in open source communities is assigning a consistent identity to users who may employ multiple variants of their name and e-mail addresses in their project interactions. Several approaches to match identities have been proposed (e.g. [4,33]). Exact name matching (either names or e-mails) or partial matching (e.g. based on edit distance) are two commonly used schemes.

Our identity matching was designed as a 3 step pipeline: formatting, name-email separation and pair-wise matching. Formatting includes the removal of symbols such as '< >', commas or replacing 'at' with '@', while avoiding modifying a name, such as Matt. Name and e-mail separation handles cases where first or last or both names are not provided, multiple word names, etc. Finally, pair-wise matching handles comparisons of name and e-mail, or reversed names. In total, the steps of formatting, name separation, and name matching amounted to 31 test cases, which were successfully implemented. At the end of this step, users in the version control system, issue tracker, and mailing list who matched via the tests we implemented were assigned an appropriate ID. Thus, given the name, and optionally the e-mail, other information sources can be matched.

Fig. 6. Reply networks combine communication networks. Here dark blue nodes are issue comments, light blue nodes are mailing list comments, and black nodes are developers. Red nodes are developers who communicate in both the mailing list and the issue tracker. (Color figure online)

An example of the utility of identity matching is shown in Fig. 6. Here, project communication occurs in parallel in both the Jira issue tracker and the project's mailing list. We fuse these information sources into a single "Reply Network".

In summary, the transformer API provides users with flexibility with respect to both temporal assumptions and sub-file granularity. Because all networks are annotated graphs, community detection algorithms in Kaiaulu can be used to identify important patterns. For example, if applied to a file-commit network over a fixed period of time, co-changed file clusters can be identified. Similarly, if the file network is derived from file to file dependencies, clusters related to modularity measures can be derived. Developer networks can be used to detect communities.

In Fig. 7, we apply the OSLOM community detection algorithm [19] to a temporal network such as the one illustrated in Fig. 4. The result is displayed by re-coloring the black nodes. Darker blue and lighter blue nodes represent two communities of developers as determined by the files that they changed in common. Developers in black represent boundary nodes, which participate of both communities. In the interactive format, researchers can "zoom in" on these nodes to identify who are the common developers, and can use this information to draw further hypotheses.

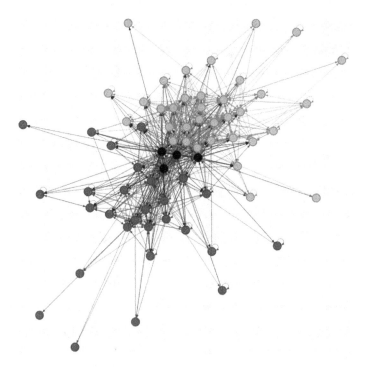

Fig. 7. OSLOM community detection algorithm [19] applied to a temporal projection. (Color figure online)

4.4 Metrics

In the metrics module, we define some commonly used metrics, such as number of bugs, churn, LOC, as well as the less well-known social metrics. Demographics are also provided to help contextualize the previously presented social networks, such as the number of developers modifying files and exchanging e-mails, number of files, threads, and different timezones[25].

---

[25] For a full analysis with the metrics, see: http://itm0.shidler.hawaii.edu/kaiaulu/ articles/social_smell_showcase.html. The source code can be found on https://github. com/sailuh/kaiaulu/blob/master/vignettes/social_smell_showcase.Rmd.

For bug counts, rather than simply interpreting these as metrics, we make it easy for users to observe their topology. This is evident in Fig. 8, where a single issue is associated with multiple files (top right). While some other files may have a lower count of issues, more complex structure (such as we can observe at the bottom left of the Figure) would be missed if only metrics were employed. Furthermore, feature issues can be discerned from bugs by examining the issue labels.

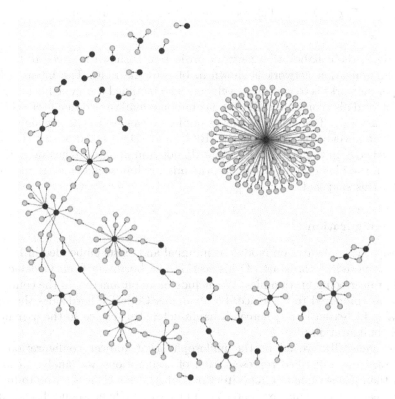

Fig. 8. Issue network. Blue nodes represent issues, and yellow nodes files. (Color figure online)

Lastly, we briefly discuss the social metrics as they leverage the previously discussed modules. For the social metrics, we adopt the definitions of social smells defined by [29]. Social smells reflect recurring sub-optimal organizational structure patterns connected to organizational behavior patterns, e.g., sub-optimal knowledge sharing, recurrent sharing delays, misguided collaboration and more. We chose to integrate three of these smells—Organizational Silo, Missing Link and Radio Silence—and two related metrics: socio-technical congruence and missing communicability [29]. Here we explain one of the social smells; additional details about these metrics can be found in [29].

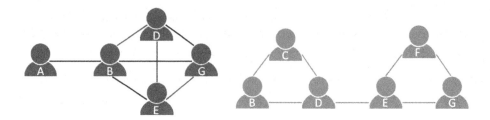

Fig. 9. Missing link social smell [20] (Color figure online)

In Fig. 9, the collaboration network projection is shown in green to the left. The communication network is shown in blue to the right. The intent behind developer networks is to capture developers who modified the same file in a given snapshot, and also communicated via a common e-mail thread in a user-specified time window (e.g. 3 months). In this example, we can see to the left highlighted in red that developers (A,B), (B,E), (B,G), and (D,G) collaborated (i.e. they have a red edge in the green graph), but do not communicate (they do not have an edge in the blue graph). Therefore, the missing link social smell is counted 4 times for this snapshot.

4.5   Configuration

Currently, the configuration module is minimal and exists embedded in R Notebooks. As noted at the start of this section, we borrowed from Codeface the idea of project configuration files. We include more parameters in the configuration file as compared to Codeface. For example, Codeface hardcodes the set of acceptable file extensions, whereas Kaiaulu defers this choice to the user in the project configuration file.

More generally, we adopt the philosophy that project configuration files should serve as a distilled representation of assumptions and analysis choices. Rather than just serving as a repository of configuration choices for reproducibility, it is readable as plain text, and so can be easily exchanged and discussed. In Kaiaulu, a project configuration file is written in YAML. An example of project configuration file can be found in the public tool repository 'conf' folder[26].

As with every design decision in Kaiaulu, the full project configuration file needs not be specified. Indeed, every R Notebook, at the beginning, clarifies which parameters are required. In future work, we plan to expand the Configuration module to tabulate multiple configuration files. For example, it is often common in software engineering literature to analyze multiple projects and present a summary statistics table of the projects to assess generalization of results. Such tables could be generated on the fly from the files. Ideally, project configuration files should suffice as supplementary material, alongside Kaiaulu's version for full reproducibility.

---

[26] https://github.com/sailuh/kaiaulu/tree/master/conf.

5 Conclusions and Future Work

In this paper, through an action research approach, we have determined a set of key design decisions mined from existing tools. Based on these lessons learned we iteratively developed Kaiaulu, an R package for mining software repositories. Our goal in creating Kaiaulu was to simplify most of the boring, repetitive, and error-prone tasks in mining software repositories, leaving the user free to focus on the true goals of their research.

In Kaiaulu we have implemented and released a comprehensive set of capabilities to mine, analyze, and visualize software repositories, including social smells [29], architecture smells and metrics [23], and bug timelines based on prior work by other authors. Kaiaulu is licensed under MPL 2.0.

While we have derived the principles for Kaiaulu from our action research, our future work is to take a more disciplined approach to Kaiaulu's design, based on the quality attributes that represent its architectural drivers. Following the approach outlined in [18] and [3] we can, in the future, attempt to more systematically collect architectural drivers, make reasoned design decisions, and support these decisions with well-established design rationale.

In terms of our design decisions, we believe that future work can more systematically expand on lessons learned and coverage, by means of a systematic mapping study to evaluate existing tools from scientific databases and conferences, instead of being limited to related work known by the authors. We have also not extensively evaluated Kaiaulu's performance on very large projects. Nonetheless, we believe the lessons learned in this work, and the exploratory capabilities of Kaiaulu, constitute a good starting point to address these limitations.

References

1. 15th IEEE/ACM International Workshop on Cooperative and Human Aspects of Software Engineering, CHASE@ICSE 2022. IEEE (2022). https://fpalomba. github.io/pdf/Conferencs/C65.pdf
2. Almeida, D.A., Murphy, G.C., Wilson, G., Hoye, M.: Do software developers understand open source licenses? In: IEEE/ACM 25th International Conference on Program Comprehension, pp. 1–11 (2017)
3. Bass, L., Clements, P., Kazman, R.: Software Architecture in Practice, 4th edn. Addison-Wesley, Boston (2021)
4. Bird, C., Gourley, A., Devanbu, P., Gertz, M., Swaminathan, A.: Mining email social networks. In: Proceedings of International Workshop on Mining Software Repositories, pp. 137–143. ACM (2006)
5. Bird, C., Rigby, P.C., Barr, E.T., Hamilton, D.J., German, D.M., Devanbu, P.: The promises and perils of mining git. In: 2009 6th IEEE International Working Conference on Mining Software Repositories, pp. 1–10 (2009). https://doi.org/10. 1109/MSR.2009.5069475
6. Broere, C.: Effects of community smells on turnover in Open Source Software projects. Ph.D. thesis, Vrije Universiteit Amsterdam (2021)
7. Carlos Paradis, R.K.: Design choices in building an MSR tool: the case of kaiaulu. In: ECSA 2021 (2021). http://ceur-ws.org/Vol-2978/msr4sa-paper1.pdf

8. Coelho, J., Valente, M.: Why modern open source projects fail. In: Proceedings of 11th Joint Meeting on Foundations of Software Engineering, pp. 186–196. ACM (2017)

9. De Stefano, M., Iannone, E., Pecorelli, F., Tamburri, D.A.: Impacts of software community patterns on process and product: an empirical study. Sci. Comput. Program. **214**, 102731 (2022). https://doi.org/10.1016/j.scico.2021.102731. https://www.sciencedirect.com/science/article/pii/S0167642321001246

10. Dueñas, S., Cosentino, V., Robles, G., Gonzalez-Barahona, J.M.: Perceval: software project data at your will. In: Proceedings of 40th International Conference on Software Engineering: Companion Proceedings, pp. 1–4. ACM (2018)

11. Easterbrook, S., Singer, J., Storey, M.A., Damian, D.: Selecting empirical methods for software engineering research. In: Shull, F., Singer, J., Sjøberg, D.I.K. (eds.) Guide to Advanced Empirical Software Engineering, pp. 285–311. Springer, London (2008). https://doi.org/10.1007/978-1-84800-044-5_11

12. Giarola, F.: Detecting code and community smells in open-source: an automated approach. Master's thesis, Politecnico di Milano (2016)

13. Gousios, G., Spinellis, D.: Alitheia core: an extensible software quality monitoring platform. In: 2009 IEEE 31st International Conference on Software Engineering, pp. 579–582 (2009)

14. Joblin, M., Apel, S., Hunsen, C., Mauerer, W.: Classifying developers into core and peripheral: an empirical study on count and network metrics. In: IEEE/ACM 39th International Conference on Software Engineering, pp. 164–174 (2017)

15. Joblin, M., Mauerer, W., Apel, S., Siegmund, J., Riehle, D.: From developer networks to verified communities: a fine-grained approach. In: 2015 IEEE/ACM 37th IEEE International Conference on Software Engineering, vol. 1, pp. 563–573 (2015)

16. Joblin, M.: Structural and evolutionary analysis of developer networks. Ph.D. thesis, Universitat Passau (2017)

17. Kalliamvakou, E., Gousios, G., Blincoe, K., Singer, L., German, D.M., Damian, D.: The promises and perils of mining github. In: Proceedings of the 11th Working Conference on Mining Software Repositories, MSR 2014, pp. 92–101. Association for Computing Machinery, New York (2014). https://doi.org/10.1145/2597073.2597074

18. Kazman, R., Bianco, P., Echeverria, S., Ivers, J.: Robustness. Technical report, CMU/SEI-2022-TR-004 (2022)

19. Lancichinetti, A., Radicchi, F., Ramasco, J.J., Fortunato, S.: Finding statistically significant communities in networks. PLoS ONE **6**(4), e18961 (2011). https://doi.org/10.1371/journal.pone.0018961

20. Magnoni, S.: An approach to measure community smells in software development communities. Ph.D. thesis, Politecnico Milano (2016)

21. van Meijel, J.: On the relations between community patterns and smells in open-source: a taxonomic and empirical analysis. Ph.D. thesis, Eindhoven University of Technology (2021)

22. Menzies, T., Williams, L., Zimmermann, T.: Perspectives on Data Science for Software Engineering, 1st edn. Morgan Kaufmann Publishers Inc., Burlington (2016)

23. Mo, R., Cai, Y., Kazman, R., Xiao, L., Feng, Q.: Architecture anti-patterns: automatically detectable violations of design principles. IEEE Trans. Softw. Eng. **47**(5), 1008–1028 (2019)

24. Moreno, D., et al.: Sortinghat: wizardry on software project members. In: IEEE/ACM 41st International Conference on Software Engineering: Companion Proceedings, pp. 51–54 (2019)

25. Neubig, G., et al.: XNMT: the extensible neural machine translation toolkit. In: Conference of the Association for Machine Translation in the Americas Open Source Software Showcase (2018)
26. Raymond, E.S.: The Art of UNIX Programming. Pearson Education, Burlington (2003)
27. Sculley, D., et al.: Hidden technical debt in machine learning systems. In: Proceedings of 28th International Conference on Neural Information Processing Systems, NIPS 2015, vol. 2, pp. 2503–2511. MIT Press, Cambridge (2015)
28. Spadini, D., Aniche, M., Bacchelli, A.: PyDriller: python framework for mining software repositories. In: Proceedings of 26th ACM Joint Proceedings of ESEC/FSE, pp. 908–911. ACM Press (2018)
29. Tamburri, D., Palomba, F., Kazman, R.: Exploring community smells in open-source: an automated approach. IEEE Trans. Softw. Eng. **47**(3), 630–652 (2019)
30. Trautsch, A., Trautsch, F., Herbold, S., Ledel, B., Grabowski, J.: The smartshark ecosystem for software repository mining. arXiv preprint arXiv:2001.01606 (2020)
31. Trautsch, F., Herbold, S., Makedonski, P., Grabowski, J.: Addressing problems with replicability and validity of repository mining studies through a smart data platform. Empir. Softw. Eng. **23**(2), 1036–1083 (2017). https://doi.org/10.1007/s10664-017-9537-x
32. Valiev, M., Vasilescu, B., Herbsleb, J.: Ecosystem-level determinants of sustained activity in open-source projects: a case study of the PyPI ecosystem. In: Proceedings of 26th ACM Joint Proceedings of ESEC/FSE, pp. 644–655. ACM (2018)
33. Zhu, J., Wei, J.: An empirical study of multiple names and email addresses in OSS version control repositories. In: IEEE/ACM 16th International Conference on Mining Software Repositories (MSR), pp. 409–420 (2019)

1st International Workshop on Software Architecture and Machine Learning (SAML)

Self-adaptive Machine Learning Systems: Research Challenges and Opportunities

Maria Casimiro[1,2]([✉]), Paolo Romano[2], David Garlan[1], Gabriel A. Moreno[3], Eunsuk Kang[1], and Mark Klein[3]

[1] Institute for Software Research, Carnegie Mellon University, Pittsburgh, PA, USA
[2] INESC-ID, Instituto Superior Técnico, University of Lisbon, Lisbon, Portugal
maria.casimiro@tecnico.ulisboa.pt
[3] Software Engineering Institute, Carnegie Mellon University, Pittsburgh, PA, USA

Abstract. Today's world is witnessing a shift from human-written software to machine-learned software, with the rise of systems that rely on machine learning. These systems typically operate in non-static environments, which are prone to unexpected changes, as is the case of self-driving cars and enterprise systems. In this context, machine-learned software can misbehave. Thus, it is paramount that these systems are capable of detecting problems with their machined-learned components and adapting themselves to maintain desired qualities. For instance, a fraud detection system that cannot adapt its machine-learned model to efficiently cope with emerging fraud patterns or changes in the volume of transactions is subject to losses of millions of dollars. In this paper, we take a first step towards the development of a framework for self-adaptation of systems that rely on machine-learned components. We describe: (i) a set of causes of machine-learned component misbehavior and a set of adaptation tactics inspired by the literature on machine learning, motivating them with the aid of two running examples from the enterprise systems and cyber-physical systems domains; (ii) the required changes to the MAPE-K loop, a popular control loop for self-adaptive systems; and (iii) the challenges associated with developing this framework. We conclude with a set of research questions to guide future work.

Keywords: Self-adaptive systems · Machine learning · Model degradation · Learning-enabled systems · Learning-enabled components

1 Introduction

In recent years, Learning-Enabled Systems (LES) have become ubiquitous in domains such as enterprise and cyber-physical systems. LES are composed of one or more machine-learning components, also known as Learning Enabled Components (LEC), whose behavior is derived from training data [40]. LECs are then embedded into a larger system containing traditional computational entities such as web services, databases, and operator interfaces. Examples include:

© The Author(s), under exclusive license to Springer Nature Switzerland AG 2022
P. Scandurra et al. (Eds.): ECSA Tracks and Workshops 2021, LNCS 13365, pp. 133–155, 2022.
https://doi.org/10.1007/978-3-031-15116-3_7

fraud detection, which uses a classifier to detect fraudulent transactions [8]; medical diagnosis, which relies on Machine Learning (ML) for classifying types of diseases of patients [27]; self-driving cars, which use ML to determine whether they should brake to avoid collision with moving objects (e.g., cars, pedestrians) [4,44]; robots, which rely on ML models to predict the amount of remaining battery power [37]; targeted advertisement services, which rely on recommender systems to show users items that they may find interesting [20]; and smart homes/buildings, that rely on LECs for tasks such as face and voice recognition [34,63] or occupancy prediction for proactive heating/cooling [28,36].

Despite their widespread use, and similarly to non-machine learned components, LECs can fail to perform as expected [23,40,68], thereby reducing system utility. For instance, changes in a system's operating environment can introduce drifts in the input data of the ML components making them less accurate [57], or attacks may attempt to subvert the intended functionality of the system [33].

While the literature offers no immediate solution to guarantee the behavior of LES under changing environments [40], the large body of works on Self-Adaptive Systems (SAS) has already investigated a number of methods to tackle analogous problems for non-ML based systems. Specifically, SAS react to environment changes, faults and internal system issues to improve the system's behavior, utility and/or dependability [19]. These systems usually adopt an architecture based on the MAPE-K loop [38], which monitors the system, decides when adaptation is needed, selects the best course of action to improve the system, and executes it. In this field, the actions available for the system to execute are usually called *tactics*. This is an extensive and active research area that has made steady improvements for years and thus we propose the use of SAS to deal with environment changes and faults in the context of LESs and LECs.

In fact, there is a large number of emerging techniques that have been developed by the ML community for improving and correcting supervised ML models and that could in principle be used as adaptation tactics in a SAS. These range from off-line, full model retraining and replacement, at one extreme, to incremental approaches performed in-situ, at the other [12,35,46,56,58,67].

Unfortunately, determining when and how to take advantage of such tactics to perform adaptation is far from being trivial. First, there is a large number of possible adaptation tactics that could potentially be applied to a ML component, but not all approaches work with all forms of ML models. For example, when a new family is moving into a new smart home, all the LECs should be fine-tuned to work as expected for that family [7]. Transfer learning [52] could be leveraged in this setting to speed up the process of fine-tuning these models. Yet, this tactic would yield the expected benefits only if the families are similar [49].

Second, the value of investing in improving the accuracy of a ML component is strongly context-dependent – often depending on both domain and timing considerations. For example, while a medical diagnosis system may support model retraining at run time, the latency of this tactic may make it infeasible for self-driving cars, which rely instead on swifter tactics (such as replacing the ML component entirely) to match real-time response requirements. In a different mode of operation, however, both types of tactics may be available, e.g., if the self-driving car is stopped (parked mode of operation), it may be feasible to retrain an under-performing model without compromising safety.

Third, calculating the costs and benefits of these tactics is difficult, particularly in a whole-system context, where improving a specific component's performance may or may not improve overall system utility. Costs include time, resources (processing, memory, power), and service disruption. Benefits derive for instance from increased accuracy or fairness of the ML component, which can in turn lead to better performing down-stream components and support overall business goals (e.g. by improving advertisement revenue). Yet, both costs [16,45] and benefits [17] can be hard to quantify, thus making it challenging to reason about whether executing a ML adaptation tactic will improve system utility.

We argue that in order to harness the potential of the rich space of ML adaptation mechanisms, it is necessary to develop methods aimed to: i) identify which tactics, among the ones available to adapt an LES, are the most effective in a given context to maximize system utility, and ii) integrate them into modern adaptive systems architectures. Specifically, in this paper we attempt to bring some clarity to this emerging but critical aspect of SAS by outlining: **(i)** a set of causes of ML component performance degradation and a set of adaptation tactics derived from research on ML (Sect. 3), providing examples from the domains of enterprise systems (Sect. 4) and cyber-physical systems (Sect. 5); **(ii)** the architectural and algorithmic changes required to incorporate effective ML adaptation into the MAPE-K loop, a popular framework for monitoring and controlling self-adaptive systems (Sect. 6); and **(iii)** the modeling and engineering challenges associated with realizing the full potential for adaptation of LESs (Sect. 6). We conclude by introducing a set of open research questions and directions for future work. This work is an extended version of [14] which provides: **(i)** a more detailed and general discussion on the causes of ML component performance degradation; and **(ii)** a second use-case from the cyber-physical systems domain. This work further extends the original running example by mapping the detailed discussion on the causes of ML component performance degradation to examples in the enterprise systems domain.

2   Background and Related Work

Current literature on SAS focuses on managed systems that do not embed (nor rely upon) ML models [39]. That is, although the self-adaptation mechanism (i.e. managing system) may rely on ML to perform a given function (e.g., decide which tactic to execute), the actual system that is adapted (i.e. the managed system) does not rely on any ML component. These systems have at their disposal a set of tactics that, for instance, change a system's architecture (e.g., adding/removing servers) or the quality of the service they provide (e.g., increasing/decreasing the rendering quality of images) in response to environment changes [21]. Usually, tactic outcomes have some uncertainty that can be modeled via probabilistic methods given assumptions on the underlying hardware/software platforms and their characteristics. Further, one can measure the properties of such systems through the use of metrics such as latency, throughput and content quality.

Determining the costs and benefits of such adaptation tactics has been well researched and there are numerous techniques and algorithms to that end [11,25, 30]. Yet, new challenges arise when considering managed systems that depend on LECs. Not only are we missing a well-understood and generally applicable set of tactics that SASs can use to adapt LESs, but also the properties of ML components, such as accuracy and fairness, may not change consistently with the tactic that is executed. For example, if we retrain a ML model, its accuracy is not always affected in the same way, but may depend on the samples available to retrain the model, on the duration of the retraining process, and on the model's hyper-parameters [16]. Similarly, model fairness may also be affected in different ways due to the training samples that are used during re-training [24].

To improve the self-adaptive capabilities of systems and their performance, recent research has proposed SASs that rely on ML techniques and models to adapt the system [32,59]. Specifically, ML can be used in the adaptation manager to: update adaptation policies, predict resource usage, update run-time models, reduce adaptation spaces, predict anomalies, and collect knowledge. Further, learning can be leveraged to improve the Analysis and Plan components of the MAPE-K loop [32].

In this paper, we focus on the complementary problem of how to leverage self-adaptation to correct and adapt supervised ML components of a managed system. The goal is to increase overall utility of ML-based systems when their ML components are under-performing. This vision is aligned with the one presented by Bures [10] who claims that *"self-adaptation should stand in equal-to-equal relationship to AI. It should both benefit from AI and enable AI."* Extending this vision further, we argue that the techniques developed in this context could also be applied, in a recursive fashion, to self-adapt adaptation managers that rely on ML components to enhance their effectiveness and robustness. For instance, a planner that relies on ML to reduce the adaptation space could have its own self-adaptation manager to ensure that the ML component is working as expected.

Our vision ties in the field of self-adaptive systems with the field of life-long/continual learning [41,61], which deals with open-world learning problems. In fact, dealing with open-world changes was identified [32] as an open problem in the SAS domain. Specifically, Lifelong Learning deals with the problem of leveraging past knowledge to learn a new task better and Continual Learning is focused on solving the problem of maintaining the accuracy of old tasks when learning new tasks [41]. The techniques developed in these fields can be leveraged by SASs to improve ML components when unexpected changes occur in the environment or when the performance of the ML component is degraded and affecting overall system utility. Our focus is on SASs and on how to integrate techniques from these research domains into a generic, yet rigorous/principled framework that can decide which ML component to adapt, how and when.

Finally, Gheibi et al. [31] have recently proposed a framework that aims at enhancing the quality of ML-based adaptation managers in scenarios where the managed system is not ML-based. The proposed system reacts to concept drifts that lead the ML models to perform sub-optimally (hence hindering the effectiveness of the adaptation manager) and automatically generates alternative ML-models (e.g., using different features) to replace the ones currently in use. Our framework targets a broader class of systems in which ML-components are part of the managed system and not only of the adaptation manager. Further, the conceptual framework presented in this work considers a broader set of adaptation tactics for ML-components, such as unlearning or having humans in the loop (see Sect. 3.2). The next section provides details on possible causes of ML component degradation and repair tactics inspired by this field of research.

3 Degradation and Repair of Learning-Enabled Components

Similarly to traditional components, LECs can fail, leading systems to undesirable states and to require repair of the under-performing components [40]. Thus, in this section we are interested in understanding what can lead an LEC to fail or produce erroneous outputs (Sect. 3.1), and what tactics are available to repair the components that are deteriorating system utility (Sect. 3.2). The different causes of degradation and the applicability of the tactics introduced in Sect. 3.2 will be exemplified in Sects. 4 and 5 using two use-cases from the fraud detection systems' and cyber-physical systems' domains, respectively.

3.1 Causes of Degradation of ML Components' Accuracy

ML approaches rely on a data-set composed of multi-dimensional input data and labels. Since this data-set is used for training the ML model, the environment from which these data-points are collected is usually known as the training environment. Then, once the ML model has been trained, it can be used by the system to make predictions in run-time. This is typically considered the testing environment as the model has never seen the current data-points. We will use the notions of training and testing environments throughout this section to introduce typical causes of degradation of ML components.

It is generally assumed that the distribution $p(y, \mathbf{x})$ of labels y and multi-dimensional input data $\mathbf{x}$ does not change between training and testing environments. However, when this assumption does not hold, and hence the prior distribution $P(\mathbf{x})$, or the posterior distribution $P(y)$, or any of the conditional distributions $P(y|\mathbf{x})$ or $P(\mathbf{x}|y)$ changes, one may be in the presence of a problem commonly known as data-set shift [51,56–58]. This raises the question of whether the current model is still fit for the current environment. As recent work has shown, not all data-set shifts are malign [58]. Thus, an effective SAS should not only detect shifts, but also assess their actual impact on system utility.

The literature on ML has investigated several types of data-set shifts that have different characteristics. These different characteristics influence the impact that each type of shift has on a given system, and also how easy it is to deal with/detect the shift. Specifically, problems such as anomaly detection, novelty detection, open set recognition, out of distribution detection, and outlier detection [70] are specific instances of the most common types of shift. We argue that the different types of shift are general enough to be representative of most of the issues addressed by the existing ML literature. The following paragraphs introduce these types of shift and give examples of typical sources of shift that can affect an LEC.

Covariate Shift. When the distribution of the inputs to a model changes, such that it becomes substantially different from the distribution on which the model was trained, we find ourselves in the presence of a problem commonly known as covariate shift. That is, the distribution $P(\mathbf{x})$ changes but the conditional distribution $P(y|\mathbf{x})$ remains the same. More formally, $P(\mathbf{x})_{train} \neq P(\mathbf{x})_{test}$ and $P(y|\mathbf{x})_{train} = P(y|\mathbf{x})_{test}$ [48]. This type of shift is usually analyzed to evaluate how a model generalizes and how robust it is when the feature space is altered at test time, i.e. while the system is executing.

Prior Probability Shift (Label Shift). Differently, when we are in the presence of prior probability shift, also known as label shift, this means that the distribution $P(y)$ of the labels/outputs has changed, i.e., the class proportions differ between training and test. More formally, $P(y)_{train} \neq P(y)_{test}$ and $P(\mathbf{x}|y)_{train} = P(\mathbf{x}|y)_{test}$ [48]. This can be seen as the inverse of covariate shift in the sense that now the distribution of features is the same between training and testing while the distribution of the labels changes. Dealing with this type of shift is particularly challenging when the new distribution $P(y)_{test}$ is unknown.

Concept Shift. Finally, concept shift corresponds to a change in the relationship between input and output distributions, although each remains the same. More formally, when this type of shift occurs, we can have $P(y|\mathbf{x})_{train} \neq P(y|\mathbf{x})_{test}$ and $P(\mathbf{x})_{train} = P(\mathbf{x})_{test}$ or $P(\mathbf{x}|y)_{train} \neq P(\mathbf{x}|y)_{test}$ and $P(y)_{train} = P(y)_{test}$ [48].

Although these are the most common types of shift, it is also possible that other types of shift occur. We list them for completeness but give examples only of the most common ones in the remainder of the paper. Other types of shift that can happen are for instance when both the conditional distribution and the features/labels distribution changes. Formally, this would correspond to $P(y|\mathbf{x})_{train} \neq P(y|\mathbf{x})_{test}$ and $P(\mathbf{x})_{train} \neq P(\mathbf{x})_{test}$ or $P(\mathbf{x}|y)_{train} \neq P(\mathbf{x}|y)_{test}$ and $P(y)_{train} \neq P(y)_{test}$ [48]. These types of shift are typically less investigated in the literature since they are not so common in real world applications and also because they are extremely difficult to detect and deal with.

Sources of Data Shift. During the normal operation of a system, shift in the data can occur due to several reasons: to the passing of time, incorrect data or sample selection bias. Next, we provide details on each of these sources of shift.

Natural Drift due to Time. An effect of the natural passing of time is that people's tastes and behavior patterns change [7,43]. For example, due to the passing of time and due to inflation, the value of money decreases. A static LEC, that is never adapted and does not account for these natural changes will gradually start producing worse predictions.

Incorrect Data. This problem arises when there are samples in the model's training set that are incorrectly labeled [66] or when test data is tampered with, thus leading the model to mispredict for inputs with specific characteristics. The former can happen for instance when unsupervised techniques are used to label examples in order to bootstrap the training set of a second supervised model [66]. Incorrect data can also make their way into a model's training set due to attackers that intentionally pollute it (e.g., by maliciously altering some of the input features) so as to cause the ML component to incorrectly predict outputs for certain inputs [33,35]. Finally, noise and uncertainty, due to sensor errors or due to errors from upstream components, may also change the input data to an LEC, possibly causing drift and mispredictions.

Sample Selection Bias. This occurs when selecting data-points for a training set or when performing data cleaning[1]. While selecting data-points, there may be environmental factors that cause some inputs or labels to be sampled more often. For example, when selecting participants for a survey, steps must be taken to ensure that the population of interest is accurately represented. Similarly, when performing data cleaning, for example for a digit recognition task, less clear digits may be thrown away. However, this may prevent the model from learning that some digits are intrinsically harder to write than others [57]. During these, arguably critical, phases of model construction, sample selection bias will cause the training distribution to follow a different distribution than the test distribution, hence causing data shift and potentially a drop in system utility.

3.2 Repair Tactics

Table 1 illustrates a collection of tactics that can be used to deal with issues introduced by ML-based components caused by the different types of shift previously introduced. These tactics were inspired by research on ML [12,46,52,61,67]. Next, we describe the tactics presented in the table, discussing their costs and benefits, and motivating them in the following sections with scenarios from enterprise systems (Sect. 4) and cyber-physical systems domains (Sect. 5).

Component Replacement. This tactic assumes the existence of a repository of components and respective meta-data that can be analyzed to determine if there exists a component that is better suited for the current system state, i.e., that is expected to lead to a higher system utility. If such a component exists, then this

---

[1] In ML, data cleaning corresponds to the process of identifying and correcting errors in a dataset that may negatively impact a predictive model.

Table 1. Examples of general adaptation tactics for ML-based systems with their strengths ('+') and weaknesses ('−').

Tactic	Description	Properties
Component replacement	Replace an under-performing component by one that better matches the current environment	+ Fast and inexpensive, when possible − Alternative components may not be available in all scenarios − Alternative estimators, when available, may be more robust but less precise
Human-based labeling [46]	Rely on a human to classify incoming samples or to correct the labeling of samples in the training set	+ Accuracy of human-based labels expected to be high − Expert knowledge may be expensive to obtain and/or introduce unacceptable latency
Transfer learning [52]	Reuse knowledge gathered previously on different tasks/problems to accelerate the learning of new tasks	+ Less data-hungry than plain retrain − Effectiveness dependent on the similarities between old and new tasks/data − Computationally intensive process
Unlearning [12]	Remove samples that are no longer representative from the training set and from the model	+ Fast when ratio between data to forget and data-set size is small − Cost/latency for identifying examples to unlearn can be large and context-dependent
Retrain [67]	Retrain with new data and maybe choose new values for the ML model's hyper-parameters	+ Generic and robust method − Computationally intensive process − Accuracy and latency of the retrain process may vary significantly − Effective only once a relatively large number of instances of the new data are available

tactic will replace the under-performing component by the one that is expected to be better. A benefit of this tactic, whenever it is available, is to enable a swift reaction to data-set shifts. Its main cost depends on the latency and resources used for the analysis of the candidate components available in the repository. Additionally, alternative components may not always be available and, when they do exist, they may be less precise albeit more robust.

Human-Based Labeling. Humans are often able to recognize patterns, problems, and objects more accurately than ML components [46]. Thus, depending on the domain, humans may play a role in correcting these components or giving them correct samples [46,65]. For example, when an LEC is highly uncertain about a specific input, it may rely on a human to provide a label. Similarly, if incorrect data is found on a model's data-set, a human may be asked to correct those samples. While this tactic may provide high benefit if the human is an expert, it also has a high cost, since humans are expensive. Also, if there is a significant amount of samples to label, the latency of the process may be unacceptable.

Transfer Learning. Transfer learning (TL) techniques leverage knowledge obtained when performing previous tasks that are similar to the current one so that learning the current task becomes easier [42,52]. For this tactic to be applicable, it is necessary to evaluate the similarity between the source and target tasks/domains. Transferring knowledge between dissimilar tasks will not provide benefits. In order to compute this similarity, metrics such as LEEP [49] can be used. The advantages of this tactic are that it requires less data than is needed to retrain a model from scratch, thus allowing for a quicker model initialization phase. However, the process of TL, similarly to a model retrain, is also computationally intensive.

Unlearning. This tactic corresponds to unlearning data that no longer reflects the current environment/state of the system and its lineage, thus eliminating the effect of that data on current predictions [12], while avoiding a full model retrain. A key problem that stands in the way of the execution of this tactic is the identification of incorrect labels. In scenarios in which the identification of incorrect samples is not readily available, one may leverage automatic techniques, such as the one described in [13], which are faster but typically less accurate than relying on humans. As such, the cost and complexity of this adaptation tactic vary depending on the context. Then, after identifying the incorrect samples, the model must be updated to accurately reflect the correct data. The advantage of unlearning techniques with respect to a typical full model retrain is the time savings (up to several orders of magnitude [12]) that can be achieved.

Retrain and/or Hyper-parameter Optimization. This is a general tactic that involves retraining the model with new data that reflects recent relevant data-set shifts. There are many types of retraining, ranging from a simple model refresh (incorporate new data using old hyper-parameters), to a full retrain (including hyper-parameter optimization, possibly encompassing the search for different model types/architectures [26]). These imply different computational costs and lead to different benefits in terms of model accuracy improvements. In the presence of data-set shifts, when there is new data that already incorporates the new input distribution, this tactic often represents a simple, yet possibly expensive, approach to deal with this problem. However, this tactic usually requires a substantial amount of data to yield highly accurate models and is computationally intensive. The benefits of this tactic are dependent on the type of retrain process and on the quality of the new data. As for its cost, if retraining is performed on the cloud, it can be directly converted to the economic cost of the virtual machines. Several techniques exist to predict such costs [2,16,45,69].

4 Adaptation of ML-Based Enterprise Systems

We now motivate the need for self-adaptive Learning-Enabled Systems through an example from the enterprise systems domain. We provide examples of situations in which each type of shift can occur as well as of scenarios in which each repair tactic can be applied.

4.1   Running Example – Fraud Detection System

Consider a fraud detection system that relies on ML models for determining whether credit/debit card transactions are legitimate or fraudulent. These ML models typically attribute a score to each transaction, which corresponds to the likelihood of the transaction being fraudulent [56]. The score attributed by the ML model is then used by a rule-based model to decide whether transactions are legitimate or fraudulent. Typical clients of companies that provide fraud detection services are banks and merchants. In this setting, system utility is typically defined based on attributes such as the cost of losing clients due to incorrectly declined transactions, fairness (no user sees its transactions declined more often than others) [24] and the overall cost of service level agreement (SLA) violations (these systems have strict SLAs to process transactions in real time, e.g. at most 200 ms on the 99.999th percentile of the latencies' distribution [8]).

While cost and revenue are directly affected by the ML model's mispredictions, response time is affected by model complexity, i.e., more complex models may introduce higher latencies that compromise SLAs. Thus, when adapting an LEC in this domain, it is necessary to account for the impact of increased complexity on the fulfillment of the SLAs. Further, the impact of LEC mispredictions varies not only from client to client, with whom different SLAs may have been agreed upon, but also in time, since during specific periods, e.g., Black Friday, the volume of transactions is substantially increased. During busy days such as these, since there is an increase in the number of legitimate transactions and the spending patterns are altered, it is crucial that ML models are less strict and reduce false alarms. At the same time, having less strict models may lead to more fraudulent transactions being accepted. Hence, mispredictions come at huge penalties and a delicate tradeoff is required to ensure an acceptable system utility. Finally, these systems are subject to constantly evolving fraud patterns, to which the ML components must adapt [3].

4.2   Causes of Degradation of ML Components' Accuracy

This section illustrates each type of data-shift with examples from the fraud detection systems domain.

Covariate Shift. In a fraud detection system, covariate shift occurs when patterns of legitimate transactions change, for instance due to busy shopping days like Black Friday and Christmas [3]. Although the actual features used for classification may not change, their distribution does. For example, suppose a user usually purchases items online from shop **A**. The distribution of fraud given the feature *online shop* is 10% for shop **A**. The user then discovers that shop **B** actually sells the same items but at a cheaper price, so they start purchasing from shop **B**. In such a setting, the distribution of the feature *online shop*, given by $P(\mathbf{x})$ is altered, but the distribution of fraud given the feature, $P(y|\mathbf{x})$, remains the same, i.e., there is the same amount of fraud in shops **A** and **B**, regardless of where the user buys. This scenario will possibly lead the fraud detection system to suspect that the change in the user's behavior is actually fraud because it learned that the user typically buys from shop **A**.

As an example of incorrect data leading to shifts, security breaches could lead attackers to poison the data used for training ML models, hence causing them to make incorrect predictions.

Prior Probability Shift (Label Shift). In the context of fraud detection systems, this type of shift occurs for example when the proportion of fraudulent transactions in the training set is different than for the test set [43], i.e., $P(y)_{train} \neq P(y)_{test}$. This type of shift requires assuming that the distribution of input data given fraud, $P(\mathbf{x}|y)$, does not change between training and testing environments. This corresponds to a mathematical abstraction over the power of an adversary that is capable of generating fraudulent transactions that follow the same pattern as legitimate transactions. Since the model has learned the typical distribution of fraud, it's predictions will follow that distribution, which is no longer representative of the system's environment.

Concept Shift. This is the most common type of data-set shift in the fraud detection domain and occurs when fraudsters adapt their strategies and new fraud patterns emerge, such that the ML model is no longer able to effectively distinguish fraudulent from legitimate transactions [43]. In this case, it is the distribution $P(y|\mathbf{x})$ that changes while $P(\mathbf{x})$ remains the same.

4.3   Repair Tactics

This section motivates the applicability of each repair tactic by providing examples of their usage when different causes of degradation have affected the system's LECs.

Component Replacement. When the volume of transactions changes, for instance during special days such as Black Friday, ML models may consider the increased frequency of transactions as an indicator of fraud and erroneously flag legitimate transactions as fraudulent. Such mispredictions can lead to significant financial losses [8], thus requiring timely fixes that render the use of high latency tactics infeasible (note that in this context transactions need to be accepted/rejected within a few hundreds milliseconds [8]). As such, only low latency tactics can be applied. An example is to replace the under-performing models with rule-based models, e.g., developed by experts for specific situations, and/or to switch to previously trained models that are known to perform well in similar conditions.

Human-Based Labeling. Whenever the ML component suspects a transaction of being fraudulent it can automatically block that transaction. Then, the user can be informed of the decision and asked whether the transaction should be authorized or declined in the future. Another possibility is to add humans to the loop when adding samples to the ML component's training set. In this scenario, an expert can be asked to review the most uncertain classifications so as to improve the quality of the training samples. In the former scenario, the benefits are easily quantifiable, since the risk of accepting a possibly fraudulent transaction can be measured via its economic value. However, users may get annoyed if their transactions are canceled too often, to the extent that they may stop purchasing using that credit card provider. As for relying on experts to review uncertain classifications, having an on-demand expert performing this task is expensive and the latency of the manual labeling process may be unacceptable[2].

Transfer Learning. Suppose that: (i) a fraud detection company has a set of clients (such as banks), (ii) the company has a unique ML model for each client, so that it complies with data privacy regulations, and (iii) one of its clients is affected by a new attack pattern, which is eventually learned by that client's model. In this scenario, TL techniques can be used to improve other clients' models so that they can react to the same attack pattern. In fact, since privacy is important in this domain, there are techniques that can be used to deal with the problem of ensuring data confidentiality and anonymity in information transfer between clients [29,42] instead of typical TL techniques that do not provide this assurance [52]. Estimating the benefits of executing this tactic for a given client boils down to estimating the likelihood that this client may be targeted by the same attack, which comes at an added cost and time. Yet, the execution of this tactic typically implies high computational costs (e.g., if cloud resources are used) and non-negligible latency, which may render this tactic economically unfavorable, or even inadequate, e.g., if the attack on a different client is imminent and the TL process is slow.

Unlearning. In the domain of fraud detection, if after a specific amount of time (e.g. 1 month) the fraud detection system does not receive complaints about a set of transactions, these will be labeled as legitimate. However, since users typically take a long time reviewing their statements and complaining when they do not recognize some transactions, it is possible that there are incorrectly labeled transactions in the data-set. In this scenario, and if a model has been trained with the incorrect samples, it is possible to leverage this tactic to remove the incorrect samples from the model without requiring a full model retrain.

Retrain and/or Hyper-parameter Optimization. Full model retraining can be leveraged for example when there is a new fraud pattern for which there is already enough data. By retraining the model with this data, the model is likely to increase the amount of fraudulent transactions detected, thus also increasing system utility. However, as this is a slow tactic, while it executes system utility is likely to either drop or remain as unsatisfactory as it was prior to the execution of the tactic. To prevent such situations, hybrid planning approaches can be leveraged [53] to execute a swift tactic that slightly improves system utility while the slow tactic is executing.

---

[2] Fraud detection systems normally rely on a fixed set of humans at any given time. This determines a maximum load of transactions that can be processed with a human in the loop.

5   Adaptation of ML-Based Cyber-Physical Systems

Turning now to a different domain, in the context of learning-enabled cyber-physical systems (CPS) [4,6,18,55] self-adaptation of its constituent LECs can also be seen as a mechanism through which system utility can be maintained. Thus, in this section we: present a motivating example from this domain; exemplify how the causes of degradation of ML component's accuracy presented in the previous section could occur in this context; and give examples of settings in which each adaptation tactic could be applied to improve overall system utility.

5.1   Running Example – Smart Homes

As a second example, consider a smart home that relies on ML to perform tasks such as face recognition for home security [63]; voice recognition for home entertainment [34]; occupancy prediction for proactive heating, cooling, lighting [28,36,60]. For each of these components, different system utility definitions are possible. For example in the case of an occupancy prediction LES, system utility could be defined in terms of user thermal comfort: if the temperature in the house is set according to the user's preferences, system utility will be high. In this scenario, and in situations in which the number of inhabitants changes drastically, for example due to Covid-19 that forced a significant number of people to stay home, the occupancy predictor can make incorrect predictions that will cause discomfort to users. In such a setting, adapting the occupancy predictor could improve user comfort and thus maintain system utility at a desired level.

5.2   Causes of Degradation of ML Components' Accuracy

Similarly to the enterprise systems domain, in the CPS domain one must also analyze the possible causes of ML mispredictions. As such, we now provide examples of each type of ML misprediction for the smart home example.

Covariate Shift. An example of covariate shift in the context of smart homes consists of noise/uncertainty in sensors that measure air quality. This noise changes the distribution of features that go into the predictive model possibly leading a ML classifier to mispredict air quality and thus mispredict the need to ventilate a room. Noise and uncertainty could also affect smart meters used to reduce energy consumption. Finally, different types of light (night versus day, dusk versus dawn) illuminating faces may lead a face recognition system to mispredict whether someone is an intruder. This example is an instance of covariate shift since the distribution of the features is altered due to the different types of light but the distribution of labels is the same and the conditional distribution of labels given the features also remains the same. It is also possible, in both domains (CPS and enterprise systems), that faults in the input data fed by some system component (LEC or non-LEC) to an LEC lead to mispredictions. This highlights the need for a system-wide perspective that considers both LEC and non-LEC aspects of the system.

As an example of LEC mispredictions in the CPS domain due to incorrect data, the literature on adversarial ML has shown how if a data point has been adversarially manipulated, a classification model using smart-meter data as input may not correctly identify which appliances are functioning in a smart home, thus not being able to properly reduce energy consumption [62].

Prior Probability Shift (label shift). Voice controllers in smart homes serve the purpose of executing commands issued by users. In such a setting, a voice controller in a smart home is subject to label shift when a command which was very rarely used is now used very often. Since the voice controller does not account for a change in its frequency of use, it will often mispredict the required action to execute when the command is issued. In this situation, the features and the relationship between features and labels is the same, but the actual correct class that should be derived from those features has changed, thus leading to an error.

Concept Shift. Smart homes rely on models that predict inhabitants' activity patterns. When these patterns are altered [7] this corresponds to concept shift. This can happen for instance due to big life events such as the birth of a child, adoption of a new pet, or having visitors stay over for a few days. When the patterns change, the features that are fed to the model do not change, neither do the labels. The only change is the relation between the two distributions which can cause the LEC to incorrectly predict the need for different tasks/settings.

5.3 Repair Tactics

This section illustrates in which scenarios each of the previously introduced adaptation tactics could be applied in the context of smart homes.

Component Replacement. This tactic could be applied to enhance system utility in cases when the face recognition system behaves poorly for example due to low lighting at night, or due to sun rays illuminating faces at different angles at dusk or dawn. In such situations, the face recognition LEC could be replaced by a different component (LEC or non-LEC) that is known to perform better under the current environmental conditions. A benefit of this tactic, for example when compared with a retrain tactic that could potentially be applied in the same situation, is a quick improvement of system utility due to a speedy replacement of the under-performing component by one that is guaranteed to achieve a minimum desired system utility.

Human-Based Labeling. When adversaries have manipulated smart meters, such that the appliances currently working in a home cannot be properly detected, a human can be queried to clarify which appliances are working, thus improving the accuracy of the LEC and enabling an increase of system utility by contributing to reducing energy consumption.

Transfer Learning. This tactic can be applied to bootstrap LECs of houses/rooms with new inhabitants [7]. Specifically, since different homes can have different configurations of sensors, rooms, and occupancy, the LECs will require fine-tuning not only to each user but also to each house. In this setting, TL techniques (e.g., based on multi-task Bayesian Optimization [64]), can exploit knowledge gathered from homes with similar configurations and whose LECs have already been optimized.

Unlearning. This tactic could be applied for example when adversaries change smart meter data. In this context, this tactic could be applied to forget these incorrect data points so as not to pollute the LEC's training set. Similarly, this tactic could also be applied when the behaviors of the inhabitants have changed. In such a situation, unlearning old behaviors may be a suitable tactic to prevent mispredictions. However, the benefits of applying this tactic are dependent on the amount of data that needs to be forgotten: in case there are plenty of examples to forget, retraining may actually be faster at achieving the same results [12].

Retrain and/or Hyper-parameter Optimization. In a smart home, the tactic of retraining an LEC could be available in a self-adaptive LES repertoire to deal with scenarios such as when inhabitants have new routines, which may cause occupancy prediction LECs to misbehave. In this situation, the LEC can be retrained on new examples that represent these new routines, thus improving the quality of its predictions and, ultimately, user satisfaction and thermal comfort. Similarly, whenever a voice recognition system fails to recognize a voice or a control, it is possible to retrain the model with examples of the voice/control such that it learns to predict them. This tactic can also be applied in settings in which modifying the model structure also yields better predictions. For example, for face recognition systems used for security purposes, which have more stringent deadlines and require higher accuracies, a retrain tactic could train a new type of model to replace the old one, ensuring that the new model is faster (e.g., replacing neural networks by decision trees) or train a set of models to increase confidence in the predictions [9].

Table 2 summarizes the examples of situations provided in the previous sections that can occur in each domain (enterprise systems and cyber-physical systems). Each situation is an instance of each type of shift, and each tactic exemplifies how to deal with the shift in the different situations.

6   MAPE-K Loop for Learning-Enabled Systems

In SAS, the MAPE-K loop typically actuates over a system composed of traditional components, i.e., non-LEC components. However, as illustrated in Fig. 1, LESs generally encompass both non-LEC and LEC components. We argue that the MAPE-K loop should be revised in order to be able to cope with the unique issues described in Sect. 3.1 that affect LECs by effectively leveraging the adaptation tactics presented in Sect. 3.2. In the following, we discuss the research

Table 2. Examples of causes of ML misbehavior within each domain—enterprise systems (ES) and cyber-physical systems (CPS)—and tactics available for adaptation in each scenario.

Problem	Domain	Example situation	Applicable tactics
Covariate shift	ES	Transaction patterns change	• Component replacement
		Adversaries poison data	• Unlearning
	CPS	Noise/uncertainty in sensors	• Transfer learning
		Different lighting conditions for face recognition LEC	• Component replacement
		Adversaries manipulate Smart meter data	• Human-based labeling • Unlearning
Label shift	ES	Variable fraud rate	• Human-based labeling
	CPS	Unknown command for voice controller	• Human-based labeling
Concept shift	ES	New fraud strategies	• Transfer learning
	CPS	Inhabitant's living patterns	• Retrain • Unlearning

challenges and opportunities that arise in each of the MAPE-K loop stages due to the LEC specific adaptation tactics.

6.1 Monitor

The *Monitor* stage has to keep track of the inputs received by the ML components because shifts of the input distributions may affect the predictions. For instance, the detection of out-of-distribution inputs may mean that there has been a change in the environment and thus the model used by some ML component may no longer be representative of the current environment. The challenge here is not only detecting the occurrence of shifts in a timely and reliable fashion, but also how to effectively characterize them—since different types of shifts require different reaction methods.

As in other SAS, typical attributes that contribute to the system's utility (e.g., latency, throughput) or the satisfaction of required system properties must be monitored. In addition to these, the *Monitor* stage must also gather the outputs of the ML component to account for situations in which changes in the inputs go by unnoticed, perhaps because they are too slow, but that manifest themselves faster in the outputs [72]. Examples of outputs to monitor are, for instance, shifts in the output distribution, model's accuracy and error—obtained by comparing predictions with real outcomes. A relevant challenge here is that often real outcomes are only known after a long time, if ever. For instance, in fraud detection, false negatives (i.e., undetected real fraud) are known only when users file a complaint. Approaches such as those proposed in [56,71,72] provide a good starting point for the implementation of a *Monitor* for self-adaptive learning-enabled systems.

Challenges. Monitoring input and output distributions requires keeping track of a multitude of features and parameters, which would otherwise be disregarded. This is already challenging due to the amount of data that needs to be stored,

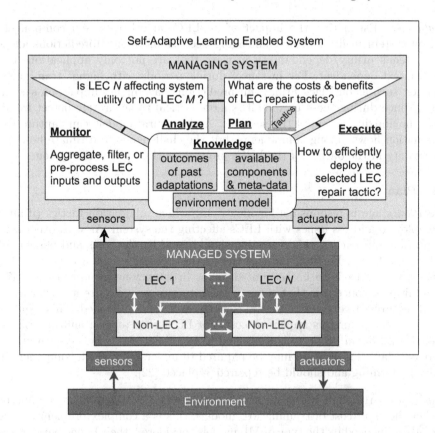

Fig. 1. MAPE-K loop over an LES with a mix of LECs and components that are not learning-enabled, with specific challenges for each MAPE-K stage. White arrows represent dependencies between components.

maintained, and analyzed. Finding suitable frequencies to gather these data and adapting them in the face of evolving time constraints is an even bigger challenge in time-critical domains [5,56].

6.2 Analyze

The *Analyze* stage is responsible for determining whether degradations of the prediction quality of LECs are affecting (or are predicted to affect) other system components and system utility to such an extent that adaptation may be required. To accomplish this, one can leverage techniques developed by the ML community to detect possible issues in the inputs and outputs of the LEC [56–58,72], errors in its training set [1] and the appearance of new features relevant for prediction [54]. These techniques must then be adjusted for each system, which includes adapting them to different ML models and tasks.

Challenges. Estimating the impact of an LEC on other system components and on system utility can be challenging because often (mis)predictions affect the system's utility/dependability in ways that are not only application- but also context-dependent. For instance, during periods with higher transaction volumes, such as on Black Friday, mispredictions have higher impact on system utility, since during these periods it is more critical to accurately detect fraud, while maximizing accepted transactions. Architectural models can capture the information flows among components, but the challenge is to estimate how the uncertainty in the output of the LECs propagates throughout the system.

6.3   Plan

The *Plan* stage is responsible for identifying which adaptation tactics (if any) to employ to address issues with LECs affecting the system. As with other self-adaptation approaches, this reasoning should consider the costs and benefits of each viable tactic. Further, most of the proposed tactics have a non-negligible latency, which needs to be accounted for as in latency-aware approaches [47]. An additional concern is that some of these tactics may require a considerable use of resources to execute, either in the system itself or offloaded. This requires *Plan* to account for this impact or cost. For LESs that rely on multiple LECs, whenever a system property is (expected to be) violated or when system utility decreases, fault localization may be required to understand which component is under-performing and should be repaired/replaced [22].

Challenges. Although there are several approaches [2,16,69] that attempt to predict the time/cost of training ML models, this is a complex problem that is strongly influenced by the type of ML models considered, their hyper-parameters and the underlying (cloud) infrastructure used for training. These techniques represent a natural starting point to estimate the costs and benefits of adaptation tactics such as the ones presented. Yet, developing techniques for predicting the costs/benefits of complex tactics, e.g., unlearning, remains an open challenge.

One interesting direction is to exploit techniques for estimating the uncertainty [51] of ML models to quantify both the likelihood of models' mispredictions as well as the potential benefits deriving from employing corrective adaptation tactics. While some ML models can directly estimate their own uncertainty [50], others require additional techniques (e.g. ensembles [9]) to obtain uncertainty estimations. Still, existing techniques can suffer from significant shortcomings in practical settings [51].

Finally, tactics that modify LECs are typically computationally expensive (e.g., non-negligible latency). Thus, *Plan* must have mechanisms to verify that the system can execute the tactic without compromising other components/properties, or even the entire system.

6.4   Execute

To execute a given adaptation tactic, the *Execute* stage must have access to mechanisms to improve or replace the LEC and/or its training set. As in the conventional MAPE-K loop, we require implementations of adaptation tactics that are not only efficient to execute, but also have predictable costs/benefits and are resilient to run-time exceptions.

Challenges. A key challenge is how to enhance the predictability of the execution of the ML adaptation tactics, which often require the processing of large volumes of data (e.g., to re-train a large scale model) possibly under stringent timing constraints. We argue that the community of SAS would benefit from the availability of open-source software frameworks that implement a range of generic adaptation tactics for LECs. These frameworks would allow to mask complexity, promote interoperability and comparability of SAS. Further, it would also provide an opportunity to assemble, in a common framework, techniques that have been proposed over many years in different areas of the AI/ML literature.

6.5 Knowledge

Finally, the *Knowledge* module is responsible for maintaining information that reflects what is known about the environment and the system. As in traditional systems, in the case of self-adaptive LESs *Knowledge* also needs to maintain information about the environment so that trends can be observed. These trends can be crucial to detect the shifts that may lead to mispredictions. Additionally, for LESs, the *Knowledge* component should evolve in order to keep track of the costs/benefits of each tactic on the affected LECs and system's utility. This corresponds to gathering: knowledge on how each tactic altered an LEC and on the context in which the tactic was executed; and meta information on training sets, for instance characterizing the most important features for predicting the costs and benefits of the different tactics. This added knowledge should be leveraged to improve the decision making process and thus improve adaptation. By gathering knowledge on how each tactic altered an LEC and on the context in which the tactic was executed, the *Analyze* and *Plan* stages can take more effective decisions on when to adapt and which tactic to execute, respectively. Finally, for a tactic that replaces under-performing LECs, *Knowledge* must contain a repository of the available components and their meta-data. This meta-data, we argue, should provide information to enable reasoning on whether the necessary preconditions to enable a safe and timely reconfiguration hold.

7   Conclusions and Future Work

This work introduced a vision for a new breed of self-adaptive frameworks that brings together techniques developed by the ML literature (used here as adaptation tactics), and reasons about the cost/benefit tradeoffs of each, with the end goal of adapting LECs of learning-enabled systems to maintain or improve system utility. With the aid of two running examples we showed how different adaptation tactics can be applied to repair LECs when different real-life situations hinder system utility.

Further, we identified a set of key requirements that should be supported by the various elements of the classic MAPE-K control loop and a set of challenging research problems, such as: **(i)** How to estimate the costs and benefits of each tactic? **(ii)** How to reason about the impact of LEC mispredictions on system utility? **(iii)** How to determine whether changes to one LEC impact other components in the system? **(iv)** How to reason about the long-term impacts of adaptation tactics on system utility?

We have started to address these research questions by developing a framework to reason about the costs and benefits of executing a repair tactic [15]. This framework relies on probabilistic model checking to determine whether repairing an LEC at a specific point in time will improve overall system utility in the future. As next steps, we plan to study the benefits of executing retrain tactics in the context of a fraud detection system. We aim to develop simple models that are able to estimate the benefits of retrain within acceptable bounds. These models can then be integrated into the model checking framework to determine when to adapt the fraud detection system.

Acknowledgements. Support for this research was provided by Fundação para a Ciência e a Tecnologia (Portuguese Foundation for Science and Technology) through the Carnegie Mellon Portugal Program under Grant SFRH/BD/150643/2020 and via projects with references POCI-01-0247-FEDER-045915, POCI-01-0247-FEDER-045907, and UIDB/50021/2020. The contributions of Gabriel Moreno and Mark Klein are based upon work funded and supported by the Department of Defense under Contract No. FA8702-15-D-0002 with Carnegie Mellon University for the operation of the Software Engineering Institute, a federally funded research and development center. Such contributions are used with permission, but ownership of the underlying intellectual property embodied within such contributions is retained by Carnegie Mellon University. DM22-0149.

References

1. Abedjan, Z., et al.: Detecting data errors: where are we and what needs to be done? Proc. VLDB **9**(12), 19993–1004 (2016)
2. Alipourfard, O., et al.: CherryPick: adaptively unearthing the best cloud configurations for big data analytics. In: Proceedings of NSDI (2017)
3. Aparício, D., et al.: Arms: automated rules management system for fraud detection. arXiv preprint arXiv:2002.06075 (2020)
4. Badue, C., Guidolini, R., et al.: Self-driving cars: a survey. Expert Syst. App. **165**, 113816 (2021)
5. Bartocci, E., et al.: Specification-based monitoring of cyber-physical systems: a survey on theory, tools and applications. In: Bartocci, E., Falcone, Y. (eds.) Lectures on Runtime Verification. LNCS, vol. 10457, pp. 135–175. Springer, Cham (2018). https://doi.org/10.1007/978-3-319-75632-5_5
6. Bojarski, M., et al.: End to end learning for self-driving cars. arXiv preprint arXiv:1604.07316 (2016)
7. Bouchabou, D., Nguyen, S.M., Lohr, C., LeDuc, B., Kanellos, I.: A survey of human activity recognition in smart homes based on iot sensors algorithms: taxonomies, challenges, and opportunities with deep learning. Sensors **21**(18), 6037 (2021)

8. Branco, B., et al.: Interleaved sequence RNNs for fraud detection. In: Proceedings of KDD (2020)
9. Breiman, L.: Bagging predictors. Mach. Learn. **24**, 123–140 (1996). https://doi.org/10.1007/BF00058655
10. Bureš, T.: Self-adaptation 2.0. In: 2021 International Symposium on Software Engineering for Adaptive and Self-Managing Systems (SEAMS) (2021)
11. Cámara, J., Lopes, A., Garlan, D., Schmerl, B.: Adaptation impact and environment models for architecture-based self-adaptive systems. Sci. Comput. Program. **127**, 50–75 (2016)
12. Cao, Y., Yang, J.: Towards making systems forget with machine unlearning. In: Proceedings of S&P. IEEE (2015)
13. Cao, Y., et al.: Efficient repair of polluted machine learning systems via causal unlearning. In: Proceedings of Asia CCS (2018)
14. Casimiro, M., Romano, P., Garlan, D., Moreno, G., Kang, E., Klein, M.: Self-adaptation for machine learning based systems. In: Proceedings of SAML (2021)
15. Casimiro, M., Garlan, D., Cámara, J., Rodrigues, L., Romano, P.: A probabilistic model checking approach to self-adapting machine learning systems. In: Procseedings of ASYDE, Co-located with SEFM 2021 (2021)
16. Casimiro, M., et al.: Lynceus: cost-efficient tuning and provisioning of data analytic jobs. In: Proceedings of ICDCS (2020)
17. Chen, T.: All versus one: an empirical comparison on retrained and incremental machine learning for modeling performance of adaptable software. In: Proceedings of SEAMS. IEEE (2019)
18. Chen, Z., Huang, X.: End-to-end learning for lane keeping of self-driving cars. In: Proceedings of IV (2017)
19. Cheng, B.H.C., et al.: Software engineering for self-adaptive systems: a research roadmap. In: Cheng, B.H.C., de Lemos, R., Giese, H., Inverardi, P., Magee, J. (eds.) Software Engineering for Self-Adaptive Systems. LNCS, vol. 5525, pp. 1–26. Springer, Heidelberg (2009). https://doi.org/10.1007/978-3-642-02161-9_1
20. Cheng, H.T., et al.: Wide & deep learning for recommender systems. In: Proceedings of DLRS (2016)
21. Cheng, S.W., et al.: Evaluating the effectiveness of the rainbow self-adaptive system. In: Proceedings of SEAMS. IEEE (2009)
22. Christi, A., et al.: Evaluating fault localization for resource adaptation via test-based software modification. In: Proceedings of QRS (2019)
23. Cito, J., Dillig, I., Kim, S., Murali, V., Chandra, S.: Explaining mispredictions of machine learning models using rule induction. In: Proceedings of ESEC/FSE (2021)
24. Cruz, A.F., et al.: A bandit-based algorithm for fairness-aware hyperparameter optimization. CoRR abs/2010.03665 (2020)
25. deGrandis, P., Valetto, G.: Elicitation and utilization of application-level utility functions. In: Proceedings of ICAC (2009)
26. Elsken, T., Metzen, J.H., Hutter, F.: Neural architecture search: a survey. J. Mach. Learn. Res. **20**(1), 1997–2017 (2019)
27. Erickson, B.J., et al.: Machine learning for medical imaging. Radiographics **37**(2), 505 (2017)
28. Esrafilian-Najafabadi, M., Haghighat, F.: Occupancy-based HVAC control systems in buildings: a state-of-the-art review. Build. Environ. **197**, 107810 (2021)
29. Gao, D., Liu, Y., Huang, A., Ju, C., Yu, H., Yang, Q.: Privacy-preserving heterogeneous federated transfer learning. In: 2019 IEEE International Conference on Big Data (Big Data), pp. 2552–2559. IEEE (2019)

30. Ghahremani, S., Giese, H., Vogel, T.: Improving scalability and reward of utility-driven self-healing for large dynamic architectures. ACM Trans. Auton. Adapt. Syst. **14**(3), 1–41 (2020)
31. Gheibi, O., Weyns, D.: Lifelong self-adaptation: self-adaptation meets lifelong machine learning. In: Proceedings of SEAMS (2022)
32. Gheibi, O., et al.: Applying machine learning in self-adaptive systems: a systematic literature review. arXiv preprint arXiv:2103.04112 (2021)
33. Gu, T., et al.: BadNets: evaluating backdooring attacks on deep neural networks. IEEE Access **7**, 47230–47244 (2019)
34. Guo, X., Shen, Z., Zhang, Y., Wu, T.: Review on the application of artificial intelligence in smart homes. Smart Cities **2**(3), 402–420 (2019)
35. Huang, L., et al.: Adversarial machine learning. In: Proceedings of AISec (2011)
36. Huchuk, B., Sanner, S., O'Brien, W.: Comparison of machine learning models for occupancy prediction in residential buildings using connected thermostat data. Build. Environ. **160**, 106177 (2019)
37. Jamshidi, P., et al.: Machine learning meets quantitative planning: enabling self-adaptation in autonomous robots. In: Proceedings of SEAMS (2019)
38. Kephart, J.O., Chess, D.M.: The vision of autonomic computing. Computer **36**(1), 46–50 (2003)
39. Krupitzer, C., et al.: A survey on engineering approaches for self-adaptive systems. Pervasive Mob. Comput. **17**, 184–206 (2018)
40. Langford, M.A., Chan, K.H., Fleck, J.E., McKinley, P.K., Cheng, B.H.: MoDALAS: model-driven assurance for learning-enabled autonomous systems. In: Proceedings of MODELS (2021)
41. Liu, B.: Learning on the job: online lifelong and continual learning. In: Proceedings of the AAAI Conference on Artificial Intelligence, vol. 34 (2020)
42. Liu, Y., et al.: A secure federated transfer learning framework. Proc. IS **35**(4), 70–82 (2020)
43. Lucas, Y., Jurgovsky, J.: Credit card fraud detection using machine learning: a survey. CoRR abs/2010.06479 (2020)
44. Mallozzi, P., Pelliccione, P., Knauss, A., Berger, C., Mohammadiha, N.: Autonomous vehicles: state of the art, future trends, and challenges. In: Dajsuren, Y., van den Brand, M. (eds.)Automotive Systems and Software Engineering, pp. 347–367. Springer, Cham (2019). https://doi.org/10.1007/978-3-030-12157-0_16
45. Mendes, P., et al.: TrimTuner: Efficient optimization of machine learning jobs in the cloud via sub-sampling. In: MASCOTS (2020)
46. Miller, B., et al.: Reviewer integration and performance measurement for malware detection. In: Proceedings of DIMVA (2016)
47. Moreno, G.A., et al.: Flexible and efficient decision-making for proactive latency-aware self-adaptation. ACM Trans. Auton. Adapt. Syst. **13**(1), 1–36 (2018)
48. Moreno-Torres, J.G., Raeder, T., Alaiz-Rodríguez, R., Chawla, N.V., Herrera, F.: A unifying view on dataset shift in classification. Pattern Recogn. **45**(1), 521–530 (2012)
49. Nguyen, C., Hassner, T., Seeger, M., Archambeau, C.: LEEP: a new measure to evaluate transferability of learned representations. In: Proceedings of ICML. PMLR (2020)
50. Osborne, M.A., et al.: Gaussian processes for global optimization. In: LION (2009)
51. Ovadia, Y., et al.: Can you trust your model's uncertainty? evaluating predictive uncertainty under dataset shift. In: Proceedings of NIPS (2019)
52. Pan, S.J., Yang, Q.: A survey on transfer learning. IEEE TKDE **22**(10), 1345–4350 (2009)

53. Pandey, A., Moreno, G.A., Cámara, J., Garlan, D.: Hybrid planning for decision making in self-adaptive systems. In: Proceedings of SASO (2016)
54. Papamartzivanos, D., et al.: Introducing deep learning self-adaptive misuse network intrusion detection systems. IEEE Access **7**, 13546–13560 (2019)
55. Peng, Z., Yang, J., Chen, T.H., Ma, L.: A first look at the integration of machine learning models in complex autonomous driving systems: a case study on Apollo. In: Proceedings of ESEC/FSE (2020)
56. Pinto, F., et al.: Automatic model monitoring for data streams. arXiv preprint arXiv:1908.04240 (2019)
57. Quionero-Candela, J., et al.: Dataset Shift in Machine Learning. The MIT Press, Cambridge (2009)
58. Rabanser, S., et al.: Failing loudly: an empirical study of methods for detecting dataset shift. In: Proceedings of NIPS (2019)
59. Saputri, T.R.D., Lee, S.W.: The application of machine learning in self-adaptive systems: a systematic literature review. IEEE Access **8**, 205948–205967 (2020)
60. Shi, J., Yu, N., Yao, W.: Energy efficient building HVAC control algorithm with real-time occupancy prediction. Energy Proc. **111**, 267–276 (2017)
61. Silver, D.L., Yang, Q., Li, L.: Lifelong machine learning systems: beyond learning algorithms. In: 2013 AAAI Spring Symposium Series (2013)
62. Singh, A., Sikdar, B.: Adversarial attack for deep learning based IoT appliance classification techniques. In: 2021 IEEE 7th World Forum on Internet of Things (WF-IoT). IEEE (2021)
63. Surantha, N., Wicaksono, W.R.: Design of smart home security system using object recognition and PIR sensor. Proc. Comput. Sci. **135**, 465–472 (2018)
64. Swersky, K., et al.: Multi-task Bayesian optimization. Proc. NIPS **26**, 1–9 (2013)
65. Wang, Z.J., Choi, D., Xu, S., Yang, D.: Putting humans in the natural language processing loop: a survey. arXiv preprint arXiv:2103.04044 (2021)
66. Wu, D., et al.: A highly accurate framework for self-labeled semisupervised classification in industrial applications. IEEE TII **14**(3), 1–12 (2018)
67. Wu, Y., et al.: DeltaGrad: rapid retraining of machine learning models. In: Proceedings of ICML (2020)
68. Xiao, Y., et al.: Self-checking deep neural networks in deployment. In: Proceedings of ICSE (2021)
69. Yadwadkar, N.J., Hariharan, B., Gonzalez, J.E., Smith, B., Katz, R.H.: Selecting the <i>best</i> vm across multiple public clouds: a data-driven performance modeling approach. In: Proceedings of SoCC, pp. 452–465 (2017)
70. Yang, J., Zhou, K., Li, Y., Liu, Z.: Generalized out-of-distribution detection: a survey. arXiv preprint arXiv:2110.11334 (2021)
71. Yang, Z., Asyrofi, M.H., Lo, D.: BiasRV: uncovering biased sentiment predictions at runtime. CoRR abs/2105.14874 (2021)
72. Zhou, X., Lo Faro, W., Zhang, X., Arvapally, R.S.: A framework to monitor machine learning systems using concept drift detection. In: Abramowicz, W., Corchuelo, R. (eds.) BIS 2019. A Framework to Monitor Machine Learning Systems Using Concept Drift Detection, vol. 353, pp. 218–231. Springer, Cham (2019). https://doi.org/10.1007/978-3-030-20485-3_17

4th Context-Aware, Autonomous and Smart Architectures International Workshop (CASA)

Behavioral Maps: Identifying Architectural Smells in Self-adaptive Systems at Runtime

Edilton Lima dos Santos$^{(\boxtimes)}$, Sophie Fortz , Pierre-Yves Schobbens ,
and Gilles Perrouin

PReCISE, NaDI, Faculty of Computer Science, University of Namur, Namur, Belgium
{edilton.limados,sophie.fortz,pierre-yves.schobbens,
gilles.perrouin}@unamur.be

Abstract. Self-adaptive systems (SAS) change their behavior and structure at runtime, depending on environmental changes and reconfiguration plans and goals. Such systems combine architectural fragments or solutions in their (re)configuration process. However, this process may negatively impact the system's architectural qualities, exhibiting architectural bad smells (ABS). Also, some smells may appear in only particular runtime conditions. This issue is challenging to detect due to the combinatorial explosion of interactions amongst features. We initially proposed the notion of *Behavioral Map* to explore architectural issues at runtime. This extended study applies the *Behavioral Map* to analyze the ABS in self-adaptive systems at runtime. In particular, we look for Cyclic Dependency, Extraneous Connector, Hub-Like Dependency, and Oppressed Monitor ABS in various runtime adaptations in the Smart Home Environment (SHE) framework, Adasim, and mRUBiS systems developed in Java. The results indicate that runtime ABS identification is required to fully capture SAS architectural qualities because the ABS are feature-dependent, and their number is highly variable for each adaptation. We have observed that some ABS appears in all runtime adaptations, some in only a few. However, some ABS only appear in the publish-subscribe architecture, such as Extraneous Connector and Oppressed Monitor smell. We discuss the reasons behind these architectural smells for each system and motivate the need for targeted ABS analyses in SAS.

Keywords: Architectural smells · Dynamic software product lines · Runtime validation · Self-adaptive systems · Behavioral maps

1 Introduction

Self-adaptive systems (SAS) must adjust their structure or behavior, depending on environmental changes and (re)configuration plans to work in such environments. Moreover, (re)configurations may also negatively affect architectural qualities at runtime. It happens because the (re)configuration process combines different architectural fragments or solutions via feature binding/unbinding at runtime. Thus, Architectural Bad Smells (ABS) may emerge, implying reduced

© The Author(s), under exclusive license to Springer Nature Switzerland AG 2022
P. Scandurra et al. (Eds.): ECSA Tracks and Workshops 2021, LNCS 13365, pp. 159–180, 2022.
https://doi.org/10.1007/978-3-031-15116-3_8

system maintainability [1,12]. ABS result from a set of architectural design decisions that negatively impact system lifecycle properties, such as understandability, testability, maintainability, extensibility, and reusability [1,6,9]. Consequently, ABS indicate possible design and implementation issues and fixing them can improve the system's quality. ABS are well-studied for single systems [1,6,8,9,12,13]. Yet, fewer works exist for SAS [15,16,19–21]. Additionally, these studies do not analyze the impact of runtime variability on smell detection and evolution as the SAS adapts.

In this paper, we extend our previous work [19] to analyze the Architectural Bad Smell in self-adaptive systems at runtime. In particular, we described the feature identification process used to instrument the source code of the self-adaptive systems to detect architectural bad smells at runtime. We look for Cyclic Dependency (CD), Extraneous Connector (EC), Hub-Like Dependency (HL), and Oppressed Monitor (OM) architectural bad smells in various runtime adaptations in the Smart Home Environment (SHE) framework [17], Adasim [24], and mRUBiS [23] systems developed in Java.

Our results suggest that runtime ABS assessment is required to fully capture SAS architectural qualities because the ABS occurrences vary along each self-adaptation. In summary, this paper provides the following contributions:

1. A first study to identify architectural bad smells for SAS at runtime;
2. An analysis based on two runtime adaptations of SHE, 40 runtime adaptations of Adasim, and 16 runtime adaptations of mRUBiS, demonstrate that runtime variability affect the type and occurrence of smells found;
3. A replication package containing the results and scripts to process behavioral maps is also available:
   https://github.com/edilton-santos/BehavioralMapExtendedStudy.

The remainder of the paper is as follows. Section 2 formally defines the Behavioral Map (BM) and presents the framework. Section 3 discusses the studied systems, and the architectural bad smells identified through the **BM** and illustrated on the SHE framework [17]. We describe our results in Sect. 4. Section 5 addresses the threats to validity. Section 6 presents the related work. Finally, Sect. 7 wraps up the paper.

2   Behavioral Map

Inspired by Dynamic Software Product Lines (DSPLs) [3–5,17], we consider SAS adaptations as *configurations of interacting features*. In a (D)SPL, one describes features and their dependencies in Feature Model (FM) [11] and trace their realization in the code via *e.g.,*, annotations. Not all SASs are DSPLs, and FM as well as traceability of features throughout the implementation may be absent. Our BM process copes with this issue (see Sect. 2.2). Then, the role of a **Behavioral Map** is to capture interactions between features of a specific (re)configuration to be analyzed before it gets deployed [18]. Such configurations are produced within

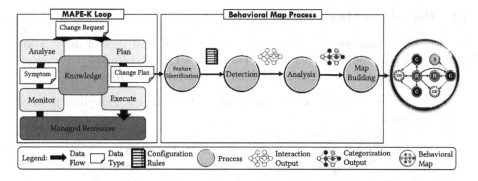

Fig. 1. Behavioral Map (BM) process overview.

an adaptation loop. We rely on the well-known MAPE-K loop (*Monitor, Analyze, Plan,* and *Execute* over a shared *Knowledge* base) proposed by IBM in [10]. We depicted it left side of Fig. 1, though any type of control loop may interact with a **BM**. Thus, the **BM** needs to interact with the component responsible for defining the *Change Plan* used in the adaptation process at runtime and retrieving the configuration rules. We used the *Change Plan* of the self-adaptive system selected to create the map based on its configuration rules. This strategy was adopted because we assume that the system implements a MAPE-K loop [10] to manage the adaptation process at runtime. We thus avoid building a **Behavioral Map** for an invalid configuration. Furthermore, the Behavioral Map can look for architectural bad smells in a self-adaptive system independently of the adaptation mechanism employed in the reconfiguration process at runtime. However, to facilitate the presentation of the Behavioral Map process, we decided to use MAPE-K loop because it is more intuitive and the most used adaptation mechanism for developing SASs.

To build a **BM**, we follow the process described in Fig. 1. The MAPE-K loop *monitors* continuously a set of managed resources and gathers the results in *symptoms*. Then the loop *analyses* symptoms and determines if an adaptation is necessary based on *Knowledge* (which in our case includes the DSPL feature model). If such an adaptation is necessary, it will issue a *change request* for the plan phase that will determine the appropriate configuration (a set of enabled and disabled features) to *execute* as prescribed by its *Change Plan*. The **BM** building process (right side of Fig. 1) interacts with this *Change Plan* containing, besides the candidate configuration, a set of *configuration rules* noted $\mathbb{CR}$. These rules contain information on the features and their dependencies (versions, imported and exported packages) obtained via extraction (see Sect. 2.3). The map building process comprises the following steps: *Feature Identification, Detection, Analysis* and *Map Building*. In the following, we define the **BM** formalism and explain the **BM** building process.

2.1   Behavioral Map Definition

A **BM** is a hybrid structure, mixing structure, data, and control information about one configuration of the DSPL. Formally, a **BM** is a tuple:

$BM = (C, V, VTypes, vtype, E, ETypes, A, vattributes)$, where:

- C is a configuration, i.e. a selection of interacting features in a given planned SAS adaptation,
- $V \subseteq C$ is a set of vertices,
- $VTypes = \{$Core, Controller, Sensor, Actuator, Presenter$\}$,
- $vtype : V \times \mathcal{P}(VTypes) \setminus \emptyset$ is a function giving the types of a vertice. We suppose that a vertice/feature can have multiple types. For example, a feature can be core (*i.e.,* present in all configurations) and also serves as a controller,
- E is a set of edges such as $\forall e \in E$, $e = (v, v', r)$ where $v, v' \in V$ and $r \in ETypes = \{$Controls, Reads, Suppresses, Requires$\}$,
- A is the set of all attributes,
- $vattributes : V \times P\{A\}$ is a function giving the value of all the attributes for a given vertice.

2.2   Behavioral Map Building Process

In the remaining, we describe the **BM** process shown in the right side of the Fig. 1.

Feature Identification. We describe the manual process used to identify features in source code based on information available in the system's repository. The feature identification process uses the *Feature Trace* provide by Data Extractor (see Sect. 2.3 for details) to track features at runtime. This process is necessary because the self-adaptive systems available in Self-adaptive System Community[1] do not use a feature model to define their features. The feature identification process consists of four steps.

Step 1 - Identifying the Features: We first identify the features available in the selected systems by examining articles (published in the literature), software requirements documents, architecture descriptions, and other information provided by developers in the software repository (*e.g.,* GitHub) used to describe the software requirements and implementation. These documents describe the systems, including adaptive mechanisms, applicability, test scenarios, and source code.

Step 2 - Identifying the Core Features in the Source Code: We used the feature name (or description) identified in step 1 and adaptive mechanisms (see the Table 1) implemented in the system to guide the identification of the core features in the source code. The Core features are executed in every (re)configuration of the system. In addition, we selected only the main concrete class responsible for implementing the feature behavior because the class is the

---

[1] https://www.hpi.uni-potsdam.de/giese/public/selfadapt/exemplars/.

main point for the feature implementation. Consequently, we use this class to identify the hierarchy of dependencies at runtime via Data Extractor.

Step 3 - Identifying the Optional Features in the Source Code: We used the feature name (or description) and the scenario where each feature is activated to define the optional features in the source code. Also, we analyzed the source code comments used to describe the class or method implementation to support feature identification in the source code. Thus, we associated the information collected in step 1 with the source code information to find each feature. We selected the main concrete class responsible for implementing the optional feature.

Step 4 - Behavioral Map Feature Trace: The features (class) identified in steps 2 and 3 are included in the *Feature Trace* provided by the Data Extractor.

Detection. *Detection* determines interacting features using pairwise analysis [22] and their directed relationships based on the configuration rules $\mathbb{CR}$. Moreover, we assume that in the $\mathbb{CR}$, there are all features and their configuration policy (including feature dependencies) required to address a specific context at runtime. For example, the feature installation process used the constraints available in the manifest file to identify the feature and its dependencies. Besides, this process can use complementary information defined in the *Change Plan* to guide the installation, configuration, and adaptation processes at runtime.

In this context, we will use the $\mathbb{CR}$ defined in the *Change Plan* to identify the features and directions of each relationship. Thus, the Detection process selects a feature in the $\mathbb{CR}$ and identifies its dependencies based on the configuration information of the feature. Let us consider a *Feature A*, which requires loading a *Feature B* at runtime. This dependency is defined in the $\mathbb{CR}$ file and used by the Detection process to create an arrow from feature A to feature B, indicating the direction of the relationship between the features. The process repeats for each feature until all interactions are detected and created on the map.

Analysis. During the analysis stage, we further refine the interactions identified during detection in categories. We identify several relationship types (*ETypes*) as relevant to highlight runtime interaction problems. The currently supported types are: **i) Controls:** a relationship where a feature has control over another feature, but does not suppress its behavior; **ii) Suppresses:** a relationship where a feature suppresses the behavior of another one. Also, we consider as suppressed the relationship between features where one controlled feature needs to be uninstalled or unbound by its controlling feature; **iii) Requires:** a relationship in which a feature is part of another feature's implementation. In this relationship, there is no suppression or control over the feature's behavior that is part of the main feature; **iv) Reads:** This type of relationship occurs when one feature reads data produced by another feature, but there is no control or suppression of the feature's behavior.

Map Building. Based on interaction detection and analysis, we can build the Behavioral Map for a configuration of the SAS. We represent this map as a directed graph where features form the vertices and relationships form the edges.

```
1  table ← loadConfigurationRulesFile(CRfile);
2  verticesOnMap ← createVerticesOnMap(table);
3  foreach vertex in verticesOnMap do
4      foreach row in table do
5          if row.name.equals(vertex.name) then
6              foreach relation in row.getAllRelationships() do
7                  if relation.relationship is not null then
8                      createEdge(vertex, relation.relationship_type, relation.featureName);
9                  end
10             end
11         end
12     end
13 end
```

Algorithm 1: Behavioral Map algorithm.

Algorithm 1 captures the whole BM building process. The algorithm begins by loading the CR file as a **table** (line 1 at Algorithm 1) and instantiates the vertices (features) on the map (**createVerticesOnMap**, line 2). The next step is to look for each created vertex (feature) and identify its relationships in the *Configuration Rules* (**table**). Consequently, we create three loops, as shown lines 3, 4, and 6. The first loop selects a vertex on the map and then looks for its information in the **table** using the second loop. Line 5 checks whether each **row** of the table contains the selected vertex. Line 6 retrieves all relationships (**row.getAllRelationships()**) related to the selected vertex on the map. For each relationship, **createEdge** creates an edge in the map based on the following arguments: **i)** the vertex from which the edge starts; **ii)** the relationship type represented by the edge; **iii)** the destination vertex (**relation.featureName** in line 8). The loop on line 6 will repeat until all edges are created.

2.3   Framework Implementation

We conceived a framework to infer Behavioral Maps whose architecture is shown in Fig. 2. The framework uses the Neo4J[2] platform and its Cypher[3] query language. The top-most layers, **Map Builder**, **Analyzer**, and **Interaction Detector** perform the processes defined in Sect. 2. In the following, we focus on the remaining elements of the framework.

The **Integration Layer (IL)** serves as an interface between the DSPL and the map building components, receiving the data used to build the map. Also, this layer defines the CR *file* data type used to build the map as follows: **i) name** is the feature name in the system; **ii) friendly_name** is friendly name of feature

---

[2] Neo4j - https://neo4j.com/product/.

[3] Cypher - https://neo4j.com/docs/cypher-manual/current/introduction/.

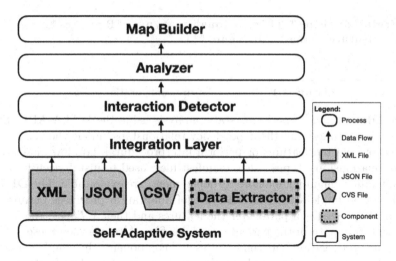

Fig. 2. Behavioral Map architecture overview.

shown to the user; **iii) exported_packages** lists the exported packages or services offered via features; **iv) imported_packages** lists the packages used by features to compose their functionality; **v) version** represents the feature version; **vi) status** defines if the feature is active or inactive; **vii) type** defines the feature type; **viii) relationships** is a collection composed of relationship types and associated features as describe as follows: **a) relationship_type** represents the relationship type, as defined in *ETypes*; **b) feature_name** is the *feature name* associated with the *relationship_type* field. The **IL** reads data via *Data Extractor* or ℂℝ*file* in formats *XML, JSON,* or *CSV.*

The **Data Extractor (DE)** realizes the runtime integration between the *Integration Layer* and the Self-Adaptive system. The **DE** runs over the *Plan* function (see Fig. 1), reading the *Change Plan* information at runtime and relating the features and ℂℝ after the system triggers the adaptation process. Hence, the **DE** identifies all features used and their relationships regarding the *Change Plan* configuration to be deployed. Thereafter, the **DE** builds a ℂℝ *file* including all involved features and sends it to the *Integration Layer.* Listing 1.1 shows a small part of the ℂℝ (in JSON format), created by **DE** with one feature (Presence), some properties (*e.g.,* name, status, and type), and relationships at runtime (*e.g.,* line 9).

```
1  {
2    "name":"Presence",
3    "friendly_name":"presence"
4    "exported_packages":["com.she.core.presence"],
5    "imported_packages":["com.she.core.listener"],
6    "version":"1.0.0",
7    "status":"Active",
8    "type":"Sensor",
```

```
 9    "relationships":[{"relationship_type":"Requires","
         feature_name":"Listener"}]
10  }
11  ...
```

Listing 1.1. Presence feature configuration rules.

The **DE** component performs static analysis using the WALA API[4]. Static analysis allows to identify the dependency relationships among the class hierarchy used by selected features or perform interprocedural dataflow analysis and identify relationships' types. Also, manifest files, used to install each feature of the candidate configuration before its deployment, are exploitable. The **DE** component can be implemented for all types of adaptation processes because this component receives as a parameter the features and their *VTypes*, the features implementation path in the packages, and Jar files. Also, we used these parameters to maps the relation between features and components that implements each feature. Besides, the **DE** provides a *Feature Trace* used to identify the features executed at runtime based on the features identified in the source code by the developers or researchers following the process defined in Sect. 2.2. The *Feature Trace* gets all the information used to build the ℂℝ file at runtime and sends all collected information to **DE** for each monitored adaptation.

The BM framework allows to compute a graph depicting core and variable features as well as the different interactions between them (see the Figs. 3, 4, 5, 6, 7, and 8). Though these maps may be used for visual inspection, they mainly serve as support for further analyses thanks to the Neo4J graph database[5].

3   BM-Based ABS Detection

This section presents the SAS under study and describes the architectural bad smells that the Behavioral Map can identify. Furthermore, we describe the process for identifying each architectural smell and discuss its impact on the SAS' architecture.

3.1   SAS Under Study

We applied our **BM** framework on SHE [17], Adasim [24] and mRUBiS [23] systems, all written in Java programming language. The motivation for these choices also relies on the fact that these systems have different adaptive mechanisms, and their description and implementation are available. Furthermore, the last two systems were selected as part of a previous study on ABS for SAS [15]. Table 1 shows the main characteristics of each selected system as follows: i) System - the name of the system; ii) Architectural Model - The type of architectural model used to

---

[4] WALA - https://github.com/wala/WALA.
[5] https://neo4j.com/product/neo4j-graph-database/.

Table 1. Systems used in this study.

System	Architectural model	Adaptive mechanisms	Application domain
SHE	Publish-Subscribe	MAPE-K	Internet Of Things
Adasim	Agent-based	Parameter-based routing algorithm	Automated traffic routing
mRUBiS	Architectural model-based	Architecture-based MAPE-K Event-Condition-Action State based feedback loop	Marketplace

implement the system under evaluation; iii) Adaptive Mechanisms - The mechanisms used to trigger the adaptations at runtime; iv) Application Domain - Information about the application domain of the systems selected in this study. These characteristics are essential to help us understand the impact of each smell in the selected systems. We present each selected system and its configurations under evaluation in the following.

SHE is a smart home system that uses the MAPE-K loop to identify changes (such as a new sensor being plugged in) and make the appropriate changes to the dashboard (*e.g.,* display data coming from that sensor). The SHE core is composed by *Manager, Listener, Loader, Installer*, and *Presentation Layer*. These layers are responsible for controlling the adaptation, communication, and data presentation at runtime. Also, we included four optional features as follows: i) **Luminosity**: used to read data from the luminosity sensor; ii) **Presence**: used to read data from the presence sensor; iii) **lampController**: responsible for controlling Lamp feature's behavior using the information read from *Luminosity* and *Presence* features; iv) **Lamp**: an actuator used to switch on and off lights based on the *lampController* feature's data. This configuration of SHE is depicted Fig. 3. Also, we analyzed a second version of the SHE that uses the same features described above and includes the *water, climateController, temperature,* and *airConditioner* features.

Adasim is a simulator for the Automated Traffic Routing Problem (ATRP)[6], implemented as an agent-based system [15,24]. The system is composed of six abstract components: i) a map; ii) vehicles; iii) agents - make routing decisions; iv) sensors; v) uncertainty filters - utilized to control the noise and other sources of uncertainty in the sensor; and vi) data privacy policies - used by vehicles and streets to restrict part or all information about themselves from sensors [24]. The system employs adaptive mechanisms to deal with the scalability problems and the unpredictable changes in the environment, for instance, an accident.

---

[6] https://www.hpi.uni-potsdam.de/giese/public/selfadapt/exemplars/model-problem-atrp/.

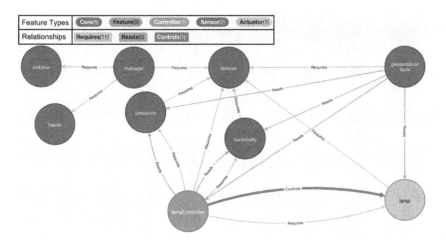

Fig. 3. Behavioral Map (BM) for one SHE configuration.

mRUBiS is a marketplace based on RUBiS [14], comprising 18 components and can arbitrarily host many shops. These shops manage items, users, auctions/purchases, inventory, and authenticate users. mRUBiS[7] allows different adaptive mechanisms [23], as showed in Table 1.

3.2   Identifying Architectural Bad Smells

Table 2. Selected architectural bad smells for self-adaptive systems.

Smell name	Detection
Cyclic Dependency (CD) [2]	Full
Extraneous Connector (EC) [8]	Full
Hub-Like Dependency (HL) [2,15]	Full
Oppressed Monitors (OM) [21]	Partial

While ABS catalogs exist in the literature [2,8], their role in self-adaptive architectures is less known [15,21]. Table 2 presents a list of smells we believe to be relevant for assessing self-adaptive architecture as well as their level of support through the **BM**. For each of them, we briefly describe how they can be identified via the **BM**, and we provide a short discussion on their impact. We also provide a replication package on GitHub[8] with a tutorial to configure the Neo4J platform, CR files, and the scripts used to create the map and analyze ABS.

---

[7] https://www.hpi.uni-potsdam.de/giese/public/selfadapt/exemplars/mrubis/.
[8] https://github.com/edilton-santos/BehavioralMapExtendedStudy.

Cyclic Dependency [2]: This smell occurs when two or more components depend on each other directly or indirectly [2]. Components involved in a dependency cycle can hardly be released, maintained, or reused in isolation [7].

Identification Guidelines. We determine cycles in the sub-graph of the BM formed by the features and the relationships of type *Requires* using a Depth-First traversal strategy.

Discussion. Based on relationship categories, other forms of cyclic dependencies may be uncovered, such as control ones which may cause concurrent accesses to resources and/or deadlocks.

Extraneous Connector (EC) [8]: This smell happens when two connectors of different types are used to link a pair of components [8]. This paper focuses on only the impact of combining procedure call and event connectors (*e.g.,* communication via publish-subscribe).

Identification Guidelines. The automatic identification of extraneous connectors proceeds by analyzing paths between pairs of vertices in the **BM**. In a complementary way, a designer can visually identify EC smells on the **BM**. The *lampController* (Fig. 3) uses two types of connectors to connect with the features *Presence, Luminosity,* and *Lamp.* The *lampController* uses the *Listener* (*Publish-Subscribe* client to implement the Reads edge) and procedure call communication (represented by the Requires edge) with *Presence, Luminosity,* and *Lamp.*

Discussion. This smell increases the coupling between features of the DSPL, negatively impacting its variability, and thus its adaptability [9]. However, a direct connection may be justified for concurrent operation [8] and may increase the system's resiliency in case of failure of the publish-subscribe architecture.

Hub-Like Dependency (HL): This smell appears when a component has (incoming or outgoing) dependencies with a large number of other abstractions (*e.g.,* other components) or concrete classes [2,15].

Identification Guidelines. Thanks to its graph structure, the **BM** allows to automatically compute the in/out-degree (number of incoming or outgoing edges) for each vertex (feature). Features having high in/out-degrees are subjected to the HL smell. In Fig. 3, we see that the *Listener* feature is subjected to the HL smell since it is involved in most of the *Requires* relationships of the **BM**. Besides, if a feature has only many outgoing Requires edges, it is a Hub type called *Overreliant Class* [2].

Discussion. The presence of the HL smell in the Listener feature is motivated by the publish-subscribe architecture adopted by the SHE framework. The *Listener* centralizes all the communication processes in this software architecture and works as a communication broker. It is therefore acceptable in this case [2,7]. However, hubs form points of attention in case of failure.

Oppressed Monitors [21] **(OM):** According to [21], this smell is characterized by a set of monitors (retrieving information from sensors) independent from each other that are managed with the same data polling rate and predefined execution order, yielding sub-optimal data acquisition and failure of subsequent monitors if one monitor in the sequence fails.

Identification Guidelines. Fully identifying this smell involves delving into the source code and getting information about polling rate since sequencing of sensor calls is not present on the map. Yet, if several sensors are controlled by the same controller, the map can help locating the features to look for this smell.

Discussion. In some cases, this smell is acceptable, especially when there are simple monitors with similar polling rates [21]. However, this smell limits the adaptability and resiliency of the system, which are important criteria for self-adaptive systems.

These examples illustrate the two complementary usages of the **BM**. First, the BM is a formal model amenable to automated detection of smells using graph algorithms. Second, visual representations help designers and engineers to visualize runtime configurations.

Identification Process: The **BM** framework thus comes with dedicated algorithms to identify ABS [19], as described in Sect. 3.2. These algorithms are implemented via the Cypher[9] language, allowing to query the graph. We used provided queries to identify CD, EC, HL, and OM on the map created for the SASs under study. For example, Listing 1.2 shows how to compute cyclic dependencies on the map. All queries used in this study are available on GitHub[10].

```
1 MATCH ( f : Feature )−[ : Requires ]−>(f 2 : Feature )−[ : Requires ]−>(
      f )
2 OPTIONAL MATCH ( f 2)−[ : Requires ]−>(f 3 : Feature )−[ : Requires ]
      −>(f )
3 RETURNf ,  f 2 ,  f 3
```

Listing 1.2. Cypher query used to look for CD in the BM.

4   Results

The following sections describe the results and discuss the reasons behind each architectural smell identified in the self-adaptive systems under study.

4.1   SHE Framework Results

The **SHE Framework** performed two self-adaptations and activated 22 features at runtime, nine in the first adaptation and 13 in the last adaptation. Table 3 presents in detail the features involved in ABS during the SHE Framework adaptations. The *listener* is involved in HL smell in both adaptations, but the number of outgoing increases in the second adaptation. This situation occurred

---

[9] Cypher - https://neo4j.com/docs/cypher-manual/current/introduction/.

[10] https://github.com/edilton-santos/BehavioralMapExtendedStudy.

Table 3. ABSs identified adaptation 1 and 2 of the SHE.

Feature name	Feature type	Adaptation 1			Adaptation 2		
		EC	HL	OM	EC	HL	OM
listener	Core		Yes (6)			Yes (10)	
lampController	Optional	Yes (3)		Yes	Yes (3)		Yes
climateController	Optional				Yes (2)		

because the *water*, *climateController*, *temperature*, and *airConditioner* features were activated at runtime, increasing the number of the *Requires* relationships on the *listener* feature, as shown in Fig. 4.

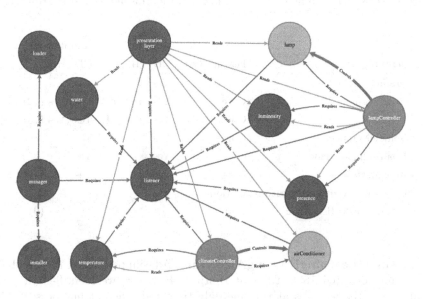

Fig. 4. Behavioral Map for SHE in adaptation 2.

Also, the BM identified *lampController* as involved in EC and OM smells in both adaptations. The EC smell occurred because the *lampController* uses the *listener* (the communication broker) and procedure call to exchange messages with *presence*, *luminosity*, and *lamp*. The procedure call is represented as the relationship *Requires* or *Controls* on the BM, as illustrated in Fig. 4. The *Requires* relationships among *lampController* and *presence*, *luminosity*, *lamp* represent an architectural bad smell.

The BM identified the *lampController* and *presentation layer* as a possible OM smell. However, after analyzing the source code together with the SHE Framework developers, we identified that only the *lampController* uses the same data polling rate and predefined execution order to retrieve data from the sensors. Thus, only *lampController* feature was classified as OM smell. Finally, the *climateController* feature activated in adaptation two was classified as EC smell. While the BM supports the identification of potential OM smells, manual source code analysis is necessary to eliminate false positives.

4.2 Adasim Results

The Adasim system was executed using two different parameter files because we identified two adaptation modes: *QLearningRoutingAlgorithm* and *AdaptiveRoutingAlgorithm*.

Table 4. ABSs identified in adaptation 1 and 2 of the Adasim - QLearningRoutingAlgorithm.

Feature name	Feature type	Adaptation 1		Adaptation 2	
		CD	HL	CD	HL
TrafficSimulator	Core	Yes		Yes	
RoadSegment	Core	Yes	Yes (13)	Yes	Yes (12)
Vehicle	Core	Yes	Yes (14)	Yes	Yes (13)
VehicleManager	Core	Yes		Yes	
RoadVehicleQueue	Core	Yes		Yes	
AdasimMap	Core	Yes		Yes	
QLearningRoutingAlgorithm	Optional	Yes			
SimulationXMLBuilder	Core		Yes (9)		Yes (9)

Adasim QLearningRoutingAlgorithm. Adasim performed 13 self-adaptations and activated 18 features at runtime. However, we identified that the variability of the features at runtime only triggered different numbers of ABS detected between adaptations one and two. Such behavior was observed because Adasim did not enable/disable other features (after adaptation two), which may add new ABS at runtime. It means that the system continued executing the adaptations process using the features and data produced by each loop until it completed its adaptation cycles.

Table 4 presents in detail the features involved in ABS during the two first adaptations. The *QLearningRoutingAlgorithm* is an optional feature involved in CD only in adaptation one with the feature *RoadSegment*, and *Vehicle*, as shown in Fig. 5. Such figures show all features involved in CD, the features in green are core features and the optional feature in pink. The relationship defined as Requires amongst features in CD indicates that all features involved can hardly be released, maintained, or reused in isolation. Thus, if the developers decide to reuse the feature *Vehicle*, they should reuse all features presented in Fig. 5.

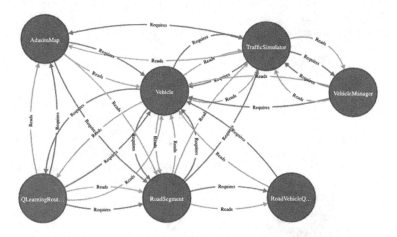

Fig. 5. CD identified in Adasim QLearningRoutingAlgorithm in adaptation 1.

Nevertheless, the absence of the *QLearningRoutingAlgorithm* (in adaptation two) reduces the numbers of dependency in the features *RoadsSegment* and *Vehicle* involved in HL, see Table 4. This situation occurred because *RoadSegment* and *Vehicle* are not sharing *QLearningRoutingAlgorithm* in adaptation two. Also, performing evolutionary or corrective maintenance on the *RoadSegment* and *Vehicle* features is an arduous task, as poorly planned maintenance can trigger unexpected behavior in the system, like bugs. Moreover, a hub (as *RoadSegment* and *Vehicle*) with a mixture of ingoing/outgoing dependencies could be a problem because of its lack of architectural logic [7]. These aspects negatively impact system maintenance and reusability. In addition, the *SimulationXMLBuilder* feature has been identified as HL. Thus, we have identified three features involved in HL, as shown in Fig. 6.

Adasim AdaptiveRoutingAlgorithm. The Adasim executed 27 self-adaptations and activated 20 features at runtime. We observed that the variability of the features at runtime impacted the numbers of ABS detected between adaptation 1 and 2, as identified in the Adasim QLearningRoutingAlgorithm. Table 5 presents the ABS identified during adaptations 1 and 2. Additionally, it is possible to observe that the number of CD identified increase or decrease depending on the number of optional features required in each adaptation process. This situation also impacts the number of HL identified in each adaptation, mainly because the features identified as CD and HL concentrated on the core features. Also, there is a strong relation of dependency among them at runtime. Thus, we detected that the *Vehicle* feature identified as HL in Adaptation 1 was not identified in Adaptation 2. Such a situation occurred because the optional features *AdaptiveRoutingAlgorithm*, *QLearningRoutingAlgorithm*, and *LookaheadShortestPathRoutingAlgorithm* are not used in adaptation 2. Consequently, the BM identified in adaptation 2 the *RoadSegment* feature as a new HL.

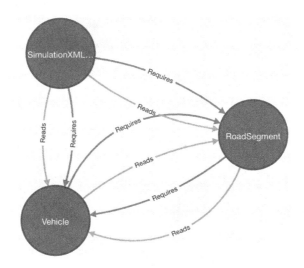

Fig. 6. Features involved in HL identified in Adasim.

However, we did not identify the Extraneous Connector and Oppressed Monitors smells in Adasim because the system does not use publish-subscribe architecture or loops to collect data in the sensors.

4.3   mRUBiS Results

The mRUBiS system is divided into self-healing and self-optimization versions. However, during the feature identification process, we identified four versions of mRUBiS: i) self-healing with adaptation mechanism Event-Condition-Action (ECA) feedback loop is composed of 22 features; ii) self-healing with adaptation mechanism State-Based Feedback Loop (SBFL) is composed by 18 features; iii) self-healing with adaptation mechanism MAPE-K is composed of 22 features, and iv) self-optimization with adaptation mechanism MAPE-K is composed by 27 features.

mRUBiS Self-optimization: Figure 7 depicts the first configuration of mRUBiS self-optimization with one optional feature (in pink). We started looking for ABS in the system based on this configuration. The BM identified the *SelfOptimizationConfig*, *MRubisModelQuery*, and *EventBasedMapeFeedbackLoop* as HL in four adaptation loops. Thus, these features are core used in all configurations of mRUBiS self-optimization. We observed in the *SelfOptimizationConfig* a decrease in the numbers of dependencies used in the second adaptation. This situation occurred because the feature is responsible for adding the validators and other parameters for self-optimization to the simulator. However, the number of validators used at runtime decreases, impacting the dependencies identified. The *MRubisModelQuery* and *EventBasedMapeFeedbackLoop* maintain the same numbers of dependencies in all adaptations. Also, the BM framework did not identify other types of ABS during the adaption loop.

Table 5. ABSs identified in adaptation 1 and 2 of the Adasim AdaptiveRoutingAlgorithm.

		Adaptation 1		Adaptation 2	
Feature name	Feature type	CD	HL	CD	HL
TrafficSimulator	Core	Yes		Yes	
RoadSegment	Core	Yes		Yes	Yes (13)
Vehicle	Core	Yes	Yes (17)	Yes	
VehicleManager	Core	Yes		Yes	
RoadVehicleQueue	Core	Yes		Yes	
AdasimMap	Core	Yes		Yes	
AdaptiveRouting Algorithm	Optional	Yes			
QLearningRouting Algorithm	Optional	Yes			
LookaheadShortest PathRoutingAlgorithm	Optional	Yes			
SimulationXMLBuilder	Core		Yes (11)		Yes (11)

mRUBiS Self-healing: The BM does not identify ABS in the self-healing version with adaptation mechanism ECA and SBFL after four reconfiguration processes at runtime. The BM identified one instance of HL in the core feature *StateBasedMapeFeedbackLoop* in four adaptations loops to mRUBiS self-healing version with adaptation mechanism MAPE-K. The feature is the main entry point to other features such as *Monitor, Action, Plan, Execute, SelfHealingConfig, SelfHealingScenario*, and *MRubisSelfHealingUtilityFunction*. Also, the knowledge is captured in the model described in CompArch [23] language, provided by the framework CompArch implemented outside the mRUBiS implementation. This model is utilized as a parameter on the feature *StateBasedMapeFeedbackLoop* to validate the self-healing issues at runtime. Thus, the HL identified is a feature of the architecture instead of an issue. This situation happened because the *StateBasedMapeFeedbackLoop* has been chosen as a controlled entry point to separate the adaptive mechanism (MAPE-K) logically from the self-healing configuration (implemented via *SelfHealingConfig*). We can observe this situation in Fig. 8 through the relationship between *StateBasedMapeFeedbackLoop* (highlighted in red) and *SelfHealingConfig* (highlighted in blue). Also, Fig. 8 presents all features available in adaptation 1 of the mRUBiS Self-Healing MAPE-K loop. The features *CF1_Injector* (in pink) and *LightWeightRedeployComponent* (in yellow) are optional features activated at runtime.

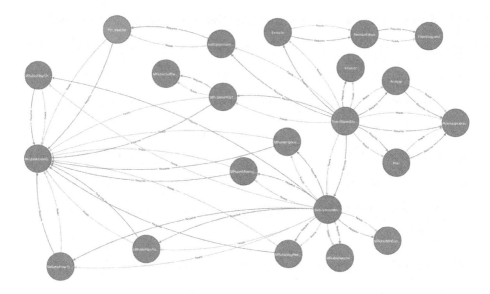

Fig. 7. Behavioral map of the first configuration of mRUBiS Self-optimization.

5   Threats to Validity

As for any empirical study, we consider threats to the internal validity of results themselves or their generalization.

5.1   Internal Validity

The absence of a feature model and feature annotations in the source code may reduce the precision of the feature identification process in the source code. To mitigate this threat, we used the Eclipse IDE[11] tool to verify the feature implementation and to debug the systems' source code to check the execution of each feature identified using the process defined in Sect. 2.2. Also, the systems under study provide a log system that we used to check whether the main class used to implement the features identified using our methodology were present in the system log. Thus, we checked whether each core or optional feature was correctly identified in the source code.

5.2   External Validity

Our results may not generalize to all SAS since we selected only three systems in our study. Additionally, it is impossible to run all possible system adaptations or estimate their number. We selected systems with different architectural models, adaptation mechanisms, and application domains, as presented in Table 1.

---

[11] Eclipse IDE - https://www.eclipse.org/downloads/packages/.

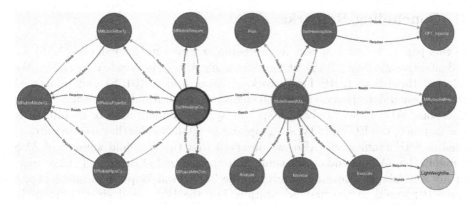

Fig. 8. Behavioral map of the first configuration of mRUBiS Self-Healing MAPE-K loop.

This diversity contributes to the mitigation of this threat. In this study, our goal was to reveal and explain the existence of the runtime architectural bad smells using the Behavioral Map. We left for future work with a more quantitative assessment.

6 Related Work

We found two works dedicated to the identification of ABS in self-adaptive systems. The first study [15] relies on the Arcan [7] tool to identify ABS in 11 self-adaptive systems. Arcan creates a graph database with the structure of classes, packages, and dependencies of the analyzed project, allowing the execution of algorithms on the graph to detect the ABS at design time. Our approach also uses a graph for ABS detection, but there are two differences: i) we create a map for each SAS configuration identified at runtime; and ii) we identify the ABS at the level of features defined in the system's feature model. Thus, to analyze the architecture, we associate the features defined in the model with the structure of classes, packages, and dependencies implemented in the source code. This process allows us to relate a feature to its implementation. Our work in progress involves the comparison of Acran and the BM for runtime smell detection [20].

The second study [21] presents two new ABSs specific to self-adaptive systems: the Obscure Monitor and the Oppressed Monitors. Also, it defines the algorithms to identify each smell at design time. To validate the proposed smells, the authors identified the proposed smells in 8 SASs in the manual and discussed how to refactor the system affected for those smells. We believe that our work on smells identification at runtime may uncover new ABS specific to SAS.

7   Concluding Remarks

In this paper, we made a case for assessing architectural bad smells (ABS) for self-adaptive systems (SAS) at runtime using the Behavioral Map (BM). We selected three SAS (SHE Framework, Adasim, and mRUBiS) and performed runtime smell detection on several systems reconfigurations. Our results showed that some ABS appear only in a specific system configuration or architecture. For instance, the EC and OM smell appear in publish-subscribe architecture, as used in SHE Framework. Also, we observed that the type and amount of ABS found in the SAS depend on the configuration analyzed at runtime. For instance, in Adasim AdaptiveRoutingAlgorithm, the Behavioral Map found nine CD and three HL smells in the first adaptation, but the BM found six CD smells in the second. We could explain this variation by binding and unbinding certain runtime features. Thus, the Behavioral Map framework offers interesting support for assessing the architectural qualities of a given runtime adaptation. However, instrumenting the systems for runtime ABS identification requires expertise and time because the core and variable features are not documented.

We envision three future works: i) we would like to conduct an empirical study to investigate differences between smells one detects at design time and smells occurring at runtime in self-adaptive systems; ii) we would like to reduce the cost of engineering involved in analyzing SAS at runtime. In particular, we will design a dedicated ABS tool operating at the bytecode level, easing runtime analyses; iii) we will generalize our findings by assessing more self-adaptive systems.

Acknowledgements. Edilton Lima dos Santos is funded by a CERUNA grant from the University of Namur. Sophie Fortz is supported by the FNRS via a FRIA grant. Gilles Perrouin is an FNRS Research Associate.

References

1. de Andrade, H.S., Almeida, E., Crnkovic, I.: Architectural bad smells in software product lines: an exploratory study. In: Proceedings of the WICSA 2014 Companion Volume, pp. 1–6 (2014)
2. Azadi, U., Fontana, F.A., Taibi, D.: Architectural smells detected by tools: a catalogue proposal. In: 2019 IEEE/ACM International Conference on Technical Debt (TechDebt), pp. 88–97. IEEE (2019)
3. Baresi, L., Quinton, C.: Dynamically evolving the structural variability of dynamic software product lines. In: Proceedings of the 10th International Symposium on Software Engineering for Adaptive and Self-Managing Systems, pp. 57–63. IEEE Press (2015)
4. Bencomo, N., Sawyer, P., Blair, G.S., Grace, P.: Dynamically adaptive systems are product lines too: using model-driven techniques to capture dynamic variability of adaptive systems. In: SPLC, vol. 2, pp. 23–32 (2008)
5. Capilla, R., Bosch, J., Trinidad, P., Ruiz-Cortés, A., Hinchey, M.: An overview of dynamic software product line architectures and techniques: observations from research and industry. J. Syst. Softw. **91**, 3–23 (2014)

6. Fontana, F.A., Avgeriou, P., Pigazzini, I., Roveda, R.: A study on architectural smells prediction. In: 2019 45th Euromicro Conference on Software Engineering and Advanced Applications (SEAA), pp. 333–337. IEEE (2019)
7. Fontana, F.A., Pigazzini, I., Roveda, R., Zanoni, M.: Automatic detection of instability architectural smells. In: IEEE International Conference on Software Maintenance and Evolution (ICSME), pp. 433–437. IEEE (2016)
8. Garcia, J., Popescu, D., Edwards, G., Medvidovic, N.: Identifying architectural bad smells. In: 13th European Conference on Software Maintenance and Reengineering, pp. 255–258. IEEE (2009)
9. Garcia, J., Popescu, D., Edwards, G., Medvidovic, N.: Toward a catalogue of architectural bad smells. In: Mirandola, R., Gorton, I., Hofmeister, C. (eds.) QoSA 2009. LNCS, vol. 5581, pp. 146–162. Springer, Heidelberg (2009). https://doi.org/10.1007/978-3-642-02351-4_10
10. IBM: An architectural blueprint for autonomic computing. IBM White Paper, vol. 31, pp. 1–6 (2006)
11. Kang, K.C., Cohen, S.G., Hess, J.A., Novak, W.E., Peterson, A.S.: Feature-oriented domain analysis (foda) feasibility study. Tech. rep, CMU-SEI (1990)
12. Lippert, M., Roock, S.: Refactoring in Large Software Projects: Performing Complex Restructurings Successfully. John Wiley & Sons, Chichester (2006)
13. Mumtaz, H., Singh, P., Blincoe, K.: A systematic mapping study on architectural smells detection. J. Syst. Softw. **173** (2020)
14. Patikirikorala, T., Colman, A., Han, J., Wang, L.: A systematic survey on the design of self-adaptive software systems using control engineering approaches. In: 2012 7th International Symposium on Software Engineering for Adaptive and Self-Managing Systems (SEAMS), pp. 33–42. IEEE (2012)
15. Raibulet, C., Arcelli Fontana, F., Carettoni, S.: A preliminary analysis of self-adaptive systems according to different issues. Softw. Qual. J.l **28**(3), 1213–1243 (2020). https://doi.org/10.1007/s11219-020-09502-5
16. Raibulet, C., Fontana, F.A., Carettoni, S.: SAS vs. NSAS: analysis and comparison of self-adaptive systems and non-self-adaptive systems based on smells and patterns. In: ENASE, pp. 490–497 (2020)
17. Santos, E., Machado, I.: Towards an architecture model for dynamic software product lines engineering. In: IEEE International Conference on Information Reuse and Integration (IRI), pp. 31–38. IEEE (2018)
18. dos Santos, E.L.: Stars: software technology for adaptable and reusable systems. In: Proceedings of the 25th International Systems and Software Product Line Conference (SPLC), ACM (2021)
19. dos Santos, E.L., Fortz, S., Perrouin, G., Schobbens, P.Y.: A vision to identify architectural smells in self-adaptive systems using behavioral maps. In: 15th European Conference on Software Architecture (ECSA 2021), p. 1. CEUR Workshop Proceedings (2021)
20. dos Santos, E.L., Schobbens, P.Y., Perrouin, G.: Featured scents: towards assessing architectural smells for self-adaptive systems at runtime. In: 19th International Conference on Software Architecture, pp. 71–74. IEEE (2022)
21. Serikawa, M.A., et al.: Towards the characterization of monitor smells in adaptive systems. In: X Brazilian Symposium on Software Components, Architectures and Reuse (SBCARS), pp. 51–60. IEEE (2016)
22. Soares, L.R., Meinicke, J., Nadi, S., Kästner, C., de Almeida, E.S.: VarXplorer: lightweight process for dynamic analysis of feature interactions. In: Proceedings of the 12th International Workshop on Variability Modelling of Software-Intensive Systems, pp. 59–66 (2018)

23. Vogel, T.: mRUBIS: an exemplar for model-based architectural self-healing and self-optimization: an exemplar for model-based architectural self-healing and self-optimization. In: Proceedings of the 13th International Conference on Software Engineering for Adaptive and Self-Managing Systems, pp. 101–107 (2018)
24. Wuttke, J., Brun, Y., Gorla, A., Ramaswamy, J.: Traffic routing for evaluating self-adaptation. In: 2012 7th International Symposium on Software Engineering for Adaptive and Self-Managing Systems (SEAMS), pp. 27–32. IEEE (2012)

An Architectural Approach for Enabling and Developing Cooperative Behaviour in Diverse Autonomous Robots

Simo Linkola(✉), Niko Mäkitalo, Tomi Laurinen, Anna Kantosalo,
and Tomi Männistö

Department of Computer Science, University of Helsinki, Helsinki, Finland
{simo.linkola,niko.makitalo,tomi.laurinen,anna.kantosalo,
tomi.mannisto}@helsinki.fi

Abstract. The paper introduces an architecture for robot-to-robot cooperation which takes into consideration how situational context augmented with peer modeling fosters cooperation opportunity identification and cooperation planning. The presented architecture allows developing, training, testing, and deploying dynamic cooperation solutions for diverse autonomous robots using ontology-based reasoning. The architecture operates in three different worlds: in the Real World with real robots, in a 3D Virtual World by emulating the real environments and robots, and in an abstract Block World that enables developing and studying large-scale cooperation scenarios. We describe an assessment practice for our architecture and cooperation procedures, which is based on scenarios implemented in all three worlds, and provide initial results of stress testing the cooperation procedures in the Block World. Moreover, as the core part of our architecture can operate in all the three worlds, development of the robot cooperation with the architecture can regularly accommodate insights gained from experimenting and testing in one world as improvements in another. We report our insights from developing the architecture and cooperation procedures as additional research outcomes.

Keywords: Robot software architecture · Robot cooperation · Ontology-based reasoning · Peer modeling · Autonomous robots

1 Introduction

Understanding the context of the robots plays a key role in autonomous robot cooperation. Situational context is a term used to describe why some phenomenon occurs in a specific situation and what actions can be associated with this situation [4]. This paper presents an extended and revised version of an architecture that fosters the situational awareness of cooperative robots, originally presented in 2021 CASA Workshop [14].

Information relevant to autonomous cooperation is pivotal in our approach to cooperation planning: A robot must be able to form an understanding of

© The Author(s), under exclusive license to Springer Nature Switzerland AG 2022
P. Scandurra et al. (Eds.): ECSA Tracks and Workshops 2021, LNCS 13365, pp. 181–204, 2022.
https://doi.org/10.1007/978-3-031-15116-3_9

both (a) the other robots and their resources and (b) the environment where
the cooperation is intended to take place. Our architectural approach does not
provide a solution to form a complete or joint contextual understanding between
the robots. Instead, the architecture enables each robot to form its own view of
the situation. The robots then use their situational context model and understanding as a basis for forming joint action plans for meeting their personal
goals.

In most autonomous robot approaches, the goal of the individual robot and its
cooperation behavior is fixed during the design. This leaves little room for novel
dynamic cooperation where new (joint) actions and plans could be formed or
goals adjusted after deployment in heterogeneous encounters with diverse peers
or other computational actors. Nonetheless, this kind of creative use of complementary capabilities could highly benefit the whole robot population associated
with a specific location, especially when the population is sparse and consists of
low-end consumer robots built for singular tasks, e.g., cleaning, with ample idle
time to allocate to other goals.

To optimize the use of context, and to develop the capabilities of the robots to
understand their situation and cooperation possibilities, the architecture enables
development in three conceptually and operationally different worlds. The development approach involves the Real World, a 3D Virtual World, and a 2D Block
World, and a shared associated software architecture and frameworks, which can
operate in all of the three worlds. Each of the worlds allows the designer to focus
on different aspects of the development effort.

The 2D Block World works as a test bed for developing an ontology-based
understanding of the cooperation context for the robots as it allows the simulation of large number of diverse robots in different cooperation scenarios.
Ontology-based reasoning and planning provide robots a shared understanding
of "how the world works" and thus are crucial in our approach for multi-robot
cooperation.

We adopt DUL (DOLCE+DnS Ultralite)[1] as our base ontology. DUL is well
suited for autonomous robot reasoning (see, e.g., KnowRob 2.0 [3]), where it
serves as a *top-level ontology*, which specific applications are supposed to extend
through their own ontology classes and relations. For this work we have developed a preliminary extension to DUL to showcase the applicability of our general
approach.

In the Real World and the 3D Virtual World implementations, we have
focused on robots based on the Robot Operating System (ROS), specifically
ROS2 [18]. Briefly put, ROS2 is an open-source robot development framework
where different nodes, or programs, communicate asynchronously using DDS,
allowing nodes to *subscribe* and *publish* to *topics* shared over a network. Being
a leading open-source project in robotics, ROS (and ROS2) has an active development community.

Our approach to autonomous robot cooperation aims to support ad hoc
encounters between heterogeneous autonomous robots, each of which have their

---

[1] http://ontologydesignpatterns.org/wiki/Ontology:DOLCE+DnS_Ultralite.

own individual goals. These goals can be used to define various plans, or work-flows, which include different types of tasks. Typically, the cooperation tasks can be categorized into loosely and tightly coupled cooperation tasks [7]: *Tightly coupled tasks* cannot be performed by one robot but require multiple robots to work cooperatively; *Loosely coupled tasks*, on the other hand, can be performed by a single robot but the task can be performed more efficiently with cooperation.

The proposed software architecture enables cooperation in both tightly coupled and loosely coupled tasks mainly through *peer modeling*, which has been argued to be a requirement for cooperation [5]. The robots can exchange, learn, use and evaluate models of themselves and their peers to identify and exploit cooperation opportunities. Although the architecture proposes means for coordination and communication, implementing tightly coupled tasks, however, requires more work from the developer.

The rest of this paper is structured as follows. In Sect. 2, we introduce the relevant cooperation concepts related to our architecture. In Sect. 3, we describe our solution – a software architecture that enables the development, training, and testing of cooperation between autonomous robots. In Sect. 4, we explain the current status of two core elements of our cooperation solution: the ontology extension and the planner which uses the ontology. In Sect. 5, we describe the scenario-based assessment practice of our architecture, and results of preliminary stress tests of the architecture in the 2D Block World. In Sect. 6, we report our insights on developing the autonomous robot cooperation with the three-world approach. In Sect. 7, we cover related work and discussion. Finally, in Sect. 8, we draw the conclusions for this work.

2   Cooperation Concepts

To understand our architecture, we first introduce the ontological concepts we use to enable cooperation. The basic concepts introduced here are part of the DUL ontology, but we extend them in our work to provide concrete solutions and a better understanding of the situational context at hand (see Sect. 4.1).

The robots' essential operation revolves around *goals*, which we model as *environment states*, describing desirable situations the robot should find itself in. A goal can be, e.g., to keep a room clean or deliver a package to a specific place. A robot may have multiple or even conflicting goals.

To achieve its goals (either by itself or in cooperation), a robot forms *plans* which consist of *tasks*. A plan describes how a certain goal is achieved, i.e., which tasks should be done and their (partial) order. To make a plan concrete, each task needs to be assigned to a robot (or a set of robots). In DUL this type of plan, where each task has a designed executor(s), is called a *workflow*.

Tasks are the individual elements from which plans and workflows are composed of. Each task includes some objective(s) to be achieved, e.g., open a particular door, move to a specific place, etc. Tasks can be hierarchically nested in two ways. First, there can be general tasks (open a door) and refinements of those tasks (open a door by pulling the handle). Second, lower-level tasks may be combined to compose higher-level tasks, e.g., moving, opening a door, and moving again can be seen as one higher-level moving task. These task structures are used when generating and communicating workflows.

Tasks have defined start and end conditions. However, the actions (see below) can be partly responsible for checking these conditions. The start condition is checked before the task can be attempted, e.g., to open a door manually, the robot must be next to it. The end conditions are checked to see if the task was completed successfully, e.g., if the door is open. The task end conditions can be modeled as individual, low-level goals.

To achieve tasks, each robot has *actions* by which the tasks can be completed. The robot may have multiple (sets of) actions that achieve the same task, and an action may be utilized in multiple tasks. Where goals, plans, workflows, and tasks are platform-independent, actions need to be implemented on each platform (and world) separately.

To allow cooperation, robots communicate their goals, suggested workflows, and tasks to develop workflows, including multiple robots. To make this communication more fluent, robots maintain a model of themselves and each of the peers they have encountered. In general, these models may hold any important information of the robot in question, such as their physical properties, *capabilities*, i.e., which tasks they can perform, the robot's goals, and the history of the workflows they have been included in and their success.

3   Software Architecture for Autonomous Robot Cooperation

At the core of our research is the *CACDAR architecture* (Creative and Adaptive Collaboration between Diverse Autonomous Robots). The architecture, with its components and the leveraged services, is depicted in Fig. 1. The architecture can operate in all three worlds, the 2D Block World, the 3D Virtual World, and the Real World, and it also enables feedback loops for the developers between these three different worlds, allowing them to manually – or automatically – incorporate insights gained from one world to another in order to advance the situational context awareness that fosters the robot cooperation (see Sect. 6).

Next, we introduce the high level descriptions of all the components and their development end goals. The current status of (some of) the main elements enabling cooperation are explained in the next section.

3.1   Cooperative Brain Service

The critical enabling service for the novel and valuable cooperation is the platform-agnostic *Cooperative Brain Service*, which encloses several components. The *Cooperative Brain Service* is responsible for the high-level functionality of the robot such as the planning of future tasks and cooperation (see *Planner*), scheduling of tasks to be executed (see *Scheduler*) by *Task Runtime*, and it gathers information from sensors, the operation and communication of the robot with

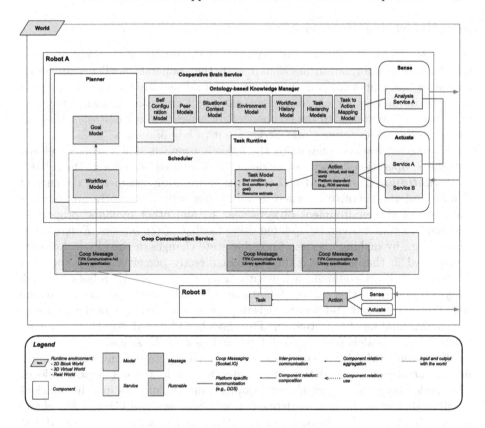

Fig. 1. CACDAR architecture.

other robots into *Knowledge Manager* which it uses in its reasoning. For cooperation, the service needs to be able to understand the requests of another robot for help, and then try to reason if it would (a) have the missing resources, or (b) would have free resources or less important tasks so that it could free up the resources for the cooperation. The availability of such resources (e.g., time and battery) are estimated in collaboration with the *Scheduler* and the *Task Runtime* components.

However, the most crucial responsibility of the service is to estimate whether it will meet its own goals. It constantly keeps track of its resources and what resources other robots have allocated for helping it to meet its goals. Hence, it leverages *Knowledge Manager* and *Task Runtime* components by observing changes in the models that represent the other robots and environment, and then notifies the *Planner* which can alter its workflow and tasks (e.g., by replanning tasks with missing resources or reorganizing tasks in its workflow).

3.2   Knowledge Manager

Knowledge Manager takes care of maintaining the robot's understanding of the world and the information associated with the cooperation. The main input source for the component is the robot's (platform-dependent) service components that the robot uses for observing and sensing. *Knowledge Manager* may also exchange information with the components of other robots *Knowledge Manager* via respective *Cooperative Brain Services* with *Coop Messages*.

Knowledge Manager maintains the following models that enable novel and valuable cooperation as well as individual goal-oriented behavior of the robot:

Situational Context Model captures information considering the current situation of the robot, e.g., where it and other robots currently are, what is the state of the environment objects near it, and other dynamic properties. The model's contents can be updated using feedback from sensors, *Environment Model* (e.g., by making queries of possible state changes in the physical objects represented in the ontology if they are not directly perceived), *Self* and *Peer Models*, and direct communication with other actors, such as robots, through *Coop Messages*. To this extent, *Situational Context Model* operates in tandem with the environment and peer models to provide a unified view of the most current understanding of the situation. This model can be used directly in *Planner*, whereas other models provide more fractured view of the situation.

Environment Model connects actions in the operating environment, e.g., moving or object manipulation, into state changes in the ontological objects. The model should represent the environment and the objects in it in sufficient detail so that it can be used to derive reasonable *Situational Context Model* and reason about possible consequences of actions in particular situations. It can be updated using feedback from the environment (either perceived or received through communication). The level of detail in the *Environment Model* varies across the different *world types*. In 2D Block World, the model is sufficient to possess simple logical states, e.g., is the door open or closed, while in Virtual and the Real World the model may be more elaborate, e.g., a door can be partially closed and currently opening. However, to keep the "backward functionality" intact from Real World back to 2D Block World, individual object states and actions that manipulate them in Real World model should be mappable into the 2D Block World model.

Self Model and Peer Models contain information about the robot itself and its peers. In general, each peer has its own model, but aggregate models, e.g., considering certain classes of robots, are possible. Robots exchange information considering themselves (drawn from their *Self Model* and other knowledge sources) when they first meet their peers and update and replace this information through communication and observations. Where *Situational Context Model* offers current information of the state of the world, and *Environment Model* offers an understanding of how the world works, these models provide knowledge of what are the goals of each robot, which tasks are possible for the robot, and what restrictions the robot may have for performing specific tasks, e.g., if the robot can only open specific types of doors. From the cooperation perspective, these models are highly relevant, as their information is needed in *Planner* when determining which peers can perform a particular *Task*.

Task to Action Mapping Models contains knowledge about mapping the task realizations to actions. This knowledge is mainly about the robot's tasks, but peers' tasks to action mapping information can also be partially stored. This applies especially to cases if the robots are of the same type. Additionally, other peers may provide some information about their action mapping for a particular task, e.g., resource estimates, timing information, or constraints that can be used in reasoning.

Workflow History Model contains the information on earlier cooperation situations, such as performed task sequences, their configurations, and execution results. The information is used for improving the quality of the cooperation by analyzing which workflows have previously worked well and which ones have failed.

Task Hierarchy Models are used as configuration models for creating task hierarchies (consisting of task-goal-plan nodes), e.g., options for decomposing tasks or goals and constraints for valid hierarchy configurations. The model can be used to determine whether a particular task hierarchy configuration is valid, and the hierarchies can, then, be used by *Planner* or other components in *Knowledge Manager*, e.g., to represent aggregated high-level capabilities of the peers.

3.3   Planner

Planner is responsible for constructing *Workflows* which are then, e.g., passed to *Scheduler* for execution or stored for later use. As input, *Planner* is given some starting situation, e.g. the current *Situational Context*, a desired end condition, e.g. the current *Goal*, and other related parameters, e.g. restrictions for the workflow. *Planner* leverages the information maintained by *Knowledge Manager* in its attempts to select the robot and its peers to specific roles and to assign them *Tasks*. For actually assigning *Tasks* for its peer robots, *Planner* negotiates with the *Planner* components of different robots. The purpose is to ensure that the robot has a correct understanding of the capabilities of its peer (i.e., *Tasks* it can perform) and that the peer has sufficient resources, e.g., time and battery power, to participate in the workflow.

Goal Model defines a single mission (e.g. a task) that is expected to be carried out by a single robot or a set of robots. However, it does not define how the actual plan and the mission is expected to be performed. Instead, a *Goal Model* can set some ground rules for the robot behavior, like time constraints or quality attributes. A *Goal Model* is used for deriving start and end conditions for specific tasks. It may also affect what types of robots get selected into the roles of the cooperation.

Workflow Model consists of a *Goal Model* and a partially ordered list of *Task Models* where each task is assigned to a (set of) robots. By default, *Planner* tries to put together a *Workflow Model* where the robot itself is in the primary role, and its peers are assigned only if the robot cannot meet the *Goal*.

However, the *Goal Model* can affect how the workflow is put together: As the *Goal Model* contains information regarding the mission of a single robot, it can then define the mission to be highly cooperative or act as a leader. For example, consider that one robot is expected to act as a supervisor for the other robots – its mission is then defined to coordinate the others and their cooperation.

3.4   Task Runtime

Different types of robots can feature very differing underlying platforms for development and interfacing in general. Therefore, the platform is essentially what dictates how actions have to be implemented. The *Task Runtime* is accordingly designed so that support for new platforms can be added at will, in the form of *platform modules*. However, special care needs to be taken when implementing 2D Block World platforms, as they operate in discrete time and not in continuous time. Currently supported platforms are ROS2 and a simple iterative simulation platform for 2D Block World built on top of Creamas[2].

Task. The self-adaptive aspects of the architecture come into play when the autonomous operation or cooperation requires certain resources. Each robot describes its capabilities by communicating to others what kind of *tasks* they can execute. A task may consist of other tasks, that is, a task may group together other tasks to obtain a higher-level behavior. As an example, consider that a robot can perform a task Guide. Such task then consists of other tasks, like Move, Turn, Navigate, etc.

Action is the mapping from the behavior modeled with tasks to the actual implementation of a specific task. Actions are generally platform-specific, but there can be alternative versions of actions for different robots even within the same platform. Similar to the tasks, also actions can be composed of a set of other actions. For instance, conforming Action: Guide may leverage various other action implementations.

3.5   Robot's Services

For actuating and sensing the events coming from the world, the architecture enables leveraging various services and communication between them. In Fig. 1, such services have been illustrated: an imaginary actuating *Service A* is used, for example controlling the robot, and at the same time, it sends data to *Analysis Service A*. While we have mainly used ROS2 based services in our current implementation, the Cooperation Brain is not tied to any specific robot technology. Hence the services may also be realized as ROS1 services or any other type of service technology (e.g., as a Docker-based microservice), or, in case of 2D Block World, simple asynchronous function calls.

---

[2] https://creamas.readthedocs.io/en/latest/.

3.6   Scheduler

Scheduler component is part of the Task Runtime component. Scheduler's main duty is to fetch tasks to be executed in Task Runtime. To this end, it queries from the Brain if there are tasks to be executed, which may cause the Planner to plan a new workflow, converts the responded tasks to their platform specific implementations, and delivers the runnable Actions to the Task Runtime. The Scheduler also ensures that the situation is correct for running the task, i.e. the task's start conditions are satisfied, and it communicates back to the other Brain components if that is not the case. The Scheduler can also use the resource estimates to ensure that the robot has the promised resources for performing the task.

3.7   Coop Communication Service

In order to cooperate effectively in varying situations and environments, the robots require a communication platform that can relay messages between the components deployed on various robots. The base technology for inter-robot communication is Socket.IO. It provides a relatively reliable and fast enough communication channel for negotiating about the cooperation-related activities, like tasks and roles in workflows, and providing feedback.

In our present research, we mainly leverage ROS2-based robots. ROS2, on the other hand, leverages DDS technology for communication between the ROS2 services. Hence, in the future, our implementation may change using DDS also for the cooperation communication to make the architecture more streamlined. The downside, however, is that setting up a DDS-based communication infrastructure can be challenging for robots that lack the required resources, and as there are several different DDS implementations, incompatibility issues may emerge and issues with licensing. For this reason, the implementation yet relies on our service and Socket.IO technology. Additionally, to support also non-ROS2 based robots, we have been discussing implementing a communication bridge that would allow ROS and other types of robots and smart objects and resources (e.g., sensors, existing facility service systems, smart home systems, etc.) in the environments to participate and enhance the cooperation.

Coop Message is the base unit of the communication in the *CACDAR architecture*. Two other base message types – *BroadcastMessage* and *Direct Message* – are inherited from the base. The idea is that the communication language is extended by inheriting new subtypes. The only requirement is that each message has a sender. The actual communication messages are based on FIPA Communicative Act Library Specification [8] from which we use a subset.

Broadcast Messages are sent publicly to all robots and services connected to the Coop Communication Service. Typical use cases for these messages are when a new robot arrives at a specific venue and then gets connected to the Coop Communication Service located at this venue. The robot may then greet other connected robots by broadcasting its name and the tasks it considers capable of performing. The robot may also request help from other robots by trying to describe its goal to other robots.

Direct Messages, on the other hand, are sent directly from one robot to a set of recipients. These messages are mainly used for negotiating a cooperation plan and communicating during the execution of the plan.

4   Current Status

In this section, we present the current implementation status of our ontology extension and the *Planner* component, two of the main elements enabling the cooperative behaviour.

4.1   Ontology

The collaboration of our robots is based on ontological reasoning. While rigorous ontology development is not the main focus of our study, developing an ontology based on a well-known general ontology enables new collaboration possibilities for the robots: As long as the robots are familiar with the top level ontology, they can reason about the concepts presented to them, even if they are not familiar with the exact ontological classes used by another robot. Here we explain our ontology development process and illustrate a few classes from our ontology.

In our ontology development effort we have consulted the approach advocated by Noy and McGuinness [15]. They describe an iterative process of creating an ontological model of the world in a specific domain. After considering the scope and domain of the ontology, Noy and McGuinness encourage defining competency questions[3] to guide the ontology development before considering existing ontologies, enumerating terms, defining classes and hierarchies, properties, their value types, and finally creating instances of the ontology classes.

As stated before, we decided to extend the domain general DUL (DOLCE+DnS Ultralite) ontology to fit collaboration in the intended sample use cases. The domain of our work thus is general robot-to-robot collaboration and from the use case we derive that the collaboration in this case considers planning of navigation in a physical space. To aid our design we considered the following competency questions:

1. What objects in the environment are important for the robot to recognize and how will the robot tell them apart? (e.g. a door or a room in our use case of package delivery)
2. Which concepts are necessary for the robot to conduct a simple task alone? (e.g. moving from one room to another)
3. Which concepts are essential for collaborative plan construction?
4. How will the robot ask for help?

---

[3] After Gruninger, M. and Fox, M.S. (1995). Methodology for the Design and Evaluation of Ontologies. In: Proceedings of the Workshop on Basic Ontological Issues in Knowledge Sharing, IJCAI-95, Montreal.

5. How will the robot maintain an understanding of its capabilities?
6. How will the robot maintain an understanding of its peers' capabilities?

The first two questions (1–2) deal directly with the physical properies of the domain and suggest additions to the ontology supporting the description of spaces and their relations through doorways. The two following questions (3–4) relate to the ability of the robot to plan and initiate collaboration. Finally the last two questions (5–6) deal with the robots ability to recognize and model itself and its peers as agents in the world. In our current ontology development effort we have focused on questions 1–4.

The existing DUL ontology has general classes which can be used to describe any domain. The full DUL ontology is out of the scope of this paper, but we describe some general principles that support our extension. The DUL ontology offers several classes to represent physical objects and agents, which we extend in our own implementation. Examples of our extensions can be seen in Table 1. The DUL ontology also has several classes for representing social concepts, such as the class `Task`, which is inherited by our extensions describing specific kind of tasks in the domain, such as `OpenDoorTask`. Finally some classes represent information rather than events or physical objects.

The separation between `PhysicalObject` and subclasses of the `Information Entity` class in the DUL Ontology means that some aspects of our ontological extension need to be represented by two separate classes to connect the information and the physical object representing it in the simulations or the real world. This is linked to the problem of symbolic grounding. We chose to circumvent it by using QR codes to tag the physical objects in our simulations and the real world. In our ontology the `QRCode` class represents the information stored in a QR Code tag, while the `QRCodeTag` represents the physical or virtual entity. These further link to other ontological objects, such as doors. The grounding problem could also have been solved by using for example machine learning to recognize the objects, but as it is not the focus of our project, we chose the QR code + tag approach.

Our ontology development effort is a living project and it is developed further to raise to the challenge of creative collaboration as we move on to investigate the ontological questions 5–6.

4.2 Planner

We have implemented the first working version of the planner, where emphasis has been given to forming operational plans for physical navigation in enclosures consisting of rooms which are connected with doors, i.e. floor plans resembling typical offices and other buildings. We chose to implement our own planner software as it needs to constantly communicate with the peers in the context, therefore making the existing software solutions for ontology-based reasoning, e.g. KnowRob 2.0 [3], only partially suitable for our needs. In the future, some of the subroutines of the planner may be refactored to utilise existing solutions. Next, we briefly describe the operation of the current planner. The full description of the component is out of the scope of this paper.

Table 1. Examples of ontological concepts used in planning and other reasoning.

Class (DUL inheritance)	Description	Current Usage
NavigateToTask (DUL:Task)	General task to move around in the world	Used to move between two points
DeliverObjectTask (DUL:Task)	Task to deliver objects to their destinations	Used to deliver packages to their destination locations. The robot must check it is next to the destination before it can deliver an object
Point2D (DUL:SpaceRegion)	Singular point with (x, y) coordinates	Represents the location of any DUL:PhysicalObject. The coordinates are internal to the robot
Room (DUL:SpaceRegion)	General area construct. Rooms are connected to other rooms (or areas) by doors (or other portals)	The robot can move between any two points in the same room using only NavigateToTask
Door (DUL:DesignedArtifact)	Any object which can act as a closeable portal between two (or more) rooms	A robot with proper capabilities can open a door between two rooms to move between them, but it must be next to the door to do this
DeliveryObject (DUL:DesignedArtifact)	Objects to be delivered	Used to represent the real objects with knowledge of their destinations, etc.
QRCode (DUL:InformationObject)	Represents a QR code which can be attached to any DUL:PhysicalObject	Robot identifies objects, e.g. doors and delivery locations, in its environment by recognising and reading QR codes

The current planner closely follows the famous A* heuristic search algorithm [10], which is quaranteed to find the shortest path in a graph (for us, a sequence of tasks) if the search's properties conform to some general assumptions. For now, the path cost is simply the time estimated to complete all the tasks in it, but it can be expanded to take into account other resources as well. A* search uses a heuristic function to guide the search to more promising directions. In our current implementation, with the focus for physical navigation, the heuristic is the time estimated for travel from current position to the goal position via straight line distance.

The A* algorithm operates on (directed) weighted graphs. We can construct the search graph using the instances of ontology classes and their relations. Starting from a single node, the starting location, the algorithm considers which tasks are possible to execute from the current node and adds them to the task graph as edges between nodes representing states. For example, in a room we can ask which all other points are in this room and expand the search with instances of NavigateToTask to those points, or in points next to doors, we can expand the search with OpenDoorTasks allowing the search procedure to cover also other rooms.

To better accommodate our needs, we have made a few modifications to the basic A*. First, for some of the tasks it is crucial to verify if their starting conditions are satisfied before the task can be expanded, e.g. the manual OpenDoorTask can be added as an edge to the graph only, if the robot is next to a door it can open manually. Second, the planner communicates with peers to find executors for tasks which the robot can not do itself. In such cases it can use the time estimates of the peers to compute the path cost estimates. Third, for some closely associated task sequences, the planner utilises task hierarchies to achieve more complete behaviour. For example, if the current goal is to find a route to a certain point, and the robot is not guiding anybody, then OpenDoorTask, NavigateToTask and CloseDoorTask are added automatically to the task graph as tasks related to entering a new room before a new search expansion is done.

After a task sequence required to achieve the goal task is found, the planner communicates to the peers which tasks are done by which peers based on their request responses. The planner also inserts into the robot's own task sequence WaitTask with proper end condition before any task that (1) is done by a peer and (2) is required to be completed before the robot can continue to its next task towards its goal.

5   Asessing Cooperative Behaviour in the Three Worlds

To evaluate the implementation of our architecture we developed scenarios that represent the desired qualities of the system: autonomy, cooperation with diverse peers, self-adaptation and functioning in changing or uncertain environments. First, we elaborate on our scenario development process, and then we discuss the implementation and results of testing our architecture using randomised scenarios in the 2D Block World.

5.1   Scenario Development

In this section we describe the assessment practice of our architecture revolving around *scenarios*, and the properties we have identified as preliminary requirements for the scenarios. We report our insights on developing the architecture using an example scenario in Sect. 6.3.

We defined a scenario to consist of a context and an activity (associated with some goals) in one of the worlds. Both the context and the activity can have variable properties. Variables of the context include the physical context, e.g. a floor plan and objects residing in it, and the participants of the scenario, e.g. the robots operating in it. The variables for the activities include parameters specific to that activity, such as goal states and start locations for the participants. A scenario that is executed forms a situation. A situation describes how things are at a particular time in a particular context when the robots are performing particular activities. The situation defines the current status of the system and can consider also the inner states of the robots.

These scenarios were developed to be implementable in the three different worlds: 2D Block World, 3D Virtual World, and Real World. The main purpose of developing the system for all three platforms was to evaluate its feasibility similar to building a skeleton system for evaluating software architecture (see e.g. Rozanski and Woods [17, p. 225]). The use of the different worlds allows us to evaluate further aspects of the system: Through building a sample system for Real World we evaluate the feasibility of our system. Simulating the system in the 3D Virtual World allows us to test the variability and deployability of the system as we can change the simulated hardware and the environment of the system easily. Finally evaluating the system in the 2D Block World allows us to test the logic with different single-agent service configurations, as well as the robustness of the system with large sets of agents. Together the multiple worlds, multiple scenarios approach allows us to achieve reliability through iterative development and experimentation.

We conducted our scenario development iteratively starting from a simple 'follow me' scenario in which one robot follows the other to a target (see Mäkitalo et al. [14]). From this simple scenario we derived alternative activities and contexts to enable for more robust testing that would allow us to validate the capability of the system in working autonomously under variable scenarios including changes and uncertainty.

After implementing the initial scenario in the three worlds, we decided on the materials for the physical context of the scenarios. We selected 3 mm thick cellular board as the physical building material and designed the physical scenario creation based on 50 cm × 50 cm modular wall pieces supporting easy implementation in all three worlds. The modularity allows for building various enclosures, which we also call floor plans. The enclosures can be used to test how cooperation and the base software function in changing or uncertain environments, supporting our goals of self-adaptation and autonomy. In our scenarios the enclosures resemble house floor plans, which typically include rooms. The different rooms (as well as other physical objects relevant for robots) are labeled using QR codes to facilitate their recognition.

Next we defined a number of activities to be implemented in an enclosure built from the physical or simulated modular squares. These activities focused on the collaboration aspects of testing. These activities are described in detail in Table 2. The first three tasks are variations of the same theme. The value of separating the guiding task into three different activities becomes apparent if additional restrictions are posed on the system, such as access rights. The first

Table 2. Set of test activities for our scenario-based assessment practice.

Label	Task	Description
Guide 1	Guide robot from point A to point B	In this task one robot guides another from a point to another in a situation where the first robot does not know the location or route to point B. The robots need to communicate using ontological concepts. The guidance could be for example related to a package delivery scenario, or regular maintenance performed by a robot visiting a new environment
Guide 2	Guide robot from room A to room B where there are two or more routes available that are equally good	In this task one robot guides another from one room to another, but there are more than one optimal route. This can be used to test additional constraints, e.g. situations in which access rights required to complete the two routes are different
Guide 3	Guide robot from room A to room B, when there are several routes available with different assessments of route quality or cost	In this task one robot guides another from one room to another, but there are routes with varied levels of optimality. This can be used to test additional constraints, e.g. situations in which the required access to complete the routes is different
Pickup	Pick up a package in room A and bring it back to room B.	In this task one robot picks up a package stored in a room. It can be combined with the guiding task. As the robot picks up the package its weight and dimensions may change, meaning it may need to select an alternative route back

three activities are suitable for *static* scenarios, in the sense that the properties of the participating robots or the environment do not change during the scenario involving the activity. They can still be used to test for autonomy, cooperation with diverse peers, self-adaptation and functioning in uncertain environments, as the participating robots and the context, or the start or end locations of the guiding activity can be changed before each test run. Any of these activities can be used to construct a *dynamic* scenario by blocking the route from one room to another during the activity, or changing access rights. However, the fourth activity, 'Pickup' has some inherent dynamism as the properties of the participating robot can change if it picks up a large delivery. This can for example prevent the use of certain doors on the way back.

In our scenarios the differences between participating robots are defined through *robot capabilities*. E.g. one robot is able to follow, one to guide and

Table 3. Results of tests in 2D Block World simulations. The setting on each row has been run 10 times and run averages are reported. Size is the scenario's floor plan size, #DL is the number of delivery locations, #DO is the number of delivery objects, #Objects is the number of Point2D and Door objects in the scenario, Delivered% is the percentage of successful deliveries, Steps is the average number of simulation steps required to deliver all the objects, and Time is the average time the simulation took to complete with time per step in parentheses.

Size	#DL	#DO	#Objects	Delivered%	Steps	Time
20×20	4	10	440	100%	129	0.279 (0.002)
50×50	10	10	2720	100%	351.5	2.326 (0.007)
200×200	20	10	43280	100%	1487.5	112.3 (0.076)
400×400	50	10	172960	100%	3084.7	953.6 (0.309)

a third to open doors. It is however possible also to further derivate between robot properties by allowing them different access levels to different areas of the physical enclosure. This can enable more complex collaborative tasks, such as a robot having to be lead by two others to reach a final destination going through areas the two other robots are not allowed to be in alone. The use of differently capabled robots in our scenarios makes them suitable for evaluating tightly coupled cooperation, but they could be used for evaluating loosely coupled cooperation, if the same capabilities were given to all robots.

5.2   Stress Testing in 2D Block World

We conducted stress testing of our architecture, and especially the *Planner* component, by building on top of the basic scenarios described above in 2D Block World iterative simulations. We created a diverse set of floor plans consisting of different sized rooms, doors between them, and a few delivery points spawned in random locations across the floor plan. Specifically, we created 10 floor plans for each 2D Block World size: 20×20, 50×50, 200×200 and 400×400. For each floor plan, we spawned two robots to random places with different capabilities: one that could open doors and guide, and one that could follow and deliver objects. The delivery robot did not have an understanding of the floor plan, i.e. it had to ask for guidance to the delivery points, and it was initialised with 10 delivery objects with random, specific delivery point destinations.

The purpose of the expanded scenario was to verify that (1) the planner was able to find a proper cooperation plan for each DeliveryTask, (2) the robots were able to execute the plan so that the object was delivered in the end, and (3) to ensure that the execution time of the planner did not grow too much as a function of the floor plan size. We report our results in Table 3.

We make two main observations from Table 3. First and foremost, the planner is able to construct a proper cooperative plan and the agents are able to execute it in all the randomly initialised scenarios (see Delivered% for each row). This is strong evidence that both the planner is working correctly and that the

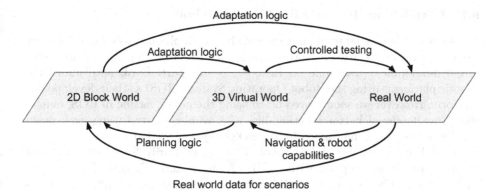

Fig. 2. Examples of lessons learned feedback loops between three development and evaluation worlds. The three worlds each bring their own development properties, but some of these properties also affect other worlds. For example data from the Real World, including robot types and configurations, guide the work on the simulated worlds.

2D Block World implementations of the actions are properly implemented. Second, we see that the time to execute each simulation step grows as the scenario size grows (both the size and the number of ontological objects). However, the growth is non-existent when dividing the step time with the number of ontological objects in the scenario. This indicates that the planner is able to consider the plan candidates in an efficient way and expand the search to the most promising directions, and that the number of ontological objects in the agent's knowledge does not affect (on this scale) the performance too much. However, based on these observations, we have already identified certain bottlenecks in our architecture implementation where inefficient list lookups of ontology objects could be refactored to more efficient solutions.

6   Three-World Development Process

We chose to develop our architecture for three different worlds the Real World, the 3D Virtual World and a simple 2D Block World to facilitate different development targets. The 2D Block World offers a simple environment to test the architectural adaptation logic, as well as for stress testing. The 3D Virtual World offers a way to progressively transfer the implementations to the Real World via controlled platforms featuring 3D physics simulation. Finally, the Real World helps us to identify potential gaps left by the simulations as well as test the applicability of the architecture in real scenarios. We began with simple tests run in the Real World, and now conduct our development concurrently on the different worlds, creating feedback loops from one world to the other. The effect of this feedback loop on our development effort is illustrated in Fig. 2. In this section we describe some of the lessons learned in our development efforts on the three worlds.

6.1   Introducing ROS and Real-World Robots

We deemed it beneficial to familiarize ourselves with physical robot development from early on and started by prototyping with robots in the Real World. Our initial development was done on Rosbot 2.0 and TurtleBot3, both affordable robotic platforms using the Robot Operating System (ROS) as their development platform. However we soon moved on to using the newer version of ROS, named ROS2, as it offered better functionality, and we also started using exclusively the TurtleBot3, as it had much better ROS2 support at that point.

TurtleBot3 is an economical robot intended primarily for educational and research use. It is equipped with a pair of wheels and a LIDAR for scanning surroundings. The system is modular and the composition of different robots can be changed with relative ease. For example, cameras can be added to the robots to enable more complex sensing of the world. This proved important, as in our project the robots do not share any common understanding of the world, such as a common map or even a common coordinate system. Therefore one of the preliminary coordinated Actions we implemented consists of one robot following another with the help of QR codes [14].

During experimentation in the Real World, several realities of robot development became apparent: Lighting conditions would affect the detection of QR codes greatly, even the slightest of obstacles such as cables were insurmountable for the TurtleBot3, and having to reset the positions of the robots manually every attempt was also rather inconvenient in the long run. We also did not have the equipment or means for complicated feats such as having the robots carry objects. Finally, the worsening COVID-19 pandemic shut down Real World development, so we focused on the 3D Virtual World environment next.

6.2   Bringing Cooperation from Real World to 3D Virtual World

As the intermediate world of the three-world approach, we chose Gazebo[4] for our first simulation environment, as it integrates well with ROS2, supporting the reuse of the implementation of our architecture in the three worlds. Gazebo also supported a smooth transition from the Real World to the 3D Virtual World, as it already includes a well implemented, accurate model for Turtlebot3. Therefore the QR code based robot following method, for one, worked in the 3D Virtual World as-is (see Fig. 3 for cooperation development in Gazebo with Turtlebots).

However, we did face some challenges with the 3D Virtual World implementation when trying to run multiple robots in a single Gazebo simulation. When using ROS2 in Real World, each robot is typically assigned its own ROS2 domain. However, when using Gazebo with ROS2, all the simulated robots have to use the same ROS2 domain. Unfortunately, this means the ROS2 topics used by the simulated robots would overlap by default, making it impossible to communicate with the robots separately. To avoid this overlap issue, separate namespaces had

---

[4] http://gazebosim.org/.

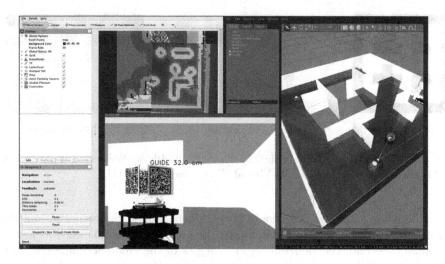

Fig. 3. Cooperation scenario running in the 3D Virtual World: Gazebo.

to be assigned to differentiate the topics of the robots. However, while this names-pace approach is commonly used in ROS1, support for it is much more limited in ROS2, so the platform change required developing some code workarounds.

Currently we can run several Turtlebots in the same simulation in Gazebo. However increasing the number of robots increases the processing power required to run the simulation significantly. This limits the current simulation run on a virtualized Ubuntu 20.04 on a business laptop to 3 robots, and even then the simulation runs between 0.4–0.7 times of the normal speed.

Despite the initial challenges, the benefits of the 3D Virtual World approach are clear: The simulation environment can be edited and reset at will, although we are currently experiencing some Gazebo-specific bugs with these features. Troublesome aspects of the real world such as light conditions causing problems with QR code detection are not an issue in Gazebo, and delivery of objects can be simulated with ease by spawning and despawning items.

6.3   Building Example Scenario for Cooperation Development

After getting the first scenario in Gazebo working, we built an example scenario following the ideas explained in Sect. 5.1 in all three worlds (see Fig. 4). After building the scenario we soon observed that the following method, which worked in our previous scenario, was bound to break in the 3D Virtual World and the Real World in the new scenario due to two main factors.

First, the interoperation of navigation and SLAM (simultaneous localisation and mapping) implementations in ROS2 were prone to create artifacts from previous observations in the follower's navigation map. That is, the follower continuously observed spaces previously occupied by the guide still as occupied even though the guide had already moved away. This resulted in poor behaviour

(a) Block world　　　　　(b) Gazebo　　　　　(c) Physical world

Fig. 4. An example enclosure in the three worlds: 2D Block World with iterative discrete time simulation, Gazebo 3D Virtual World, and Real World.

in tight spaces as the follower could not navigate around the artifacts, and the underlying implementations did not clear the artifacts if the follower was nearly stationary. Second, the sharp navigation angles of the guide accompanied with the thinness of the walls was causing problems for the following method, which was implemented by keeping the guiding robot's QR code as close to the center of the camera stream as possible. Due to this the follower repeatedly bumped into walls.

Fortunately, due to our three world development approach, we could still continue the development of other parts of the architecture and cooperation procedures even though a single platform (Turtlebot3 with ROS2) *Action* achieving single *Task* was temporarily broken. It was easy to verify that the problem was in the underlying action implementation and not in the core workings of the architecture. Moreover, we could begin to test how to circumvent these kind of problems in the future by making the following method more robust. For this, we could temporarily eased the properties of the 3D Virtual World, e.g. by making the corridors of the scenario wider and making the walls thicker.

7   Related Work and Discussion

In this section, we discuss related research on architectures enabling autonomous robot cooperation, leveraging ontologies for forming an understanding of the cooperation possibilities and situations, task planning and decision making in the context of autonomous robot cooperation, as well as changing environment in our development approach.

7.1   Architectures for Autonomous Robot Cooperation

Autonomous robots cooperating in uncertain and constantly changing environments have been studied for many years. The general interest in the overall topic has spawned several research subfields, e.g., swarm robotics [1], collaborative robotics (cf. [9]) and unmanned autonomous vehicles (UAV) (cf. [13]).

We find that the closest works related to our work from the architectural perspective are related to tightly coupled multi-robot cooperation. For example,

Chaimowicz et al. [6] have studied an architecture in which the key feature is flexibility, which enables changes in leadership and assignment of roles during the execution of a task. While their approach allows dynamical behavior, the cooperation is still tightly coupled. In our approach, each robot is expected to individually execute their tasks and then ask for help when needed. Hence, the cooperation is less tightly coupled. In addition, the aim is not to jointly execute predefined tasks but instead, enable the robots to model their environment and their peers so that they could independently form new cooperative plans and meet their personal goals.

The use case of transportation of objects has been studied by several researchers over the years, including Chaimowicz et al. [6]. Recently, Zhang et al. [20] as well as Manko et al. [12] have studied control architecture that is using deep reinforcement learning in the transportation of large or heavy objects with a particular focus on decentralized decision making. While these approaches have similarities to our work, our work aims to enable individual robots to fulfill their personal goals instead of the group's goal. Hence our architecture would likely not be well-suited for such tightly coupled cooperation. However, we can learn from their experiences on how they use deep learning technologies and Q-learning-based algorithms for training the robots to execute a tightly coupled task, and in the future, we could try a similar approach in our 2D Block World.

7.2 Ontologies for Cooperation

Ontologies have been widely used to make agents and robots understand the structures of the physical and social world around them [3, 16], and initiatives considering their usage to build robot collectives that can communicate and cooperate have been suggested before, e.g., RoboEarth [2]. In contrast to RoboEarth, where most of the reasoning happens in the cloud, cooperation understanding and planning in our architecture take place inside the individual robots. The robots do not share their world views in general as they are assumed to hold also information that should not be shared with others, such as maps of restricted areas or passwords. Instead, they will only exchange information relevant to the current situation and goals directly with each other. That said, cloud-based solutions, such as RoboEarth, could be integrated into the architecture as optional components.

Mainly due to the advent of IoT, ontologies prove to be an exciting starting point for robots to understand the world as the built environment is getting populated with intelligent devices capable of communicating with other computational actors. This means that, e.g., a door can be opened using software communication alone and does not have to rely on physical door manipulation, and that sensors and other IoT devices may send information of their physical composition, purpose, and capabilities using ontological representations. Especially on low-end robots this benefits cooperation, as the robot does not need to perceive these attributes from its raw sensor inputs such as camera streams.

7.3   Planning for Agents and Robots

Single robot planning may be approached from multiple perspectives. Two often used ones are heuristic shortest path search, such as the famous A* algorithm [10] and its dynamic counterparts, and solutions used for logical optimization problems, e.g. (weighted) maximum satisfiability solvers. The shortest path search provides (estimates) for moving from one node to another in a graph and aims to find the path of nodes with the shortest length, and logical optimization aims to find a (maximal or minimal) set of clauses that satisfy certain conditions. Dynamic shortest path algorithms fit well in environments where the robot may not fully understand its situation, e.g., the robot does not have a complete map or the map is bound to change, and logical optimization excels in cases where it is crucial to ensure the correctness of the solution beforehand.

However, our goal is to provide a planner that uses both logical verifications of the workflows through the fulfillment of each tasks' start and end conditions and a heuristic estimate of its execution resources through peer models and communication. Our approach differs from typical multi-robot task planning (see, e.g., [19]) in that one robot initiates the planning of the workflow phase (task decomposition), and it communicates, based on its peer models, with other robots to find suitable members to execute the tasks (task allocation).

7.4   Changing Environment and Three-World Develoment

In Real World, there are innumerable factors that can potentially affect the robots' ability to perform, such as the lighting conditions and cables on the floor. Of course, for our project's purposes, this would not seem a significant issue, as we can perform our tests also in carefully designed, controlled environments. However, this does not remove the fundamental issue of unexpected factors. How would this uncertainty be dealt with within a hypothetical practical environment? One possible approach would be introducing some degree of self-healing (see, e.g. Kounev et al. [11]) properties in the design, both in terms of the robots' performance and the cooperation context. Currently, extensive work on this aspect is beyond the scope of this project, however.

In contrast to the unpredictable Real World, the simulated 3D environments are inherently about control and thus easier to work with. Nevertheless, there can still be considerable effort to set up a simulation the desired way, as seen with the difficulties in deploying multiple robots simultaneously in Gazebo. It also became apparent that multi-robot simulation can involve substantial hardware requirements. Still, we have found the Gazebo 3D simulation fulfills its purpose satisfactorily as a platform where cooperative actions can be developed for Real World (ROS2) robots in a more controlled manner.

However, it could also be noted that while the usage of 3D simulation does simplify some aspects, designing *Actions* for the *Task Runtime* remains an endeavor that relies on detailed knowledge in leveraging a particular robot's inner workings. Contrary to how the primary interests of this project are in the dynamic and creative aspects of robot cooperation, there remains a nontrivial effort necessary in creating the actual units of implementation, *Actions*. For this purpose, ROS2 has been of great help with its high quality open source solutions for features such as robot navigation. Yet conversely, it became apparent that it can be even impractically laborious to implement new *Actions* where the ROS2 support falls short.

8 Conclusions

In this paper, we presented a new software architecture and development approach for diverse multi-robot cooperation. The core ideas of our approach include (a) improving the robot's understanding of its situational context for cooperation by peer modeling, (b) an ontology that enables the robots to understand and share information about the world and (c) three conceptually and operationally different worlds where the development of cooperative behaviour takes place: 2D Block World, 3D Virtual World, and Real World. The peer models enable the robots to take the capabilities and goals of their peers into account in their reasoning, the ontology can be used as a shared basis for communication and forming cooperation plans, and the different worlds serve different development purposes, e.g. testing different components and services, in the overall cooperation development process.

To test the feasibility of our architecture's core, we conducted stress testing in 2D Block World and verified that the ontology-based reasoning and planning is able to find and execute suitable cooperation plans in all the random scenarios encountered. This gives our architecture implementation a stable starting point to improve its other aspects, e.g. situational context awareness through peer modeling, which in turn should result in better suited cooperation plans.

Acknowledgments. The work was supported by the Academy of Finland (project 328729).

References

1. Bayındır, L.: A review of swarm robotics tasks. Neurocomputing **172**, 292–321 (2016)
2. Beetz, M., Civera, J., D'Andrea, R., Elfring, J., Galvez-lopez, D.: RoboEarth: a world wide web for robot. IEEE Trans. Robot. Autom. **6**(14), 69–82 (2011)
3. Beetz, M., Beßler, D., Haidu, A., Pomarlan, M., Bozcuoğlu, A.K., Bartels, G.: Know rob 2.0 - a 2nd generation knowledge processing framework for cognition-enabled robotic agents. In: 2018 IEEE International Conference on Robotics and Automation (ICRA), pp. 512–519 (2018)
4. Berrocal, J., Garcia-Alonso, J., Galán-Jiménez, J., Murillo, J.M., Mäkitalo, N., Mikkonen, T., Canal, C.: Situational context in the programmable world. In: 2017 IEEE SmartWorld, pp. 1–8 (2017)
5. Castelfranchi, C.: Modelling social action for AI agents. Artif. Intell. **103**(1), 157–182 (1998)

6. Chaimowicz, L., Sugar, T., Kumar, V., Campos, M.: An architecture for tightly coupled multi-robot cooperation. In: Proceedings 2001 ICRA. IEEE International Conference on Robotics and Automation (Cat. No.01CH37164). vol. 3, pp. 2992–2997 (2001)
7. Chaimowicz, L., Campos, M., Kumar, V.: Simulating loosely and tightly coupled multi-robot cooperation. In: V Brazilian Symposium on Intelligent Automation. The Electrical Engineering Department of the Federal University of Rio Grande do Sul (2001)
8. Edwardes, A., Burghardt, D., Neun, M.: FIPA Communicative Act Library Specification. Foundation for Intelligent Physical Agents. University of Maine, Oronom, pp. 377–387. John Wiley & Sons (2000)
9. El Zaatari, S., Marei, M., Li, W., Usman, Z.: Cobot programming for collaborative industrial tasks: an overview. Robot. Auton. Syst. **116**, 162–180 (2019)
10. Hart, P.E., Nilsson, N.J., Raphael, B.: A formal basis for the heuristic determination of minimum cost paths. IEEE Trans. Syst. Sci. Cybern. **4**(2), 100–107 (1968)
11. Kounev, S., Kephart, J., Milenkoski, A., Zhu, X.: Self-Aware Computing Systems. Springer, Cham (2017). https://doi.org/10.1007/978-3-319-47474-8
12. Manko, S.V., Diane, S.A.K., Krivoshatskiy, A.E., Margolin, I.D., Slepynina, E.A.: Adaptive control of a multi-robot system for transportation of large-sized objects based on reinforcement learning. In: 2018 IEEE Conference of Russian Young Researchers in Electrical and Electronic Engineering (EIConRus), pp. 923–927 (2018)
13. Mathew, N., Smith, S.L., Waslander, S.L.: Planning paths for package delivery in heterogeneous multirobot teams. IEEE Trans. Autom. Sci. Eng. **12**(4), 1298–1308 (2015)
14. Mäkitalo, N., Linkola, S., Laurinen, T., Männistö, T.: Towards novel and intentional cooperation of diverse autonomous robots: an architectural approach. In: Proceedings of the Context-Aware, Autonomous and Smart Architecture Workshop, pp. 1–10. CEUR Workshop Proceedings (2021)
15. Noy, N.F., McGuinness, D.L.: Ontology Development 101: A Guide to Creating Your First Ontology, Stanford University, Stanford (2001)
16. Olivares-Alarcos, A., et al.: A review and comparison of ontology-based approaches to robot autonomy. Knowl. Eng. Rev. **34** (2019)
17. Rozanski, N., Woods, E.: Software Systems Architecture: Working with Stakeholders Using Viewpoints and Perspectives, 2nd edn. Addison-Wesley, Boston (2012)
18. Thomas, D., Woodall, W., Fernandez, E.: Next-generation ROS: Building on DDS. In: ROSCon Chicago 2014. Open Robotics, Mountain View, CA, September 2014
19. Yan, Z., Jouandeau, N., Cherif, A.A.: A survey and analysis of multi-robot coordination. Int. J. Adv. Robot. Syst. **10**(12), 399 (2013)
20. Zhang, T., Liu, G.: Design of formation control architecture based on leader-following approach. In: 2015 IEEE International Conference on Mechatronics and Automation (ICMA), pp. 893–898 (2015)

A Probabilistic Model for Effective Explainability Based on Personality Traits

Mohammed N. Alharbi[1], Shihong Huang[1(✉)], and David Garlan[2]

[1] Florida Atlantic University, Boca Raton, FL, USA
{malharbi2016,shihong}@fau.edu
[2] Carnegie Mellon University, Pittsburgh, PA, USA
garlan@cs.cmu.edu

Abstract. It is becoming increasingly important for an autonomous system to be able to explain its actions to humans in order to improve trust and enhance human-machine collaboration. However, providing the most appropriate kind of explanations – in terms of length, format and presentation mode of explanations at the proper time – is critical to enhancing their effectiveness. Moreover, since explanation entails costs, such as the time it takes to explain and for humans to comprehend and respond, the actual improvement in human-system tasks from explanations (if any) is not always obvious, particularly given various forms of uncertainty in knowledge about the human. In this paper, we describe an approach to address this issue. The key idea is to provide a structured framework that allows a system to model and reason about *human personality traits* as critical elements to guide proper explanation in human and system collaboration. In particular, we focus on the two concerns of *modality* and *amount* of explanation in order to optimize the explanation experience and improve overall system-human utility. Our models are based on probabilistic modeling and analysis to determine at run time what is the most effective explanation under uncertainty. To demonstrate our approach, we introduce a self-adaptive system called the Stock Prediction Engine (SPE), which allows an automated system and a human to collaborate on stock investments. Our evaluation of this exemplar through simulation demonstrates that a human subject's performance and overall human-system utility is improved when considering the psychology of human personality traits in providing explanations.

Keywords: Explainability · Self-adaptive systems · Human system co-adaptation · Human-computer interaction (HCI) · Personality traits · Human-in-the-loop · Model checking · Probabilistic modelling

1 Introduction

As autonomous and self-adaptive systems provide more and more automated capabilities, it is becoming increasingly important for them to "explain" themselves to humans [1, 2]. Explainability serves four primary purposes in particular: justification, control, improvement, and discovery [2]. These purposes can be defined as follows: (1) In explanation for *justification*: explanations are used to demonstrate certain findings to humans,

© The Author(s), under exclusive license to Springer Nature Switzerland AG 2022
P. Scandurra et al. (Eds.): ECSA Tracks and Workshops 2021, LNCS 13365, pp. 205–225, 2022.
https://doi.org/10.1007/978-3-031-15116-3_10

especially when judgments are made quickly; (2) In explanations for *controlling*: explanations may assist in not only justifying, but also preventing systems from malfunctioning; (3) In explanations for *improvement*: explanations help to constantly improve systems through human interaction; (4) In explanations for *discovery*: explanations help with finding and accumulating new information that aid in our knowledge and learning. Concerning purpose (3) this research focuses on explanations for improvement. In context, explainability is employed to *improve* a system's overall co-adaptation, and it describes the degree to which the actions and solutions of a software system can be comprehended by humans.

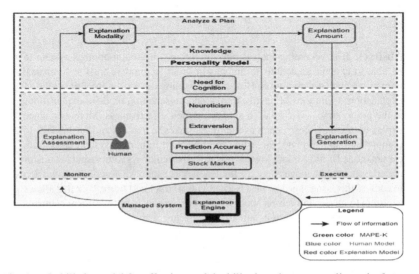

Fig. 1. A probabilistic model for effective explainability based on personality traits framework.

Although explanation is becoming a more desired – and arguably necessary – feature of a semi-autonomous or self-adaptive system, it is not always clear when and how it should be provided. When considering the cost of human attentiveness, system-human interaction delays, and the reality that different individuals may require various types of explanations, an immediate problem arises. The findings of our prior research, published as a short paper in [3] indicated that there is a need to look beyond the duration of explanations (i.e., their amount) and look more closely at detailed questions such as whether the presentation of explanations should be visual, textual, or verbal.

The work presented in this paper represents a significant extension of that prior research. In this extension we incorporate more complex models of human personality traits to enable the system to additionally decide optimal choices for "modality and amount" of explanation.

Our overall framework provides a coordinated set of mechanisms for understanding the right optimal "modalities and amounts" of explanation that a system should give to humans – dependent on their personality traits. Specifically, we adopt a MAPE-K architecture [4]. In Fig. 1, *Knowledge* refers to the information that maintains a model of the managed system (Explanation engine). The three personality traits incorporated in this framework, are Neuroticism, Extraversion, and Need for Cognition (explained in detail later). As critical components of the human model, they serve as a guideline for the system while making decisions regarding the optimal modalities and amounts of explanation. The explanation engine *monitors* the human's personality traits to determine the optimal "modalities and amounts" of explanation. The managed system *analyzes* and *plans* what explanation should be. Within the *execute* stage, we command the managed system to generate an explanation that will be given to humans. Finally, the explanation engine *monitors* the explanation's assessment (through feedback) about human satisfaction for each given explanation.

To assess the accuracy of predictions, projections, and overall approach we use an example man-machine collaborative system called Stock Prediction Engine (SPE), initially developed in [5]. The SPE is a self-adaptive system to predict stock's trend and recommend actions to "Buy" or "Sell". In this context the human and machine collaborate to develop an investment plan that can be quantified by profits and losses.

The organization of the rest of the paper is as follows: Sect. 2 describes the research problem and goals, Sect. 3 represents background information and related work, Sect. 4 shows methodology, Sect. 5 shows the Stochastic Multi-player Games (SMG) model while Sect. 6 shows results and analysis, Sect. 7 presents discussion and future work and the last section focuses on the conclusion.

2 Problem Statement and Research Goals

2.1 Problem Statement

For many systems the activities of system and humans are mutually dependent upon the behavior of each other in completing coherent tasks, human-system collaboration is essential to attain collective objectives [5]. In such "human-in-the-loop" systems, the human must be provided with reasonable explanations in order to optimize the co-adaptation outcomes [6]. The optimization of human-system co-adaptation outcomes refers to the development of a partnership between human and system, or a formation of a cooperative relationship where both the human and system work semi-autonomously as opposed to conventional systems that function in response to human inputs and orders [5], or alternatively, are completely automatic.

The main argument of this research revolves around the fact that systems are more capable of demonstrating adequate explanations when these explanations for a particular human are tailored to that person's personality traits, and as a result, increase the efficiency of the co-adaptation system. In particular, we hypothesize that there is a different impact of "modalities and amounts" of explanations upon different humans. Specifically, the efficacy of collaboration among humans and systems can be enhanced by providing multiple "modalities" of explanations (i.e., graphic, verbal, or textual) and different amounts (i.e., short or long). However, a drawback of such an effort is that it may take humans longer to comprehend and respond to these explanations. As a result, one of the most important problems that a system must answer is what "modalities and amounts" can be utilized for an explanation, and how long should they be given? Moreover, what is the standard procedure of decision-making that could be utilized by the system while answering such questions?

2.2 Research Goals

The objective of this research is to address these prior problems by developing a conceptual framework that analyzes how explanations should be provided by a self-adaptive system depending on the personality traits of a particular human. Based on a formal human model that contains psychologically relevant characteristics of human personality, this framework utilizes probabilistic analysis to reason about how the explanations should be given. We are particularly interested in addressing the following research question:

RQ: How the information of an individual's personality traits is used to improve the overall system's co-adaptation?

Therefore, the prime contribution of this research is: a conceptual framework that includes (models of) personality traits of humans and assists adaptive human-in-the-loop systems in determining which "modality and amount" of explanation should be provided to improve the effectiveness of human-system co-adaptation.

3 Background and Related Work

The current section begins with background details of personality traits as well as summarizing the latest research on human-system co-adaptation and explainability.

3.1 Personality Traits

Personality traits of a human have a significant impact on human behavior, as indicated by psychological studies [7]. Human traits that form personalities are relatively consistent human features that impact behavior. The combination set of qualities and patterns that impact a person's behavior, cognition, motivation, and emotion is often referred to as his or her personality. Humans are motivated to think, feel, and act in certain ways regularly due to certain traits.

Individuals, of course, differ in a variety of ways. But personality traits are among the most important quantitative features that may be used to differentiate one individual from another. The Big Five (also known as the Five-Factor) model of personality is one of the most commonly recognized personality classifications in psychological research. Neuroticism, Extraversion, Agreeableness, Openness to Experience, and Conscientiousness are the five characteristics of personality in the Big Five model [8]. In this research we focus specifically on Neuroticism, Extraversion, and the Need for Cognition.

Neuroticism (or emotional stability) is characterized as "a propensity for worry, despair, self-doubt, and other unpleasant feelings." [8]. Audio listening is positively linked to Neuroticism. Neurotic humans prefer to listen to music (i.e., audio) rather than watch movies (i.e., video) [9]. A visual-verbal learning method is adversely associated with Neuroticism [10].

Extraversion is a personality trait that indicates how spontaneous and sociable a person is. A human with high Extraversion is characterized by excitability, friendliness, talkativeness, aggressiveness, and a high level of emotional expressiveness [8].

Extraversion is linked to movie watching positively (i.e., video) [10]. Extraversion is further linked to a visual-verbal learning methods positively as well [8].

Need for Cognition (NFC) is defined as the "individual's tendency to engage in and enjoy effortful cognitive tasks." People with higher NFC levels typically prefer more detail, while those with low levels of NFC want to quickly understand the big picture and avoid engaging through more detail [11, 12].

A score of 80 or above on the NFC 10-item assessment instrument indicates a high personality characteristic, whereas a score of 50 or lower indicates a low personality trait [8].

In this research, these three basic personality traits (Neuroticism, Extraversion, and Need for Cognition) have been adopted as critical elements of a human model. The utilization of Neuroticism and Extraversion traits assists in guiding the system to determine the appropriate "modalities" of explanation that needs to be given to humans in order to increase overall effectiveness of the system, while the utilization of Need for Cognition from our previous research [3] assists in guiding the system to determine the appropriate "amount" of explanation.

3.2 Human-in-the-Loop Self-adaptation and Explainability

The fields of human-system interaction are being advanced as a result of human-system integration or human-system co-adaptation. The term "integration" refers to a partnership or bilateral interaction between humans and systems in which both the entities work together rather than the system relying upon the inputs and directions by the human for taking an action. In this context, over time the system and the human "co-adapt" to each other. A process in which an integrated system co-adapts its behavior to a human depending on its inner human model, dynamic information obtained about the human, the context of usage, and the environment around it is often referred to as self-adaptation [4–6].

Several studies have examined the notion of explainability from the human-system co-adaptation standpoint. A methodology has been proposed by [13] to produce verbal explanations of multi-objective probabilistic planning. The method aims to demonstrate the reasoning behind the system selecting a specific behavior based on a set of optimization goals. The author's explainability method is based on describing the values of a generated behavior and, as a result, explaining tradeoffs made to balance conflicting goals.

In [14], the authors developed a systematic framework to support reasoning about the explainability of co-adaptive system behaviors and the circumstances in which explanation is justified. The authors classified explainability based on three categories: cost, impact, and content. They propose a dynamic adaptation strategy that uses a probabilistic reasoning mechanism, similar to ours, to identify when we use explanations to improve system utility.

The authors in [15], employ a similar paradigm to [14] to describe the explainability of adaptive system behaviors and the circumstances in which they are justified. Explainability has been characterized by the authors as to how it affects the ability of a human to engage effectively in co-adaptive actions. The authors propose a mechanism for making decisions for the planning of self-adaptation that involves a probabilistic reasoning tool for determining when there is a need to use explanations in adaptation.

In contrast to these approaches, the research described in this paper uses human personality traits as a basis for reasoning about how best to use explanation for specific types of humans as determine by their traits. Although prior studies have utilized a probabilistic reasoning to capture the uncertainties involved in the human model and logic of explanations with regards to human-system co-adaptation, none of these have explored how to incorporate and exploit human traits in those models.

In earlier work we defined a systematic framework [3], for reasoning about the proper "amount" of explanation that should be provided by a system to humans depending on their personality traits. The framework specifically involves two prime personality traits (Need for Cognition and Openness) belonging to a human model, which are critical properties that a system can use as guidance while making decisions regarding the proper "amount" of explanation that needs to be provided to humans in order to improve overall system utility. This framework has relied upon research conducted regarding the psychology of human personality. Specifically, the Opportunity-Willingness-Capability (OWC) model has been used to represent the impact of these human personality traits based on explanations in human-system co-adaptation [16]. The OWC is a model that has been used widely for reasoning about the human-in-the-loop behavior of adaptive systems. In that previous work to illustrate the approach we developed Grid, a virtual game involving human-system interaction [3]. In the current research we use the Stock Market Prediction, a much richer co-adaptive system, as the basis for investigation and validation of the modeling and exploitation of human personality traits.

4   Methodology

The current section illustrates our use of explanation as a technique that is based on human personality traits and is used by our system to improve the overall effectiveness of human-system co-adaptation. Next, we show how a probabilistic planner [17] can use models of personality traits to determine appropriate "modality and modality".

4.1   Selection of Personality Traits

Certain personality traits should be taken into account with respect to explanations. As previously noted, human personality has been defined in the psychological literature through a number of established differentiating characteristics. Not all characteristics, though, are related to explainability. In the current research, three personality characteristics have been utilized (*Neuroticism* and *Extraversion)* because there is a clear link among these characteristics and explanation 'modalities' (in terms of audio and video) [9, 10]. We also adapted *Need for Cognition (NFC)* trait, from our previous research [3], since there is a direct relationship between NFC and explainability amount [18]. The reason for excluding the *Openness* trait from current research is because we do not use the OWC model here where there is a direct relationship between Openness and capability in OWC [16].

In this work we make a number of simplifying assumptions. First, we assume in that the personality traits of humans can be determined through some instrument (for instance, using the NFC 10-item assessment instrument in [11, 12]), and second that do not vary throughout the time horizon of specific interactions with the system. However, it is worth noting that while the traits need to be determined *a priori*, there remains considerable uncertainty concerning the influence of different "modalities and amounts" of explanation that should be provided to the human in a given context. Finally, we will also assume, for the sake of clarity, the relevance of both personality traits and that their weights hold equal importance (although adjustments can be made in their relative importance within the model in a straightforward way).

4.2   Utilizing Model Checking Stochastic Multiplayer Games (SMG)

Probabilistic model checking has been used to evaluate systems that display unpredictable and stochastic behavior. In a multi-agent system, Stochastic Multi-player Games (SMG) is a type of probabilistic modeling that enables us to reason quantitatively about reward-based properties and probability such as time, consumption, and resources [19–21]. SMG models have been used to explain the optimal explanation "modalities" and "amounts" for humans depending on their personality traits, where the humans and system have been modeled as (cooperative) players in a game.

Specifically, we use the probabilistic model checker PRISM-games [17]. PRISM-games is particularly well suited to our research because it enables us to explain quantitatively in the face of volatility and unpredictability as to which "modalities" and "amounts" of explanation should be provided. With regards to the current study, uncertainty is related to the appropriate explanation "modalities" and "amounts" and the effect of different explanation forms to be provided to humans.

The SPE system (described in Sect. 4.3 below) has been modeled as a turn-based SMG, which implies that in each state of the represented system, precisely one player can pick an action with a probabilistic outcome. In an SMG, players can work together to achieve a shared objective or compete to accomplish distinct goals. We simulate three players (the system, the human, and the surrounding environment) in our examples while assuming that a common objective is shared by them (namely, optimizing system utility).

4.3   Stock Prediction Engine (SPE) System

As a proof-of-concept, we developed the Stock Prediction Engine (SPE) as a co-adaptive system for stock prediction. SPE is fed with stock data and personality traits (*Neuroticism, Extraversion*, and *Need for Cognition*) to dynamically determine if a human would likely or not enhance stock market decisions.

The SPE involves the use of different *tactics*[1], as shown in Table 1 and Fig. 2, for interacting with humans. The SPE predicts the direction of a given stock for the next trading day, i.e., whether its price will go *up* or *down* (SPE_Predict tactic). Based on the prediction, a decision to *buy* or *sell* that asset is presented to the human through

---

[1] *strategy* is the action plan that takes you where you want to go, the *tactics* are the individual steps and actions that will get you there.

Table 1. The SPE tactics

Tactic	Role
SPE_Predict	The system decides for a given stock
LessAudioExp	Gives less amount (shorter) of an audio explanation
MoreAudioExp	Gives more amount of an audio explanation
LessVideoExp	Gives less amount (shorter) of a video explanation
MoreVideoExp	Gives more amount of a video explanation
Buy	The system creates an order to *buy*
Sell	The system creates an order to *sell*
Human_Predict	The human makes a decision for a given stock
assessExp	Human feedback is collected about satisfaction for each given explanation (*satisfy* or *dissatisfy*)

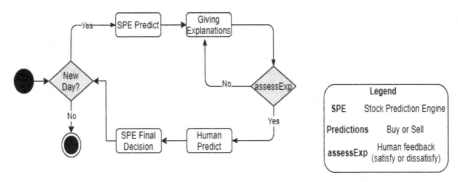

Fig. 2. The SPE tactics

the use of the proper "modality and amount" of explanation (**LessAudioExp, More-AudioExp, LessVideoExp,** and **MoreVideoExp** tactics), which is based on human personality traits. After an explanation is presented, an explanation assessment is performed based on human feedback (**assessExp** tactic). The human then gives his decision/recommendation to either *buy* or *sell* that stock based on the given information (**Human_Predict** tactic). Lastly, the SPE makes a final decision based on its initial prediction and the human's decision to evaluate the value of its decision.

Figure 3 shows the trading *strategy* we used to model our SMG. The final decision of the SPE for stock prediction mainly depends on the prediction accuracy of the system and the human (explained in Sect. 4.3). The SPE will exclude the human (from the human-in-the-loop) if the human prediction accuracy is less than the SPE, in case they have conflicting predictions. Otherwise, the SPE will include the human if the human prediction accuracy is equal to or greater than the SPE. The SPE needs to compare its prediction accuracy (80%) with the human in case they have opposing decisions.

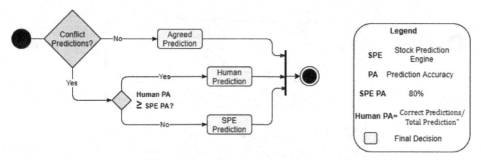

Fig. 3. Trading strategy

The human prediction accuracy is determined through the *Prediction accuracy* utility (explained in the following subsection).

Figure 4 shows the explainability strategy we used to model the SMG. The proper "modality and amount" of explanation are determined based on three personality traits of the human (*High Neuroticism, High Extraversion,* and *High in Need for Cognition*). First, the proper modality (audio or video) is determined based on Neuroticism and Extraversion traits. Then, the amount of explanation (more or less) is determined based on the Need for Cognition.

First step: determining the modality of explanation:

- An audio explanation is given to humans with high Neuroticism.
- A video explanation is given for humans with high Extraversion. These two modalities are determined based on research in the psychology of human personality explained in Sect. 3.1.
- The SPE gives an audio explanation for humans with High in both Neuroticism and Extraversion traits since processing audio data needs less storage and data processing than video data [22].

Second step: determining the amount of explanation:

- Less amount (shorter) of explanation (lExp) will be given to humans with a low Need for Cognition.
- More amount of explanation (mExp) will be given to humans with a high Need for Cognition.

If the human is dissatisfied with the given explanation (through assessExp tactic), the SPE will further explain through the other "modality and amount" of explanation (i.e., the SPE gives MoreAudioExp instead of LessAudioExp, MoreVideoExp instead of LessVideoExp, MoreVideoExp instead of MoreAudioExp, and MoreAudioExp instead of MoreVideoExp). An example of one of the explanations using more amount is an audio or video clip containing, "Based on the given information, the analyst expects the price of the asset to rise in the future and strongly recommends investors to increase your holdings of the asset and buy".

Utility Attributes:

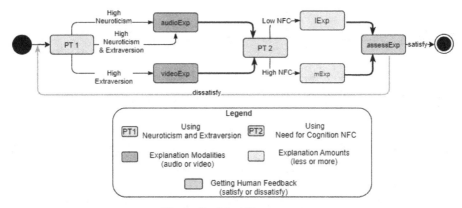

Fig. 4. Explainability strategy

The three utility attributes of the SPE system are:

- Time consumption: the number of explanations given.
- Explanation assessment: human satisfaction feedback for each given explanation (through **assessExp** tactic).
- Prediction accuracy: the rate of correct decisions from the human and SPE.

Utility Function for Prediction Accuracy:

To compare different explainability tactics, we used probabilistic temporal logic with rewards, rPATL, which enabled us to analyze the utilities of the system that explainability can influence. rPATL is used to reason about the ability of a group of players (system, human, and environment) to collectively achieve a specific goal [23].

In the formal model, we define a formula that represents the accrued utility (i.e., prediction accuracy) as the maximum real immediate utility that the human and SPE can achieve along with the whole task.

In the formal model, we defined a formula that represents the accrued utility (i.e., prediction accuracy) as the maximum real immediate utility that the human and SPE can achieve throughout the whole task. The prediction accuracy function, as shown in function (1), maps high utility derived by dividing the number of correct predictions made (*CorrectPredictions*) by the total number of predictions (*TotalPrediction*):

$$Prediction\_Accuracy = CorrectPredictions/TotalPrediction \qquad (1)$$

5   The Stochastic Multi-player Games (SMG) Model

The SMG has been designed with three players where all the players are attempting to maximize cumulative reward(s) in a collaborative manner: (1) The Stock Prediction Engine (**SPE**) system is represented by Player SPE, which outlines the activities that are controlled by the system. (2) The human's activities are specified by the player **HUMAN**. (3) The **ENVIRONMENT** player keeps track of time. The models depict the behavior of a group of agents (or "players") who take turns making trading decisions (of buying or selling); the decision choice is determined stochastically or non-deterministically. An optimal strategy has been determined for the players by a game solver (such as PRISM-games [17]) for such a system through resolving non-deterministic transitions in a way that the expected reward for every player is maximized.

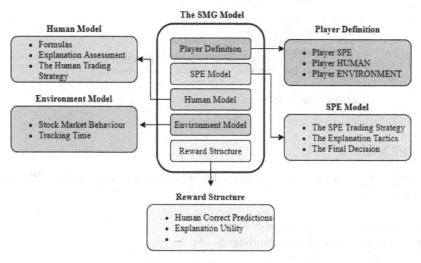

Fig. 5. SMG model contents

The Stochastic Multi-player Games (SMG) model[2] consists of the following five parts, as shown in Fig. 5:

5.1 Player Definition

Player definition includes the declaration of the three players in the SMG and different modules that each player has control of. The three players in our game are shown in Listing 1. Player **SPE** (lines 1–7) specifies the actions that are controlled by the system. For example, the "FinalDecision" module (line 5) can only be controlled by the SPE. Player **HUMAN** (lines 8–11) specifies the actions belonging to the human. Player **ENVIRONMENT** keeps track of time (lines 12–14). The SMG is played in turns by the three players **SPE, HUMAN,** and **ENVIRONMENT** (lines 15–16). Tactics are executed sequentially in our model.

---

[2] A module in PRISM contains two parts: its variables and its commands [20]. The *variables* describe the possible states that the module can be in. The *commands* describe its behavior (i.e., the way in which the state changes over time). The false means this tactic/action is not in use and the reverse is true. The global keyword defines the variables that can be read by all modules. The const keyword expresses values that cannot be altered.

```
1.    player SPE
2.      [SPEPredict], [Explain],
3.      [LessAudioExp], [MoreAudioExp],
4.      [LessVideoExp],[ MoreVideoExp],
5.      [FinalDecision],
6.    …
7.    endplayer
8.    player HUMAN
9.      [AssessExplanation], [HumanPredict],
10.   …
11.   endplayer
12.   player ENVIRONMENT
13.     [NewDay], [DayStart], [DayEnd], …
14.   Endplayer
15.   global turn:[ENVIRONMENT..HUMAN] init ENVIRONMENT;
16.   const ENVIRONMENT=1; const SPE=2; const HUMAN=3;
17.   …
```

Listing 1. Player definition

5.2 SPE Model

Player SPE has control of the system model, illustrated in Listing 2. The SPE model consists of three parts:

- The SPE trading strategy (lines 2–7).
- The different explanation tactics (lines 9–16).
- The final decision (lines 18–26).

During the system's turn, the system executes these tactics/actions sequentially. For the sake of clarity, we will describe one tactic from the three parts to illustrate how tactic execution is modeled. The other tactics follow the same structure.

The SPE trading strategy (SPEPredict): the system predicts to *buy* or *sell* based on the stock performance (lines 2–4). This tactic executes only if:

- It is the turn of the SPE (turn=SPE).
- The stock market is going up (StockUp=true).

If the guard is satisfied:

- The system prediction will recommend buying (SPE_Predict'=Buy) with a probability of 80% (SPE_Accuracy) (line 3).
- Or the system prediction will recommend selling (SPE_Predict'=Sell) with a probability of 20% (1-SPE_Accuracy) (line 4).

The explanation tactic (Explain): the system gives an appropriate explanation to the human depending on the human trait through executing the command labeled as Explain (lines 9–10). This tactic executes only if:

- It is the turn of the SPE (turn=SPE).
- The human Neuroticism trait is high (Human_Neurot>=80).

- The other two traits are not high ((Human_Extrav<80)&(Human_NFC<80)).

If the guard is satisfied, the system will give a shorter *audio* explanation about the stock market performance by flagging LessAudioExp tactic true with probability 1, and updating the value of the variable turn, changing control to the human player (turn'=HUMAN) (line 10).

```
1.  module SPE
2.    [SPEPredict] (turn=SPE)&(StockUp=true)& …->
3.        SPE_Accuracy: (SPE_Predict'=Buy) &…
4.        + (1-SPE_Accuracy):(SPE_Predict'=Sell) &…
5.    [SPEPredict] (turn=SPE) & (StockDown=true) & …->
6.        SPE_Accuracy: (SPE_Predict'=Sell)& …
7.        + (1-SPE_Accuracy): (SPE_Predict'=Buy) &…
8.    …
9.    [Explain] (turn=SPE) &(Human_Neurot>=80)& (Human_Extrav<80)&(Human_NFC<80)&…->
10.       (LessAudioExp'= true) & (turn'=Human);
11.   [Explain] (turn=SPE) &(Human_Neurot>=80)& (Human_Extrav<80)&(Human_NFC>=80)&…->
12.       (MoreAudioExp'= true) & (turn'=Human);
13.   [Explain] (turn=SPE) &(Human_Extrav>=80)& (Human_Neurot<80)&(Human_NFC<80)&…->
14.       (LessVideoExp'= true) & (turn'=Human);
15.   [Explain] (turn=SPE) &(Human_Extrav>=80)&(Human_Neurot<80)&(Human_NFC>=80)&…->
16.       (MoreVideoExp'= true) & (turn'=Human);
17.   …
18.   [FinalDecision] (turn=SPE) &(SPE_Predict=Human_Predict)&…->
19.       (agree'=true) & (Final_Decision'=SPE_Predict) &
20.       (Decider'= BothDecide) & (turn'=ENVIRONMENT) & …
21.   [FinalDecision] (turn=SPE) & (Human_Accuracy<SPE_Accuracy)&…->
22.       (Final_Decision'=SPE_Predict) &
23.       (Decider'=SPEDecides)&(turn'=ENVIRONMENT) &…;
24.   [FinalDecision] (turn=SPE) & (Human_Accuracy>=SPE_Accuracy)&…->
25.       (Final_Decision'=Human_Predict) &
26.       (Decider'=HumanDecides) &(turn'=ENVIRONMENT) & …;
27.   …
28. endmodule
```

Listing 2. SPE model

The final decision (FinalDecision): the system finally decides which prediction to go with (the SPE or human prediction) based on the prediction accuracy and whether both of them have agreed on predictions (lines 18–26):

- The SPE and the human decision are chosen if they both agree (lines 18–20).
- The SPE decision is chosen if the human accuracy is less than the SPE (Human_Accuracy<SPE_Accuracy) (lines 21–23).
- The human decision is chosen if his accuracy is greater or equal to the SPE (Human_Accuracy>=SPE_Accuracy) (lines 24–26).

5.3 Human Model

Player HUMAN is illustrated in Listing 3. The encodings of the HUMAN module are similar to those of the SPE module. The HUMAN model consists of three parts:

- The formulas we use to calculate the prediction accuracy (lines 1–2).

- The explanation assessment tactics (lines 5–7).
- The human trading strategy (lines 9–14).

```
1.   formula Update_Human_Accuracy = HumanCorrectPredictions/Prediction_Counter;
2.   formula Remain_Update_Human_Accuracy = 1- Update_Human_Accuracy;
3.   …
4.   module HUMAN
5.   [AssessExplanation] (turn=HUMAN) & …->
6.       0.5:(Satisfy'=true)&(turn'=HUMAN)&…
7.       + 0.5:(Satisfy'=false)&(turn'=SPE)&…;
8.   …
9.   [HumanPredict] (turn=HUMAN) & (StockUp=true)&…->
10.    Update_Human_Accuracy: (Human_Predict'=Buy)
11.    + Remain_Update_Human_Accuracy: (Human_Predict'=Sell);
12.  [HumanPredict] (turn=HUMAN) (StockDown=true)&…->
13.    Update_Human_Accuracy: (Human_Predict'= Sell)
14.    + Remain_Update_Human_Accuracy: (Human_Predict'=Buy);
15.  …
16.  endmodule
17.  …
```

Listing 3. Human model

During the human's turn, the human can execute one of these tactics sequentially. We will describe one tactic from each part to illustrate how tactic execution is modeled.

The explanation assessment tactic (**AssessExplanation**): human feedback is collected about his satisfaction for each given explanation (lines 5–7):

- Fifty percent of the time the human will be *satisfied* with the given explanation (0.5:(Satisfy'=true)) (line 6).
- Fifty percent of the time the human will be *dissatisfied* with the given explanation (+0.5:(Satisfy'=false)) (line 7).

The Human trading strategy (**HumanPredict**) (lines 9–11): the Human predicts to *buy* or *sell*. This tactic executes only if (line 9):

- It is the turn of the Human (turn=HUMAN).
- The stock market is going up (StockUp=true).

If the guard is satisfied:

- The human will decide to *buy* (Human_Predict'=Buy) with probability (Update_Human_Accuracy) (line 10).
- Or the human prediction will be *selling* (Human_Predict'=Sell) with probability (1-Remain_Update_Human_Accuracy) (line 11).

5.4 Environment Model

Player Environment, illustrated in Listing 4, Keeps track of the time.

- Lines 5–7: check the behavior of the stock market:

  – Fifty percent of the time the stock market will go up (0.5: (StockUp'=true)), and the correct prediction to be buying (Correct_Prediction'=Buy) (line 6).
  – Fifty percent of the time the stock market will go down (+0.5: (StockUp'=false)), and the correct prediction to be selling (Correct_Prediction'=Sell) (line 7).

Lines 8–11: "Is it the end of the simulations?" If the guard is not satisfied (meaning that Days < AllPredictions) (line 8), then, switch to a new day (line 9). If the guard is satisfied (meaning that Days > = AllPredictions) (line 10), then, ends the simulation by flagging (step'=PredictionsEnd) (line 9).

```
1.    Days: [0..AllPredictions] init 0;
2.    predictions: [0..AllPredictions] init 1;
3.    ...
4.    module ENVIRONMENT
5.    [DayStart] (turn=ENVIRONMENT)& ...->
6.       0.5: (StockUp'= true) & (Correct_Prediction'=Buy) & (turn'=SPE) & ...
7.       + 0.5: (StockDown'= true) &(Correct_Prediction'=Sell) & (turn'=SPE) & ...;
8.    [DayEnd] (turn=ENVIRONMENT) & (Days < AllPredictions)&...->
9.         (step'= NewDay);
10.   [DayEnd] (turn=ENVIRONMENT) & (Days >= AllPredictions)&...->
11.       step'= PredictionsEnd);
12.   ...
13. endmodule
```

Listing 4. Environment model

5.5 Reward Structure

A probabilistic model developed in PRISM can be augmented with *costs or rewards,* which are real values associated with states or transitions of the model [23]. Listing 5, shows some of the rewards structures. For the sake of clarity, we will describe two rewards and their properties to illustrate how are modeled. The other rewards follow the same structure:

- "Human Correct Predictions" reward (Lines 1–3): adds 1 as a reward for each time the human made a correct prediction by the end of the day. PRISM can help us to ask a variety of questions such as: What is the expected number of correct predictions within a certain period of time (500 predictions)? (Related reward lines 1–3, and property line 18),
- "Explanation Utility" reward (Lines 4–9): adds 1 as a reward for each time the SPE explains. We can ask PRISM the following question "what is the expected number of given explanations within a certain period of time (500 predictions)? (Related reward lines 4–9, and property line 19).

```
1    rewards "Human_Correct_Predictions"
2      [DayEnd] (Human_Predict=Correct_Prediction):1;
3    endrewards
4    rewards "Explanation_Utility"
5      [LessAudioExp] true:1;
6      [MoreAudioExp] true:1;
7      [LessVideoExp] true:1;
8      [MoreVideoExp] true:1;
9    endrewards
10   rewards "Satisfy_Utility"
11     [DayEnd] (Satisfy=true):1;
12   endrewards
13   rewards "Human_Helps_SPE"
14     [DayEnd] (Final_Decision=Human_Predict) & (Human_Predict=Correct_Prediction) &
       (Human_Predict!=SPE_Predict): 1;
15   Endrewards
16   ...
17   label "PredictionsDone" = Predictions=500;
```

```
18.  R{"Human_Correct_Predictions"}=? [ F "PredictionsDone"]
19.  R{"Explanation_Utility"}=? [ F "PredictionsDone"]
20.  R{"Satisfy_Utility"}=? [ F "PredictionsDone"]
21.  R{"Human_Helps_SPE"}=? [ F "PredictionsDone"]
22.  ...
```

Listing 5. Rewards structure

6 Results and Analysis

Our results and analysis that are illustrated in this section demonstrate how adaptive systems can provide appropriate explanations to humans based on personality traits. We compare the outcome of different utilities of explainability (that are described in Sect. 4.3) through our SMG models to determine the best "modality and amount" of explanation for the proper personality trait types. Our modeling is done as a simulation (or set of "experiments" in PRISM terms). We ask PRISM a variety of questions through rPATL, such as "what is the expected number of correct predictions within a certain period of time (500 predictions)?".

Figure 6 shows the results of 500 simulations (i.e., predictions) run on PRISM for the three human groups: High Neuroticism (Plot a), High Need for Cognition (Plot b), and High Extraversion (Plot c). We use three different utilities, including correct human predictions (left graphs), satisfaction rate (middle graphs), and explanations utility (right graphs) (see Sect. 4.3). We compare the three utilities with consideration of personality traits when the SPE gives explanations based on research conducted regarding the psychology of human personality (in blue) (see Sect. 3.1). On the other hand, we observe the outcome of the three utilities without considering personality traits when the SPE gives explanations randomly (in gray). The percentage represents the rate of the 500 predictions conducted on PRISM for each utility.

Table 2 summarizes the results of 500 simulations run on PRISM. As shown in Fig. 6 and Table 2, the number of correct predictions of the human subjects was better when we gave explanations based on the personality traits (72–73% out of 500 predictions; versus 70–71% without considering the personality traits). The average satisfaction rate was

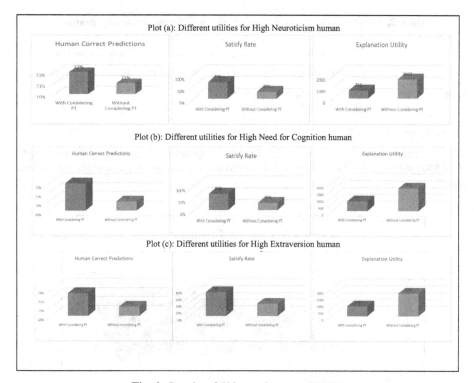

Fig. 6. Results of 500 rounds run on PRISM

much better when we gave explanations based on personality traits (satisfied with 68–70% of the given explanations; versus satisfied with 30–36% of the given explanations without considering the personality traits). Moreover, the explanation utility (i.e., the amount of given explanations) was preferable when we considered the human personality traits (711–714 versus 1663–1670 when we gave explanations randomly). Furthermore, the human subjects who were high in Neuroticism and NFC had the best outcome of the correct predictions and explanation utility. For satisfaction rate, humans high in Neuroticism and Extraversion had better results than NFC human subjects. It can be seen therefore that the overall performance of all human subject groups was improved when we employed the psychology of human personality in our study.

Figure 7 shows the final cumulative SPE correct predictions for the final decisions based on the accuracy of both the human subjects (horizontal axis) and the SPE (z-axis). The highest cumulative reward 300–500 (represents the final cumulative SPE correct predictions; represented in gray) happened when the humans subjects have accuracy greater than 70.

Table 2. Comparing utility performance among different personality groups*

	Correct predictions		Satisfaction rate		Explanation utility	
	With PT	Without PT	With PT	Without PT	With PT	Without PT
High neuroticism	72%	**71%**	**70%**	30%	**711**	**1663**
High NFC	72%	70%	68%	30%	**711**	1666
High extraversion	**73%**	70%	**70%**	**36%**	714	1670

*PT is an abbreviation for personality traits. The percentage means the number of achieved utility out of 500 predictions in total. Bold numbers refer to the best performance among the three human groups.

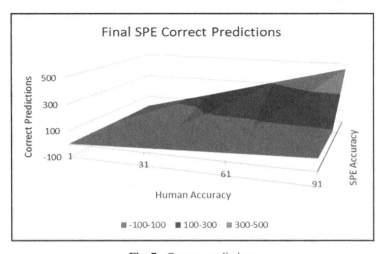

Fig. 7. Correct predictions

7   Discussion and Future Work

In this paper we have presented a probabilistic model checking approach using SMGs to determine which "modality and amount" of explanations should be provided to human subjects based on their personality traits. For the optimization and improvement of human-system co-adaptation throughout their interaction, it is critical to match the right human subjects with the right explanation "modality and amount". This research went beyond the *amount* of explanations (from our previous research [3]), and examined in more detail the *modality* of explanations based on three personality traits (Neuroticism, Extraversion, and Need for Cognition). In this research, we utilized three relative personality traits instead of only two in our previous research [3].

There are some limitations to this research that can be addressed in future research based on the foundations provided here. These choices of explanation are ideal possibilities that have yet to be proven in reality through direct human-subject testing. The most critical next step in addressing this is to perform empirical research to test these models on practical cases with humans-in-the loop.

Explainability serves four primary purposes: justification, control, improvement, and discovery (see Sect. 1). This research focuses on explanations for *improving* a system's overall utility. For future work, explainability can be used also to *justify* some of the information provided to humans. Justifying some information improves the overall co-adaptation between the human and the system, and therefore, increases the human's capability. In addition, *controlling* and *preventing* systems from going wrong is another area of potential future work. *Discovering*, the last primary purpose of explainability, is a gathering of new facts that help us learn and gain knowledge.

A natural extension of this study is the development of more sophisticated models that allow the system to decide the optimum contents for the explanation. The contents would be examined in a more nuanced manner through the consideration of additional personality traits.

8 Conclusion

This research presents a formal framework that incorporates three human personality traits (Neuroticism, Extraversion, and Need for Cognition) as one of the important elements in guiding automated decision-making about the proper "modalities and amounts" of explanation that should be provided to the human subjects to improve the overall co-adaptation utility.

As we have elaborated, our focus is on answering the following research question: How can the information of an individual's personality traits be used to improve the overall human-machine system's behavior? The indicators provided through these results allows us to answer the research question through improving the overall system utility (represented through the different utility attributes explained in Sect. 4.3).

To carry out our objective of this research, the Stock Prediction Engine (SPE) was adopted to illustrate our approach in order to illustrate typical scenarios for human-system co-adaptation, and to demonstrate through simulation how human personality traits can be used as a factor to consider for systems in providing appropriate explanations. As future work, we plan to conduct an empirical study to validate these models on real-world systems with actual humans in the loop. A further extension of this research will be the development of more sophisticated models by considering other related personality traits and other uses of explanation.

References

1. Vilone, G., Longo, L.: Explainable Artificial Intelligence: a Systematic Review. arXiv preprint arXiv:2006.00093 (2020)
2. Adadi, A., Berrada, M.: Peeking inside the black-box: a survey on explainable artificial intelligence (XAI). IEEE Access **6**, 52138–52160 (2018)
3. Alharbi, M.N., Huang, S., Garlan, D.: A probabilistic model for personality trait focused explainability. In: Proceedings of the 4th International Workshop on Context-aware, Autonomous and Smart Architecture, co-located with the 15th European Conference on Software Architecture (2021)
4. Kephart, J.O., Chess, D.M.: The vision of autonomic computing. Computer **36**(1), 41–50 (2003)

5. Lloyd, E., Huang, S., Tognoli, E.: Improving human-in-the-loop adaptive systems using brain-computer interaction. In: Proceedings - 2017 IEEE/ACM 12th International Symposium on Software Engineering for Adaptive and Self-Managing Systems, SEAMS 2017, pp. 163–174 (2017)

6. Alharbi, M., Huang, S.: A survey of incorporating affective computing for human-system co-adaptation. In: Proceedings of the 2020 the 2nd World Symposium on Software Engineering, pp. 72–79 (2020)

7. Jung, C.G.H.: Psychological factors determining human behaviour. Collected Works of C.G. Jung, Volume 8: Structure & Dynamics of the Psyche, pp. 114–126 (2015)

8. de Raad, B., Perugini, M.: Big Five factor assessment: Introduction. Big Five Assess, no. January 2002, pp. 1–27 (2002)

9. Hall, A.: Audience personality and the selection of media and media genres. Media Psychol. **7**(4), 377–398 (2005)

10. Arockiam, L., Selvaraj, J.C.: User interface design for effective e-learning based on personality traits. Int. J. Comput. Appl. **61**(14), 28–32 (2013)

11. Sadowski, C.J., Cogburn, H.E.: Need for cognition in the big-five factor structure. J. Psychol. **131**(3), 307–312 (1997)

12. Petty, R.E., Cacioppo, J.T., Petty, R.E., Feinstein, J.A., Jarvis, W.B.G.: Dispositional differences in cognitive motivation: the life and times of individuals varying in need for cognition dispositional differences in cognitive motivation: the life and times of individuals varying in need for cognition. Psychol. Bull. **119**, 197–253 (2015)

13. Sukkerd, R., Simmons, R., Garlan, D.: Towards explainable multi-objective probabilistic planning. In: Proceedings of International Conference on Software Engineering, pp. 19–25 (2018)

14. Li, N., Adepu, S., Kang, E., Garlan, D.: Explanations for human-on-the-loop: a probabilistic model checking approach. In: Proceedings - 2020 IEEE/ACM 15th International Symposium on Software Engineering for Adaptive and Self-Managing Systems, SEAMS 2020, pp. 181–187 (2020)

15. Li, N., Cámara, J., Garlan, D., Schmerl, B.: Reasoning about when to provide explanation for human-in-the-loop self-adaptive systems. In: Proceedings of the 2020 IEEE Conference on Autonomic Computing and Self-organizing Systems (ACSOS), Washington, DC, pp. 19–23 (2020)

16. Eskins, D., Sanders, W.H.: The multiple-asymmetric-utility system model: a framework for modeling cyber-human systems. In: Proceedings 2011 8th International Conference on Quantitative Evaluation of Systems, QEST 2011, pp. 233–242 (2011)

17. Kwiatkowska, M., Norman, G., Parker, D., Santos, G.: PRISM-games 3.0: stochastic game verification with concurrency, equilibria and time. In: Lahiri, S.K., Wang, C. (eds.) CAV 2020. LNCS, vol. 12225, pp. 475–487. Springer, Cham (2020). https://doi.org/10.1007/978-3-030-53291-8_25

18. McCrae, R.R.: Openness to experience as a basic dimension of personality. Imagin. Cogn. Pers. **13**(1), 39–55 (1993)

19. Kwiatkowska, M., Norman, G., Parker, D.: Probabilistic model checking: advances and applications. In: Drechsler, R. (ed.) Formal System Verification, pp. 73–121. Springer, Cham (2018). https://doi.org/10.1007/978-3-319-57685-5_3

20. Baier, C.: Probabilistic model checking. Dependable Softw. Syst. Eng. **45**, 1–23 (2016)

21. Cheng, S.W., Garlan, D.: Stitch: a language for architecture-based self-adaptation. J. Syst. Softw. **85**(12), 2860–2875 (2012)

22. Sivarajah, U., Kamal, M.M., Irani, Z., Weerakkody, V.: Critical analysis of big data challenges and analytical methods. J. Bus. Res. **70**, 263–286 (2017)
23. Kwiatkowska, M., Norman, G., Parker, D.: PRISM 4.0: verification of probabilistic real-time systems. In: Gopalakrishnan, G., Qadeer, S. (eds.) CAV 2011. LNCS, vol. 6806, pp. 585–591. Springer, Heidelberg (2011). https://doi.org/10.1007/978-3-642-22110-1_47

5th International Workshop on Formal Approaches for Advanced Computing Systems (FAACS)

Interactive Elicitation of Resilience Scenarios Based on Hazard Analysis Techniques

Sebastian Frank[1,2]([⊠]), Alireza Hakamian[2], Lion Wagner[2], Dominik Kesim[2], Christoph Zorn[2], Jóakim von Kistowski[3], and André van Hoorn[1]

[1] Department of Informatics, University of Hamburg, Hamburg, Germany
{sebastian.frank,andre.van.hoorn}@uni-hamburg.de
[2] Institute of Software Engineering, University of Stuttgart, Stuttgart, Germany
[3] DATEV eG, Nürnberg, Germany

Abstract. *Context.* Microservice-based architectures are expected to be resilient. *Problem.* In practice, the elicitation of resilience requirements and the quantitative evaluation of whether the system meets these requirements is not systematic or not even conducted. *Objective.* We explore (1) the usage of the scenario-based Architecture Trade-Off Analysis Method (ATAM) and established hazard analysis techniques, i.e., Fault Trees and Control Hazard and Operability Study (CHAZOP), for interactive resilience requirement elicitation and (2) resilience testing through chaos experiments for architecture assessment and improvement. *Method.* In an industrial setting, we design a structured ATAM-based workshop, including the system's stakeholders, to elicit resilience requirements. To complement the workshop, we develop RESIRIO—a semi-automated, chatbot-assisted, and CHAZOP-based approach—for elicitation. We evaluate RESIRIO through a user study. The requirements from both sources are specified using the ATAM scenario template. We use and extend Chaos Toolkit to transform and automate two scenarios. We quantitatively evaluate these scenarios and suggest resilience improvements based on resilience patterns. *Result.* We identify 12 resilience scenarios in the workshop. We share lessons learned from the study. In particular, our work provides evidence that an ATAM-based workshop is intuitive to stakeholders in an industrial setting and that stakeholders can quickly learn to use RESIRIO in order to successfully obtain new scenarios. *Conclusion.* Our approach helps requirements and quality engineers in interactive resilience requirements elicitation.

Keywords: Interactive elicitation · Requirements engineering · Resilience · Hazard analysis

1 Introduction

Context and Problem. An intrinsic quality property of the microservices architectural style is resilience, i.e., the system meets performance and other Quality

© The Author(s), under exclusive license to Springer Nature Switzerland AG 2022
P. Scandurra et al. (Eds.): ECSA Tracks and Workshops 2021, LNCS 13365, pp. 229–253, 2022.
https://doi.org/10.1007/978-3-031-15116-3_11

of Service (QoS) requirements despite different failure modes or workload variations [21]. However, real-world postmortems [13] often show that systems suffer either unacceptable QoS degradation or recovery time. It is necessary to assure system resilience in the context of microservice-based architectures. The first step is to elicit resilience requirements, which is the focus of this paper.

Practitioners who use Chaos Engineering [2,18], including tools such as Chaos Toolkit (CTK) [8] for resilience testing, require to (1) think about hazards [17] as causes of QoS degradation, (2) set up chaos experiments by specifying failure mode types and hypotheses of expected quality behavior, and (3) execute each experiment to detect deviations from the hypotheses. This approach lacks the systematic identification of causes of a hazard through hazard analysis methods.

Objective. We contributed to this problem in our previous work [15], which serves as a foundation for this paper, but lacks a systematic process for elicitation and specification. In the context of an industrial system, we now integrate hazard analysis techniques [17], i.e., Fault Tree and Control Hazard and Operability Study [10] into more systematic, interactive requirement elicitation processes and use scenarios as a more formal description of requirements. Scenarios enable resilience testing through resilience experiments (aka chaos experiments) for architecture assessment and improvement. Therefore, our research question is: *How to leverage hazard analysis techniques to interactively elicit resilience scenarios, which can be utilized to evaluate resilience through resilience experiments and suggest architectural improvements quantitatively?*

Research Overview. To answer our research question, we devise a method consisting of three main activities (as illustrated in Fig. 1). Our main contributions lie in interactive resilience requirements elicitation, where we propose an ATAM-based workshop and chatbot-assisted tooling for elicitation purposes. The outcome of the elicitation activity is a set of structured scenarios that are the basis for requirements assessment and architecture design improvement.

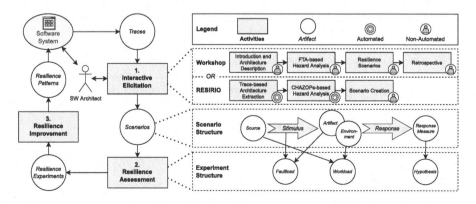

Fig. 1. Overview of this work and its contributions

Main Contribution 1: *Workshop-based Elicitation.* The Architecture Trade-Off Analysis Method scenario template [3] is a mechanism for eliciting quality requirements and consists of the following elements: (1) source, (2) stimuli, (3) artifact(s), (4) system's environment, (5) its response, and (6) response measure. ATAM has already been used in practice to elicit and specify quality requirements other than resilience, e.g., availability, performance, and maintainability. Thus, we hypothesize that ATAM can be adopted for effectively eliciting resilience requirements and evaluating them through chaos experiments. Therefore, we use the ATAM scenario template to describe resilience requirements in semi-structured textual language. The aim of the ATAM method is to assess architectural design decisions to find trade-offs between quality requirements and identify risks early. Therefore, (1) eliciting precise statements over quality requirements, (2) eliciting precise statements over architectural design decisions, and (3) evaluating whether the architectural design decisions satisfy the quality requirements are major goals in ATAM. In this paper, we do not perform a trade-off analysis, but use an ATAM-based workshop to elicit and specify resilience requirements by involving system stakeholders. Our structured workshop also comprises a hazard analysis based on the Fault Tree Analysis (FTA) [17].

Main Contribution 2: *Chatbot-Based Elicitation.* Traditional elicitation techniques, such as interviews or our workshop, impose a high amount of time on participants, require locations to meet, and the presence of expert analysts. Therefore, as also outlined by various researchers, e.g., Rietz [26], there is a strong need for novel elicitation approaches. We designed an interactive elicitation technique called RESIRIO that utilizes a combination of a chatbot and an architecture visualization. First, RESIRIO extracts the system's architecture and applies a CHAZOP-like method to identify hazards from Jaeger and Zipkin traces. Then, the chatbot assists the engineer in the scenario specification. To evaluate RESIRIO's usability and effectiveness, we conduct an expert user study.

Results. The workshop's result is a set of 12 resilience scenarios. We use CTK to transform two scenarios into experiments, and conduct a measurement-based resilience evaluation. The evaluation results suggest that the architecture does not take temporary failures when services communicate with each other into account. Resilience patterns [1] describe architectural changes to enable applications to handle failures gracefully and recover from them. We improve system resilience by applying the *retry* pattern [21,22]. We validate the improvement by re-executing the respective scenario. Furthermore, our user study gives evidence that RESIRIO helps novice requirements engineers in fast requirements elicitation, but has limitations in specifying various and precise scenarios. Regarding the chatbot, engineers preferred the fast input of Quick Replies over writing text.

Summary of Further Contributions. In addition to the interactive elicitation techniques, the paper makes the following contributions:

– Automating scenario execution using CTK for measurement-based evaluation.

- We share lessons learned that benefit both practitioners and researchers regarding resilience requirement elicitation, evaluation, and improvement.
- Artifacts—including scenarios, resilience experiments, and results of the experimentation—are available online [27].

This paper is a revised and extended version of our workshop paper [11]. Our new contribution is the RESIRIO approach and its evaluation. Due to space limits, we consolidated parts of the workshop-based elicitation and the experiments.

2 Industrial Setting: Domain Context and System

The system's purpose is to calculate payments. An accounting department's wage clerks use the payment accounting system to calculate each registered employee's income taxes. The payment accounting system has to gather data from health insurance providers and send its results to the corresponding tax office to execute the calculations. This process presumes that a company that wants to use the payment accounting system provides its employee and tax information to the health insurance provider and tax offices.

All of the payment accounting system's tasks are currently taken care of by a monolithic legacy system. In peak times, up to 13 million calculation requests have to be handled in a day or single night. Under normal circumstances, this number is significantly lower. In order to handle such varying loads more efficiently, stakeholders desire a better scaling system. Therefore, the old system is being replaced by a more scalable microservice-based Spring application. The investigated part of the system under study, which is still under development, consists of seven services as detailed later. The system is deployed to a Platform as a Service (PaaS), i.e., Cloud Foundry (CF). Together with the industrial partner, we decided on a scenario-based approach, as our industrial partner already employed ATAM for other quality attributes.

3 Workshop-Based Elicitation and Specification

This section elaborates on the planning, execution, and results of the workshop.

3.1 Structured Workshop Approach

Before the workshop, we received documentation regarding the architecture of the system. This allowed us to specify an architecture model of the system, including a component diagram and an explanation of the implemented components. Using ATAM, we required to know key architectural design decisions. Therefore, knowing the architecture description in advance allowed us to focus more on the hazard analysis and developing resilience scenarios.

The full-day workshop consisted of four sessions leveraging different methods. The moderators explained each technique and method at the beginning of each session. The participants were stakeholders of the system and comprised two software architects, one product owner, and one quality assurance engineer.

Session 1: Introduction and Architecture Description for achieving a common understanding of the workshop process and the system's architecture. (1) We resolved misunderstandings regarding the elicited architecture description through asking questions, and (2) refined the prepared architectural models.

Session 2: Hazard Analysis to identify potential causes for degradation in QoS. Index cards were used as a means to collect hazards. Afterward, the participants arranged the hazards and their causes in a fault-tree-like fashion. To not break the participants' creative flow, we relaxed the strict construction rules of fault trees, e.g., we allowed events having multiple parents, which resulted in a graph. For this reason, we refer to this session's result as a *fault graph*. Note that the (directed acyclic) fault graph can be transformed into an equivalent fault tree by creating duplicate sub-trees for nodes having more than one parent.

Session 3: Resilience Scenarios for collecting and prioritizing resilience scenarios based on the previously identified hazards. We provided a table based on the ATAM scenario template. Then, the stakeholders jointly created scenarios by informally analyzing the fault graph in a sequence driven by the associated severity (in descending order) of the hazards.

Session 4: Retrospective to collect feedback about the workshop from the participants and to inform them about the next steps, which comprise (1) refinement resilience requirements, and (2) execution of resilience experiments.

3.2 Workshop Results

Elicited Architecture Description: Figure 2 shows the component diagram of the system as specified in the first session of the workshop. It describes a snapshot of the system as used in the workshop and the subsequent activities. It represents a typical microservice-based architecture. As such, the system is deployed to a CF and contains several services. Each service has its own PostgreSQL database. The only exception is the *Calculations* service, which employs a Mongo database. The *API-Gateway* service handles all incoming connections and routes all communications. A *Eureka* service is employed to provide service discovery for all internal components. The *Frontend* service is the only external component that a user can access directly. The *Calculations* service is the central hub of the system since the calculation of payments is the system's main feature. Once this

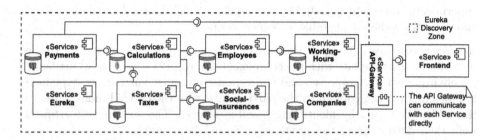

Fig. 2. Component diagram of the payment accounting system

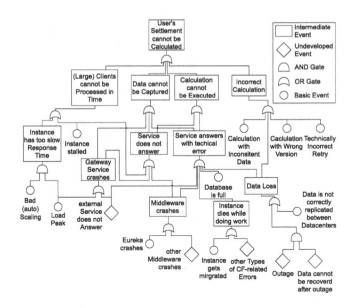

Fig. 3. Cleaned fault graph

service receives a calculation request from the gateway, it collects all necessary data asynchronously from the other services. The *Companies* service is used to handle data the *Frontend* displays, but is not relevant for the calculation.

Hazard Analysis: Figure 3 shows the fault graph created in the second workshop session. The stakeholders agreed on unavailability or long response of settlement calculations as the main system hazard. Therefore, *user's settlement can not be calculated* is the top event in the fault graph. The stakeholders analyzed possible causes from the top event until we reached basic events that we could not further decompose. We connected different causes by logical operators, i.e., *AND* and *OR*. For example, users can not calculate their settlement if it is not processed in time. This can occur when the assigned *instance stalls* OR *responds to slow*. We argue that the latter can be experienced if the system receives a sudden *(work)load peak* AND its *(auto) scaling does not work correctly*. The hazards at the leaf nodes are potential candidates for fault/failure injection during resilience experiments and can be initiated by tools such as CTK. The stakeholders selected and prioritized the set of resilience experiments.

Resilience Scenarios: We gave the participants an empty table according to the ATAM scenario template with the columns (1) source, (2) stimulus, (3) artifacts, (4) environment, (5) response, and (6) response measure. Further, we explained the meaning of each column to the participants, who then added index cards to the table. We began by identifying possible *sources*. The *stimuli* and *artifacts* were then derived from the previously created fault graph. The *environment* represents different time periods when the identified stimuli occur. The *responses* are the stakeholders' assumptions about how the system should respond to the

Table 1. Scenarios created during the workshop

ID	Short name	Source	Stimulus	Artifact	Environment	Response	Response measure
01	Peak(LinCo)/ Ser/Abr	User	Linear increasing load peak (cold start)	Service	Payslip calculation period	All requests are handled correctly and in time	Wage calculation $\leq$ 1 s, in 99% of the cases, payslip calculation $\leq$ 20 s (300 Employees)
02	Peak(ExCo)/ Ser/Abr		Exponentially increasing load peak (cold start)				
03	Peak(LinCo)/ Ser/NoAbr		Linear increasing load peak (cold start)		Not during payslip calculation period		
04	Peak(ExCo)/ Ser/NoAbr		Exponentially increasing load peak (cold start)				
05	Failure(CF)/ Ins/Ber	Cloud Foundry	Instance terminates	Instance	During wage calculation	User unaware, calc. correct & in time, $\geq$1 instance running	
06	Bug/Ins/Ber	Bug				Developer gets notified	Developer gets notified within 5 min
07	Failure(MW)/ Bac/Ber	Middleware Operator	Middleware terminates	Backend	During wage calculation	Abort calculation, caller will be notified	Notification arrives within 1 s in 99% of the cases
08	Failure(MW)/ Bac/Abr		Middleware terminates but recovers		Async. payslip calculation	Process is aborted but can be picked up	Restarts and SLOs are satisfied
09	Depl(GW)/ FroBac/NoIdle	Deployment	Gateway terminates	Front- and Backend	Not Idle	Frontend shows error, gateway restarts	Downtime of gateway instance is below 1 min
10	Failure(GW)/ FroBac/NoIdle	Technical Issue					
11	Failure(SerE)/ Ser/Ber	Receiving Service	Service terminates	Sending Service S, Receiving Service R	During wage calculation, no instance available	Error message and services R restarts	Downtime is below 1 min
12	Failure(SerE)/ Ins/Ber				During wage calculation, one instance not available	Calculation correct and in time	Wage calculation response time is below 2 s

particular stimulus. The *response measures* are based on their internal Service Level Objectives (SLOs). For example, a workload peak resulting in a system failure was transposed into multiple scenarios. Users of the system are the source since they cause the load peak. The respective stimulus is the workload peak itself. A service was chosen as the artifact to represent that a load peak can influence all service instances. As the environment, the payslip calculation period was chosen to imply an existing base workload. At last, the stakeholders chose the responses and response measures based on their SLOs.

The stakeholders elaborated 12 resilience scenarios, summarized in Table 1. Scenarios 01 to 04 are different variations of an unexpected load peak, including linear and exponentially increasing loads. Scenarios 05 and 06 describe the failure of a single service instance. Scenarios 07 and 08 are about middleware failures. Scenarios 09 and 10 revolve around gateway failures. Lastly, Scenarios 11 and 12 describe the failure of multiple instances. Actors such as end-users, elements of the CF platform, different bugs, and technical issues caused by the middleware or deployment artifacts and issues intrinsic to individual services of the system comprise the established sources. In total, all scenarios can affect all services. The environments cover different states of the system according to the identified system domain context, e.g., payslip calculation periods or simply services being non-idle independent of the different calculations. The response and response measures were specified by the stakeholders based on their internal SLOs.

Retrospection: The brief retrospective at the end of the workshop showed that the participants were satisfied with the agenda, content, and outcomes. However, comments were made concerning time management.

3.3 Key Lessons Learned

After the workshop and the retrospective session, this section presents the key lessons learned. For more details on each lesson, please refer to [11].

- Elicitation of resilience requirements involves hazard analysis.
- ATAM is a useful method to adopt resilience elicitation.
- Loose adoption of formalisms is already good enough.
- The workshop requires considerable refinement that can be done "offline".
- A tightly planned one-day workshop is sufficient.
- The resilience elicitation helps to refine "classical" QoS requirements.

4 Chatbot-Based Elicitation and Specification

Although we tried to design the workshop (see Sect. 3) to be lightweight, its execution still requires significant time and effort. We also noticed that some of the elicited scenarios, particularly their triggering conditions, are rather generic, e.g., Scenarios 11 and 12 describe that a service terminates due to a service failure. Therefore, we designed an approach called RESIRIO to complement the workshop. RESIRIO aims to accelerate the elicitation of simple resilience scenarios through automation and interaction with visualizations and chatbots.

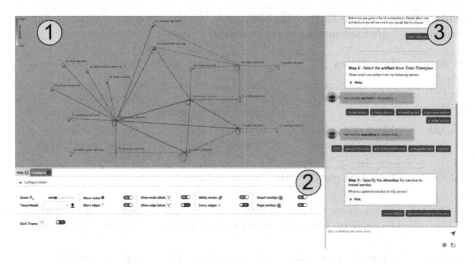

Fig. 4. The graphical interface of the RESIRIO prototype (Color figure online)

Similar to the workshop sessions, the RESIRIO process consists of three steps: architecture analysis, hazard analysis, and scenario creation. However, the first two steps are fully automated. In the *architecture analysis*, RESIRIO extracts the system's architecture from Jaeger or Zipkin execution traces [23]. This analysis substitutes the workshop session for the architecture elicitation, specification, and refinement. Since the fault tree analysis is difficult to automate, RESIRIO applies a CHAZOP-like technique in the *hazard analysis* to identify potential hazards and prioritize suggestions. Finally, in the *scenario creation*, the architecture is visualized, and a chatbot assists the user in the specification of concrete scenarios. The following sections detail these three steps.

We implemented the RESIRIO approach as a prototype. Figure 4 shows the graphical interface of the prototype, which consists of the (1) architecture graph, the (2) configuration view, and the (3) chatbot. Regarding the architectural documentation, including architectural views, design decisions, and use of technologies, please refer to the work by Zorn [30].

4.1 Architecture Analysis

Traces from Zipkin and Jaeger are the source of the architecture description for two reasons: (1) there is an existing basis of literature and academic work and (2) both frameworks are widely used in the industry and open-source projects.

To unify both representations of Zipkin and Jaeger into one format, we developed a generic meta-model for the system's architecture. This model captures the system's services, operations, and dependencies. Individual parsers for Zipkin and Jaeger transform the JSON-formatted traces into a representation described by our meta-model. This method allows for an extension regarding other tracing tools, given that the necessary parsers are implemented.

Table 2. Interpretations for the CHAZOPs guide words in the context of traces. Entries marked with * are implemented in the prototype.

Guide word	Description	Operation level effect	Service level cause
NO	No Information	Response Time Spike*, No Response	Service Failure*
MORE	More data passed than expected	Response Time Deviation*	Decreased Service Performance*, High Utilization
LESS	Less data passed than expected	Response Time Deviation (harmless)	-
PART OF	Information incomplete (for group flows)	Failed Operation/Exception	Software Bug, Service Failure, API Change
REVERSE	Flow of information in wrong direction	Response Send To Wrong Service	Software Bug
OTHER THAN	Information complete, but incorrect	Exception After Operation Response	Software Bug, API Change
EARLY	Data arrives earlier in a sequence	One Operation Call With Quick Response (harmless)	-
LATE	Data arrives later in a sequence	One (Async) Operation Call With Slow Response	Decreased Service Performance, High Utilization

Since our data is relational, a graph is suitable for the representation. The spans from a trace describe dependencies between services and are represented by directed edges. The graph is visualized as node-link-diagram, as displayed in Fig. 4. It is extended with tooltips and a context menu for further inspection of trace details. Once the graph is opened, it creates a list of available meta-information. Nodes display names of processes and the endpoint information (hostname and port). Edges display the spans' execution details, such as the duration of a call, logs, and tags. In addition, we apply a force-directed layout and extended it with a zooming function and the option to drag the graph.

4.2 Hazard Analysis

We base our hazard analysis on CHAZOP [10] to automatically identify hazards, generate suggestions, and prioritize services in the specification. CHAZOP is a risk assessment technique. It requires iterating over all interconnections, data-flows, and attributes in a system. Then, predefined guide words are interpreted, and causes, consequences, and protection mechanisms are derived.

In our approach, we iterate over the dependencies in the graph. In a brainstorming session, we interpreted the CHAZOP guide words. We did not explicitly select particular data-flows or attributes but treated a dependency like a request.

Furthermore, we thought about how a deviation could be detected in traces on the operation level. We considered the calling and called operation, the response time, and the request status as known information. Next, we tried to identify the deviations' causes on the service level. For practical reasons, we did also consider interpretations that did not fully match the guide words, e.g., we see a *Response Time Spike* as interpretation for the guide word *NO*, since the complete absence of a request cannot be detected from a trace alone. The (non-exhaustive) list of interpretations from our brainstorming session can be found in Table 2.

For the prototypical implementation of RESIRIO, we selected two different hazard types on the operation level (*Response Time Deviation, Spike Response Times*) and two derived hazard types on the service level (*Service Failure, Degraded Service Performance*). These hazard types can easily be detected by inspecting response times in spans. We classify response times that deviate by 50% filtered by three times the standard deviation as *Response Time Deviation*. Furthermore, a *Response Time Spike* denotes outliers in the response times. If a hazard is detected in a service's operation, the algorithm suggests *Service Failure* as service hazard in case of *Response Time Spike*. For *Response Time Deviation*, the algorithm suggests *Decreased Service Performance* on the service level.

The identified hazards are involved in the computation of a priority value. The priority value depends on the number of incoming and outgoing edges and the number of hazards found in the architectural element. A service with many connections to other services has a higher priority than services with fewer connections. The priority of an edge is defined by the two services it connects. If hazards are found in a service or operation during the analysis, the service's priority is multiplied by the number of found hazards. The resulting formula is loosely based on the formula of the Risk Priority Number in Failure Modes and Effects Analysis (FMEA) hazard analysis method [17].

In RESIRIO, the priority value is used in two different ways in the scenario specification process: On the one hand, the chatbot suggests the five services and five operations with the highest priority to the engineer. On the other hand, each service and dependency in the graph representation is assigned a color from white (low priority) to blue (high priority). The color palette is interpolated from the lowest priority to the highest priority in the graph.

Instead of triggering deviations to the component's parameter based on expert knowledge, we examine response times from previous executions of the system to extract hazards. This kind of hazard analysis requires two prerequisites. First, it is necessary that the system ran before and went into a hazardous state. For some systems, this is not tolerable. Second, it requires that the hazard type is defined in advance. Therefore, very system-specific hazards are usually not detectable. We emphasize that the inspection of trace metrics and resulting hazards provides resilience engineers only with suggestions. Resilience engineers may still use their expertise to define custom stimuli types.

4.3 Scenario Creation

In order to enable the engineer to specify resilience scenarios, we present her an architecture graph and a chatbot, as displayed in Fig. 4. The chat follows the design of a typical messenger interface and has three kinds of content types. The user content (blue) is on the right side of the chat component. The left side of the chat component contains the chatbot responses (yellow). Rich content guides the interaction and covers the middle of the chat content, rendering *Card Responses*, *Accordions*, and *Quick Replies*. The architecture and chatbot components are linked with each other, for example, selecting a service in the architecture graph, will be interpreted by the chatbot as choice of an artifact in the specification. Furthermore, the chatbot highlights the corresponding graph artifact when choosing an artifact for the scenario specification.

The goal of the specification process is to output fully specified scenarios. Our work extends the original resilience scenario with the parameters *component*, *normal availability*, *normal response times*, *normal response cases*, and *recovery time*. The *artifact* and the *component* are always used in combination with each other. While the *component* describes a concrete service or operation name, the *artifact* contains the type, e.g., whether a service or operation is selected. We limit the use of the extended scenario structure to trace metrics in favor of a more detailed scenario description. Thus, we divide the *response measure* further into sub-parameters. A *response measure* for services has *normal availability* and *recovery time*. The *response measure* for operations has *normal response time*, *normal response case*, and *recovery time*. The parameters *normal availability*, *normal response time*, and *normal response cases* describe a system's normal operation state. Quantitative measures are used to specify these parameters (e.g., 100 ms or 99%) that can easily be checked against runtime metrics of the inspected system. If system metrics deviate from the given metrics of the normal operation state, a return to the normal state is necessary. The *recovery time* parameter describes the maximum tolerable time to return to the normal state, also using a quantitative measure (e.g., 5 min, or 4 s).

The interaction concept is rather simple. The chatbot aims to elicit one element of the extended scenario format in one step. For each step, the engineer selects default responses, which are predefined or generated from the previous analysis phases, or enters custom values. In a regular interaction, the chatbot first encourages the engineer to select services or operations to determine the *artifact* and *component*. Next, it proceeds with the description of the incident, followed by the description of the desired system response. In the end, the scenario can be edited or saved. In the latter case, the scenario appears in the configuration view in a separate tab. This tab summarizes the responses and is equipped with an export button that downloads the scenario in the JSON format.

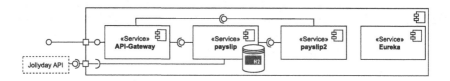

Fig. 5. Mocked payroll accounting system

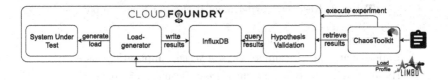

Fig. 6. Used structure of the experiment framework

5   Resilience Evaluation

This section aims to evaluate the resilience of the system under study. Therefore, we implemented a subset of the previously elicited resilience scenarios into resilience experiments using CTK. We compare the system's behavior against the expected behavior described in the scenarios' response part.

5.1   Experiment Setup

Examined Software System. Due to legal constraints and to maintain anonymity, our industrial partner provided us with a mocked version as a proxy for the real payroll accounting system. This version, shown in Fig. 5, is used throughout this paper as the system under test. It implements a similar business logic but with less computational overhead. The system uses typical patterns of the microservice architectural style, i.e., *API-Gateway-service* as a central gateway that manages all incoming requests and *Eureka* [20] to provide service discovery. The *payslip-service* utilizes an H2 in-memory database and the third-party API *Jollyday*. It can forward requests to the *payslip-service2*. Requests can also be sent directly to *payslip-service2* using a different endpoint.

The following six endpoints are used during the experiments:

INTERNAL_DEP—Calls the *payslip-service2* via *payslip-service*.
DB_READ—Reads an entry from the database of the *payslip-service*.
EXTERNAL_DEP—Calls the third-party API *Jollydays* via *payslip-service*.
DB_WRITE—Writes an entry into the database of the *payslip-service*.
GATEWAY_PING—Checks whether the *API-Gateway-service* responds.
UNAFF_SERVICE—Sends a request directly to *payslip-service2*.

The actual payment accounting system is deployed to a paid CF. Due to financial constraints and legal issues, the mock system is deployed to a local CF environment [9], which has similar properties as a paid CF. As CF is a constraint given by the stakeholders, we did not consider other cloud providers.

Experiment Tools. Figure 6 shows our experiment framework comprising three tools, i.e., CTK, load generator, and hypothesis validator. During an experiment, these tools interact with the system to monitor the experiments and provide detailed insights, e.g., response times of calls to individual endpoints.

Table 3. Resilience experiment design for Scenario 05'

Target service	*payslip-service*
Experiment type	Terminate *payslip-service* application instance
Hypothesis	Response measure of Scenario 05 holds
Blast radius	*payslip-service*

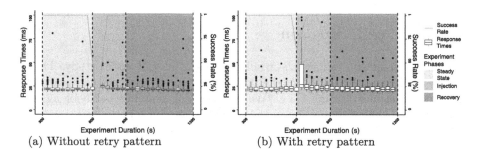

(a) Without retry pattern   (b) With retry pattern

Fig. 7. Comparison of experiment results at endpoint INTERNAL_DEP

To execute the experiments, we used CTK [8], which can execute and monitor chaos tests and has drivers for various PaaS solutions. We leveraged the CF driver to terminate a service instance at a specific point in time and validate the steady-state hypothesis. The load that the system receives is controlled by an adapted version of the load generator from the TeaStore microservices benchmark [16] that monitors response times, number of successful, dropped, and failed requests. The collected data is written into an InfluxDB [14]. During the evaluation, a Spring service collects the data from the InfluxDB and calculates whether a hypothesis holds. We also created a dashboard application that provides convenient features, like synchronized starting of CTK and the load generator, live monitoring, and automated CTK setup. Since the dashboard does not add functionalities in executing experiments, it is not part of Fig. 6.

5.2   Experiment Execution

Based on Scenarios 04 and 05, we implemented three resilience experiments. The first experiment investigates a load peak with an exponential increase (Scenario 04), while the remaining two investigate instance termination due to an internal CF error for random instances (Scenario 05) and specifically the *payslip-service* (Scenario 05'). The selection of experiments is based on the industrial partner's preferences. In all experiments, the effect on all endpoints is examined. In the following, we will only discuss the results of a subset of endpoints for Scenario 05'. The residual results can be found in the supplementary material [27].

The design of the experiment related to Scenario 05' is given in Table 3. The target service of this experiment is the *payslip-service*, which holds the core business logic of the mock system. We use CTK to terminate running CF application instances to simulate the scenario's stimulus. The stimulus refers to an error that occurs in CF, which leads to a loss of an application instance. We assume that the blast radius only affects the *payslip-service* and that CF registers the loss of the *payslip-service* instance and starts a new instance. Our hypothesis is that the response measure of Scenario 05 still holds.

During the experiments, the system is exposed to an almost constant, synthetic load. We generated a load profile with a target load of 20 requests per second and some noise. The requests are evenly distributed over all six endpoints. To assess whether the system still responds correctly and in time, we measure response times of the requests and compute their success rate.

5.3   Experiment Results

The measurements for endpoint INTERNAL_DEP are visualized in Fig. 7a. In the steady-state phase, we assume that the system is working as expected, i.e., the response times satisfy the SLOs. In the injection phase, CTK terminates the *payslip-service* instance. In the recovery phase, we assume that the system returns to a steady state, i.e., the response times satisfy the SLOs. We omitted the load generator's warmup and cooldown phase due to readability and analysis reasons, which refers to the overall first and last 300 s. Further, a 30 s binning was applied, and extreme outliers (>100 ms) are not shown.

The success rates at the endpoint INTERNAL_DEP (Fig. 7a), DB_READ, EXTERNAL_DEP, and DB_WRITE drop to 0% as the *payslip-service* is terminated after 600 s and rises back to 100% as it recovers in about 1.5 min. During this downtime, no response times are recorded since no requests arrive at the *payslip-service*. During the steady-state and recovery phase, the response times are stable at around 20 ms and 15 ms, respectively. During the injection phase, there is a slight increase as the *payslip-service* has restarted.

5.4   Discussion of Results

As visible in Fig. 7a, the response time and success rate values are almost identical in the steady state phase and the recovery phase. Furthermore, the increase in the success rate indicates that the *payslip-service* becomes available after 30 s to 60 s. Thus, the CF platform can re-instantiate the *payslip-service* quickly, leading to a quick recovery of the system.

Response times are slightly higher while the *payslip-service* is re-instantiated, which was expected as normal cold-start behavior. Endpoints GATEWAY_PING and UNAFF_SERVICE should remain unaffected during the injection because the *payslip-service* is not required to answer the requests. Nevertheless, response times at endpoint GATEWAY_PING are affected, which indicates a propagation of the failure effects from the *payslip-service* to the *API-Gateway-service*.

After the injection started, the success rate drops to 0% at the endpoints INTERNAL_DEP, DB_READ, EXTERNAL_DEP, and DB_WRITE. The CTK terminates the single *payslip-service* instance. The load generator flags all requests as failed, leading to a success rate of 0%.

We hypothesized that the response measure of Scenario 05 holds, i.e., requests are answered in time (99% in less than 1 s) and correctly. As the response times are far below 1 s, our hypothesis regarding the response times is technically fulfilled. However, several requests are not answered at all, which is indicated by the dropped success rate. We consider these as incorrect response. Therefore, we assume that the hypothesis regarding correctness is not fulfilled.

6   Resilience Improvement

The previous section's experiments showed that the system does not respond as described in Scenario 05 to a failure of an instance of the *payslip-service*. While the response times are technically below 1s in 99% of all cases, requests are temporarily not answered at all. We consider that an incorrect response. Therefore, we aim to improve the system's success rate concerning Scenario 05 by applying resilience pattern(s). Resilience patterns [1] describe architectural changes to enable applications to handle failures gracefully and recover from them. A request may fail due to temporary failures in network components. Retrying requests is one well-known resilience pattern, which provides a solution to the problem of temporary failures within the application. Hence, we hypothesize that adding retry improves overall system resilience. We determine the efficacy of improvements to the system's resilience by re-executing the experiments.

6.1   Architectural Modifications

The system under test was fortified with a retry pattern [22], i.e., the *API-Gateway-service* sends another request to the *payslip-service* if a request fails or remains unanswered. The retry pattern seems to be a reasonable choice since response times are far below the threshold of 1 s, as indicated by the previous experiment. Due to its specific purpose, the system has to accept requests near real-time and always answer correctly. Thus, resilience patterns that rely on backup or restricting behavior, like circuit breakers or flow limiters, are unsuited. To avoid bad retry behavior, we configured the Spring-Retry as follows. We set the maximum number of retries of each *payslip-service* request to be 4, the initial delay to 10 ms, the factor for the exponential increase to 3, and the maximum delay to 150 ms—resulting in retries after 10 ms, 30 ms, 90 ms, and 150 ms.

6.2   Experiment Results and Discussion

Figure 7b visualizes the system's response times and success rates with the retry pattern for endpoint INTERNAL_DEP. Table 4 shows the associated statistical

Table 4. Statistical summaries of the three experiment phases. p_α: α-th percentile; $\tilde{x}$: median; and $\bar{x}$: mean. Values are given in ms.

	Steady state								Injection								Recovery							
	w/o Pattern				w Pattern				w/o Pattern				w Pattern				w/o Pattern				w Pattern			
Endpoint	p_5	$\tilde{x}$	$\bar{x}$	p_{99}	p_5	$\tilde{x}$	$\bar{x}$	p_{99}	p_5	$\tilde{x}$	$\bar{x}$	p_{99}	p_5	$\tilde{x}$	$\bar{x}$	p_{99}	p_5	$\tilde{x}$	$\bar{x}$	p_{99}	p_5	$\tilde{x}$	$\bar{x}$	p_{99}
INTERNAL_DEP	19	22	22.5	33	19	22	24.0	51	19	21	22.4	32	19	22	24.6	90	19	21	22.1	31	19	22	23.0	34
DB_READ	11	12	13.3	21	11	12	13.0	24	11	12	13.1	20	11	12	13.2	30	11	12	12.9	20	11	12	12.8	19
EXTERNAL_DEP	11	12	12.6	21	10	12	13.3	23	11	12	12.5	21	10	12	14.1	31	11	12	12.3	19	10	12	12.2	19
DB_WRITE	11	13	13.4	21	11	12	13.1	22	11	12	13.1	20	11	12	13.3	27	11	12	13.0	20	11	12	12.7	19
GATEWAY_PING	11	12	13.3	21	11	12	13.3	24	11	12	13.1	20	11	12	13.6	32	11	12	12.9	19	11	12	12.9	21
UNAFF_SERVICE	10	11	11.9	19	10	11	11.6	19	10	11	11.7	18	10	11	11.6	19	10	11	11.8	18	10	11	11.5	19

values. In general, similar behavior can be observed at all the endpoints. Comparing the plots of Fig. 7 shows that the mean response times in the steady state phase do not vary significantly when the retry pattern is added. Although, at the beginning of the injection phase, far more high response times can be observed. In addition, the boxplots show a slightly higher interquartile range in the plot where the retry pattern is integrated.

The plots also show that the success rate does not drop to zero anymore with the active pattern. For endpoint INTERNAL_DEP, the success rate drops to approximately 70%. For the endpoints GATEWAY_PING and UNAFF_SERVICE, the success rate remains at 100%. The two endpoints do not depend on the *payslip-service*, which explains the high success rate at these endpoints.

The application of the retry pattern can explain the response time spikes during the injection (see the Fig. 7). Requests sent shortly before the restart of the *payslip-service* fail, but are retried by the *API-Gateway-service* until the *payslip-service* recovered after approximately 10 s. However, as several retries have been aggregated, the *payslip-service* has to handle a high amount of requests upon recovery, resulting in a visible spike in response times.

In contrast to the system without the retry pattern, the success rate drops less. Thus, the retry pattern improves the scenario satisfaction as it increases the percentage of correct responses while the response times stays below 1 s.

7   RESIRIO User Study

To evaluate the developed prototype on usability and effectiveness, we designed an expert user study. In the following, we give an overview of the procedure and results. Artifact and more results can be found in the supplementary material. The user study aimed to get feedback from inexperienced engineers and experts. Separate research question and hypotheses are investigated. The goal is to accept a hypothesis H_{x1} by rejecting the corresponding null-hypothesis H_{x0}. The research questions and derived hypotheses are:

- **RQ1:** Are users of RESIRIO able to create resilience scenarios successfully?
    - H_{11}: Study participants can complete the study tasks successfully.

- **RQ2:** How effective is RESIRIO compared to traditional elicitation processes?
  - H_{21}: Study participants create ATAM-based scenarios faster with RESIRIO than with a traditional approach, e.g., the workshop.
- **RQ3:** How supportive is RESIRIO during the elicitation process?
  - H_{3a1}: RESIRIO supports inexperienced engineers in the elicitation process.
  - H_{3b1}: RESIRIO supports experienced engineers in the elicitation process.
- **RQ4:** How usable are ATAM-based scenarios created with RESIRIO for resilience assessment?
  - H_{41}: RESIRIO's scenarios can be used for system resilience assessment.

7.1   Design and Methodology

We perform a qualitative study, since there is a limited number of domain experts for scenario-based resilience engineering. The study has three different strategies to collect feedback. First, subjective feedback is collected through interview-style and open-ended questions. Secondly, the prototype measures metrics like the duration of the study, the number and type of interactions, interactions with features besides the chatbot, and the number of elicited scenarios. To support the measurement of effectiveness and the quality of the prototype, we include close-ended questions. Finally, usability is measured based on a Likert scale from questions as suggested by Brooke [4] in the System Usability Study. If participants have a particular interest in a feature or make suggestions for improvements, the study conductor asked additional questions to get more insights.

We created two tasks. At the beginning of each task, the participants are given a general description of the inspected system, which introduces a failure to the system. In each task, an ATAM-based scenario to fix the failure needs to be created. In the first task, which was considered beginner-friendly, we present a predefined solution. The only challenge in this task is to create the scenario through the use of the chatbot. Additionally, it is possible to create the resilience scenario only with the use of *Quick Replies*. The second is designed to be more challenging. On the one hand, the correct solution was not shown to the participants. On the other hand, the task description contains names of services and operations that are not available through *Quick Replies*. The absence of *Quick Replies* requires participants to use the architecture graph and the text input.

7.2   Study Execution

We invited participants from the industry and academia for the evaluation. Five employees from the industry company did take part in the study: two software architects, one DevOps Engineer, one quality assurance engineer, and one doctoral researcher. Four participants already participated in the workshop. Three participants are considered experts of the system since they were involved in its development. The system is the industrial system as described in Sect. 3.2. We also requested the participation of researchers familiar with the Train Ticket system [29]. Seven researchers agreed to participate. Four participants are considered experts of the system since they were involved in its development.

We informed the participants beforehand that the study takes place virtually and requires approximately 45–60 min to complete. After their verbal agreement to the consent form, they were sent the task description. In the first part, the goal and purpose of the study are given. In the second part, the prototype is introduced. The third part contains the actual tasks fitted to each system. After the participants read the first two parts of the task description, they were given a link to the prototype. The participants were encouraged to describe their actions with the prototype, which was done in most cases. The study conductor stayed passive and just reminded the participants to carefully reread the task description, which resolved the problems in all cases. After completing the practical part, the study conductor started a verbal conversation with the participants and asked them about noticeable events during the practical part. Examples of noticeable events were not using the chatbot text interactions or creating a new scenario from the beginning. These questions usually led to a discussion with open-ended questions. After all noticeable events were covered, the study conductor asked the participants to fill out the questionnaire.

7.3 Results and Discussion

All participants claimed that they completed the given tasks successfully. The questionnaire confirms that the first task was perceived easier than the second task (see Fig. 8d), as intended. We created a set of solutions for the more complex second task before the study was executed. In the evaluation, we compared the elicited scenarios of the participants with the prepared solutions. Overall, six participants had to reconfigure the parameters of a scenario because they were not satisfied with their initially chosen parameters, or the chatbot did not assign the specified parameters as intended. Three of the 24 final scenarios contained invalid parameters. Therefore, H_{10} is rejected, and H_{11} can be accepted.

The fastest participant used 7 min to complete both tasks, while the slowest used more than 24 min. The median lies at approx. 16 min. Although the second task is the difficult task, recordings indicate an approximated median of only five minutes to complete the second task. This can be ascribed to the learning effect that users had for solving the first task. The workshop required several participants to elicit 12 scenarios over a working day. In contrast to that, a single person can elicit a scenario within 5 min after little training. Therefore, H_{20} is rejected, and H_{21} can be accepted. Three participants did not agree with this conclusion. However, all participants who had previously taken part in the workshop confirmed our conclusion.

Six participants got stuck during the elicitation process, but three of them could return to the conversation without the help of the Chatbot Reset functionality. Nevertheless, most of the participants agreed that they were provided with enough assistance (see Fig. 8c). Additionally, the results of the System Usability Study confirmed that RESIRIO (i) was perceived as easy to use, (ii) does not require too much knowledge to use, and (iii) has well-integrated features.

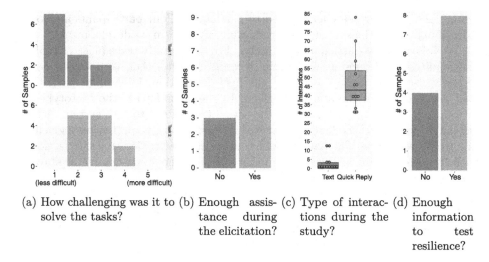

(a) How challenging was it to solve the tasks? (b) Enough assistance during the elicitation? (c) Type of interactions during the study? (d) Enough information to test resilience?

Fig. 8. Results from questions and measurements of the user study.

A significant finding is an overall preference of using Quick Replies over the use of text interactions (see Fig. 8b), which is an explanation for the quick elicitation. While six participants did not use text interactions, the other six used only three to thirteen text interactions. Quick Replies were the prototype's most used and liked feature, followed by the Architecture Graph. Two participants requested general documentation of the prototype and wanted to see all the available functionalities of the prototype. Other suggestions for improvements were more Quick Replies, role assignment (i.e., software architect, testing engineer), and displaying the scenario at all times. In general, experts responded with more critical feedback. While they were happy with the prototype's usability, they stated that features were missing to highlight details of a scenario and give more insights into the technical background of the analysis process. Therefore, H_{3a1} can be accepted and H_{3a0} is rejected. However, we can not reject H_{3b0} for the current state of the approach based on the experts' feedback.

Overall, most participants agreed that the elicited scenarios are sufficient to test a system's resilience (see Fig. 8a). For this reason, we accept H_{41} and reject H_{40}. However, especially the experts noted that the available options for stimuli and responses as too limited to create usable scenarios in practice. Half of the participants agreed that more quick replies are necessary.

7.4 Key Lessons Learned

This section presents the key lessons learned from the user study.

- Engineering teams in traditional elicitation processes such as workshops are concerned about the documentation process. Automated interactive tooling such as RESIRIO address that concern.

- The tendency to interact through the architecture graph and quick replies is higher than having time-consuming conversations with a chatbot.
- Chatbot-assisted tooling such as RESIRIO, which involves interaction between one person and a chatbot, does not replace traditional elicitation processes because traditional methods involve discussions between people, leading to more coverage of stimuli and response measures.

8 Related Work

We explored (1) the usage of the scenario-based ATAM and established hazard analysis techniques for interactive resilience requirement elicitation and (2) testing through resilience experiments for architecture assessment and improvement. This section classifies research areas and existing works close to us.

8.1 Measurement-Based Resilience Evaluation

A workshop is an effective technique for requirement elicitation [24]. In our case, the workshop's preparation and conduction are based on the scenario template of Bass et al. [3]. Our difference to existing works on measurement-based resilience evaluation is that we have an explicit step on eliciting resilience requirements. In the next paragraphs, we elaborate on this in more detail.

Cámara et al. [5–7] propose an approach for resilience analysis of self-adaptive systems. The core idea consists of three parts: (1) specification of resilience properties using Probabilistic Computation Tree Logic, (2) modeling causes of a hazard, e.g., high-load using experimentation and collecting traces of system behavior, and (3) verification of resilience properties using model checking. In contrast to model checking-based verification, we evaluate a scenario's response measure by analyzing measurements. Furthermore, Cámara et al. do not focus on the elicitation of resilience requirements.

In Chaos Engineering [2,18], system resilience is evaluated through failure injection [19]. There are works on both (1) using engineering methods to identify failure modes [15], i.e., causes of a hazard systematically before failure injection, and (2) ad-hoc failure injection with no systematic failure mode identification [13]. However, they do not explicitly specify resilience requirements and lack a methodical way for requirement elicitation. Our work is a step toward closing this gap.

In the context of resilience requirement elicitation, Yin et al. [28] propose a goal-oriented technique for representing resilience requirements. The high-level idea is to represent a resilience goal—e.g., all requests are processed correctly—and identify possible causes of hazards that act as obstacles for achieving a resilience goal—e.g., node failure. However, they do not discuss how to identify hazards and their causes. Goal orientation and developing scenarios are two activities in requirements engineering [24] that benefit the elicitation process. According to Pohl [24], scenario development benefits elicitation by making goals understandable for stakeholders and may refine or identify new goals. Our work uses scenario development without goal-oriented modeling as all stakeholders know the system's high-level quality goal.

To our knowledge, this is the first work using ATAM for eliciting and specifying resilience requirements before evaluating the resilience through experiments.

8.2   Chatbot-Based Requirements Elicitation

Rietz [26] proposes a conversational interface called chatbot for requirements elicitation, which is applicable for novice users in requirements engineering. The core idea is to guide users in the elicitation process by asking questions from abstract to more precisely. The user interaction, including questions and answers, is stored in a knowledge base for later re-use and interaction improvements.

Friesen et al. [12] proposed the CORDULA approach. Users of the approach need to use special text format to interact with the chatbot, which identifies domain concepts and imprecise statements such as *a big file*. Afterward, in a separate debugging window, users can edit the specification. In contrast to previous works, we use the structured template of ATAM for requirements specification. In addition, we use architecture visualization and hazard analysis techniques to guide the users in the elicitation process.

The work by Surana et al. [25] allows users to elicit and classify requirements as functional or non-functional requirements. The authors benefit from machine learning algorithms for the elicitation and classification tasks. However, the chatbot expects users' familiarity with the system's requirements and is more usable for classification tasks than the elicitation process.

9   Threats to Validity

9.1   Workshop

Conclusion Validity. One threat is the reliability of measures, which means repeating the workshop yields the same resilience requirements list. Elicitation of resilience requirements involves human judgment. Hence, it is a subjective measure. Therefore, we can not entirely rule out this threat.

Internal Validity. One threat is instrumentation, which means our tools and techniques were not suitable. We conducted a one-day structured workshop and used the scenario template of Bass et al. [3] for eliciting resilience requirements. We refined all the resilience requirements through several iterations after the workshop and validated them against the workshop participants.

Construct Validity. For us, the main threat in this category is mono-method bias, which means we did not use other elicitation methods. Therefore, there is a threat that elicited resilience requirements are biased. We can not entirely rule out this threat as we did not apply other methods and cross-check the results.

External Validity. The heterogeneity poses a threat, i.e., different roles and expertise of participants. Workshops with less heterogeneity in the stakeholders could lead to no resilience requirements. We can not entirely rule out this threat. Although our study is based on a microservice architectural style, we argue that our approach of resilience requirements elicitation is independent of the architecture style. The important is eliciting resilience requirements and understanding design decisions that satisfy the requirements.

9.2 RESIRIO User Study

Conclusion Validity. As most questions asked during the study were open-ended, and of qualitative nature, it is hard to prove whether our conclusions are correct. The number of participants was limited, resulting in ambiguous conclusions from measurements and general uncertainty in the evaluation.

Internal Validity. The target group consisted of participants with different levels of experience. The knowledge of the participants is hard to compare. Four participants had previously seen the prototype in a demonstration. Although they did not use the prototype, some transfer of knowledge might have happened.

Construct Validity. The comparison of RESIRIO's efficiency to traditional elicitation processes is limited for the lack of existing measurements. We do not think that values extracted from experience reports and other literature reviews provide a good enough basis for a thorough comparison. Feedback from users is always subjective. They could, for example, not be able to judge whether created scenarios can be used for a specification in practice.

External Validity. Participants came from the same institutions and companies, complicating the generalization of results in surroundings that are different from those found in the participants' environments.

9.3 Experiment Design

We used the mock system for quantitative evaluation of resilience requirements that are based on the actual system. There is a threat that evaluation results are inaccurate. However, the purpose of the experiments is to exemplary show how elicited requirements and derived experiments can help to improve the system— we do not claim the accuracy of the quantitative results. Furthermore, due to legal issues, we used CF Dev [9]. We faced instability, e.g., resource drainage of Dev nodes, in the environment during experimentation. There is a threat of a negative impact on results due to this instability. To counteract this threat, we re-executed experiments to gain insight into approximate measurements, ensuring reliable data with no unintended node or service crash.

10   Conclusion

The successful development of resilience scenarios depends on the outcome of the hazard analysis. Our workshop approach to scenario-based resilience evaluation assumes business domain experts to derive an initial list of hazards. FTA can then be a means to analyze the hazards and derive resilience scenarios. Our semi-automated approach RESIRIO is a means for quicker and easier elicitation of such scenarios, but it can not fully replace the workshop. We plan to (1) extend our process with an explicit formalization step after the elicitation for refinement of the scenarios, (2) formally verify response measures of resilience scenarios, and (3) create processes for continuous hazard analysis when a system faces changes, e.g., updates and refinement/development of resilience scenarios.

Acknowledgment. This work has been supported by the Baden-Württemberg Stiftung (ORCAS—Efficient Resilience Benchmarking of Microservice Architectures) and the German Federal Ministry of Education and Research (dqualizer and Software Campus 2.0—Microproject: DiSpel).

Data Availability Statement. Our artifacts [27] comprise (i) the resilience scenarios, (ii) the RESIRIO project and user study documents, and (iii) the data and R scripts as a CodeOcean capsule. We are working on making parts of the created/modified experiment tools available as open-source software. For confidentiality reasons, the system under test cannot be published.

References

1. Microsoft Azure (2021). https://docs.microsoft.com/en-us/azure/architecture/framework/resiliency/reliability-patterns
2. Basiri, A., et al.: Chaos engineering. IEEE Softw. **33**(3), 35–41 (2016)
3. Bass, L., Clements, P., Kazman, R.: Software Architecture in Practice, 4th edn. Addison-Wesley Longman Publishing Co., Boston (2021)
4. Brooke, J.: SUS: a 'quick and dirty' usability scale. Usability evaluation in industry 189 (1996)
5. Cámara, J., de Lemos, R.: Evaluation of resilience in self-adaptive systems using probabilistic model-checking. In: Proceedings of 7th International Symposium on Software Engineering for Adaptive and Self-Managing Systems (SEAMS), pp. 53–62 (2012)
6. Cámara, J., de Lemos, R., Laranjeiro, N., Ventura, R., Vieira, M.: Robustness-driven resilience evaluation of self-adaptive software systems. IEEE Trans. Dependable Secure Comput. **14**(1), 50–64 (2017)
7. Cámara, J., de Lemos, R., Vieira, M., Almeida, R., Ventura, R.: Architecture-based resilience evaluation for self-adaptive systems. Computing **95**(8), 689–722 (2013)
8. Chaos Toolkit: Chaos Toolkit (2020). https://chaostoolkit.org
9. Cloud Foundry Foundation: Cloud Foundry dev documentation (2020). https://github.com/cloudfoundry-incubator/cfdev
10. Dunjó, J., Fthenakis, V., Vílchez, J.A., Arnaldos, J.: Hazard and operability (HAZOP) analysis. A literature review. J. Hazard. Mater. **173**(1–3), 19–32 (2010)
11. Frank, S., Hakamian, M.A., Wagner, L., Kesim, D., von Kistowski, J., van Hoorn, A.: Scenario-based resilience evaluation and improvement of microservice architectures: an experience report. In: ECSA 2021 Companion Volume, vol. 2978 (2021)

12. Friesen, E., Bäumer, F.S., Geierhos, M.: CORDULA: software requirements extraction utilizing chatbot as communication interface. In: Joint Proceedings of REFSQ-2018 Workshops (2018)
13. Heorhiadi, V., Rajagopalan, S., Jamjoom, H., Reiter, M.K., Sekar, V.: Gremlin: systematic resilience testing of microservices. In: Proceedings of 36th IEEE International Conference on Distributed Computing Systems (ICDCS), pp. 57–66 (2016)
14. InfluxData Inc.: InfluxDB website (2020). https://www.influxdata.com/
15. Kesim, D., van Hoorn, A., Frank, S., Häussler, M.: Identifying and prioritizing chaos experiments by using established risk analysis techniques. In: Proceedings of 31st International Symposium on Software Reliability Engineering (ISSRE) (2020)
16. von Kistowski, J., Eismann, S., et al.: Teastore: a micro-service reference application for benchmarking, modeling and resource management research. In: Proceedings of MASCOTS, pp. 223–236 (2018)
17. Leveson, N.G.: Safeware - System Safety and Computers: A Guide to Preventing Accidents and Losses Caused by Technology. Addison-Wesley, Boston (1995)
18. Miles, R.: Learning Chaos Engineering - Discovering and Overcoming System Weaknesses through Experimentation. O'Reilly Media, Inc., Sebastopol (2019)
19. Natella, R., Cotroneo, D., Madeira, H.: Assessing dependability with software fault injection: a survey. ACM Comput. Surv. (CSUR) **48**(3), 44:1–44:55 (2016)
20. Netflix Inc.: Eureka (2020). https://github.com/Netflix/eureka
21. Newman, S.: Building Microservices. O'Reilly, Sebastopol (2015)
22. Nygard, M.T.: Release It!: Design and Deploy Production-ready Software. Pragmatic Bookshelf (2018)
23. Okanović, D., van Hoorn, A., Heger, C., Wert, A., Siegl, S.: Towards performance tooling interoperability: an open format for representing execution traces. In: Fiems, D., Paolieri, M., Platis, A.N. (eds.) EPEW 2016. LNCS, vol. 9951, pp. 94–108. Springer, Cham (2016). https://doi.org/10.1007/978-3-319-46433-6_7
24. Pohl, K.: Requirements Engineering - Fundamentals, Principles, and Techniques. Springer, Heidelberg (2010)
25. Rajender Kumar Surana, C.S., Shriya, Gupta, D.B., Shankar, S.P.: Intelligent chatbot for requirements elicitation and classification. In: 2019 4th International Conference on Recent Trends on Electronics, Information, Communication and Technology (RTEICT), pp. 866–870. IEEE (2019)
26. Rietz, T.: Designing a conversational requirements elicitation system for end-users. In: 2019 IEEE 27th International Requirements Engineering Conference (RE), pp. 452–457. IEEE (2019)
27. S. Frank et al.: Supplementary material (2022). https://doi.org/10.5281/zenodo.6077724; Code Ocean capsule: https://doi.org/10.24433/CO.0520280.v1
28. Yin, K., Du, Q., Wang, W., Qiu, J., Xu, J.: On representing and eliciting resilience requirements of microservice architecture systems. CoRR abs/1909.13096 (2020). https://arxiv.org/abs/1909.13096v3
29. Zhou, X., et al.: Latent error prediction and fault localization for microservice applications by learning from system trace logs. In: Proceedings of the 2019 27th ACM Joint Meeting on European Software Engineering Conference and Symposium on the Foundations of Software Engineering, pp. 683–694. ACM (2019)
30. Zorn, C.: Interactive elicitation of resilience scenarios in microservice architectures. Master's thesis, University of Stuttgart (2021)

2nd International Workshop on Model-Driven Engineering for Software Architecture (MDE4SA)

Towards an Extensible Approach for Generative Microservice Development and Deployment Using LEMMA

Florian Rademacher⬥, Jonas Sorgalla^(✉)⬥, Philip Wizenty⬥, and Simon Trebbau⬥

IDiAL Institute, University of Applied Sciences and Arts Dortmund,
Otto-Hahn-Straße 27, 44227 Dortmund, Germany
{florian.rademacher,jonas.sorgalla,philip.wizenty,
simon.trebbau}@fh-dortmund.de

Abstract. Microservice Architecture (MSA) is an approach to implement scalable and maintainable software systems. However, when compared to monolithic applications, MSA adoption also increases architecture complexity significantly. To cope with this complexity, we investigate the application of Model-driven Engineering to MSA engineering and developed an ecosystem of architecture modeling languages (AMLs), which supports the holistic capturing of stakeholder concerns towards heterogeneous parts of a microservice architecture.

This paper enriches our AML ecosystem with an extensible approach for generating adaptable microservice code and deployment specifications from MSA models. To this end, we first derive requirements for such an approach from MSA characteristics and present two compliant realizations. Next, we integrate the approach with our AML ecosystem by defining a process for MSA model construction and processing, and the manual adaptation of generated artifacts. We validate the effectiveness of our extended AML ecosystem with a case study from the Electromobility domain.

Keywords: Microservice Architecture · Model-driven Engineering · Architecture modeling languages · Code generation

1 Introduction

Microservice Architecture (MSA) is an approach to implement service-based software architectures [17]. MSA emerged from Service-oriented Architecture (SOA) [5,7] and promotes to decompose software architectures into *microservices*. A microservice is a *service* [7] that puts particular emphasis on (i) cohesion by fulfilling a single, distinct task; (ii) independence in terms of its implementation, data management, testing, and deployment; and (iii) responsibility concerning its interaction with other components and team ownership [16,17].

Based on these characteristics, MSA adoption is expected to benefit a software architecture's (i) performance efficiency because microservices are

© The Author(s), under exclusive license to Springer Nature Switzerland AG 2022
P. Scandurra et al. (Eds.): ECSA Tracks and Workshops 2021, LNCS 13365, pp. 257–280, 2022.
https://doi.org/10.1007/978-3-031-15116-3_12

independently scalable; (ii) maintainability by allowing targeted modification or replacement of functionality given microservices' high cohesion and loose coupling; and (iii) reliability due to microservices' constrained functional scope and their self-responsibility for fault handling [3,17,27].

On the other hand, MSA tends to increase the complexity of a software architecture because it poses significant challenges concerning architecture design, development, and operation [24]. For example, regarding design, MSA requires microservice identification and afterwards careful balancing of microservices' granularity. Too fine-grained microservices increase network load, thereby decreasing performance [24], whereas too coarse-grained services counteract scalability. In addition, MSA fosters *technology heterogeneity* [17] by enabling teams to independently decide for implementation technologies, e.g., frameworks and databases, which may result in additional maintainability cost [26]. Moreover, MSA assumes a sophisticated deployment infrastructure including specialized components, e.g., for service discovery, API provisioning, and monitoring [2].

In previous works [19,20,25] we investigated the adoption of techniques from Model-driven Engineering (MDE) [4] to cope with MSA's increased complexity. As an initial enabler for the MDE paradigm in MSA engineering, we first developed a set of *architecture modeling languages* (AMLs), i.e., architecture description languages that constitute modeling languages in the sense of MDE [23]. These languages provide MSA stakeholders, e.g., domain experts, service developers and operators, with dedicated abstractions to efficiently express their concerns towards a microservice architecture. Among others, models constructed with the languages (i) facilitate reasoning about granularity by reifying service boundaries; (ii) make technology choices explicit; and (iii) support specifying microservice deployment including operation infrastructure usage.

This paper draws on insights reported in a previous work [21] in which we showed the holistic applicability of our AMLs in the design, development, and operation stages of MSA engineering (corresponding auxiliary material can be found on Software Heritage[1]). In the following, we present recent results on how to effectively utilize the constructed models in microservice development and deployment. Compared to our previous paper, the present one provides the following additional contributions:

- Enrichment of our AML ecosystem with an approach to generate executable code and deployment specifications from MSA models. The approach is specifically tailored to MSA characteristics such as technology heterogeneity, team independence and distribution [16].
- Definition of a process to structure the activities of (i) MSA model construction and adaptation; (ii) code generation; and (iii) manual adaptation of generated artifacts.
- Validation of the effectiveness of our extended AML ecosystem with a case study microservice architecture from the Electromobility domain.

---

[1] https://archive.softwareheritage.org/swh:1:dir:ec0f3181c6f2e0ffa9295766052e067d18 079c98.

The remainder of the paper is organized as follows. Section 2 provides background information on modeling dimensions in the design, development, and operation stages of MSA engineering, and how our AMLs address these dimensions. Section 3 presents our generative approach to utilize constructed MSA models in microservice development and deployment. Sections 4 and 5 validate and discuss the extended AML ecosystem, respectively. Section 6 presents related work and Sect. 7 concludes the paper.

2 Background

This section provides background information on modeling dimensions for MSA engineering stages (cf. Sect. 2.1) and our AMLs for MSA engineering targeting these stages (cf. Sect. 2.2). Furthermore, we exemplify the usage of our AMLs (cf. Sect. 2.3).

2.1 Modeling Dimensions for Microservice Architecture

As described above, we study the applicability of MDE in MSA engineering with the goal to allow efficient coping with MSA's inherent complexity. In this context, our current focus is on the three basic stages of MSA engineering, i.e., *design*, *development*, and *deployment*, as understood by Soldani et al. [24].

In our previous paper [21], we mapped each of these stages to a *modeling dimension* [4] to identify initial MDE techniques with support for the respective stage. To make the present paper self-contained, it also includes the mapping in Table 1. The mapping motivates the adoption of MDE techniques to cope with MSA's inherent complexity by listing per modeling dimension *pains* as the drivers of MSA complexity in the respective MSA engineering stage [24]. The following paragraphs describe the mapping in Table 1 per stage.

Table 1. Mapping of modeling dimensions according to Combemale et al. [4] to MSA engineering stages and pains as per Soldani et al. [24].

#	Modeling dimension	Stage	Associated pains in MSA engineering
D.1	Exploration	Design	Service Dimensioning, Size/Complexity (S/C)
D.2	Communication	Design	Service Contracts (SCs), S/C
D.3	Construction	Design	API Versioning, Communication Heterogeneity, SCs, Microservice Separation (MS), S/C
D.4	Implementation	Development	MS, Overhead, Human Errors
		Operation	Operational Complexity, Service Coordination, S/C
D.5	Testing	Development	Integration Testing, Performance Testing, S/C
D.6	Documentation	Design	S/C

Design Stage. In microservice design, models can make a microservice's granularity explicit by reifying the structures and relationships of domain concepts in the service's responsibility (cf. Dimension D.1 in Table 1). This modeling purpose aligns to the construction of service-specific *domain models* using Domain-driven Design (DDD) [8,17]. DDD is a model-based methodology that we used in our previous paper to capture the structures and relationships of the domain concepts of an MSA-based software platform for electric vehicle charging [21].

Next to domain concepts, MSA models can capture, e.g., service APIs and their versions, or allow reasoning about communication heterogeneity (D.3).

Additionally, models are means to concisely communicate and document, e.g., domain concepts or service contracts (D.2 and D.6). In MSA, efficient communication and a common architectural understanding is crucial since teams should be decomposed along service boundaries [16].

Development Stage. Code generators can support the development of microservices by producing boilerplate code from models, thereby reducing manual overhead and human errors in recurring coding tasks like service configuration (D.4) [4]. Furthermore, code generation facilitates keeping services' design consistent with their implementation, and also makes it possible to run early integration tests on generated microservices (D.5). In fact, the MDE technique of code generation [4] is the foundation for our generative approach towards microservice development and deployment presented in Sect. 3.

Operation Stage. In the operation stage of MSA engineering, models can be used to harmonize the description of service deployment, operation infrastructure and its usage across heterogeneous technologies [21]. Model-based operation specifications also facilitate reasoning about the operational complexity of a microservice architecture (D.4) and allow for the automated derivation of deployment artifacts (cf. Sect. 3).

2.2 Modeling Microservice Architecture with LEMMA

LEMMA (Language Ecosystem for Modeling Microservice Architecture) denotes our ecosystem of AMLs for MSA engineering [19,20]. In our previous paper, we showed LEMMA's applicability for the holistic modeling of an MSA-based software platform for electric vehicle charging [21]. The present paper extends LEMMA with a generative approach to derive microservice code and deployment specifications from MSA models constructed with LEMMA's AMLs (cf. Sect. 3).

Table 2 describes the AMLs of LEMMA, and identifies per language the addressed *architecture viewpoints* [14] and stakeholder types in MSA engineering.

LEMMA's AMLs rely on an import mechanism to compose information from different models. Figure 1 shows the import relationships between the AMLs.

According to Fig. 1, domain experts and service developers can use LEMMA's DML to organize domain information in several models and then combine them via imports. This approach allows, e.g., an MSA team to construct reusable domain models on which several of its microservices rely.

Table 2. LEMMA viewpoints, and corresponding stakeholder types and AMLs.

Viewpoint	Stakeholder	Modeling language
Domain	Domain Expert, Service Developer	*Domain Data Modeling Language* [20] *(DML)*: Allows the construction of LEMMA *domain models* with domain-specific data types including the assignment of DDD patterns [8]
Technology	Service Developer, Service Operator	*Technology Modeling Language* [19] *(TML)*: Supports constructing *technology models* that capture characteristics of microservice implementation languages, communication protocols, and operation technologies. The TML also enables to define *technology aspects* to augment, e.g., modeled data structures and microservices with additional semantics
Service	Service Developer	*Service Modeling Language* [20] *(SML): Service models* constructed with the SML comprise microservice specifications including service interfaces, operations, and endpoints
Operation	Service Operator	*Operation Modeling Language* [20] *(OML)*: Enables to construct *operation models* that determine microservices' deployment and their usage of operation infrastructure

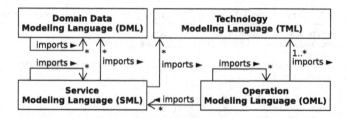

Fig. 1. Import relationships between LEMMA's AMLs in a UML class diagram. Each class denotes an AML. Associations identify import relationship between AMLs.

LEMMA's SML has import relationships to the DML, the TML, and itself (cf. Fig. 1). First, service models may import domain models to leverage domain concepts as types for microservice operation parameters. Second, the import of technology into service models allows the specification of information related to microservice implementation. However, it is optional to increase the flexibility of MSA teams by decoupling API design from technology choices. Third, service models can import other service models to capture microservice dependencies.

LEMMA's OML requires to import at least one technology model into operation models (cf. Fig. 1) as technologies, e.g., for service deployment and API provisioning, are usually prerequisites for microservice operation [2]. Furthermore, LEMMA operation models can import LEMMA service models to express services' deployment or infrastructure usage. In addition, based on the import relationship of the OML with itself, it is possible to modularize heterogeneous parts of the operation infrastructure, which is useful, e.g., when MSA teams are responsible for specifying their services' deployment while a centralized operation team maintains additional infrastructure components [25].

2.3 LEMMA by Example

We illustrate the usage of LEMMA's AMLs on the example of the coherent set of models in Listings 2.1 to 2.4. Each listing comprises a model excerpt in a different LEMMA AML and originates from our previous paper [21].

Listing 2.1. Domain model excerpt "domain.data".

```
1  context ChargingStationManagement {
2    structure ElectrifiedParkingSpace
3    <aggregate, entity> {
4      ChargingType chargingType<part>,
5      string id<identifier>,
6      string name,
7      string plugType,
8      ...
9  } ... }
```

Listing 2.2. Technology model excerpt "Spring.technology".

```
technology Spring {                              1
  protocols {                                    2
    sync rest data formats "application/json"    3
    default with format "application/json";      4
  }                                              5
  service aspects {                              6
    aspect PutMapping for operations {           7
      selector(protocol = rest);                 8
  } ... }}                                        9
```

Listing 2.3. Service model excerpt "chargingStationManagement.services".

```
1   import datatypes from "domain.data" as Domain
2   import technology from "Spring.technology" as Spring
3   @technology(Spring)
4   public functional microservice de.fhdo.puls.ChargingStationManagementCommand {
5     interface Commands {
6       @endpoints(Spring::_protocols.rest: "/ePS";)
7       @Spring::_aspects.PutMapping
8       public createElectrifiedParkingSpace(
9         sync in command : Domain::ChargingStationManagement.
10        CreateElectrifiedParkingSpaceCommand); } ... }
```

Listing 2.4. Operation model excerpt "chargingStationManagement.operation".

```
1   import microservices from "chargingStationManagement.services" as CSMM
2   import technology from "container_base.technology" as DeploymentBase
3   import nodes from "eureka.operation" as ServiceDiscovery
4   @technology(DeploymentBase)
5   container ChargingStationManagementCommandContainer
6     deployment technology container_base::_deployment.Kubernetes
7     deploys ChargingService::de.fhdo.puls.ChargingStationManagementCommand
8     depends on nodes ServiceDiscovery::Eureka ... {
9     default values {
10      serverPort=8071
11      springApplicationName="ChargingStationManagementCommandMicroservice"
12      eurekaUri="http://eureka:8761/eureka"
13      ...}}
```

Listing 2.1 shows a domain model in LEMMA's DML (cf. Sect. 2.2). The DML considers DDD patterns to enable modeling of microservices' domain concepts. Bounded Context [8] is an integral DDD pattern that shares similarities with the notion of microservice regarding boundary definition and single team ownership [17]. To define bounded contexts, the DML provides the **context** keyword by which Listing 2.1 models the bounded context `ChargingStationManagement`. It clusters the data structure `ElectrifiedParkingSpace`, which is modeled as a DDD Aggregate and Entity using corresponding DML keywords (cf. Line 3). As an aggregate, the data structure is composed of structural *parts*, whose lifetimes correspond to that of the structure [8]. As an entity, the structure also defines a domain-specific identity [8]. The part and identifier fields of the structure are marked with corresponding DML keywords (cf. Lines 4 and 5).

Listing 2.2 comprises a technology model for the Spring framework[2] expressed in LEMMA's TML (cf. Sect. 2.2). In its `protocols` section (cf. Lines 2 to 5) the technology model defines the existence of the `rest` protocol to represent synchronous, REST-based microservice interactions [9] using the JSON data format. The `service aspects` section in Lines 6 to 9 then specifies the `PutMapping` aspect. It reifies the eponymous Spring annotation and is applicable to modeled microservice `operations` that communicate via REST.

Listing 2.3 exemplifies the usage of LEMMA's SML (cf. Sect. 2.2). The service model first imports the domain and technology model from Listings 2.1 and 2.2, respectively. As a result, the `Spring` technology becomes applicable to the modeled `ChargingStationManagementCommand` (CSMC) microservice (cf. Line 3). Its definition, starting in Line 4, clusters the `Commands` interface (cf. Line 5) with its `createElectrifiedParkingSpace` operation (cf. Line 8). The operation comprises the synchronously incoming parameter `command`, whose type is a data structure of the `ChargingStationManagement` bounded context (cf. Lines 9 and 10) imported from the domain model (cf. Listing 2.1). In Lines 6 and 7 of Listing 2.3, the microservice operation is augmented with information from the imported technology model (cf. Listing 2.2). Specifically, the operation receives an endpoint for the `rest` protocol and an application of the `PutMapping` aspect so that it shall be invokable via REST and an HTTP `PUT` request [10].

Listing 2.4 shows the deployment specification of the CSMC microservice in LEMMA's OML (cf. Sect. 2.2). Lines 1 to 3 import the CSMC's service model (cf. Listing 2.3), a technology model for basic container technologies like Docker[3] and Kubernetes[4], and another operation model comprising a node definition for a Eureka-based service discovery[5]. Starting with Line 5, the operation model defines a container utilizing the imported Kubernetes technology (cf. Lines 4 and 6). The container deploys the imported CSMC microservice (cf. Line 7) and depends on the imported Eureka service discovery (cf. Line 8). Consequently, the microservice can leverage the discovery's capability to detect other microservices for interaction. For this purpose, the microservice must receive certain configuration properties, which Listing 2.4 determines in Lines 10 to 12.

To increase modeling efficiency and consider MSA's inherent support for elasticity [17], LEMMA's AMLs do not require a priori modeling, e.g., of all possible microservice instances. Instead, the runtime configuration of these artifacts, e.g.,

---

[2] https://www.spring.io.
[3] https://www.docker.com.
[4] https://www.kubernetes.io.
[5] https://github.com/Netflix/eureka.

by container orchestration platforms, determines the number of their instances. In this context, LEMMA models act as blueprints for artifact instantiation.

3   Extensible LEMMA-Based Approach for Generative Microservice Development and Deployment

This section complements our previous paper [21] with an approach to generate code and deployment specifications from MSA models expressed in LEMMA's AMLs (cf. Sect. 2.2). Therefore, we first describe the requirements and basic concepts of the approach (cf. Sect. 3.1). Next, we present two requirements-compliant realizations of the approach for LEMMA (cf. Sect. 3.2). Sect. 3.3 then defines a process that integrates the generation approach with model construction and manual adaptation of generated artifacts.

3.1   Requirements and Basic Concepts for Extensible Generation of Microservice Code and Deployment Specifications

As described in Sect. 2.2, LEMMA respects the degrees of freedom in MSA technology choices, implementation approaches, and team organization. Thus, a code generation approach for LEMMA must also respect them. Therefore, we pose the following requirements towards such an approach:

R.1 *Provisioning of a basic technology mapping:* Following the notion of code generation in MDE [4], a code generation approach for LEMMA must enable a basic mapping of coherent LEMMA models (cf. Sect. 2.2) to a technology. For instance, a basic mapping targeting Java microservices could map domain concepts and microservices modeled with LEMMA's DML and SML to Plain Old Java Objects (POJOs) and classes with the entrypoint method `main` [11], respectively.

R.2 *Flexible composition of additive technology mappings:* The code generation approach must allow the composition of the basic technology mapping with additive mappings to support MSA technology heterogeneity. For example, a mapping for Spring Boot[6] could be additive in that it extends generated Java classes with Spring annotations.

R.3 *Support for mapping sharing:* Basic and additive technology mappings must be shareable to cope with MSA team distribution. For example, several teams may rely on the Java basic mapping to derive initial Java code from LEMMA models, but then apply distinct additive mappings for their favored microservice frameworks, e.g., Spring Boot or Micronaut[7].

R.4 *Support for standalone execution of mapping compositions:* We consider a selected basic technology mapping and an additional set of additive technology mappings a *mapping composition*. For instance, the combination of

---

[6] https://spring.io/projects/spring-boot.

[7] https://micronaut.io.

a Java basic mapping with additive mappings for Spring Boot and Spring Kafka[8] constitutes a mapping composition that enables the generation of Java microservice code from LEMMA models including support for synchronous and asynchronous interactions. A mapping composition must be standalone executable to anticipate the integration of mapping compositions into continuous integration pipelines as a crucial technique in MSA projects [3].

R.5 *Production of manually extensible artifacts by mapping compositions*: The execution of a mapping composition on coherent LEMMA models must produce artifacts that are manually extensible by service developers or operators (cf. Sect. 2.2). This requirement is particularly crucial as LEMMA currently does not support behavior specification so that, e.g., business logic must be manually retrofitted into Java method bodies. There exist several approaches to allow manual extension of generated artifacts and preserve extensions upon regeneration [12]. We do not prescribe mapping compositions to use one of these approaches but expect them to ensure manual, preserving extension of generated artifacts.

R.6 *Production of syntactically correct code by mapping compositions*: Mapping compositions must produce syntactically correct code. In case the generated code is for a programming language and not for, e.g., a declarative deployment language, we also expect it to be executable. This requirement enables to integrate mapping compositions into continuous integration pipelines, e.g., to run tests on generated code (cf. Sect. 2.1) or enable microservice deployment.

Our code generation approach for LEMMA consists of two basic concepts that are compliant with the aforementioned requirements. A *LEMMA Base Generator* (LBG) provides a basic technology mapping (**R.1**) and a *LEMMA Generation Fragment* (LGF) realizes an additive mapping for the same basic technology as a certain LBG (**R.2**). To this end, the LBG and LGFs compatible to the LBG must agree on a mechanism to gather produced code and augment it with additional information. Furthermore, LBGs and LGFs represent distinct, shareable artifacts (**R.3**), e.g., Java archives. In this context, an LBG integrates means to invoke LGFs during code generation following a prescribed composition approach (**R.4**). LBGs and LGFs must also ensure manual code extension (**R.5**) and the production of syntactically correct code (**R.6**).

3.2 AST-Based and File-Based Code Generation for LEMMA

For LEMMA, we developed two requirements-compliant realizations of the code generation approach presented in Sect. 3.1. These realizations comprise distinct LBGs and LGFs for Java microservices and Docker deployment with Kubernetes. In addition, due to their respective purpose, the realizations differ in how produced code is gathered by LBGs and continuously enriched by LGFs.

---

[8] https://spring.io/projects/spring-kafka.

AST-Based Code Generation. We implemented an LBG and LGFs for Java as a microservice implementation language. Among others, the resulting LEMMA Base Generator for Java (LBG$_j$) maps (i) data structures in LEMMA domain models to POJOs with getters and setters for modeled fields; (ii) microservices in LEMMA service models to Java classes with `main` methods; and (iii) modeled microservice interfaces to Java classes with a method per modeled operation (cf. Sect. 2.3 and Requirement **R.1** in Sect. 3.1).

The LBG$_j$ first instantiates all Java classes as in-memory Abstract Syntax Trees (ASTs) [11]. Each AST represents a mutable object graph that the LBG$_j$ can pass to a LEMMA Generation Fragment for Java (LGF$_j$). An LGF$_j$ realizes an additive technology mapping (**R.2**) to, e.g., enhance generated Java classes with Spring Boot annotations. The usage of in-memory ASTs to gather produced code and augment it allows flexible mapping composition and also prevents expensive re-parsing of Java classes generated by the LBG$_j$ or a previous LGF$_j$.

The LBG$_j$ and each LGF$_j$ is packaged in its own Java archive and thus shareable across MSA teams (**R.3**). The LBG$_j$ is a standalone Java application that can load LGF$_j$ Java archives and invoke them on in-memory ASTs (**R.4**). In this case, the mapping composition comprises executing passed LGF$_j$ archives in order.

For the manual extension of generated code (**R.5**), the LBG$_j$ supports the Generation Gap pattern and its extended version [12]. That is, the LBG$_j$ modifies Java ASTs to comply with one of these patterns after all LGF$_j$ executions.

We developed the LBG$_j$ and each LGF$_j$ to generate executable Java code (**R.6**), which we achieved mainly by (i) preventing the user to generate code from incorrect LEMMA models; (ii) generating `throw` statements in method bodies hinting at yet missing business logic implementation; and (iii) integrating validations in LGF$_j$ implementations to prevent specifying unsupported values for LEMMA technology aspects (cf. Sect. 2.3). Currently, we provide LGF$_j$ implementations for the Command Query Responsibility Segregation (CQRS) and Domain Events patterns [22] as well as Spring Boot and Spring Kafka[9].

Figure 2 exemplifies the evolution of a Java AST generated for the `Commands` interface modeled in Listing 2.3 by the LBG$_j$ and the Spring Boot LGF$_j$.

In Step 1, the LBG$_j$ instantiates a basic Java AST for the `Commands` interface (`NormalClassDeclaration` object) including its `createElectrifiedParkingSpace` operation (`MethodDeclaration` object). The generated method also receives a `throw` statement as its body (`MethodBody` object).

In Step 2, the LBG$_j$ executes the Spring Boot LGF$_j$ on the basic AST. It adds the annotations `Component` and `RestController` to the `Commands` class (`NormalAnnotation` objects). The LGF$_j$ generates these annotations due to the REST endpoint specified in Line 6 of Listing 2.3. Similarly, the LGF$_j$ generates the `PutMapping` annotation with the value "/ePS" for the `createElectrifiedParkingSpace` method based on the modeled REST endpoint and the application of the LEMMA technology aspect in Line 7 of Listing 2.3.

---

[9] https://github.com/SeelabFhdo/lemma/tree/main/code%20generators.

Fig. 2. Evolution of a Java AST by the LBG$_j$ and the Spring Boot LGF$_j$. Each compartment shows an excerpt of the evolved AST as an object graph of Java language concepts [11] in UML's syntax for instance specifications.

In Step 3, the LBG$_j$ enriches the AST with classes and interfaces (`NormalInterfaceDeclaration`) following the Generation Gap pattern for the preserving integration of manual with generated code [12].

File-Based Code Generation. Next to the LBG$_j$ and LGF$_j$, we developed a second realization of the generation approach described in Sect. 3.1 for LEMMA. It focuses on the generation of artifacts for microservice deployment with Docker and Kubernetes. The realization consists of a LEMMA Base Generator for Docker and Kubernetes (LBG$_d$), and a set of corresponding LEMMA Generation Fragments (LGF$_d$). The LBG$_d$ performs a basic mapping of LEMMA operation models (cf. Sect. 2.2) to deployment specifications. More specifically, it maps (i) modeled containers to Dockerfiles and Kubernetes specifications for service deployment; and (ii) modeled configuration properties to technology-specific configuration files (cf. Sect. 2.3 and Requirement **R.1** in Sect. 3.1). An LGF$_d$ then generates additional or extends previously generated files from configuration properties of modeled LEMMA containers or infrastructure nodes (**R.2**).

By contrast to the AST-based code generation of the LBG_j (see above), the LBG_d pursues a file-based approach for mapping composition. That is due to the large degree of heterogeneity in MSA operation technologies [2]. While LEMMA's OML aims to provide a homogeneous syntax for the specification of microservice deployment and operation [21], MSA strives to also decouple infrastructure components as much as possible to increase scalability. Hence, no common format exists for the LBG_d and LGF_d implementations to agree on for in-memory AST generation, which is why deployment-related generation in LEMMA uses configuration files in different formats to synchronize basic and additive technology mappings (cf. Sect. 3.1). For example, the LGF_d can generate a build script for a container image in the Dockerfile format[10] and a required configuration file for Java microservices in the Properties format. The latter file is now re-parseable and extensible by an LGF_d for Eureka (see below).

The LBG_d and LGF_d implementations are compiled into their own Java archives to make them shareable across MSA teams (**R.3**). In addition, the LBG_d is standalone executable and controls the execution of LGF_d archives in their specified order (**R.4**). By contrast to the LGF_j archives, LGF_d archives are executable without their base generator. That is to allow, e.g., the generation of a Eureka service discovery when an MSA team does not employ Docker or is not responsible for microservice deployment but only infrastructure provisioning [25].

To comply with Requirement **R.5**, the LBG_d and each LGF_d supports the adoption of manual adaptations in generated artifacts into their newly generated versions. Since the configuration files are in formats that expect a unique identifier for each entry, reconciling manually adopted and newly generated artifacts boils down to integrating non-existing entries into newly generated artifacts and preventing the overwriting of existing entries by generated values.

The LBG_d and each LGF_d use the same mechanisms as the LBG_j and LGF_j implementations to achieve the generation of syntactically correct code (**R.6**).

Next to the LBG_d targeting Docker and Kubernetes for service deployment, we currently provide LGF_d implementations for MariaDB[11], MongoDB[12], Eureka, and Zuul[13] (see Footnote 9).

Figure 3 exemplifies the evolution of deployment specifications generated from the container modeled in Listing 2.4 by the LBG_d and the Eureka LGF_d.

In Step 1, the LBG_d generates a Dockerfile for the microservice deployed by the modeled container (cf. Listing 2.4) and a Docker Compose file[14] including the service. The latter file is common to all components of a modeled microservice architecture for coordinated application startup. In addition, since the microservice relies on Spring (cf. Listing 2.3), the LBG_d produces the `application.properties` file to incorporate the service's configuration properties from the modeled container. In case the generated Docker Compose or

---

[10] https://docs.docker.com/engine/reference/builder.

[11] https://www.mariadb.org.

[12] https://www.mongodb.com.

[13] https://github.com/Netflix/zuul.

[14] https://docs.docker.com/compose.

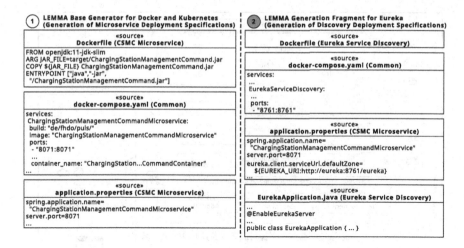

Fig. 3. Evolution of deployment specifications' file contents by the LBG$_d$ and the Eureka LGF$_d$.

Spring configuration file already existed, the LBG$_d$ would have extended them with missing entries.

In Step 2, the Eureka LGF$_d$ generates Docker and configuration files for the Eureka service discovery. While the Dockerfile is Eureka-specific and always re-generated, the LGF$_d$ extends the existing Docker Compose and `application.properties` files with entries to enable the microservice the discovery of other services. Additionally, the LGF$_d$ generates an executable Java class to run the service discovery according to the Eureka framework.

The LBG$_d$ and each LGF$_d$ can also generate Kubernetes specifications for service and infrastructure deployment, respectively. For the sake of brevity, we omit them in Fig. 3 and provide them with our validation package (cf. Sect. 4).

3.3 Integration of the Generative Approach with LEMMA Modeling Activities

This section describes the integration of the code generation approach and its two realizations (cf. Sects. 3.1 and 3.2) with LEMMA. More specifically, it complements our previous paper [21] with a process that combines holistic MSA modeling using LEMMA's AMLs with effective model processing to increase models' value [4]. Consequently, the process involves the operation of the previously introduced LBGs and LGFs on the different LEMMA model kinds (cf. Sect. 2.2) as well as the adaptation of generated artifacts. The process is organized along the three stages of MSA engineering [24] (c.f. Sect. 2.1) and intentionally abstracts from the applied process model for software development [29], e.g., incremental or waterfall, but considers all steps for an MSA team to realize its services using LEMMA's AMLs and code generation approach. Figure 4 shows the process. It indicates possible iterations within and between process

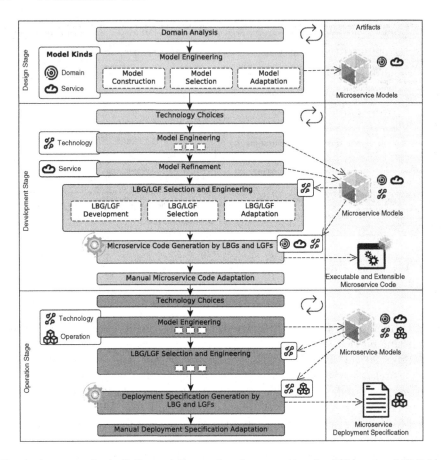

Fig. 4. A process for holistic modeling and code generation for MSA using LEMMA.

steps, which result from MSA models' enabling of exploration and communication of microservice artifacts (cf. Sect. 2.1), by an iteration icon in the upper right corner of each engineering stage.

The following paragraphs describe the process per MSA engineering stage.

Design Stage. The process starts with a Domain Analysis in which the MSA team, depending on the applied process model for software development, analyzes the portion of the application domain in its responsibility [16], e.g., using DDD [8]. Based on the Domain Analysis and aligned to the modeling dimensions described in Sect. 2.1, the process continues with the Model Engineering step. Its goal is to provide LEMMA domain and technology-agnostic service models (cf. Sect. 2.2) from the results of the Domain Analysis. Model Engineering consists of the sub-steps Model Construction, Model Selection, and/or Model Adaptation. Depending on the MSA team and its utilization level of LEMMA, it might not always be necessary to construct domain and service models from scratch, e.g., when a microservice evolves or a new microservice shall operate on an already captured bounded context (cf. Sect. 2.3).

Development Stage. This stage concerns the implementation of previously designed microservices (cf. Sect. 2.1). Therefore, the MSA team first makes Technology Choices, e.g., of the service programming language and supportive frameworks. It follows a Model Engineering step in which LEMMA technology models for the chosen technologies are constructed, or selected and adapted, e.g., to cover new annotations from frameworks (cf. Sect. 2.3). The Model Refinement step uses the technology models to augment the technology-agnostic service models from the Design stage with technology-specific information.

The LBG/LGF Selection and Engineering step involves the development of new LBGs/LGFs as well as their selection and potential adaptation. The actions performed in this step depend on the chosen technologies, their models and applications in LEMMA service models. For example, the generation support for a new microservice programming language requires the implementation of an LBG to perform the basic technology mapping (cf. Sect. 3.1). On the other hand, in case there exists an LGF for a framework but lacks new functionality of the latter, the LGF needs to be adapted.

After LBG/LGF Selection and Engineering, mapping compositions (cf. Sect. 3.1) generate microservice code from LEMMA domain and technology-specific service models (cf. Listings 2.1 and 2.3 in Sect. 2.3).

The final step of the Development stage concerns Manual Microservice Code Adaptation, e.g., to add business logic to new microservice operations. To this end, developers may import the runnable microservices into a corresponding IDE based on their chosen programming language during generation.

Operation Stage. The process covers the Operation stage in MSA engineering to leverage LEMMA's generation approach for microservice deployment (cf. Sect. 3.2). Similar to the Development stage, the MSA team first makes Technology Choices regarding, e.g., the container configuration of a microservice or the requested infrastructure capabilities. The Model Engineering step again consists of the construction, or selection and adaptation of technology models. In addition, the MSA team uses LEMMA's OML (c.f. Subsect. 2.2) to construct operation models for their microservices. As operation models are always technology-specific, model engineering and technology-specific refinement collapse in the Operation stage.

The following LBG/LGF Selection and Engineering step equals that of the Development stage, but focuses on microservice deployment rather than implementation technologies. The last two steps of the Operation stage concern the generation of deployment specifications from LEMMA operation models and their possible manual adaptation.

4   Validation

This section validates our code generation approach (cf. Sect. 3) in the context of a case study from the Electromobility domain. Sect. 4.1 briefly introduces the case study (a comprehensive description can be found in our previous paper [21]) and Sect. 4.2 applies our code generation approach to its LEMMA models.

4.1   Case Study

The case study is the Park and Charge Platform (PACP), which we are developing as part of the research project PuLS[15]. PuLS aims to increase the accessibility of charging stations for electric vehicles by enabling citizens to offer spare stations on private ground for use by other owners of electric vehicles. In addition, charging stations are equipped with sensors to contribute in urban air quality monitoring. Figure 5 shows the design of the PACP.

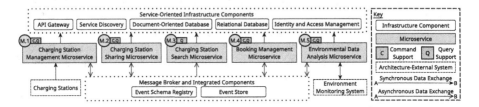

Fig. 5. Service-based design of the PACP including shared infrastructure components.

The PACP comprises five logical microservices and follows the CQRS pattern [22] to decompose each service into at least two physical microservice implementations, i.e., one for the execution of state-changing commands, e.g., database updates, and one for state-invariant queries, e.g., database reads. The microservices provide capabilities for (i) managing charging station information like location, charging and plug type (Microservice **M.1**); (ii) offering spare charging stations for use by others (**M.2**); (iii) searching spare stations (**M.3**); (iv) booking spare stations (**M.4**); and (v) analyzing air quality indicators (**M.5**).

Additionally, the PACP involves two kinds of infrastructure components. Service-oriented infrastructure components provide each microservice with capabilities for API provisioning, service discovery, data management, and identity and access management. Message Broker and integrated Components, on the other hand, are shared by all microservices to send asynchronous events, e.g., about handled command requests and resulting database updates following the CQRS pattern.

4.2   Generating Case Study Code and Deployment Specifications

We validated our code generation approach and its two realizations (cf. Sect. 3) with the five PACP microservices (cf. Sect. 4.1). Therefore, we followed the process for holistic LEMMA modeling presented in Sect. 3.3. This section illustrates the process steps for the validation of our code generation approach on the physical command microservice of the logical PACP Microservice M.1. This microservice is the `ChargingStationManagementCommand` microservice (CSMC-M) with

---

[15] Funded by the German Federal Ministry of Transport and Digital Infrastructure under grant number 03EMF0203C.

which we illustrated the usage of LEMMA's AMLs in Sect. 2.3. We provide a validation package with the LEMMA models and generated artifacts of all PACP microservice on Software Heritage[16] to enable reproduction of our validation results. We structure the following presentation of the validation results for the CSMC-M by the phases of our holistic modeling process.

Design Stage. Following our modeling process, we first performed a domain analysis of the application domain together with the industry partners of the PuLS project. Next, we used the resulting DDD domain models for model engineering. Since the PACP is a greenfield microservice architecture, we could not refer to existing LEMMA models but had to construct them from scratch. For the CSMC-M, these models comprised the domain model in Listing 2.1 and the service model in Listing 2.3, however without technology aspect applications since no technology decisions had taken place yet (cf. Sect. 3.3).

Development Stage. After all project partners had agreed on utilizing Java with the Spring framework for microservice implementation and the Kafka message broker[17] for asynchronous service interaction (cf. Sect. 4.1), we entered the Development stage of our process by first constructing a set of LEMMA technology models. Next to the Spring technology model shown in Listing 2.2, we also constructed technology models for Kafka and the CQRS pattern. We refer to our previous paper [21] for their description. With all technology models at hand, we refined the CSMC-M service model as exemplified by Listing 4.1.

Listing 4.1. Excerpt of refined LEMMA service model for the CSMC-M.

```
 1  ...
 2  @technology(CQRS)
 3  @technology(Kafka)
 4  @technology(Spring)
 5  @CQRS::_aspects.CommandSide("ChargingStationManagementMicroservice")
 6  @endpoints(Kafka::_protocols.kafka: "kafka-server1:9092";)
 7  public functional microservice de.fhdo.puls.ChargingStationManagementCommand {
 8    interface Commands {
 9    @endpoints(Spring::_protocols.rest: "/ePS";)
10    @Spring::_aspects.PutMapping
11    public createElectrifiedParkingSpace(
12      sync in command : Domain::ChargingStationManagement.
13      CreateElectrifiedParkingSpaceCommand); } ... }
```

Lines in boldface identify the technology information with which we augmented the service model for the CSMC-M as compared to its peculiarity in the Design stage. Next to the Spring-related annotations described in Sect. 2.3, we applied the CommandSide aspect from the CQRS technology model to the microservice (cf. Line 5) and also specified an endpoint for the kafka protocol originating from the Kafka technology model (cf. Line 6). While the aspect identifies the CSMC-M as a CQRS command microservice [22], the endpoint configures the address of the Kafka broker for the CSMC-M to interact with [21].

---

[16] https://archive.softwareheritage.org/swh:1:dir:a1ec70bc3a12387fde806dcb0b536426 0541b583.

[17] https://kafka.apache.org.

After model refinement, we iteratively developed the LGF$_j$ and an LGF$_j$ for each technology model (cf. Sect. 3.2). Finally, we generated Spring- and Kafka-enabled microservice code compliant to the CQRS pattern from the mapping composition consisting of the LGF$_j$ and all additive fragments. Listings 4.2 and 4.3 show the serialized version of the Java AST in Fig. 2 for the `Commands` interface of the CSMC-C (cf. Sect. 2.3).

Listing 4.2. Excerpt of the generated, manually extensible `Commands` class.

```
1  ...
2  @Component
3  @RestController
4  public class Commands
5  extends CommandsGenImpl {
6   public void
7   createElectrifiedParkingSpace
8   (@RequestBody
9   CreateElectrifiedParkingSpaceCommand
10  command) {
11   checkRequiredParameters(command);
12   super.createElectrifiedParkingSpace
13   (command);
14  } ... }
```

Listing 4.3. Continuously generated super class of the `Commands` class.

```
1  ...
2  public abstract class CommandsGenImpl
3  implements CommandsGen {
4   @PutMapping(value = "/ePS")
5   public void
6   createElectrifiedParkingSpace
7   (@RequestBody
8   CreateElectrifiedParkingSpaceCommand
9   command
10  ) {
11   throw new
12   UnsupportedOperationException
13   ("Not implemented yet");
14  } ... }
```

Both classes apply the Generation Gap pattern [12] to enable manual code extension in the next step of our modeling process. That is, the `Commands` class in Listing 4.2 can comprise custom code, whereas its super class in 4.3 is newly generated upon each execution of the mapping composition to ensure consistency with the `Commands` interface in a possibly evolved service model of the CSMC-M.

Listing 4.4 shows a generated Java class for enabling the CSMC-M to communicate with the Kafka message broker of the PACP (cf. Sect. 4.1).

Listing 4.4. Continuously generated Kafka configuration class.

```
1  ...
2  public abstract class KafkaConfigGenImpl implements KafkaConfigGen {
3  @Value(value = "${kafka.bootstrapAddress}")
4  protected String bootstrapAddress;
5   @Bean
6   public KafkaAdmin kafkaAdmin() {
7    Map<String, Object> configs = new HashMap<>();
8    configs.put(AdminClientConfig.BOOTSTRAP_SERVERS_CONFIG, bootstrapAddress);
9    return new KafkaAdmin(configs);
10  }
11  ...
12  public KafkaTemplate<String, ParkingSpaceCreated>
13   parkingSpaceCreatedEventsProducer() {
14   return new KafkaTemplate<>(parkingSpaceCreatedEventsProducerFactory());
15  } ... }
```

The generation of the configuration class originates from the application of the Kafka technology model to the CSMC-M (cf. Listing 4.1). It is responsible for setting up the broker connection (cf. Lines 3 to 10) and provides microservice developers with convenience methods like **parkingSpaceCreatedEventsProducer** (cf. Lines 12 to 15) to send message via the broker from manually implemented business logic.

Operation Stage. In the operation stage, we constructed technology models for the Docker, Eureka, Kubernetes, MariaDB, and MongoDB technologies as at the time of writing they represent the chosen deployment and infrastructure technologies in the PuLS project. Moreover, we constructed an operation model for the CSMC-M's deployment (cf. Sect. 2.3) and operation models containing infrastructure nodes based on the aforementioned technologies. Next, we developed the LBG_d and corresponding LGF_d implementations (cf. Sect. 3.2), and generated the deployment specifications with the resulting mapping composition as illustrated in Fig. 3. By contrast to the generated microservice code in the Development stage, the deployment specification did not require manual adaptations as all relevant information could be extracted from the configuration properties provided by the technology models, and instantiated and configured in the containers and nodes of the operation models.

Result Summary. Table 3 summarizes our validation results by comparing the lines of code (LOC) of manually constructed LEMMA models (M) with those generated by LBG_j/LGF_j and LBG_d/LGF_d mapping compositions (G) per case study microservice M.1 to M.5 (cf. Sect. 4.1) and common deployment specifications I, e.g., for Docker Compose (cf. Sect. 3.2). Next to the models, the generated Java code and deployment specifications, our validation package (see footnote 16) also comprises the scripts to derive the listed figures.

Table 3. Manual model LOC and generated LOC for the PACP case study.

MS	DML LOC (M)	SML LOC (M)	OML LOC (M)	Total Manual LOC	Java LOC (G)	Deployment LOC (G)	Total Generated LOC	Total LOC	Share of Gen. Code
M.1	290	132	60	482	3549	130	3679	4161	88.42%
M.2	180	138	60	378	2472	135	2607	2985	87.34%
M.3	73	157	30	260	1182	72	1254	1514	82.83%
M.4	347	483	57	887	5617	150	5767	6654	86.67%
M.5	238	183	62	483	3038	135	3173	3656	86.79%
I	n/a	n/a	117	117	n/a	463	463	580	79.83%

5 Discussion

Validation Results. As can be seen from Table 3, the presented code generation approach and its integration with LEMMA (cf. Sect. 3) is efficient. That is, we were able to derive a significantly greater amount of Java and deployment specification LOC than comprised in the input LEMMA models. This is evident from the comparison between the Total Generated LOC and Total Manual LOC columns (cf. Table 3). In addition, since we implemented the LBGs and LGFs involved in code generation, the generated code is syntactically correct and, in the case for Java, immediately extensible by custom business logic following the modeling process in Fig. 4. However, while our validation shows the efficiency of the presented approach, it also motivates further studies.

Added Value of Code Generation. While the utilization of models to document, communicate, and construct software architectures is recognized beneficial (cf. Sect. 2.1) [13], a general answer about the added value of code generation is often not possible. On the one hand, the development and maintenance of generators like LEMMA LBGs and LGFs requires knowledge and time. On the other hand, existing generators can enable a productivity increase that grows by the amount of generator usage [13]. These factors require contextualized evaluation per project. However, empirical evidence about MSA engineering also suggests that organizations are consistent across team and service boundaries w.r.t. technology choices [3]. Hence, we see potential for investigating our approach in MSA engineering projects that exceed the complexity of the PACP (cf. Sect. 4.1), and potentially require the development of new LBGs and LGFs.

MSA and Agile Development Processes. MSA's application in large-scale agile development processes [16] also motivates further research of our approach. In such processes it is particularly important to enable sharing and extension of common artifacts across teams. As per the requirements formulated in Sect. 3.1, LBGs and LGFs take team distribution and artifact sharing into account. However, it also requires MSA teams, which develop an LBG or LGF, to also consider its usage by other teams for their LEMMA models. Technology models may provide a basic guidance for other teams concerning the features supported by an LBG or LGF. Nonetheless, an LBG or LGF constitutes a *shared artifact* [17] between MSA teams, and thus requires an agreement on provided and required capabilities. Therefore, we consider it necessary to reason about means to ensure such an agreement. A popular approach in MSA engineering for this purpose is the definition of *consumer-driven contracts* [17] for which a consuming team expresses its requirements towards a microservice API in the form of tests. Similarly, the provisioning of testable APIs by code generators could allow for the conclusion of consumer-driven contracts between LBG/LGF providers and users.

Threats to Validity. The conducted validation of our approach (c.f. Sect. 4) can be classified as an empirical study and, thus, the results' validity may be threatened [30]. Regarding the *Internal Validity*, we are confident that internal validity is given with respect to LOC as a measurement for efficiency because there is an inherent causal relationship between the constructed models and generated source code. For future studies, we plan to use other metrics, such as time measurement, which will require consideration of other threats to internal validity. Concerning the *Conclusion Validity*, our validation does not take into account the amount of time necessary to learn LEMMA to a degree that models can be constructed as fast (or faster) as writing source code. Although the notations of LEMMA's different modeling languages have been designed to be easily learnable, we need further empirical studies which take the initial learning effort into account. However, for an experienced LEMMA user, our data indicates that the time required to create the software artifacts is less when using our generative approach. The *Construct Validity* of our case study could be threatened by the fact that we only used LOC as means to measure the outcome of our approach.

Since not every line of code is equally difficult to write and expressiveness can vary depending on the language used and personal style, LOC can only be taken as an initial indicator of the quality of our approach. Therefore, we aim to evaluate LEMMA in an industrial-scale empirical study for future work (c.f. Sect. 7). Because our validation only comprises one system with five microservices, the *External Validity*, i.e., the generalizability of our results to other MSA-based systems, is only partially given. We addressed this issue by selecting technologies for our case study that are widely adopted in industry for MSA engineering [3]. However, we are aware that further research with more cases and larger sample size is needed to increase external validity.

6 Related Work

Le et al. [6] present the DcSL modeling language that, similar to LEMMA's DML (cf. Sect. 2.2), focuses on capturing domain information. However, DcSL uses UML to model domain concepts, and neither supports DDD pattern nor addresses distributed domain models as required for MSA engineering [17]. Le et al. also define a generator function for DcSL that maps domain concepts to code. Like our LBG_j (cf. Sect. 3.2), this generator function produces executable Java classes (cf. Requirement **R.6** in Sect. 3.1). The behavior of the generator function can be influenced by metadata as is the case for LBGs and LGFs with LEMMA technology aspects. While DcSL's generator function performs a basic, standalone executable Java mapping (**R.1**, **R.3**, **R.4**), it does not anticipate flexible additive technology mappings (**R.2**) and manual code extension (**R.5**).

Context Mapper [15] is a modeling language for DDD with an initial focus on DDD *context maps* [8]. That is, Context Mapper allows capturing the relationships between bounded contexts and their semantics. In addition, Context Mapper integrates with Sculptor[18], a modeling language for *tactical DDD* [8], i.e., the internals of a bounded context. For MSA engineering, Context Mapper models are transformable to the MDSL modeling language [15], which concerns the declaration of microservice contracts and their data representations. Both Context Mapper and MDSL share similarities with LEMMA's DML and SML [21]. First, they support the expression and usage of bounded context internals in MSA engineering. Second, they enable domain data and microservice code generation from models. However, while an import mechanism integrates LEMMA's DML and SML on the language level, the integration of Context Mapper and MDSL is based on model transformation and thus comparatively loose. Specifically, this integration approach does not permit the recognition of linkage errors resulting from missing imported model elements during model construction. Concerning code generation, the generators of Context Mapper and MDSL fully comply with our Requirements **R.1**, **R.3**, **R.4**, and **R.6**. Regarding flexible mapping composition (**R.2**) only MDSL supports code generator chaining. However, generation chains are predefined and not alterable. Context Mapper, on the other hand,

---

[18] https://www.sculptorgenerator.org.

relies on the JHipster Domain Language (JDL)[19] for code generation. JDL does not anticipate manual code extension (**R.5**),

Similar to LEMMA, the MicroBuilder tool by Terzić et al. [28] aims to facilitate MSA engineering by MDE. MicroBuilder combines the MicroDSL language with a code generator. MicroDSL enables to model data structures, service endpoints, and REST APIs for microservices, and thus integrates information from the Domain, Technology and Service viewpoints in MSA engineering (cf. Sect. 2.2) into models. By contrast, LEMMA's DML, TML, and SML constitute dedicated modeling languages for these viewpoints, so that, e.g., domain models can remain technology-agnostic to foster their comprehension by domain experts and modeling languages do not require technology-specific keywords. MicroBuilder's generator module produces Java code that utilizes the Spring framework to make derived microservices executable. MicroBuilder thus fulfills our Requirements **R.1**, **R.3**, **R.4**, and **R.6**. However, there exists no approach for additive technology mappings (**R.2**). We could not find any information whether MicroBuilder supports manual code extension (**R.5**).

DICER [1] is a model-driven approach to develop Infrastructure-as-Code (IaC) solutions for big data applications. DICER defines a UML profile to abstract from IaC specification and programming languages. Like LEMMA's OML, DICER enables to express different types of operation nodes and their environments. However, the OML puts a strong emphasis on microservice and thus artifact deployment, while DICER focuses on modeling physical deployment characteristics. DICER also integrates a code generator to derive executable and extensible TOSCA blueprints [18] from models. Hence, the DICER generator complies with our Requirements **R.1**, **R.5**, and **R.6**. However, it does not support flexible provisioning of additive technology mappings (**R.2**) and is realized as an Eclipse plugin, thereby aggravating mapping sharing (**R.3**) and preventing standalone execution (**R.4**).

7   Conclusion and Outlook

This paper presented the integration of an extensible code generation approach for microservices and their deployment into an existing ecosystem of AMLs. To this end, we first posed requirements towards such an approach taking typical characteristics of MSA, e.g., technology heterogeneity or team distribution, into account. Next, we described two requirements-compliant realizations of the approach. The first realization maps MSA models to basic Java code with the possibility to flexibly extend it with additive technology information. The second focused on the generation of deployment specifications for Docker and Kubernetes, and infrastructure configurations, e.g., for service discovery. Additionally, we defined a process for holistic modeling and code generation in MSA engineering based on our AMLs. We validated our generation approach and the process in a case study from a research project in the Electromobility domain, thereby showing their feasibility and potential for developers' productivity increase.

---

[19] https://www.jhipster.tech/jdl.

In future works we plan to evaluate our code generation approach and process in an industry-scale study. We also anticipate the development of further additive generators focusing on blockchain and security aspects as these are highly relevant in the aforementioned research project. Furthermore, we aim to facilitate the implementation of code generators adhering to our approach by microservice developers and operators. To this end, it could be beneficial to enable the generation of extensible code generator implementations from technology models in our AMLs. These code generators could also provide APIs for consumer-driven tests to guide generator evolution across MSA team boundaries.

References

1. Artač, M., Borovšak, T., Nitto, E.D., Guerriero, M., Perez-Palacin, D., Tamburri, D.A.: Infrastructure-as-code for data-intensive architectures: a model-driven development approach. In: 2018 IEEE International Conference on Software Architecture (ICSA), pp. 156–165. IEEE (2018)
2. Balalaie, A., Heydarnoori, A., Jamshidi, P.: Migrating to cloud-native architectures using microservices: an experience report. In: Celesti, A., Leitner, P. (eds.) ESOCC Workshops 2015. CCIS, vol. 567, pp. 201–215. Springer, Cham (2016). https://doi.org/10.1007/978-3-319-33313-7_15
3. Bogner, J., Fritzsch, J., Wagner, S., Zimmermann, A.: Microservices in industry: insights into technologies, characteristics, and software quality. In: 2019 IEEE International Conference on Software Architecture Companion (ICSA-C), pp. 187–195. IEEE (2019)
4. Combemale, B., France, R.B., Jézéquel, J.M., Rumpe, B., Steel, J., Vojtisek, D.: Engineering Modeling Languages: Turning Domain Knowledge into Tools. CRC Press, Boca Raton (2017)
5. Di Francesco, P., Malavolta, I., Lago, P.: Research on architecting microservices: trends, focus, and potential for industrial adoption. In: 2017 IEEE International Conference on Software Architecture (ICSA), pp. 21–30. IEEE (2017)
6. Le, D.M., Dang, D.H., Nguyen, V.-H.: Domain-driven design using meta-attributes: a DSL-based approach. In: 2016 Eighth International Conference on Knowledge and Systems Engineering (KSE), pp. 67–72. IEEE (2016)
7. Erl, T.: Service-Oriented Architecture (SOA): Concepts, Technology and Design. Prentice Hall, Hoboken (2005)
8. Evans, E.: Domain-Driven Design. Addison-Wesley, Boston (2004)
9. Fielding, R.T.: Architectural styles and the design of network-based software architectures. Ph.D. thesis (2000)
10. Fielding, R.T., Reschke, J.F.: Hypertext Transfer Protocol (HTTP/1.1): Semantics and content. RFC 7231, RFC Editor (2014)
11. Gosling, J., Joy, B., Steele, G., Bracha, G., Buckley, A., Smith, D.: The Java language specification: Java se 13 edition. Specification JSR-388 Java SE 13, Oracle America, Inc. (2019)
12. Greifenberg, T., et al.: Integration of handwritten and generated object-oriented code. In: Desfray, P., Filipe, J., Hammoudi, S., Pires, L.F. (eds.) MODELSWARD 2015. CCIS, vol. 580, pp. 112–132. Springer, Cham (2015). https://doi.org/10.1007/978-3-319-27869-8_7

13. Hutchinson, J., Whittle, J., Rouncefield, M.: Model-driven engineering practices in industry: social, organizational and managerial factors that lead to success or failure. Sci. Comput. Program. **89**, 144–161 (2014)
14. ISO/IEC/IEEE: Systems and software engineering – Architecture description. Standard ISO/IEC/IEEE 42010:2011(E) (2011)
15. Kapferer, S., Zimmermann, O.: Domain-driven service design. In: Dustdar, S. (ed.) SummerSOC 2020. CCIS, vol. 1310, pp. 189–208. Springer, Cham (2020). https://doi.org/10.1007/978-3-030-64846-6_11
16. Nadareishvili, I., Mitra, R., McLarty, M., Amundsen, M.: Microservice Architecture: Aligning Principles, Practices, and Culture. O'Reilly, Sebastopol (2016)
17. Newman, S.: Building Microservices: Designing Fine-Grained Systems. O'Reilly, Sebastopol (2015)
18. OASIS: Topology and orchestration specification for cloud applications version 1.0. Standard, Organization for the Advancement of Structured Information Standards (2013)
19. Rademacher, F., Sachweh, S., Zündorf, A.: Aspect-oriented modeling of technology heterogeneity in microservice architecture. In: 2019 IEEE International Conference on Software Architecture (ICSA), pp. 21–30. IEEE (2019)
20. Rademacher, F., Sorgalla, J., Wizenty, P., Sachweh, S., Zündorf, A.: Graphical and textual model-driven microservice development. In: Bucchiarone, A., et al. (eds.) Microservices, pp. 147–179. Springer, Cham (2020). https://doi.org/10.1007/978-3-030-31646-4_7
21. Rademacher, F., Sorgalla, J., Wizenty, P., Trebbau, S.: Towards holistic modeling of microservice architectures using LEMMA, pp. 11–20 (2021). http://ceur-ws.org/Vol-2978/mde4sa-paper2.pdf
22. Richardson, C.: Microservices Patterns. Manning Publications, New York (2019)
23. Ruscio, D.D., Malavolta, I., Muccini, H., Pelliccione, P., Pierantonio, A.: Developing next generation ADLs through MDE techniques. In: 2010 ACM/IEEE 32nd International Conference on Software Engineering, vol. 1, pp. 85–94. IEEE (2010)
24. Soldani, J., Tamburri, D.A., Heuvel, W.J.V.D.: The pains and gains of microservices: a systematic grey literature review. J. Syst. Softw. **146**, 215–232 (2018)
25. Sorgalla, J., Wizenty, P., Rademacher, F., Sachweh, S., Zündorf, A.: Applying model-driven engineering to stimulate the adoption of DevOps processes in small and medium-sized development organizations. SN Comput. Sci. **2**(6), 459 (2021)
26. Taibi, D., Lenarduzzi, V.: On the definition of microservice bad smells. IEEE Softw. **35**(3), 56–62 (2018)
27. Taibi, D., Lenarduzzi, V., Pahl, C.: Processes, motivations, and issues for migrating to microservices architectures: an empirical investigation. IEEE Cloud Comput. **4**(5), 22–32 (2017)
28. Terzić, B., Dimitrieski, V., Kordić, S., Milosavljević, G., Luković, I.: Development and evaluation of MicroBuilder: a model-driven tool for the specification of REST microservice software architectures. Enterp. Inf. Syst. **12**(8–9), 1034–1057 (2018)
29. Tsui, F., Karam, O., Bernal, B.: Essentials of Software Engineering. Jones & Bartlett Learning (2016)
30. Wohlin, C., Runeson, P., Höst, M., Ohlsson, M.C., Regnell, B., Wesslén, A.: Experimentation in Software Engineering. Springer, Heidelberg (2012). https://doi.org/10.1007/978-3-642-29044-2

Tools and Demonstrations Track

Applying Knowledge-Driven Architecture Composition with Gabble

Fabian Burzlaff[1]($\boxtimes$)(ID), Maurice Ackel[2], and Christian Bartelt[2](ID)

[1] osapiens Services GmbH, Julius-Hatry-Straße 1, Mannheim 68163, Germany
fabian.burzlaff@osapiens.com
[2] Institute for Enterprise Systems (University of Mannheim),
Schloss, Mannheim 68131, Germany
m.ackel@icloud.com, bartelt@es.uni-mannheim.de
https://osapiens.com/
https://www.institute-for-enterprise-systems.de/

Abstract. Service interoperability for embedded devices is a mandatory feature for dynamically changing Internet-of-Things and Industry 4.0 software platforms. Service interoperability is achieved on a technical, syntactic, and semantic level. If service interoperability is achieved on all levels, plug-and-play functionality known from USB storage sticks or printer drivers becomes feasible. This reduces the manual effort for system integration for home automation systems and, in the case of the producing industry, allows for micro-batch size production, individualized automation solution, or job order production. However, interoperability at the semantic level is still a problem for the maturing class of IoT systems. In this work, we present a software engineering tool in detail that allows storing, sharing, and reusing integration knowledge between software interfaces incrementally by looking at integration cases instead of domain models.

Keywords: Knowledge-driven architecture composition · Software architecture · Component coupling · Artificial intelligence · Knowledge management · Internet of Things

1 Introduction

Architectural mismatch due to semantic differences in software interfaces is a well-known problem [10, 11]. For example, current Internet-of-Things platforms require system integrators to implement point-to-point adapters, enforce a domain standard or rely on more abstract interface description languages when coupling embedded devices. However, both standards and machine-understandable interface descriptions cannot be applied effectively to IoT systems as they rely on the assumption that the semantic domain is completely known when they are created. This assumption of complete integration models hardly holds in the real world as ever-changing environments render a complete and final description of a domain impossible. Consequently, practitioners rely

This work has been developed in the project BIoTope (Research Grant Number 011S18079C) and is funded by the German Ministry of Education and Research (BMBF).

© The Author(s), under exclusive license to Springer Nature Switzerland AG 2022
P. Scandurra et al. (Eds.): ECSA Tracks and Workshops 2021, LNCS 13365, pp. 283–305, 2022.
https://doi.org/10.1007/978-3-031-15116-3_13

on implementing software adapters manually without technical support to store, share and reuse integration knowledge between interfaces.

This work introduces an extended version the tool called Gabble initially published as a short paper [6]. Gabble explicitly allows for an incomplete semantic domain model by looking at integration cases instead of domain models. "Gabble" is inspired by the fast-growing number of connected devices which talk so quickly that devices cannot understand each other. Therefore, it assists the system integrator at design time with logical reasoning capabilities by 1) proposing interface mappings based on previous integration cases and by 2) generating a software adapter in an automated way.

In addition to the initial paper, we have added a description of the implemented theoretical concepts and its link to the underlying technical architecture. Therefore, the paper is outlined as follows. In Sect. 2, a representative use case is introduced. In Sect. 3, we will map this use case to the underlying logical architecture. Next, Sect. 4 discusses the most important aspects of the technical architecture. In Sect. 4, we focus on the software adapter generation as part of the novel engineering method and in Sect. 6 we describe safety mechanisms to the expected methodological benefits. We conclude our work by naming related research and industry efforts in Sect. 7 and a conclusion in Sect. 8.

2   Use Case

In order to solve the semantic interoperability challenge from a methodology viewpoint, the Gabble tool supports the knowledge-driven architecture composition method [5]. To illustrate the tool functionality, we will take a look at an exemplary use case. In our setting, Alice and Bob work on an app that controls a Samsung smart TV. This device has a public API which is described in a syntactic specification standard (e.g., OpenAPI). Based on this specification, the client code to interface with the device was created using existing code generators. Subsequently, the necessary client logic to work with the generated library was developed.

The development team (i.e. Alice and Bob) is now tasked to make the app work with a different device (i.e. by Phillips TV). This TV has a different, yet semantically identical API with a corresponding API specification. The interfaces of both devices are depicted in Fig. 1. This figure also shows how a different person integrated the Samsung API with the LG (another smart TV) API (at time $t = 1$), and yet another system integrator mapped the LG API to the Phillips API (at $t = 2$).

To make the LG TV work with the existing app in a practical way, Bob would have to generate new client code and adjust the application logic so that it can handle the new data model. This process has to be done manually every time such a change needs to be performed and does not allow the reuse of existing integration knowledge (see arrows that illustrate mappings in Fig. 1). The Gabble tool allows for such easy reuse of integration knowledge which is defined in a case-based manner. The main benefit of the tool support is the ability to handle simple scenarios as displayed and more complex ones with thousands of integration cases where manual knowledge extraction would get infeasible.

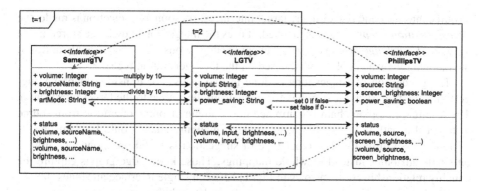

Fig. 1. Integration knowledge example

3   Logical Architecture

The underlying theoretical approach of Gabble is Knowledge-Driven Architecture Composition (KDAC) – a novel paradigm of system integration that allows reusing atomic integration knowledge preserved from previous integration cases [7]. To do this, the approach captures integration knowledge in a graph-like knowledge base, where APIs are vertices and mappings between them are edges. The approach explicitly does not assume that integration knowledge is complete once it is defined. Instead, it accepts that integration knowledge is always incomplete and aims to reuse as many mappings as possible. Gabble implements this approach, offering system integrators, and developers a new way to create integrations to make the formalization process easier, faster, and less error-prone.

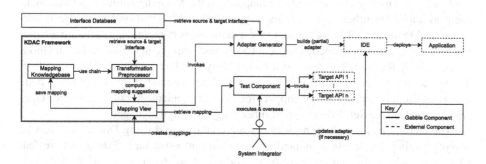

Fig. 2. Logical system architecture

The tool consists of several logical components (see Fig. 2). To start with, it allows users to add interfaces to the *Interface Database* which are then available later in the process. When adding an interface, the user has to provide either an AsyncAPI or OpenAPI specification and the interface name. Those interfaces are then available in the *Mapping View* where the user can create mappings between them. To do this, they select a source interface and one or many target interfaces. As soon as a selection is made, the *Transformation Preprocessor* is invoked. It uses the integration knowledge stored in the *Mapping Knowledgebase* to compute mapping suggestions. These are directly added to the mapping view and color coded based on the their generation type.

The generation of suggestions is done in two ways. For transitive mapping suggestions, the preprocessor searches for paths from the source to the target interface(s). The resulting mapping chain is combined into a single mapping operation from source to target if a path is found. In our example, a mapping chain would be SamsungTV → LGTV → PhilipsTV. The other type of suggestion is based on knowledge graphs on single attributes instead of whole mappings. Those knowledge graphs capture the equality relationships (e.g., arrows in Fig. 1) between single interface attributes. Invoking the Transformation Preprocessor on every update allows generating new mapping suggestions whenever the user adds new integration knowledge in the integration case at hand.

It is important to note that the generated mapping suggestions might not be able to cover all the required attributes of the target interface(s), in which case the user can also add manual mappings. Those mappings can either be one-to-one (i.e., one provided attribute to one required attribute) or many-to-one (i.e., several provided attributes to one required attribute). Mappings are created by selecting the involved attributes in the Mapping View and can either be *simple* (i.e., only value replacement, no computations) or *complex* (i.e., mathematical functions to convert or combine attribute values). In our example, this is displayed by arrows without a label or with a label.

Once all required attributes are assigned, the user can test the mapping using the *Test Component*. To do this, the user provides the input data in the source interface's data model and executing the mapping. This will transform the source to the target data model and perform the requests against the target API(s). The final result and all intermediate transformations are then shown to the user to ensure the correct functionality.

Finally, the user saves the complete mapping in the Mapping Knowledgebase, making it available for other users. In this way, case-based integration knowledge is preserved and made available for reuse. Once a mapping is completed, a software adapter can be automatically generated. This adapter encapsulates the mapping of the data models defined by the user. The result is a code library that has the same API as the client library for the source interface if it had been directly generated by an OpenAPI code generator. In our case, we added support for JavaScript adapters, but the *Adapter Generator* can also be extended to support other programming languages.

The Gabble tool's underlying services are containerized using Docker and can be deployed using one single command on any cloud infrastructure. Extensions are feasible as we rely on current software frameworks such as React, TypeScript, OpenAPI, AsyncAPI, JSONata, and Mustache templates. The benefits of the tool and the underlying method have already been demonstrated in a home automation scenario by decreasing the engineering time of software adapters and increasing the reliability of interface mappings [5,8].

4   Technical Architecture

The presented logical components are deployed using a thin client model. This means that the back-end executes all reasoning logic. We have one deployment target and one user interface (see Fig. 3). The back-end contains the Web Application, User Service, Authentication Service, API Service, Mapping Service and the Adapter Service. The Mapping Service calculates all interface mappings and the adapter service generates the software adapter. The API Service allows for create-read-update-delete operations for interface descriptions. As we deployed the docker container using Helm charts which is in turn controlling the Kubernetes layer, we required a technical API Gateway to communicate with the web application. Finally, we exploited a standard Graph Database provided by the docker infrastructure.

The Graph Database stores interfaces and mappings and hence contains an execution environment for the Interface Database and the Transformation KB. The accompanying logical component API Endpoint Instance (simulating all needed IoT devices) is realized as a component running in a web server environment.

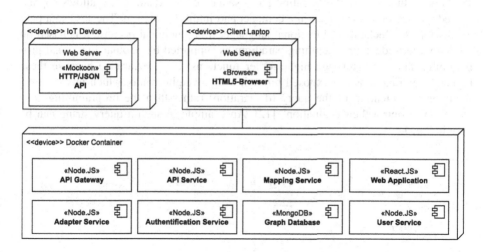

Fig. 3. Deployment diagram

4.1   Interface Description Languages

An example of an OpenAPI description can be seen in Listing 1.1. According to the creators, the goal of an OpenAPI specification is to "...define a standard, programming language agnostic interface description for REST APIs, which allows both humans and computers to discover and understand the capabilities of a service without requiring access to source code, additional documentation, or inspection of network traffic. When properly defined via OpenAPI, a consumer can understand and interact with the remote service with minimal implementation logic. Similar to what interface descriptions have done for lower-level programming, the OpenAPI Specification removes guesswork in calling a service" [3].

An example of an AsyncAPI description can be seen in Listing 1.2. According to the creators, the goal of an AsyncAPI specification is to "...make working with EDAs (Event-driven Architectures) as easy as it is to work with REST APIs. The AsyncAPI Specification is a project used to describe and document message-driven APIs in a machine-readable format. It is protocol agnostic, so you can use it for APIs that work over any protocol (e.g., AMQP, MQTT, WebSockets, ...)" [2]. Both descriptions are equipped with a specification parser, schema validators, code generators for many programming languages (e.g., JavaScript, Java, and many others), and annotation libraries for generating interface descriptions from code. We parse these specifications in the implemented prototype to render the API endpoints' interfaces within the Mapping View. Furthermore, they are stored as nodes within the knowledge graph.

4.2   Interface Mapping Language

To describe mappings between required and provided interface descriptions, we use JSONata [12]. JSONata is a "...lightweight query and transformation language for JSON data. Inspired by the 'location path' semantics of XPath 3.1, it allows sophisticated queries to be expressed in a compact and intuitive notation. The JSONata path expression is a declarative, functional language. It is functional because it is based on the map/filter/reduce programming paradigm as supported by popular functional programming languages through higher-order functions. It is declarative because these higher-order functions are exposed through a lightweight syntax which lets the user focus on the intention of the query (declaration) rather than the programming constructs that control their evaluation" [12]. An example of such a query string can be seen in Fig. 4.

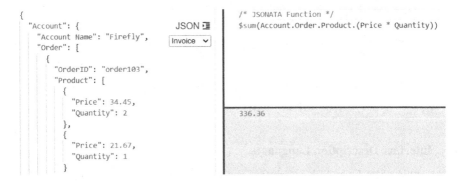

Fig. 4. JSONata example from https://try.jsonata.org/

4.3   Software Adapter Generation and API Endpoints

Both OpenAPI and AsyncAPI are equipped with code generators to generate client code to access a web service and generate server stubs. For code generation, they rely on the Moustache template engine[1]. We inject our mappings into their generation process and provide our own adapter template. A web server serves the generated code. This allows the system integrator to download a software adapter project using the Mapping View.

To manage and make IoT devices available via their interface fast, we rely on Mockoon[2]. Mockoon provides an easy way to mock APIs. Based on a configuration script, we deploy their command line interface on a web server. We started the interface instances based on the interface descriptions as provided by OpenAPI and AsyncAPI. This allows for executing the Mapping Test & Validator component on desired input and output data.

5   Software Adapter Generation

Up to now, we have seen how integration knowledge can be captured technically. In this chapter, we outline how integration knowledge (especially mapping type one-to-many) is related to two exemplary architectural styles. Consequently, we can generate the corresponding software adapter and deploy it on software systems that follow these architectural styles. The main motivation for this exercise is illustrating the applicability of mappings to different architectural styles.

5.1   Client-Server

A client-server model [13] is an architectural style where clients send requests to a server, which performs the required functions and replies with the requested information (see Listing 1.1). For example, clients initiated the communications by remote procedure calls.

Our first example deals with aggregating data produced by an action invocation (see Fig. 5). The upper part of the figure illustrates the context before, and the lower part of the figure illustrates the context after the integration has been finished. Dotted lines symbolize that these remote procedure calls are no longer used.

Before: A client sends a request to a provided action from interface A. The instance of interface A should be replaced by actions offered by interface B and interface C. Now, the request is split up into two requests.

After: After the mapping is finished, the client application logic still assumes to call actions as defined by interface description A. After deployment into the client application code, the generated software adapter transforms the mapped action requests to the available interface instances B and C.

---

[1] https://mustache.github.io/.

[2] https://mockoon.com/.

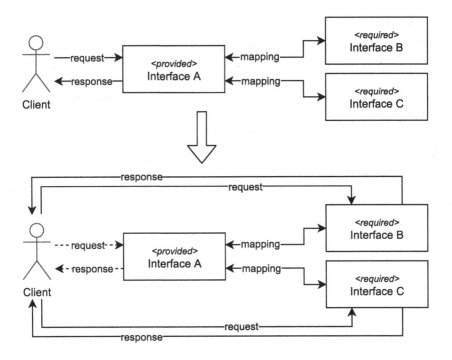

Fig. 5. Client-server split

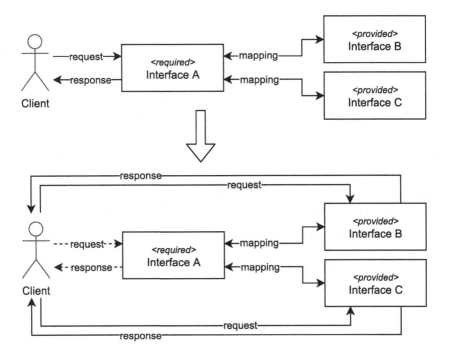

Fig. 6. Client-server aggregate

The second example deals with aggregating data produced by action invocations (see Fig. 6). In contrast to the split example, the response data is to be aggregated (please note that in contrast to Fig. 5 the roles of interfaces A,B and C changed). **Before**: A client expects response data from an action as defined in interface description A. The required output data is mapped to the provided output data from actions as offered by interface B and C. **After**: After the mapping is finished, the client application logic still assumes to call actions as defined by interface description A. After deployment into the client application code, the generated software adapter transforms the mapped actions responses as produced by the interface instances B and C.

The last example deals with extending an action invocation (see Fig. 7). In contrast to the split example, the required actions are not replaced. Hence, they act as both required and provided interfaces.

Before: A client expects input and output data as defined by an action from interface description A. Now, the client is expected to invoke actions from interface A and actions from interface B. Hence, the mappings from the required actions offered by interface A to provided actions offered by interface B are created.

After: After the mapping is finished, the client application logic still calls actions as offered by interface instance A. After deployment into the client application code, the generated software adapter extends the mapped action requests to the initial interface A and the additional interface B. It is up to the client how both responses affect the application logic. This is not part of the software adapter anymore.

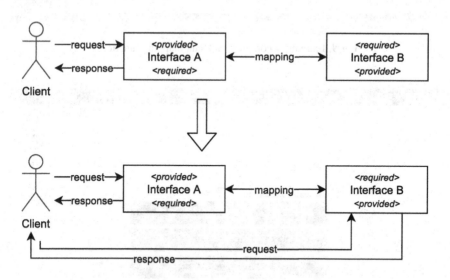

Fig. 7. Client-server extend

Exemplary Client-Server Mapping Function. An example for a simple and a more complex mapping function is visualized in Figs. 8 and 9 respectively. The depicted text editor opens when selecting a mapping from the Mapping Area. In a simple case, one required identifier can be replaced by a provided identifier. In a more complex case, all functions offered by JSONata can be used to specify an arbitrary complex mapping function. Therefore, all provided keys can be selected and are then available for usage within the text editor to compute the required key.

Fig. 8. Example – simple JSONata mapping function

Fig. 9. Example – complex JSONata mapping function

Fig. 10. One-to-one mapping using OpenAPI

Exemplary Client-Server One-to-One. In Fig. 10 a One-to-One mapping example for a OpenAPI specification is visualized. After the required source interface (left side) and provided target interface (right side) are selected, the operation to be integrated are chosen. Then, the mappings for the request as well as the response are created. Here the color code of each box within the Mapping Area indicates whether it is an invalid (red), a manual (blue), or an inferred mapping (green and brown). The respective algorithms are invoked as soon as a required operation is selected or a mapping has been modified.

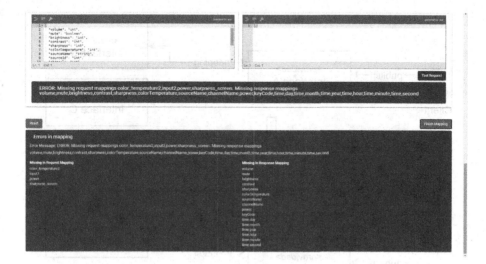

Fig. 11. Mapping test & validator using OpenAPI

In Fig. 11, the Mapping Test & Validator is displayed. The created JSONata mappings are applied by issuing a test request, and a request is made against all servers as specified in the interface specification. If a mapping function can fulfil not all required operation elements, an error listing all missing keys is displayed.

5.2 Publish-Subscribe

In contrast to the client-server model, the publish-subscribe model decouples clients from the server (see Listing 1.2). A client must not know where the requested functionally is executed. A publish-subscribe model [13] is an architectural style where subscriber register/deregister to receive specific messages or content. The publisher maintains a subscription list and broadcasts messages to subscribers either synchronously or asynchronously.

In contrast to the client-server style, requests are not directly sent to an action but to channels that contain the payload for a specific topic. This channel topic is comparable to the action invocation. Arrows from the client to other interfaces define data published from the client (i.e., a provided channel). Arrows to the client define data that the client subscribes to (i.e., a required channel). Again, dotted lines symbolize that these channels are no longer used. The first example deals with splitting published data (see Fig. 12). **Before**: The client publishes data to a channel offered by interface A. The corresponding interface instance is replaced by channels offered by interfaces B and C. Hence, the mappings based on topic and payload are created. **After**: After the mapping is finished, the client application logic still assumes to publish payload as defined by interface description A. After deployment into the client application code, the generated software adapter transforms the mapped payload and channel topics to the interface instances B and C.

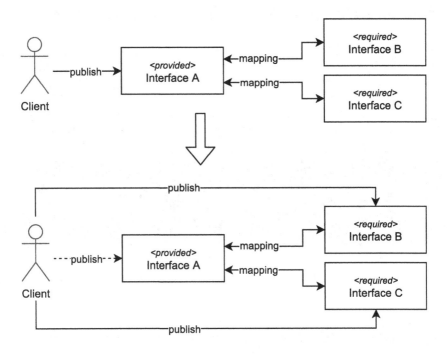

Fig. 12. Publish-subscribe split

The second example deals with aggregating payload that the client subscribes to (see Fig. 13).

Before: A client subscribes to payload from a channel as defined in interface description A. The required payload is mapped to the provided payloads from channels where B and C's interfaces publish their data.

After: After the mapping is finished, the client application logic still assumes to subscribe to channel and payload as defined by interface description A. After deployment into the client application code, the generated software adapter transforms the mapped payload and responses as published by the interface instances B and C.

The last example deals with extending a subscription (see Fig. 14). Again, the required channel is not replaced, but more payload is consumed by the client as another interface also publishes its payload to the existing channel.

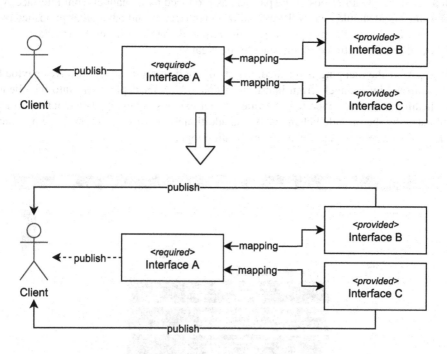

Fig. 13. Publish-subscribe aggregate

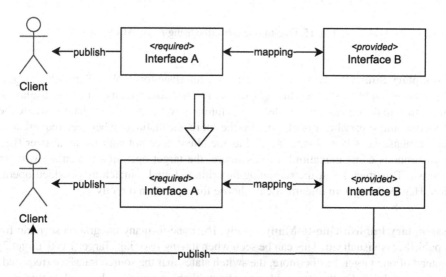

Fig. 14. Publish-subscribe extend

Before: A client subscribes to the payload as produced by a channel from interface A. Now, the client should deal with payload from interface A and payload as published by interface B. Hence, the mappings from the required channel offered by interface A to provided channels offered by interface B are created.

After: After the mapping is finished, the client application logic still receives payload as published by channels from interface instance A. After deployment into the client application code, the generated software adapter extends the mapped channel topics as published by the provided channels by the additional interface B. Again, it is up to the client how more payload affects the application logic.

Fig. 15. One-to-one subscribe using AsyncAPI

Exemplary Subscribe One-to-One. The user interface for Publish-Subscribe integration cases is slightly different. In Fig. 15 a one-to-one subscription example is displayed. In contrast to the client-server style, the operation now represents the channel where the device should subscribe or publish to. Furthermore, the distinction between request keys and response keys is no longer needed as the client does not wait for an answer (i.e., asynchronous communication). In this figure, the target operation is marked with an asterisk. This means that the reasoning algorithms found a matching provided operation. Hence, the system integrator can choose this operation directly.

Exemplary Publish One-to-Many. In Fig. 16, a one-to-many integration scenario for a publisher is visualized. This can be seen when having two (i.e., Target 1 and Target 2) instead of one target. Furthermore, the switch states that the source interface (required) is of type publish. On the target side, the new publishing setting is depicted. In this case, it is based on the extend example (see 14). For instance, the Mapping Source "Bosch

Grid" acts as a required and as a provided interface. Hence, the interface list on the right side also contains the "Bosch Grid" as a provided interface.

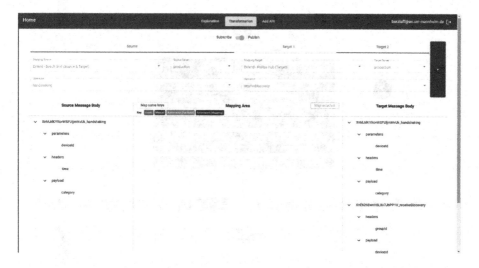

Fig. 16. Example – one-to-many publish using AsyncAPI

Overall, all features (e.g., split or extend) discussed within the examples are available for both architectural styles. What is left is the software adapter generation part.

The software adapter generation mechanism is a supportive feature for the overall process. However, it does not directly influence the integration knowledge management process. At the time of writing, we support Node.js adapters. Other programming languages are also possible but must be implemented with another template.

6 Safeguarding Expected Method Benefits

All mappings incrementally formalized over time should be defined in a reliable way (i.e., they should be trustworthy for other system integrators such that they are actually reused). Therefore, this section takes a closer look at the necessary engineering steps to identify missing mappings and mapping reliability. For a detailed empirical evaluation, please see [5] and [9].

Figure 17 illustrates situations within the formalization phase based on the reference implementation. First, the system integrator selects the required and the available provided interface from the knowledge base (see number 1). Here we already check if a provided action has already been mapped to the selected required action based on the stored integration knowledge. We indicate available action mappings with an asterisk as a prefix before the action signature.Then the reasoning algorithms are invoked. After the knowledge base is queried and the mapping calculation is finished, not all keys may have a mapping.

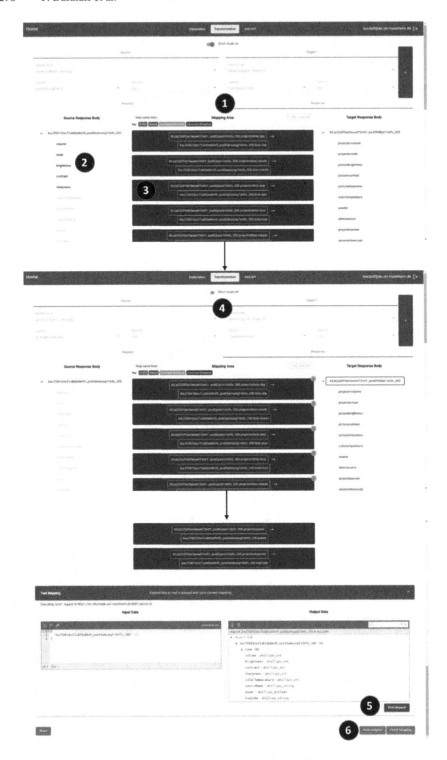

Fig. 17. Incomplete but reliable mappings

Naturally, this is the case if no mappings are found or if one of the interfaces has just been added to the knowledge base. If some but not all mappings are retrieved, then all required keys without a mapping are highlighted with black color (see number 2). Next, the missing mappings are added such that all required keys are associated with a set of provided keys (see number 3). As soon as all mappings are formalized, the following reliability checks are performed.

As a preset, mappings that are calculated or retrieved from the knowledge base can not be edited. This can only be done by deactivating the associated "strict" mode (see number 4). Assuming the provided mappings are correct, then the added mappings must be checked if they are reliable. This can be done by issuing a test request against the required interface where only the provided interface is actually available (see number 5). After the test request is executed, the system integrator inspects the result. Furthermore, the system integrator verifies if the device or mocked version of the device also exposes the desired behavior (e.g., the TV channel is switched correctly). Only then the system integrator is expected to store the defined mappings (see number 6 in Fig. 17).

Based on the presented engineering steps, we will look at the details in the next two sections.

6.1 Speed

Speed in formalizing interface mappings is mandatory as formalization effort adds to the integration time by just writing a software adapter. In order to detect missing interface mappings, all required keys must be mapped. The occurrence of incomplete mappings depends on the mapping type and the transformation function. Therefore, we look at the results that are produced by the underlying algorithms. The underlying algorithms produce incomplete mappings if there exists at least one-to-many mapping within the chain of mappings and not all intermediate nodes have a distinct path to the target action.

Assume that the running example is extended by a another device, a speaker (see Fig. 18). At t = 2, a one-to-many mapping from SamsungTV to LGTV and BTSpeaker is created. For instance, a movie's sound should not be issued by the TV but by a separate speaker. Therefore, the volume identifier of SamsungTV is mapped to the volume identifier of the BTSpeaker. At t = 3, another system integrator maps the LGTV to the PhilipsTV. This means that there exists a path within the knowledge base from $SamsungTV \rightarrow LGTV \rightarrow PhilipsTV$. In an integration case between SamsungTV and PhilipsTV, not all mappings can be calculated by the algorithms. In fact, there will not exist a mapping for the volume identifier.

Inverse of Mapping can also cause incomplete mappings. If no inverse function exists or multiple provided identifiers are used to calculate a required identifier, then the calculated reverse mapping is incomplete. As a synthetic example, we can assume that the identifier brightness of the SamsungTV interface is calculated by multiplying the brigthness_dimmer (not displayed) and the brightness identifier from the LG device. If such a mapping exists within a chain of mappings, then the inverse mapping is not calculated. The reason for this is that we cannot deal with systems of linear equations. For example, the linear equation

$$brightness_{Samsung} = brightness\_dimmer_{LG} * brightness_{LG} \qquad (1)$$

can be rewritten as

$$brightness\_dimmer_{LG} = brightness_{Samsung}/brightness_{LG} \qquad (2)$$

The algorithm can then not determine the next mapping as the LG identifier is present in both sides of the equation (i.e., there is a loop).

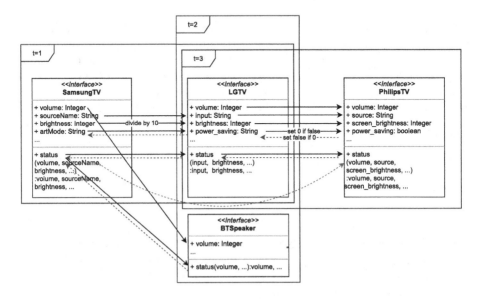

Fig. 18. Incomplete mappings

If the mentioned cases do not apply, then either no mapping or all mappings are calculated. Finally, the system integrator finishes the integration by generating the software adapter. This software adapter is then imported into the client's software project. In an ideal case, the application logic can then talk to the newly added device without changing any other piece of code. From a practical point of view, adjusting the mappings within the tooling infrastructure is generally faster than editing code within the generated software project.

6.2   Reliability

Mapping reliability over time is crucial. All mappings inserted into the knowledge base and calculated by the reasoning algorithms must be correct. Therefore, we implemented a correct by construction principle within the prototype. This principle is enforced within the prototype by the strict mode (see 4 in Fig. 17). This mode controls whether mappings can be saved or not. A mapping can only be saved if the set of mappings is incomplete for the selected required and provided action. Hence, it must be ensured that only the correct mappings are stored. If a manual mapping already exists, then only the initial creator of the mapping can change it. In order to enforce this correct by construction principle, we have implemented the following measures:

1. As soon as a mapping is formalized using the JSONata syntax, the specified syntax is validated. If the syntax is not valid, the corresponding mapping is highlighted.
2. All necessary mappings between the required and the provided interface actions must be present. For request and publish mappings, all selected actions and their identifiers for the provided interfaces must be assigned (i.e., needed to call a provided action). For response and subscribe mappings, the selected action and its identifiers for the required interface must be assigned (i.e., needed to construct the required output ultimately). Only in this case can the system integrator issue a test request.
3. When all mappings are formalized, then value transformation is inspected by issuing a test request. Therefore, a mock instance or a physical device must be present. The system integrator decided if the mapping is correct based on the received values. If a transformation fails, the corresponding error is displayed in the application (e.g., multiplying two values of type string).
4. The system integrator is allowed to save the mapping only if the values are correct.

If there are mappings that cannot be reused for any other reason, the strict mode can be deactivated. Then, all mappings can be edited regardless of their ownership. However, these mappings cannot be saved. Only the software adapter can be generated. In this way, we ensure that all mappings are correct by constructions, and thus reliability is ensured. However, there exist two cases where reliability is favoured over mapping reuse. The first case involves multiple paths from source to target actions, and the second case involves setting a static value using the interface mapping language. We will discuss both cases based on the situation as depicted in Fig. 19.

Assume four integration contexts have been formalized. At $t = 1$, a mapping from $key1_A$ to $key3_B$ is inserted. At $t = 2$, a mapping from $key1_A$ to $key5_C$ and at $t = 3$ a mapping from $key5_C$ to $key7_D$ is inserted. Lastly, a mapping from $key3_B$ to $key7_D$ is inserted. Now, a conflict arises if interface A is selected as a required interface, and interface D is selected as a provided interface. The composition algorithm for operation mappings will find two paths for $key1_A$ where the first path is $key1_A \mapsto key5_C \mapsto key7_D$ and the second path is $key1_A \mapsto key3_B \mapsto key7_D$. This case can occur without violating the correct by construction measures as each manually inserted mapping is correct. Despite this circumstance, we can choose any of the mappings as there is no mapping that is "more" correct. This is mainly achieved by not allowing to store incomplete mappings for actions.

Nevertheless, the second case involving static values renders choosing between mappings impossible. Let us assume that the mapping $key1_A$ to $key3_B$ is altered such that $key1_A$ is set to $true$ at $t = 1$. Then the mapping suggestion algorithm for operation mappings returns the paths $key1_A \mapsto true$ and $key1_A \mapsto key5_C \mapsto key7_D$. However, this static value, which can be set using a valid JSONata expression, is specific to the initial integration context (i.e., from interface A to interface B) and only set if provided the required interface exposes fewer identifiers than the other. Therefore, mapping chains that include a static value mapping are dropped by the algorithm. In the example depicted in Fig. 19 this would mean that only the mapping $key1_A \mapsto key5_C \mapsto key7_D$ is returned as a result. If only static value mappings exist, no mapping would be returned, potentially resulting in an additional mapping to be defined.

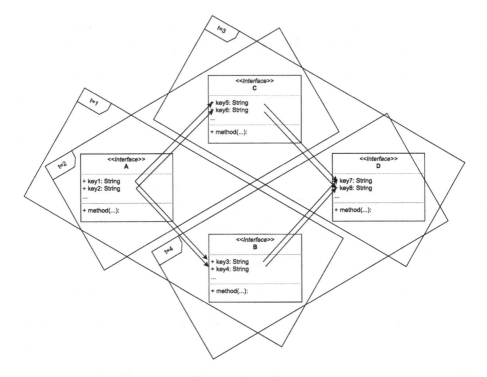

Fig. 19. Ensuring mapping reliability

The presented measures ensure high reliability regarding manual and calculated mappings. In our empirical evaluation, we focus on performance metrics, such as integration time and algorithmic performance [5,9]

However, we acknowledged that reliability must be ensured. In case of unexpected issues, we assume that these issues are solved out of band.

7   Related Research and Industry Efforts

Research-driven approaches to achieve semantic interoperability are focusing on bottom-up interface integration and can be exemplified using the tools MatchBox [14], and MICS [4]. MatchBox presents a highly customizable interface matching framework based on interface descriptions, whereas MICS enables software architectures to synthesize software connectors from formal mapping specifications automatically. The mentioned approaches and most other approaches apply formal ontologies to describe the desired domain based on the available interface descriptions. Once defined, these ontologies are hard to evolve for system integrators.

Approaches from the industry include top-down designed standards such as OPC UA in combination with ecl@ss. For instance, BaSys 4.0 [1] takes a capability-based description that contains references to an integration layer for manufacturing systems.

These approaches assume that there exists a formal vocabulary that can be used by all parties involved by linking their interfaces to it.

The Gabble tool and the underlying approach do not try to (partially) formalize a domain and link interface elements to it, but look at integration knowledge based on concrete integration cases that can evolve over time.

8   Conclusion

In this work, we presented Gabble. Gabble is a tool accompanying the knowledge-driven architecture composition approach, which resolves architectural mismatch at the semantic level for highly interconnected and dynamic IoT software platforms. We believe that Gabble can lower the amount of manually written adapter code until one domain-specific standard emerges. In the future, we plan to apply Gabble to other integration scenarios demanding a higher degree of dependability, such as automated production lines.

Online Resources

- Use Case Video: https://youtu.be/zrSsqSy_roM.
- Paper Presentation Video: https://youtu.be/dyi0eRlqu9s.
- Source Code: https://github.com/mauriceackel/Gabble/tree/demo.

```
{
"servers": [
 {
 "url": "https://iot.informatik.uni-mannheim.de:8088"
 }
 ],
 "paths": {
   "/status": {
    "post": {
    "parameters": [
        {
        "in": "body",
        "name": "body",
        "description": "Values to be updated",
        "required": true,
        "schema": {
          "$ref": "#/components/schemas/SamsungTvInfo"
        }
    ...
    ],
    "responses": {
      "200": {
       "content": {
        "application/json": {
```

```json
          "schema": {
            "$ref": "#/components/schemas/SamsungTvInfo"
            }
    ...
  },
  "components": {
   "schemas": {
    "SamsungTvInfo": {
     "type": "object",
     "properties": {
      "volume": {
       "type": "integer",
       "example": 1
      },
      "sourceName": {
       "type": "string",
       "example": "source"
      },
      ...
}
```

Listing 1.1. OpenAPI Descriptionfor Samsung TV

```json
{
   "servers": {
     "production": {
       "url": "test.mosquitto.org:1883",
       "protocol": "mqtt"
     }
   },
   "channels": {
     "samsungtv/volume/measured": {
       "publish": {
         "operationId":
         "receiveVolume",
         "message": {
           "$ref": "#/components/schemas/volumeMeasuredPayload"
     ...
     },
     "samsungtv/turn/on": {
        "subscribe": {
          "operationId": "sourceName",
          "message": {
            "$ref": "#/components/schemas/turnOnOffPayload"
          }
     ...
     },
     "components": {
       "schemas": {
         "volumeMeasuredPayload": {
```

```
"type": "object",
"properties": {
  "volume": {
    "type": "string",
    "minimum": 0,
    "description": "Sound volume measured in decibel."
  }
  ...
}
```

Listing 1.2. AsyncAPI Description forSamsung TV

References

1. Perzylo, A., et al.: Capability-based semantic interoperability of manufacturing resources: a Basys 4.0 perspective. IFAC-PapersOnLine **52**(13), 1590–1596 (2019)
2. AsyncAPI Specification (2020). https://www.asyncapi.com/. Accessed 15 Feb 2022
3. OpenAPI Specification (2020). https://swagger.io/specification/v2/. Accessed 15 Feb 2021
4. Autili, M., Inverardi, P., Spalazzese, R., Tivoli, M., Mignosi, F.: Automated synthesis of application-layer connectors from automata-based specifications. J. Comput. Syst. Sci. **104**, 17–40 (2019)
5. Burzlaff, F.: Knowledge-driven architecture composition. Ph.D. thesis, Mannheim (2021). https://madoc.bib.uni-mannheim.de/59125/
6. Burzlaff, F., Ackel, M., Bartelt, C.: Gabble: managing integration knowledge in IoT-systems with logical reasoning (2021). https://madoc.bib.uni-mannheim.de/59125/http://ceur-ws.org/Vol-2978/tool-paper89.pdf
7. Burzlaff, F., Bartelt, C.: Knowledge-driven architecture composition: case-based formalization of integration knowledge to enable automated component coupling. In: 2017 IEEE International Conference on Software Architecture Workshops (ICSAW), pp. 108–111. IEEE (2017)
8. Burzlaff, F., Bartelt, C.: Knowledge-driven architecture composition: assisting the system integrator to reuse integration knowledge. In: Brambilla, M., Chbeir, R., Frasincar, F., Manolescu, I. (eds.) ICWE 2021. LNCS, vol. 12706, pp. 305–319. Springer, Cham (2021). https://doi.org/10.1007/978-3-030-74296-6_23
9. Burzlaff, F., Bartelt, C.: Knowledge-driven architecture composition: assisting the system integrator to reuse integration knowledge. In: Brambilla, M., Chbeir, R., Frasincar, F., Manolescu, I. (eds.) ICWE 2021. LNCS, vol. 12706, pp. 305–319. Springer, Cham (2021). https://doi.org/10.1007/978-3-030-74296-6_23
10. Burzlaff, F., Wilken, N., Bartelt, C., Stuckenschmidt, H.: Semantic interoperability methods for smart service systems: a survey. IEEE Trans. Eng. Manag. **99**, 1–15 (2019)
11. Garlan, D., Allen, R., Ockerbloom, J.: Architectural mismatch: why reuse is still so hard. IEEE Softw. **26**(4), 66–69 (2009)
12. JSONata: Json query and transformation language. https://jsonata.org. Accessed 15 Feb 2021
13. Medvidovic, N., Taylor, R.N.: Software architecture: foundations, theory, and practice. In: 2010 ACM/IEEE 32nd International Conference on Software Engineering, vol. 2, pp. 471–472. IEEE (2010)
14. Platenius, M.C.: Fuzzy matching of comprehensive service specifications. Ph.D. thesis, Universitätsbibliothek, Paderborn (2016)

Tutorial Track

Architectural Optimization for Confidentiality Under Structural Uncertainty

Maximilian Walter[1]([✉]), Sebastian Hahner[1], Stephan Seifermann[1],
Tomas Bures[2], Petr Hnetynka[2], Jan Pacovský[2], and Robert Heinrich[1]

[1] KASTEL – Institute of Information Security and Dependability, Karlsruhe
Institute of Technology (KIT), Karlsruhe, Germany
{maximilian.walter,sebastian.hahner,stephan.seifermann,
robert.heinrich}@kit.edu
[2] Charles University, Prague, Czech Republic
{bures,hnetynka,pacovsky}@d3s.mff.cuni.cz

Abstract. More and more connected systems gather and exchange data. This allows building smarter, more efficient and overall better systems. However, the exchange of data also leads to questions regarding the confidentiality of these systems. Design notions such as Security by Design or Privacy by Design help to build secure and confidential systems by considering confidentiality already at the design-time. During the design-time, different analyses can support the architect. However, essential properties that impact confidentiality, such as the deployment, might be unknown during the design-time, leading to structural uncertainty about the architecture and its confidentiality. Structural uncertainty in the software architecture represents unknown properties about the structure of the software architecture. This can be, for instance, the deployment or the actual implementation of a component. For handling this uncertainty, we combine a design space exploration and optimization approach with a dataflow-based confidentiality analysis. This helps to estimate the confidentiality of an architecture under structural uncertainty. We evaluated our approach on four application examples. The results indicate a high accuracy regarding the found confidentiality violations.

Keywords: Uncertainty · Confidentiality · Design space exploration ·
Software architecture · Access control · Information flow

This work was supported by the German Research Foundation (DFG) under project number 432576552, HE8596/1-1 (FluidTrust), as well as by funding from the topic Engineering Secure Systems (46.23.03) of the Helmholtz Association (HGF) and by KASTEL Security Research Labs. Additionally, it was supported by the Czech Science Foundation project 20-24814J, and also partially supported by Charles University institutional funding SVV 260451.

© The Author(s), under exclusive license to Springer Nature Switzerland AG 2022
P. Scandurra et al. (Eds.): ECSA Tracks and Workshops 2021, LNCS 13365, pp. 309–332, 2022.
https://doi.org/10.1007/978-3-031-15116-3_14

1   Introduction

The gathering of more data and, at the same time, the exchange of existing data enables more efficient and smarter systems. This enables, for instance, the digitization of the production process [21] or eHealth services. These systems often include different stakeholders such as customers, suppliers, or public service providers. Each of these stakeholders has different systems and often different regulations. However, they exchange data and, therefore, build a complex network. Nevertheless, this exchange shall still keep the confidentiality of the involved stakeholders' data. Confidentiality is a part of information security. It is the "property that information is not made available or disclosed to unauthorized individuals, entities, or processes" [24]. It is also part of privacy such as in the General Data Protection Regulation (GDPR) [10]. However, privacy often contains more aspects like the right to forget or delete data. Violations against the GDPR can have high costs [40]. Understanding these complex networks and finding confidentiality violations is very difficult. In addition, confidentiality is not the only relevant quality of a system. Other quality attributes such as costs or performance also need to be considered, and this consideration of multiple different attributes complicates the development further.

Approaches such as Security by Design or Privacy by Design want to tackle these confidentiality issues. They propose to continuously consider the security concern in all phases of the software development [45]. These phases include especially the design-time. Additionally, finding and repairing flaws in earlier phases can reduce later costs significantly [4]. This can also be seen in cohesion with the new "Insecure Design" [37] category from the OWASP10 [38] list. This list contains the top 10 categories of security problems for web applications. Therefore, analyzing the system during design-time for confidentiality issues might reduce this type of confidentiality problem. However, not all decisions are already made during the design-time, and some remain unclear. Especially, the impact on confidentiality is unknown [19]. For instance, the concrete deployment might be unknown during the early design-time, e.g., cloud vs on-premise or within EU or outside EU. Therefore, an uncertainty exists regarding the future confidentiality of the system. In a previous publication, we classified uncertainty [6] regarding the confidentiality of software architectures. Based on this classification, we would classify the deployment as structural uncertainty. This paper is the first step to handle uncertainty and confidentiality during the design-time. Therefore, we choose first to consider structural uncertainty since it can be represented by the creation of different architecture variations. For this variation creation, there exists already approaches such as design space exploration approaches. In another previous publication, we already applied design-time confidentiality analysis for handling environmental uncertainty [5]. However, this approach is not immediately applicable to handle structural properties of software architectures.

Our contribution for tackling this problem is the combination of a design space exploration, and optimization approach [30] together with a dataflow-based confidentiality analysis [49]. This goes beyond the pure confidentiality analysis [47] by explicitly considering uncertainty. Using this combination, architects can first model different design decisions. These design decisions are then used to automatically create different architecture variations, which are analyzed for confidentiality. Since we reuse an existing approach for the design space exploration [30], our approach can consider, besides the newly added confidentiality, additional quality attributes, such as costs, and calculate the Pareto optimal candidate regarding all considered quality metrics. This optimization enables software architects to make informed trade-off decisions between different quality metrics.

We evaluated our approach based on four application examples for feasibility and accuracy regarding the consideration of confidentiality violations. All application examples are based on either the design space exploration or the confidentiality research domain. The results for these examples indicate that our approach is feasible and has a high accuracy regarding the detection of confidentiality violations in our examples.

The paper is structured as follows. We first introduce our running example in Sect. 2. Afterwards, we describe in Sect. 3 our foundations. Then, we describe the used confidentiality analysis in Sect. 4. In Sect. 5, we describe our new design space exploration integration. The evaluation follows in Sect. 6. In Sect. 7, we describe related work and Sect. 8 concludes the paper.

2   Running Example

We illustrate our approach by using a running example based on [18,32]. It represents a simplified online shop inside the European Union (EU) with EU customers. The example consists of two components and two deployment locations, shown in Fig. 1. The Online Shop component provides the basic shop system and is deployed on an On Premise Server within the EU. The Database Service component that persists data can either be deployed on the same EU-based server or a Cloud Service outside the EU. Both deployments are technically feasible.

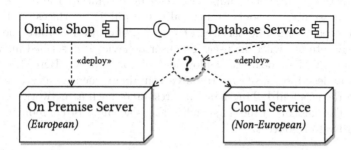

Fig. 1. Component and deployment diagram under uncertainty (denoted by "?")

However, they might not be legally possible since we need to consider the sensitivity of the data. The GDPR [10] forbids to transfer personal data outside of the EU except several conditions are met. Thus, if the `Database Service` is used to store personal data, the component cannot be deployed outside the EU. Therefore, a design decision regarding the allocation is necessary. This decision is affected by the type of the transferred data. Leaving this architectural design decision open introduces uncertainty about the structure of the system. In the worst case, this introduces confidentiality issues that violate the GDPR. This design decision is a common design decision companies face today if they consider moving from on premise solutions to cloud-based solutions. Note that this example is very basic, and the design decisions are mostly obvious. However, it helps to describe and easily understand the involved activities. The approach itself can be also used for more complicated systems that are subject to a multitude of different design decisions like multiple deployment questions or to compare different implementations.

3   Foundations

For modelling the software architecture, we use the Architecture Description Language (ADL) Palladio [43]. For the optimization of the architecture regarding different quality metrics, we use PerOpteryx [30].

3.1   Palladio

We choose the Palladio Component Model (PCM) [43] as our ADL since there exists already an optimization process, and it supports various quality analyses such as performance, reliability, and costs. Additionally, it has a well-established tooling support, which is freely available. PCM is developed for the component-based development process and consists of five different models. Architects can model components and their required and provided interfaces in the repository model. The interfaces specify services with parameters and return values. These services are implemented by components with the so-called ServiceEffectSpecifications (SEFF). Different components can be instantiated and connected in the system (assembly) model. Additionally, the public interfaces of the system are instantiated there. The services of these public interfaces are the services that directly interact with the user. The user behavior is described in the usage model. Also, PCM models the deployment of components. Here, the resource environment describes hardware resource containers such as servers and other computing devices and linking hardware resources such as network nodes (e.g., switches). The allocation model specifies the placement of components to particular hardware resources.

3.2   PerOpteryx

PerOpteryx [30] is a design space exploration and optimization approach for PCM. It supports the generation of different architectural variations and the optimization for different quality attributes. It uses evolutionary search algorithms and calculates the Pareto optimal architectural variation. The different variation points of the architecture are specified in the design decision model. Here, architects can define which entities in the software architecture can be configured. For instance, in our running example, this is the allocation of the Database Service component to the EU and the non-EU servers. The different quality attributes are defined as quality dimensions. There exist various quality dimensions, such as costs or performance.

However, there is no quality dimension for confidentiality, which would be required for our running example. The optimization approach is guided by the Quality of Service Modeling Language (QML) [15] contracts [36]. Here, architects can specify which quality dimension should be optimized and what the desired values should be. Additionally, they can specify restrictions for the optimization, e.g., that the costs cannot be higher than a certain threshold. Each generated and evaluated variation is called a candidate. Besides the optimal candidates, PerOpteryx also yields all the investigated candidates.

4   Architecture-Centric Confidentiality Analysis

For determining the confidentiality of a system, an automatic analysis based on the properties of the system, such as deployment locations or user roles, is beneficial. With this analysis, architects can analyze different scenarios regarding their confidentiality. For instance, based on our running example, an architect can model the scenario using the EU server first and the scenario using a server outside of the EU afterwards. Both scenarios could be analyzed regarding confidentiality, and afterwards, the most beneficial scenario could be chosen. To support this use case, we need to model the different scenarios and analyze the modeled scenarios. For the modeling part, we choose to extend the existing ADL PCM [43] with confidentiality annotations [46]. Based on the extended metamodel, we then create a PCM model representing the software architecture with confidentiality properties. This extended PCM model is then transformed into a dataflow diagram [48,49]. These dataflow diagrams are then combined with dataflow constraints and analyzed regarding violations of these constraints. We described this analysis method in previous publications [46,47].

4.1   Modeling Confidentiality in PCM

Modeling confidentiality aspects of software architectures in PCM serves two purposes: First, aspects, which are relevant for reasoning about confidentiality are documented. Second, a structured documentation of these aspects enables automated analyses. In the following, we focus on the second purpose since we later on use this for our analysis.

The analysis on dataflow diagrams, which we reuse to analyze software architectures given in PCM, is based on label propagation [49]. To make use of the

existing analyses [49], PCM has to provide all information to derive a label propagation graph. In our extended PCM model, we call labels *characteristics*. They
are strongly typed and defined in a so-called *data dictionary*. Listing 1.1 illustrates an excerpt of the data dictionary for our running example. We first define
an enumeration Location with the literals EU and nonEU. The same is done for
the Sensitivity levels. The enumerations define value ranges. Additionally, we
specify characteristic types (here ServerLocation and DataSensitivity), that
reference the enumerations and give the values a meaning. For instance, a location can be used as a value for a characteristic, which describes the location of a
node or the origin of data, which is allowed to flow to the node. A characteristic
always has its type and potentially multiple values.

```
1   enum Location {
2     EU
3     nonEU
4   }
5   enum Sensitivity {
6     Personal
7     Public
8   }
9
10  enumCharacteristicType ServerLocation using Location
11  enumCharacteristicType DataSensitivity using Sensitivity
```

Listing 1.1. Simplified textual representation of a data dictionary

The characteristics for nodes can be added to resources, users and deployed
components in PCM. Resources host components, so the characteristics also
apply to the components deployed on the resource. Figure 2 illustrates these
annotations for our running example by using the PCM tool support. Here
we have two servers (OnPremiseServer, CloudServer). Their characteristics
are shown as green labels. Both characteristics refer to the characteristic type
ServerLocation. One characteristic refers to the value EU and the other one
refers to the value nonEU. These characteristics are transformed to labels of the
nodes in the label propagation graph during the analysis.

The characteristics of data flows stem from the characteristics that are
assigned to parts of the system. In PCM, data is represented by parameters
or return values of services. We refer to both types of data as variables. PCM
can apply characteristics to such variables. We extended the means for modeling

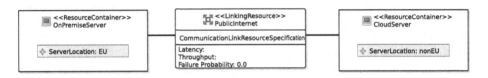

Fig. 2. Resource containers of the running example with location characteristics

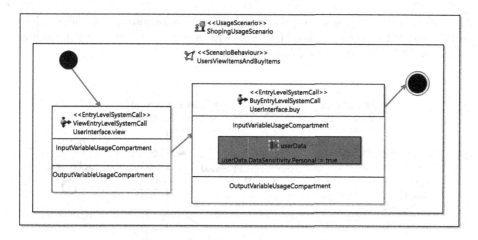

Fig. 3. Usage scenario of the running example with characteristics assignments

this application of characteristics to support the characteristic types from data dictionaries: For every variable, a software architect can define multiple assignments. An assignment applies a characteristic, which is specified on the left-hand side of an assignment, if the expression on the right-hand side of an assignment evaluates to true. The right-hand side can be a constant assignment of a truth value, a query for the existence of a characteristic on another variable or a logical connection such as a conjunction of the previously mentioned expressions. It is possible to express a characteristic propagation that uses incoming characteristics to produce outgoing characteristics. In the analysis, these assignments become label propagation functions and the characteristics are treated as labels.

Figure 3 illustrates an assignment in a usage scenario of the PCM tool support. In our running example, there is a service called *buy*. This service has, among other parameters, the parameter `userData`. For this parameter, we would like to specify that the sensitivity is *personal*. We can write this as an assignment of a constant: *userData.DataSensitivity.Personal := true*. This describes that the variable `userData` should be assigned the `DataSensitivity` `Personal`. Describing all details of the expressions and the mapping to dataflow diagrams as part of the analysis are out of scope of the paper. Instead, we refer to previous publications for details on expressions [49] and the mapping [46].

A model to model transformation transforms the extended PCM to a label propagation graph. Figure 4 illustrates a simplified graph based on the running example. We omit all edges that do not represent relevant data for our analysis. Labels on nodes, such as the *EU* label at the actor, define properties of these nodes. Labels on data, such as the *Personal* label at the dataflow originating from the actor, define properties of the exchanged data. Nodes propagate the received labels through outgoing dataflows. In our example, every node is forwarding the data without modification of its properties. The question mark indicates the structural uncertainty introduced by the unknown allocation. After the propagation, every exchanged data has a label. Afterwards, the policy, which in this particular case demands that data with a *Personal* label must never flow to nodes with a *nonEU* label, can be checked.

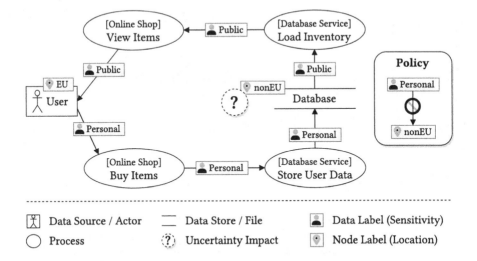

Fig. 4. Simplified label propagation graph under uncertainty of the running example

4.2   Defining and Analyzing Dataflow Constraints

To find confidentiality violations in architectural models, we have to specify prohibited behavior, first. We defined a domain-specific language (DSL) that enables software architects to model dataflow constraints on architectural abstraction [20]. Together with the modeling capabilities using characteristics and assignments, this provides means for architects to analyze confidentiality.

```
1  type DataSensitivity : DataSensitivity
2  type ServerLocation : ServerLocation
3
4  constraint NoPersonalDataToNonEUServers {
5    data.attribute.DataSensitivity.Personal NEVER FLOWS
6    element.property.ServerLocation.nonEU
7  }
```

Listing 1.2. Constraint for prohibiting flows of personal data to non-EU servers

In our running example, a confidentiality violation occurs if personal data flows to components that are located outside the EU. Listing 1.2 shows this constraint formulated using the DSL. We start by reusing the type definitions from the data dictionary. Then, we define the named constraint that shall restrict the flow of personal data to non-EU servers. Each constraint consists of at least one data selector and one element selector. In our example, we select data that has the characteristic value **Personal** of type **DataSensitivity**. We select all elements with the characteristic **ServerLocation** set to **nonEU**. The directive **never flows** implicates that selected dataflows are always forbidden. Thus, whenever a selected dataflow is detected, a violation is automatically reported. The complete analysis process is automated and transparent to software architects [47].

Please note that this only represents a very basic use case of the DSL. For example, we added capabilities to define variables and variable sets that are filled and compared dynamically during the analysis execution. By doing so, architects can describe more complex constraints such as enforcing role-based access control (RBAC) [14]. We also added selectors to reference a specific element of the architectural model or to prohibit any type of dataflow.

The tooling [47] uses Prolog to analyze the architectural model. After the modeling by software architects, both the architectural model and the constraints are automatically transformed to executable Prolog code. Here, the model is transformed into a set of clauses, that represent the dataflows in the system [49]. The dataflow constraint—formulated using the DSL—is transformed into a Prolog query and executed [20]. Besides the DSL, architects can also formulate Prolog queries directly if the DSL is too limiting. Whenever the Prolog engine successfully satisfies the query, a dataflow violation has been found. The results are translated back into the architectural domain and displayed to the architects. By doing so, the violations can be enriched with contextual information such as where the violation occurred, and which characteristics were set. Also, the complete process of transformation of models, constraints, and results as well as the analysis are automated and transparent to the architects.

5   Considering Confidentiality Under Uncertainty

With the dataflow analysis from the previous section, we can analyze architectures for confidentiality issues without taking uncertainty into account. As we discussed in previous publications [6,18] the confidentiality of the system can be influenced by uncertainty. This uncertainty can exist in different forms such as in the environment, e.g., no reliable information about the location of users, or the system structure, e.g., the deployment location assumed during the design-time [6]. There exist different means to handle uncertainty such as fuzzy policy evaluation [9] to compensate uncertainty during runtime or probabilistic model solver such as PRISM [23].

In our case, we concentrated on the uncertainty of structural elements such as the deployment or the binding of components. For this type of uncertainty, a possible solution is the creation of different variations without uncertainty. For instance, for our running example, this would involve a different variation of the software architecture for each deployment location. One solution, that uses such variations, is model averaging [39]. Here, multiple variations are created, and afterwards, the results are combined. However, using an average value for confidentiality is not useful since it is a binary decision, whether systems are confidential or not. Therefore, we want to discard solutions that have confidentiality issues. Additionally, creating these different variations manually is cumbersome and error-prone, and analyzing all variations can be very time-consuming. Besides these drawbacks, architects seldom want to optimize regarding only one quality attribute such as confidentiality but want to find the overall best architecture. Therefore, it is beneficial to integrate our dataflow analysis in an existing architecture design space exploration tool (see Subsect. 3.2). In our case, we used PerOpteryx [29], since it already supports an architectural design decision model for modeling uncertain design decisions, the optimization of multiple quality attributes such as costs or performance and is well integrated into the PCM. The first step for integrating our analysis approach is defining a new QML contract for a new quality dimension named confidentiality. These QML contracts define the quality dimensions PerOpteryx [30] can consider. Quality dimensions are the different quality attributes PerOpteryx can optimize. While PerOpteryx already contains a security dimension [8], we decided against it since we wanted to explicitly target confidentiality. The existing security domain is focused more on the costs of introducing security measures and costs of failure.

The confidentiality dimension is modeled as real values where decreasing values are better solutions, since the optimization approach of PerOpteryx currently only support real values. However, we mapped these to a binary classification for the confidentiality analysis results. For each quality dimension, PerOpteryx defines handlers, which can analyze a model for the given quality dimension. Therefore, we defined a new confidentiality handler for the confidentiality domain. This handler acts as an adapter between PerOpteryx and our original dataflow analysis. The main task is to provide the input models for our analysis, run the dataflow analysis and transform the results of our analysis as parameters for the optimization process of PerOpteryx. For the input models, we need to extract the current architecture candidate models. These are the varied architectures models based on the evolutionary search and the design decision model from PerOpteryx. The candidate model of our running example contains one concrete design decision, for instance the deployment of the database on Non-EU servers. This candidate model is now extracted from PerOpteryx and loaded into our analysis. Additionally, the adapter provides the confidentiality requirements for the dataflow analysis. After executing the analysis, we transform the results to the newly added confidentiality dimension. Our analysis can only identify violations based on confidentiality requirements. Currently, these violations are not ranked, and we cannot differentiate which violations are worse since the ranking of confidentiality is not obvious. Even obvious solutions for ranking issues, such as the number of violations, are problematic since scenarios with a higher number of violations might only leak not relevant data or leak data only in very rare cases. At the same time, scenarios with a low number could leak highly sensitive data.

The ranking of violations or quantification of confidentiality can be seen as another research area. Therefore, we choose here a binary classification with the classes *confidential* and *non-confidential*. However, because the confidentiality dimension uses real values, we need to transform the binary classifications. Also, choosing another representation than real values is not possible due to the underlying extension mechanism of PerOpteryx. Also, developing another optimization approach that supports binary classifications would come with additional drawbacks, such as missing integration of other quality metrics. Our adapter transforms confidential results to -1 and non-confidential results to 1. Despite the binary-classification of the dataflow analysis [49] results, the dataflow analysis can support multiple attributes as input values. For instance, in a previous publication [49], we successfully analyzed role-based access control or attribute-based access control approaches. The results then enable the PerOpteryx optimization to rank confidential candidates higher than non-confidential ones. Again, the value of the mapping is partly given by technical restrictions. Since we want to use the restriction option of PerOpteryx to filter/discard non-confidential candidates, the confidential result needs to be lower than the non-confidential one. PerOpteryx currently only supports filtering candidates with too high values. However, the choosing of negative values, does not affect the optimization approach since it explicitly accepts a decreasing integer range as an optimization criterion. Also, the value ∞ is reserved as an error code, as it is usually in the PerOpteryx domain.

In addition to defining the confidentiality dimension and the adapter between PerOpteryx and our dataflow analysis, we extended PerOpteryx by a new contract type for confidentiality. These types are used in the optimization definition of PerOpteryx and define which quality attributes should be optimized. In our case, these would be the confidentiality dimension.

The application of our approach looks like this: First, software architects need to specify the architectural model and extend it with our dataflow extensions (see Subsect. 4.1). For the specification, they can use our developed Eclipse tool [47], which provides graphical editors to our models. It extends the existing notions of PCM. Figure 2 illustrate how this extension looks for the resource environment and our running example. Additionally, they need to define the confidentiality constraints either with our DSL (see Subsect. 4.2) or use a Prolog constraint.

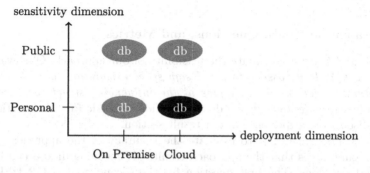

Fig. 5. Overview for possible confidentiality results based on the deployment for the database component and the sensitivity level of the stored data

For our running example, the DSL specifications looks like in Listing 1.2. The architectural variations are modeled in the design decision model from Peropteryx. For instance, for our running example, the architect can define here that the database service component can be deployed on two different servers. Besides design decisions, architects need to specify the optimization aspects. Here, PerOpteryx reuses QML contracts [15,36] (see Subsect. 3.2). For our running example, the architect creates a new QML contract with the target to achieve -1 in the confidentiality dimension. This is modeled by an objective with the value -1 as a goal. This represents a system without confidentiality violations. Afterwards, the architect will get a CSV file with the tested variations and a separate file for the Pareto optimal variation.

The possible results for our running example are illustrated in Fig. 5. On the vertical axis, the sensitivity level of the data is shown. In our case, these are `Personal` and `Public`. On the horizontal axis the deployment possibilities, i.e., `On Premise` and `Cloud`, are shown. We added the results for the database service component (`db`) by using different colored ellipses. The grey ones are configurations without confidentiality violations. The black one contains confidentiality violations. We only illustrate the database component since it is in our case the deciding factor. In our running example, we modeled that the database stores `Personal` data. Therefore, our approach returns only the variation with the `Database Service` on premise.

6   Evaluation

In the evaluation, we focus on the combination of PerOpteryx and the dataflow-based confidentiality analysis. The evaluation for PerOpteryx can be found in [30] and for the dataflow-based confidentiality analysis in [48,49]. Our evaluation exploits these results and focuses on the integration of both approaches. Our evaluation follows roughly the Goal Question Metric [3] approach. We first describe our goals, questions, and if applicable the metrics and the study design afterward. Then, we discuss the results, threats to validity, and limitations of the approach.

6.1   Evaluation Goals, Questions, and Metrics

The first goal **G1** is to evaluate the feasibility of our approach. Our evaluation question is **Q1**: *Is it possible to use design space exploration to create different architectural variations which represent the influencing structural uncertainty and required confidentiality?* We do not provide a metric for this question, but we will discuss our experience in our result section.

The second goal **G2** is to evaluate the accuracy of the approach. A high accuracy guarantees that the approach results are meaningful and can be used for design decisions. The first question for the second goal is **Q2.1**: *What is the accuracy of our approach for analyzing confidentiality based on the software architecture?* With this question, we investigate whether the integration will

affect the dataflow analysis and might change its result. The second question
is **Q2.2**: *What is the accuracy of considering confidentiality results in the software architecture optimization to identify the Pareto optimal candidate?* Here,
we investigate whether the results of the confidentiality analysis are correctly
interpreted and used for the optimization process. For both questions, we use
the metrics precision and recall [53]. For each investigated evaluation scenario,
we create a manual reference output, and this manual reference output is then
compared against the automatic result. Each incorrectly classified result is a false
positive f_p, and each correctly classified result is a true positive t_p. An expected
but missing result is counted a false negative f_n. The accuracy is then calculated
by precision $M1.1 = \frac{t_p}{t_p+f_p}$, and recall $M1.2 = \frac{t_p}{t_p+f_n}$.

6.2   Evaluation Design

We perform our evaluation based on four different application examples from
the confidentiality [27,32] or design space exploration research community [30].

For answering **Q1**, we combined the input model of PerOpteryx and the
dataflow analysis. During this, we checked the model for contradicting model
elements. After combining the input models, we run our new analysis and checked
whether an error exists.

For answering **Q2.1**, we investigate for each example the generated candidates from PerOpteryx. PerOpteryx also stores the configuration for every candidate and the results of the quality analysis. In our case, this is the classification
in confidential and non-confidential. Two authors investigated whether for each
candidate the classification is correct. A classification is correct, if the original
dataflow [49] analysis would yield the same results also without PerOpteryx. The
two authors are not the developers of the original dataflow analysis. Afterwards,
we calculated precision and recall.

For answering **Q2.2**. we used the same example as for **Q1**. However, we
now looked at the optimization process of PerOpteryx. Here, we compared the
suggested Pareto optimal candidates to all generated candidates. Based on this,
we calculated precision and recall. If the example also considered other quality
attributes as confidentiality, we also included these for our evaluation. If not, we
only considered the confidentiality.

Table 1. Original research domains and source for the application examples

Application examples	Domain	Source
TravelPlanner	Confidentiality	[27,49]
Business Trip Management	Design Space Exploration	[30]
Distance Tracker	Confidentiality	[27,49]
Online Shop	Confidentiality	[18,32]

6.3 Application Examples

Our requirements for our application examples are that they describe the system from an architectural viewpoint. Additionally, the examples need to have at least documentation about either uncertainty and different design decision or need documentation regarding the confidentiality properties. For application examples missing one of these properties, we added the missing properties manually based on our experience with similar examples and systems. For every example, there is at least one design decision that produces a confidential candidate and one decision for a non-confidential candidate. We have selected our examples from the design space exploration research or confidentiality research domain. Table 1 shows the original research domain for our application examples and their sources.

Our first example is the Travelplanner [27] scenario. It is a confidentiality research scenario and is also used in the evaluation of different similar approaches such as [31,48,49,56]. In our evaluation, we used the version from our ECSA Tutorial [47]. This variant contains 7 components. The scenario describes a flight booking system. A user can book a flight at an airline using their mobile app. The user has to send the credit card data to the airline for booking the flight. However, the credit card data is confidential and should be only accessible by the user. Therefore, the user has to declassify the credit card data manually, and only afterwards the data should be shared with the airline. We extended this basic scenario with a potential design decision that would violate the confidentiality constraint of the credit card data. In our scenario, structural uncertainty exists because it is unknown, where the credit card data should be stored.

Our second example is the Business Trip Management from PerOpteryx [30]. It describes a system to organize and book business trips. For the system, multiple design decisions are modeled. For instance, the deployment of the components can be changed, and there exist multiple implementations of components. However, these different deployment locations and implementations of components also have different costs. Here, we reused the original models from PerOpteryx [30]. It contains 4 components. Since PerOpteryx so far has not considered confidentiality, we extended this example with a confidentiality annotation. For simplicity reasons, we used low and high as values to model the confidentiality. Our confidentiality constraints describe that high data cannot flow to nodes considered low. This is similar to other information flow approaches. In this case, the uncertainty is also the deployment. Additionally, we have a design decision where we exchange some of the implemented components.

The third example is the Distance Tracker [27]. It was already used in the evaluation of our dataflow-based confidentiality analysis [48]. It models a simple mobile application, which tracks the walked distance of the user by a GPS tracker application. The walked distance is then synchronized with a service provider. However, this provider should have no access to the actual GPS data, only to the walked distance. Here, we added a design decision that would let the service provider access the GPS data. The system contains 8 components.

Our fourth example is our running example (see Sect. 2). We modeled the PCM models and constraints based on the descriptions from [18,32].

The Travelplanner and Distance Tracker [27] are both from the confidentiality research domain. They were both already investigated in previous confidentiality analysis publications [48,49]. Therefore, they fulfill our requirements. The Business Trip Management [30] is investigated in [30]. It contains an architectural model and multiple design decisions. Therefore, also our requirements are met. The running example has one design decision leading to structural uncertainty and the software architecture is modeled. Therefore, it also fulfills our requirements.

6.4   Results and Discussion

We have investigated each research question for each application example. For **Q1**, we have found no contradicting model elements. We could model every aspect necessary for the example. Additionally, we executed every example and looked for errors in the generated results. PerOpteryx marks each candidate with an error during the analysis with an ∞ value. Our results did not contain any ∞ values, therefore we assume, that no significant errors happened. This finding indicates that a combination is technically feasible.

For every question of **G2** (**Q2.1** and **Q2.2**), we get a precision and a recall of 1.0, which are the perfect results. The results are good because our example models are small, which simplifies the output. Also, most of the decisions are easily understandable and can be deduced easily without automatic tooling. However, these smaller scenarios are better to identify implementation problems or other errors easily. Additionally, in more complex scenarios, deducing the confidentiality is not that easy, especially if there are multiple different deployment decisions for components. Table 2 illustrates the results of our analysis. It shows an excerpt of the analyzed candidate models for the Business Trip Management. The first column is the cost. The second column are the confidentiality results (with -1 for confidential and $+1$ for non-confidential). The next three columns describe the deployment locations for components. The last column describes the used implementation (the normal implementation (BookingSystem) or a faster one (QuickBooking)). For brevity reasons, we only show an excerpt of the results. In this configuration the Server1 and Server3 are considered as High and Server2 as low. Based on these values we calculated precision and recall.

For **Q2.1**, the results indicate that using the architectural candidates from PerOpteryx as variations for the confidentiality analysis will not affect the confidentiality analysis. The results for our examples are the same as if we would have manually created model variations based on the uncertainty and afterwards analyzed them with our dataflow analysis [49]. For **Q2.2**, the results indicate that the optimization process of PerOpteryx can successfully consider the confidentiality results. This could enable PerOpteryx to optimize the architecture for confidential systems and even discard non-confidential architectural variations.

In summary, these results could enable architects to optimize software architectures regarding different quality metrics including confidentiality. This is indicated by our results for **G1** and **G2**. **G1** demonstrates that both analyses can be combined into one working analysis for our examples. So far there are no conceptual problems known. The results for **G2** indicate, that the found architectural candidates can be successfully analyzed regarding their confidentiality. Additionally, it indicates that the optimization process potentially can use the result from the confidentiality analysis. Therefore, our approach could optimize for confidential software architectures. Also, our approach should be less error-prone than creating manually the variations. At the manual creation of variations, architects need to manually track the different variations. In contrast, in our analysis architects need only to specify the variation points and the analysis automatically generates architecture candidates. In addition, since we used PerOpteryx which supports optimization for many other quality attributes, architects could get Pareto optimal candidates for the software architecture.

Table 2. Excerpt of results for candidates of the Business Trip Management example

Cost	Confidentiality	C1	C2	C3	BookingSystem
5734.33	−1	Server3	Server3	Server2	QuickBooking
2749.12	+1	Server2	Server2	Server3	BookingSystem
3924.26	−1	Server1	Server3	Server2	BookingSystem
3497.23	−1	Server3	Server3	Server2	BookingSystem
1570.53	−1	Server3	Server3	Server1	BookingSystem
1647.13	−1	Server3	Server2	Server3	BookingSystem
7609.77	+1	Server1	Server2	Server3	QuickBooking

...

6.5   Threats to Validity

We categories our threats to validity based on the guidelines from Runeson and Höst [44].

Internal Validity describes that only investigated factors affect the result. The internal validity is threatened by the manual creation of the reference output and the extension of the existing examples. To reduce the risk of the reference output, we compared the reference output with the output of the dataflow analysis [49] without our extension. Additionally, the small size helps to understand the results. To reduce the second risk, we added the missing properties in the examples based on our experience with similar examples, where the missing properties are modeled. Another threat to internal validity is that we only investigated the adapter and not the optimization process of PerOpteryx or the accuracy of the used confidentiality analysis. However, we integrated our integration by using the dedicated extension mechanism in PerOpteryx and only adapted the user interface. For the dataflow analysis [49], we only added an additional output method. Otherwise, we have not changed the source code. Therefore, we consider this threat to be low since both approaches are well established and are thoroughly evaluated in different publications such as [8,29,46,48,49].

External Validity describes how transferable the results are for others. The usage of application examples might provide better insights but might affect the generalizability of the results. Therefore, we chose mostly external examples from different research domains. Our first and third examples are from the confidentiality domain and the second one is originally an optimization example for performance and cost. Using different examples lowers the risk. Nevertheless, in the future, we want to investigate real application case studies and not only research examples.

Construct Validity describes whether the intended properties are relevant for the goal. Here the properties are the metrics precision and recall. These metrics are also used in the evaluation of the original confidentiality analysis [49]. Using the same metrics lowers the risk. We did not investigate the scalability of the approach. However, since the added adapter contains not too much complex logic the scalability should be similar to the foundational approaches.

Reliability is how reproducible the results are for other researchers. Using statistical metrics for G2 reduces the subjectivity of the result and increases reproducibility. Konersmann et al. [28] state the lack of reproduction packages in current software engineering research. Thus, we provide a dataset [55] containing all the relevant models and the analysis. Furthermore, the extension is published as an open-source tool[1] as well as all the necessary dependencies. This allows other researchers to reproduce the result more easily and increases the reuse.

6.6 Limitations

One limitation is currently the restricted variation creation based on the architectural decision model of PerOpteryx. While this already allows modeling structural uncertainty such as different deployments, other aspects like different variations of user roles are not possible. However, this does not mean, that our confidentiality analysis [49] approach cannot handle different roles. In fact, it can use different roles or even arbitrary attributes like in Attribute-based access control and we already demonstrated it in [49]. Only it does not support uncertainty in these attributes, yet. A possible solution might be the extension or the transformation of the design decision model to an uncertainty variation model. This would also help to create an impact analysis that identifies affected elements of uncertainty. Another limitation, so far, is the missing differentiation of confidentiality issues. Currently, the optimization of PerOpteryx only binary classifies the results and optimize to a system without confidentiality violations.

---

[1] https://github.com/FluidTrust/Palladio-Addons-DataFlowConfidentiality-DSE.

However, it might be beneficial to allow certain types of violations to get better overall system performance. This is similar to Bures et al. [7], where access control policies are adapted and sometimes lessened to guarantee a working system. Another first approach for quantifying security within PCM is presented by Reiche et al. [42]. Another problem is due to the design-time nature of our approach. Our model might differ from the actually implemented system, and therefore, the result of the analysis might not be true for the actual system. However, approaches like [35,57] try to tangle this issue. Additionally, we do not consider an explicit attacker model. Therefore, we cannot consider different attacker behaviors in the optimization process. A solution might be the integration of our attacker analysis [56].

7   Related Work

We split our related work in design space exploration, model-driven confidentiality analysis, and uncertainty.

7.1   Design Space Exploration

Sobhy et al. [50] present an overview of different design space exploration considering uncertainty. In it, PerOpteryx [30] is categorized as a search-based approach. Another design space exploration tool is ArcheOpterix [1]. It can also optimize a given architecture for multiple criteria. However, it does not support a confidentiality analysis, and the design space modeling is more restrictive. GuideArch [12] uses fuzzy logic to handle uncertainty in the design phase. This uncertainty can be reduced during the development and, therefore, GuideArch might provide more precise results. However, currently, there is no support for confidentiality. Last, there is already a PerOpteryx extension for security [8]. In contrast to our approach, they modeled these by a concept of concerns. These concerns describe which design decisions are dependent on each other. In our analysis we focus on the direct impact on confidentiality.

7.2   Model-driven Confidentiality Analysis

UMLsec [25] extends UML by defining a security profile. It supports different kinds of analyses, such as information flow or access control. In contrast to our confidentiality analysis, it does not support access control on data, and there is no support to handle structural uncertainty. Another UML security profile is SecureUML [33]. It supports role-based access control together with OCL statements to support dynamic properties. However, the analysis does also not consider structural uncertainty. SecDFD [52] is also a dataflow analysis approach. They do not support custom analysis definitions such as we with our DSL (see Subsect. 4.2) or the considering of structural uncertainty with our architectural design decision model from PerOpteryx. Gerking et al. [17] and the iFlow [26] approach are also information flow analyses. The first one targets especially

Cyber-physical systems and keeping the real-time properties. It again does not support structural uncertainty. The same applies to the iFlow approach. We also developed another confidentiality analysis for software architectures [56]. However, there the focus is on the architectural propagation of attackers and not dataflow or uncertainty.

7.3   Uncertainty

Garlan [16] discusses why it is necessary to consider uncertainty during the software engineering. Uncertainty itself is in general classified in Walker et al. [54] without special relation to software engineering. Perez-Palacin and Mirandola [39] extended this classification and combined it with other classifications, such as [2]. They also discuss mechanisms to handle different types of uncertainty. However, they do not consider confidentiality. Additionally, they focus on self-adaptive systems and do not specifically aim at handling uncertainty on architectural abstraction.

Esfahani and Malek [11] also discuss uncertainty in the context of self-adaptive systems. They highlight the problem of uncertainty in the environment of a software system, e.g., due to the deployment. Ramirez et al. [41] present different sources of uncertainty and a scheme to describe uncertainty in different development phases. Regarding design-time confidentiality, they lack in precision and name related uncertainty as *inadequate design* or *unverified design*. Still, they also list *unexplored alternatives* and *misinformed trade-off analysis* which motivates our work. Troya et al. [51] provide a current survey of different approaches regarding confidentiality. They provide another classification of uncertainty and point out the growth of research with relation to uncertainty in software models. However, they also mention the lack of repeatable results as well as tool support which we tried to also address with our work.

Mahdavi et al. [22] investigated the research community of self-adaptive systems about uncertainty. They provide an overview of the current state of the community. They find that the current state of the art lacks in including non-functional requirements both as optimization goal as well as side effects. By including confidentiality in the general PerOpteryx analysis, we can optimize towards confidentiality but also detect violations. Thus, our approach addresses this issue. We also at least partially address the mentioned problem of dealing with concurrent sources of uncertainty, at least regarding structural uncertainty.

The Design-Time Uncertainty Management (DeTUM) [13] is a tool to handle uncertainty during the design-time. It introduces uncertainty in the start phase and then resolves it in later stages. However, the authors do not mention security-related quality attributes like confidentiality. Lytra and Zdun [34] propose the use of fuzzy logic to incorporate inherent uncertainty into reusable, architectural design decisions. This shall enable software architects to share and reuse knowledge about the impact of uncertainty on quality attributes. Although this approach can also handle security-related quality attributes, violations due to integration issues remain hidden. Here, the integration of a dedicated analysis— such as our confidentiality analysis—helps identify also fine-grained problems.

Boltz et al. [5] present an approach to extend our dataflow-based confidentiality analysis to handle environmental uncertainty. They use fuzzy inference systems to calculate the impact of environmental variables on confidentiality-related attributes. Although the there discussed environmental uncertainty is another instance of known uncertainty, statements of its influence are not directly comparable to statements about an architecture's structure under uncertainty.

In summary, there exist many approaches to categorize uncertainty and some also provide approaches to handle certain uncertainty types. However, they have so far not considered confidentiality explicitly. Also, there is a focus on self-adaptive systems with a lack of systematic approaches on architectural abstraction [22].

8   Conclusion

We have presented an approach to consider structural uncertainty and confidentiality in software architectures. For this, we combined our dataflow-based confidentiality [47–49] with an architectural optimization approach [30]. Besides considering confidentiality, our approach can be used to determine Pareto optimal software architectures regarding multiple quality attributes. We demonstrated that we could detect confidentiality violations for our examples, and these exemplary confidentiality violations are correctly considered in the optimization process. This indicates that our approach could work correctly and might help architects to determine the Pareto optimal architecture candidate.

In the future, we want to extend the considered uncertainties and further investigate the accuracy with real-world case studies. We also aim to better understand the impact of different types of uncertainty on confidentiality and create a classification scheme. This shall help in discussing the impact of uncertainty and find appropriate mitigation strategies. Also, we want to extend the presented approach of handling uncertainty by analyzing different architecture variations. Last, we want to repeat the survey regarding the applicability and usability of our dataflow approach, which we conducted during a tutorial. The future study should include our new extension and address more participants.

Acknowledgement. We like to thank Oliver Liu, who helped in developing this approach during his Bachelor thesis.

References

1. Aleti, A., Bjornander, S., Grunske, L., Meedeniya, I.: ArcheOpterix: an extendable tool for architecture optimization of AADL models. In: ICSE Workshop on Model-Based Methodologies for Pervasive and Embedded Software, pp. 61–71 (2009). https://doi.org/10.1109/MOMPES.2009.5069138
2. Armour, P.G.: The five orders of ignorance. Commun. ACM **43**(10), 17–20 (2000). https://doi.org/10.1145/352183.352194
3. Basili, G., Caldiera, V.R., Rombach, H.D.: The goal question metric approach. Encycl. Softw. Eng. pp. 528–532 (1994)

4. Boehm, B., Basili, V.: Software defect reduction top 10 list. Computer **34**(1), 135–137 (2001). https://doi.org/10.1109/2.962984

5. Boltz, N., et al.: Handling environmental uncertainty in design time access control analysis. In: 2022 48th Euromicro Conference on Software Engineering and Advanced Applications (SEAA). IEEE (2022, accepted, to appear)

6. Bures, T., Hnetynka, P., Heinrich, R., Seifermann, S., Walter, M.: Capturing dynamicity and uncertainty in security and trust via situational patterns. In: Margaria, T., Steffen, B. (eds.) ISoLA 2020. LNCS, vol. 12477, pp. 295–310. Springer, Cham (2020). https://doi.org/10.1007/978-3-030-61470-6_18

7. Bureš, T., Gerostathopoulos, I., Hnětynka, P., Seifermann, S., Walter, M., Heinrich, R.: Aspect-oriented adaptation of access control rules. In: 2021 47th Euromicro Conference on Software Engineering and Advanced Applications (SEAA), pp. 363–370 (2021). https://doi.org/10.1109/SEAA53835.2021.00054

8. Busch, A., Schneider, Y., Koziolek, A., Rostami, K., Kienzle, J.: Modelling the structure of reusable solutions for architecture-based quality evaluation. In: 2016 IEEE International Conference on Cloud Computing Technology and Science (CloudCom), pp. 521–526 (2016). https://doi.org/10.1109/CloudCom.2016.0091

9. Casola, V., Preziosi, R., Rak, M., Troiano, L.: A reference model for security level evaluation: policy and fuzzy techniques. J. Univers. Comput. Sci. **11**(1), 150–174 (2005)

10. Council of European Union: REGULATION (EU) 2016/679. (general data protection regulation). https://eur-lex.europa.eu/eli/reg/2016/679/2016-05-04

11. Esfahani, N., Malek, S.: Uncertainty in self-adaptive software systems. In: de Lemos, R., Giese, H., Müller, H.A., Shaw, M. (eds.) Software Engineering for Self-Adaptive Systems II. LNCS, vol. 7475, pp. 214–238. Springer, Heidelberg (2013). https://doi.org/10.1007/978-3-642-35813-5_9

12. Esfahani, N., Malek, S., Razavi, K.: GuideArch: guiding the exploration of architectural solution space under uncertainty. In: 2013 35th International Conference on Software Engineering (ICSE), pp. 43–52. IEEE (2013). https://doi.org/10.1109/ICSE.2013.6606550, https://ieeexplore.ieee.org/document/6606550

13. Famelis, M., Chechik, M.: Managing design-time uncertainty. In: MODELS, p. 179. IEEE Press (2017). https://doi.org/10.1109/MODELS.2017.24

14. Ferraiolo, D., Cugini, J., Kuhn, D.R.: Role-based access control (RBAC): features and motivations. In: ACSAC 1995, pp. 241–248 (1995)

15. Frolund, S., Koistinen, J.: A language for quality of service specification. Tech. rep, HP Labs Technical Report, California, USA (1998)

16. Garlan, D.: Software engineering in an uncertain world. In: Proceedings of the FSE/SDP Workshop on Future of Software Engineering Research, FoSER 2010, pp. 125–128. Association for Computing Machinery, New York, NY, USA (2010). https://doi.org/10.1145/1882362.1882389

17. Gerking, C., Schubert, D.: Component-based refinement and verification of information-flow security policies for cyber-physical microservice architectures. In: ICSA2019, pp. 61–70. IEEE, March 2019. https://doi.org/10.1109/ICSA.2019.00015, https://ieeexplore.ieee.org/document/8703909

18. Hahner, S.: Architectural access control policy refinement and verification under uncertainty. In: Companion Proceedings of the 15th European Conference on Software Architecture. CEUR Workshop Proceedings, vol. 2978. RWTH Aachen (2021), 46.23.03; LK 01

19. Hahner, S.: Dealing with uncertainty in architectural confidentiality analysis. In: Proceedings of the Software Engineering 2021 Satellite Events. pp. 1–6. Gesellschaft für Informatik, Virtual (2021)

20. Hahner, S., Seifermann, S., Heinrich, R., Walter, M., Bures, T., Hnetynka, P.: Modeling data flow constraints for design-time confidentiality analyses. In: 2021 IEEE International Conference on Software Architecture Companion (ICSA-C), pp. 15–21. IEEE (2021). https://doi.org/10.1109/ICSA-C52384.2021.00009

21. Heinrich, R., et al.: Dynamic access control in industry 4.0 systems. In: Digital Transformation, Chap. 6. Springer, Heidelberg (2022, accepted, to appear)

22. Hezavehi, S.M., Weyns, D., Avgeriou, P., Calinescu, R., Mirandola, R., Perez-Palacin, D.: Uncertainty in self-adaptive systems: a research community perspective. ACM Trans. Auton. Adapt. Syst. **15**(4) (2021). https://doi.org/10.1145/3487921

23. Hinton, A., Kwiatkowska, M., Norman, G., Parker, D.: PRISM: a tool for automatic verification of probabilistic systems. In: Hermanns, H., Palsberg, J. (eds.) TACAS 2006. LNCS, vol. 3920, pp. 441–444. Springer, Heidelberg (2006). https://doi.org/10.1007/11691372_29

24. ISO Central Secretary: Information technology - security techniques - information security management systems - overview and vocabulary. Standard ISO/IEC 27000:2018. International Organization for Standardization, Geneva, CH (2018). https://www.iso.org/standard/73906.html

25. Jürjens, J.: UMLsec: extending UML for secure systems development. In: Jézéquel, J.-M., Hussmann, H., Cook, S. (eds.) UML 2002. LNCS, vol. 2460, pp. 412–425. Springer, Heidelberg (2002). https://doi.org/10.1007/3-540-45800-X_32

26. Katkalov, K., Stenzel, K., Borek, M., Reif, W.: Model-driven development of information flow-secure systems with IFLOW. In: SOCIALCOM, pp. 51–56 (2013). https://doi.org/10.1109/SocialCom.2013.14

27. Katkalov, K.: Ein modellgetriebener Ansatz zur Entwicklung informationsfluss-sicherer Systeme. doctoralthesis, Universität Augsburg (2017)

28. Konersmann, M., et al.: Evaluation methods and replicability of software architecture research objects. In: ICSA. IEEE (2022)

29. Koziolek, A.: Automated improvement of software architecture models for performance and other quality attributes. Ph.D. thesis, Karlsruher Institut für Technologie (KIT) (2011). https://doi.org/10.5445/IR/1000024955

30. Koziolek, A., Koziolek, H., Reussner, R.: PerOpteryx: automated application of tactics in multi-objective software architecture optimization. In: Proceedings of the joint ACM SIGSOFT Conference-QoSA and ACM SIGSOFT Symposium-ISARCS on Quality of Software Architectures-QoSA and Architecting Critical Systems - ISARCS, pp. 33–42 (2011)

31. Kramer, M., Hecker, M., Greiner, S., Bao, K., Yurchenko, K.: Model-driven specification and analysis of confidentiality in component-based systems. Tech. Rep. 12, KIT-Department of Informatics (2017). https://doi.org/10.5445/IR/1000076957

32. Liu, O.: Design space evaluation for confidentiality under architectural uncertainty (2021). https://doi.org/10.5445/IR/1000139590

33. Lodderstedt, T., Basin, D., Doser, J.: SecureUML: a UML-based modeling language for model-driven security. In: Jézéquel, J.-M., Hussmann, H., Cook, S. (eds.) UML 2002. LNCS, vol. 2460, pp. 426–441. Springer, Heidelberg (2002). https://doi.org/10.1007/3-540-45800-X_33

34. Lytra, I., Zdun, U.: Supporting architectural decision making for systems-of-systems design under uncertainty. In: Proceedings of the First International Workshop on Software Engineering for Systems-of-Systems, SESoS 2013, pp. 43–46. Association for Computing Machinery, July 2013. https://doi.org/10.1145/2489850.2489859

35. Monschein, D., Mazkatli, M., Heinrich, R., Koziolek, A.: Enabling consistency between software artefacts for software adaption and evolution. In: ICSA, pp. 1–12 (2021). https://doi.org/10.1109/ICSA51549.2021.00009

36. Noorshams, Q., Martens, A., Reussner, R.: Using quality of service bounds for effective multi-objective software architecture optimization. In: Proceedings of the 2nd International Workshop on the Quality of Service-Oriented Software Systems. QUASOSS 2010, Association for Computing Machinery, New York, NY, USA (2010). https://doi.org/10.1145/1858263.1858265

37. OWASP: A04:2021 - insecure design. https://owasp.org/Top10/A04_2021-Insecure_Design/

38. OWASP: Top ten web application security risks, https://owasp.org/www-project-top-ten/

39. Perez-Palacin, D., Mirandola, R.: Uncertainties in the modeling of self- adaptive systems: a taxonomy and an example of availability evaluation. pp. 3–14. In: Proceedings of the 5th ACM/SPEC International Conference on Performance Engineering, ICPE 2014, pp. 3–14. Association for Computing Machinery, New York, NY, USA (2014). https://doi.org/10.1145/2568088.2568095

40. Piper, D.: DLA Piper GDPR fines and data breach survey: January GDPR fines and data breach survey: January 2022. www.dlapiper.com/de/germany/insights/publications/2022/1/dla-piper-gdpr-fines-and-data-breach-survey-2022

41. Ramirez, A.J., Jensen, A.C., Cheng, B.H.C.: A taxonomy of uncertainty for dynamically adaptive systems. In: 2012 7th International Symposium on Software Engineering for Adaptive and Self-Managing Systems (SEAMS), pp. 99–108 (June 2012). https://doi.org/10.1109/SEAMS.2012.6224396

42. Reiche, F., Schiffl, J., Weigl, A., Heinrich, R., Beckert, B., Reussner, R.: Model-driven quantification of correctness with palladio and key. Tech. rep., Karlsruher Institut für Technologie (KIT) (2021). https://doi.org/10.5445/IR/1000128855

43. Reussner, R., et al.: Modeling and Simulating Software Architecture - The Palladio Approach. MIT Press, Cambridge. October 2016. http://mitpress.mit.edu/books/modeling-and-simulating-software-architectures

44. Runeson, P., Höst, M.: Guidelines for conducting and reporting case study research in software engineering. Emp. Softw. Eng. **14**(2), 131 (2008). https://doi.org/10.1007/s10664-008-9102-8

45. Schulz, S., Reiche, F., Hahner, S., Schiffl, J.: Continuous secure software development and analysis. In: Proceedings of Symposium on Software Performance 2021. Leipzig, Germany, November 2021

46. Seifermann, S., Heinrich, R., Werle, D., Reussner, R.: A unified model to detect information flow and access control violations in software architectures. In: Proceedings of the 18th International Conference on Security and Cryptography, SECRYPT 2021, Virtual, Online, 6 July 2021–8 July 2021. pp. 26–37. SciTePress (2021). https://doi.org/10.5220/0010515300260037

47. Seifermann, S., Walter, M., Hahner, S., Heinrich, R., Reussner, R.: Identifying confidentiality violations in architectural design using palladio. In: ECSA-C202021, vol. 2978. CEUR-WS.org (2021). 46.23.03; LK 01

48. Seifermann, S., Heinrich, R., Reussner, R.: Data-driven software architecture for analyzing confidentiality. In: ICSA, pp. 1–10. IEEE (2019). https://doi.org/10.1109/ICSA.2019.00009, https://ieeexplore.ieee.org/document/8703910

49. Seifermann, S., Heinrich, R., Werle, D., Reussner, R.: Detecting violations of access control and information flow policies in data flow diagrams. JSS **184** (2021)

50. Sobhy, D., Bahsoon, R., Minku, L., Kazman, R.: Evaluation of software architectures under Uncertainty: a systematic literature review. ACM Trans. Softw. Eng. Methodol. **1**(1), 50 (2021)

51. Troya, J., Moreno, N., Bertoa, M.F., Vallecillo, A.: Uncertainty representation in software models: a survey. Softw. Syst. Model. **20**(4), 1183–1213 (2021). https://doi.org/10.1007/s10270-020-00842-1

52. Tuma, K., Scandariato, R., Balliu, M.: Flaws in flows: unveiling design flaws via information flow analysis. In: ICSA, pp. 191–200 (2019). https://doi.org/10.1109/ICSA.2019.00028

53. Qian, M., Wang, J., Lin, H., Zhao, D., Zhang, Y., Tang, W., Yang, Z.: Auto-learning convolution-based graph convolutional network for medical relation extraction. In: Lin, H., Zhang, M., Pang, L. (eds.) CCIR 2021. LNCS, vol. 13026, pp. 195–207. Springer, Cham (2021). https://doi.org/10.1007/978-3-030-88189-4_15

54. Walker, W., et al.: Defining uncertainty: a conceptual basis for uncertainty management in model-based decision support. Integr. Assess. **4** (2003). https://doi.org/10.1076/iaij.4.1.5.16466

55. Walter, M., et al.: Dataset: architectural optimization for confidentiality under structural uncertainty. https://doi.org/10.5281/zenodo.6569353

56. Walter, M., Heinrich, R., Reussner, R.: Architectural attack propagation analysis for identifying confidentiality issues. In: ICSA (2022)

57. Yurchenko, K., et al.: Architecture-driven reduction of specification overhead for verifying confidentiality in component-based software systems. In: MODELS (Satellite Events), pp. 321–323 (2017)

Foundations and Research Agenda for Simulation of Smart Ecosystems Architectures

Valdemar Vicente Graciano Neto[1]([⊠]) [iD], Wallace Manzano[2] [iD],
Pablo Oliveira Antonino[3] [iD], and Elisa Yumi Nakagawa[2] [iD]

[1] Federal University of Goiás, Goiânia, Brazil
valdemarneto@ufg.br
[2] University of São Paulo, São Carlos, Brazil
wallace.manzano@usp.br, elisa@icmc.usp.br
[3] Fraunhofer IESE, Kaiserslautern, Germany
pablo.antonino@iese.fraunhofer.de

Abstract. The expected evolution of software-intensive systems has led to the emergence of complex systems in which smart ecosystems are representative. All life cycle phases of these ecosystems, from requirements engineering to maintenance (particularly the architectural design), are also complex. Approaches to the architecture evaluation of such complex systems are necessary, and simulation can be considered relevant and a good candidate. This work is positioned in this scenario and provides an overview of simulation of smart ecosystems architectures. We present concepts associated with simulation, known simulation technologies, such as DEVS and FERAL, and summarize our experience with the simulation of different ecosystems. Moreover, we observe several difficulties, challenges, and research opportunities that still exist and that should be carried forward to mature the field of smart ecosystems simulation.

Keywords: Simulation · Software architecture · Systems-of-Systems

1 Introduction

Software has been increasingly embedded into mechanical, electrical, hydraulic, and pneumatic systems, just to mention a few. Software supports them to offer a higher precision of their functionalities with automation of operation, which makes them sometimes *smarter*. As a result, such systems have increasingly become software-intensive, i.e., software intensively contributes, influences, and impacts on the construction, deployment, and evolution of these smart systems [24,37]. Smart ecosystems (also called as Systems-of-Systems (SoS) in the context of this work) result from the combination of multiple smart systems, resulting in alliances of systems that interoperate among them to achieve more robust behavior and create (and support) complex infrastructures and smart applications, such as Industry 4.0, smart cities, and emergency response management systems.

© The Author(s), under exclusive license to Springer Nature Switzerland AG 2022
P. Scandurra et al. (Eds.): ECSA Tracks and Workshops 2021, LNCS 13365, pp. 333–352, 2022.
https://doi.org/10.1007/978-3-031-15116-3_15

Smart ecosystems have supported several critical application domains in which failures can cause damages, losses, and financial harm. Moreover, such ecosystems often have a dynamic software architecture (DSA), i.e., their structure changes over time due to constituent systems that join and leave the ecosystem or are replaced or reorganized at run-time. Due to the critical nature of the domains that ecosystems support, they should be reliable and work without interruption or failures that could cause some of the serious aforementioned problems. However, given the dynamic nature of smart ecosystem architectures, the feasibility of each architectural arrangement that they can assume at run-time requires a prior analysis, still at design time, to assure that both smart ecosystem structure and behavior can be preserved at run-time [25].

The establishment of approaches to accordingly evaluate smart-ecosystems architectures is thus necessary [11], but the evaluation of the structure and behavior of that critical infrastructure formed by multiple constituent systems is hard. For instance, in environments such as Industry 4.0 (where we observe several instances of smart ecosystems), evaluation can be expensive and/or unfeasible to be performed at run-time. Then, approaches that allow, still at design time, to predict the smart ecosystems' properties and support decisions about their structure and behavior are necessary. In this scenario, simulation models make it possible to exercise different arrangements that smart ecosystems can assume and obtain, still at design time, a detailed analysis to support the decision-making process and recommend how to arrange constituents to maximize certain properties. At the same time, operation and quality can be preserved.

Simulation is already recognized as a relevant (and suitable) approach for software architecture assessment [9,16]. Simulations allow architects to (i) prototype large-scale systems and test their structure and behaviors at design time, (ii) anticipate/predict consequences of architectural changes on the overall systems, and (iii) offer a visual appeal to enable architects to draw new architectural alternatives to accordingly conform to the pre-established requirements [10].

This work aims to be a didactic reference about the state-of-the-art simulation techniques for evaluating smart-ecosystems architectures. For that purpose, we (i) present each involved concept, (ii) report our experience in academic and industrial projects, (iii) discuss the main difficulties and challenges involved in the adoption of simulation for smart-ecosystem architectures evaluation, and (iv) provide a research agenda with investigation opportunities. We remark that this manuscript is an extension of an ECSA 2021 tutorial paper [25].

The work is organized as follows: Sect. 2 presents background; Sect. 3 presents some remarkable simulation technologies available and often adopted; Sect. 4 presents practice perceptions and experience reports; Sect. 5 discusses the research challenges under the structure of a research agenda; and Sect. 6 concludes the work.

2   Background

Smart ecosystems refer to multiple constituent systems interoperating to accomplish common goals. Smart ecosystems share unique characteristics [44,48,53], such as (i) managerial independence of constituents, i.e., the involved systems are owned and managed by distinct organizations and stakeholders, (ii) operational independence of constituents, since they preserve their independence and also perform their activities, even when they are not accomplishing one of the ecosystems' goals, (iii) distribution, i.e., constituents are physically dispersed requiring network connectivity to communicate, (iv) evolutionary development since the entire ecosystem evolves due to the evolution of their constituents' parts, changes in environment or goals, and (v) emergent behavior, which corresponds to complex functionalities that emerge from the interoperability among constituents. Constituents cooperate with their capabilities to deliver complex functionalities; some of them deliberately planned to be accomplished as emergent behavior, which comprises the realization of a set of pre-established goals [14,36].

Smart ecosystems have their software architecture, i.e., a fundamental software-based structure that includes constituents and connections among them and properties of the constituents and the surrounding environment [49]. Given the high degree of complexity that such ecosystems can achieve, architectural models can be adopted for evaluation activities. They can also contribute to improving the overall smart ecosystem quality properties [48].

Smart ecosystems software architectures are inherently dynamic since constituents can join or leave the structure at any moment. Dynamic architectures, also known as evolutionary architectures, are considered a consequence of the inherent operational and managerial independence of constituents [50]. A DSA consists of a software architecture that exhibits dynamic reconfiguration ability, i.e., the ability to self-adapt its structure at run-time due to various reasons, including fault tolerance. Such ability is essential to minimize system disruptions while new or modified constituents are being joined to the ecosystem. Therefore, such a characteristic is inherent to the smart ecosystem and required to provide trust for its operation [45]. To evaluate smart ecosystem DSA, it should be precisely captured first, including its dynamic reconfigurations. Several notations have been proposed and adopted for specifying smart ecosystems architectures [34]. Nonetheless, despite the existence of several Architectural Description Languages (ADL) that can support the specification and evaluation of software architectures, as far as we are aware, most of them have not supported the specification of both structure and behavior of smart ecosystems and their dynamic properties (emergent behavior and dynamic architecture). For evaluation of DSA, we are aware of two main strategies: (i) a visual approach, in which an animation of the system dynamism is provided so that system architects can visually observe the ecosystem structure and behavior and monitor them at run-time supported by an execution log; or (ii) a statistical model checking approach, in which a model checker is connected to an execution mechanism so that the execution traces are monitored and a diagnosis of the ecosystem status is provided for the architects. Both have advantages and drawbacks and could even be combined. Executable models can support the former [41], while the latter demands an execution mechanism and a statistical model checker, such as UPPAAL or PLASMA [12].

In regards to the adoption of executable models for modeling DSA, we are aware of some approaches, such as GEMOC [13] and Executable UML [46]. GEMOC requires that the entire infrastructure for executing a model is defined and demands a deep knowledge of the technical details to implement it in the GEMOC platform. Executable UML does not offer abstraction capabilities to represent multiple systems' interoperation but a set of diagrams to represent multiple views of a given system being specified. Then, another option should be evaluated such as the simulation models [33]. Simulation platforms (aka simulators), in general, provide a valuable resource: model animation. The ability to animate models can support a better understanding of the modeled structure and behavior of systems. Both novices and experienced developers will benefit from the visualization of models. Model animation can provide visual feedback to novice modelers and can thus help them identify improper use of modeling constructs. Experienced modelers can use model animation to understand designs created by other developers better and faster [21]. Simulation corresponds to an imitation of the operation of a real-world process or system over time. It involves the input of (natural or artificial) stimuli and observation of outcomes to draw inferences about the operation of real-world systems that they represent [3,59]. As such, modeling and simulation (M&S) promotes [4]: (i) a visual and dynamic viewpoint for software architectures, reproducing stimuli the system can receive from a real-world environment; (ii) prediction of errors, diagnosing them, and enabling corrections; and (iii) observation of expected and unexpected emergent behavior of systems.

Some popular simulation platforms and formalism offer abstractions that can match smart ecosystems representation requirements, such as (i) animation, which provides visualization of the system structure and behavior besides its dynamics, interoperability among the composing parts, and the overall architecture evolution over time, (ii) composite pattern, which represents the system in terms of a general structure that can be itself composed of other refined parts, which can recursively compose with other structures, forming a concise whole, and (iii) execution mechanism, which enables the architect to exercise different architectural arrangements (also referred to as coalitions) and predict at design time the consequences that changes can cause at run-time. Hence, simulation is one of the approaches recognized by the software engineering community to evaluate software architectures [16]. In particular, DEVS and Systems Dynamics formalism are the well-known notations used in the software engineering context [19,20]. Remarkable simulation formalism and how they match smart ecosystems' representation demands (and requirements) are addressed in Sect. 3.

Another important issue for representing (and executing) smart ecosystems architectures regards co-simulation. Co-simulation consists of a technique in which the simulation of multiple interoperating systems can be achieved by composing the simulations of its parts, frequently involving multiple simulators [23].

Co-simulation has been increasingly demanded by industry to provide a type of holistic simulation, i.e., simulation that considers software aspects and the interplay between software with elements of other domains, such as electrical components, mechanical counterparts, thermic elements, and all the sort of integrated parts that compose a smart ecosystem. Then, different simulators are required, each representing each different part from different domains. The diagnosis of the entire smart ecosystem can be provided as the result of the interplay among all simulators connected via co-simulation techniques. Co-simulation techniques also involve mappings between simulation paradigms, varying, for instance, from continuous to discrete-event simulation timing techniques and domain-specific measures.

The following section provides details on how industrial technologies have been employed to support the simulation of smart ecosystems.

3   Industrial Simulation Technologies

A diversity of simulation technologies is available for several domains and purposes. Some of them have attracted attention over the years and have been more intensely adopted in software engineering and software architecture contexts. This section provides technical details on specific industrial simulation technologies that we have used to conduct academic and industrial projects or glimpsed as potential technologies in forthcoming projects. Section 3.1 presents details of DEVS simulation formalism; Sect. 3.2 introduces FERAL, a simulation technology developed by Fraunhofer IESE, Germany; and Sect. 3.3 discusses other general-purpose simulation technologies.

3.1   DEVS

DEVS (Discrete-Event System Specification Formalism) was created in the 1970's by Bernard Zeigler, and there are several different implementations and platforms available. DEVS is an M&S formalism based on the idea of atomic and coupled models [59]. Figure 1 depicts the DEVS metamodel. A DEVS model can be (and is formed by) Atomic Models or Coupled Models. Atomic Models represent individual entities (for instance, constituent systems), while Coupled Models represent a combination of Atomic Models. Atomic Models have the following elements: (i) a State Machine, which specifies state transitions due to input or output events; (ii) Data Types definition; (iii) Functions; (iv) Ports definition; and (v) Events definition. An Atomic Model with only a state machine specification and the ports definition is plainly executable. Coupled Models are expressed as a System Entity Structure (SES), i.e., a formal structure governed by a small number of declarative axioms that express how Atomic Models communicate to form a Coupled Model.

DEVS can offer a helpful matching and close abstraction to represent smart ecosystem architectures. Constituents are mapped to Atomic Models, and the entire architecture is represented as a Coupled Model. When a constituent is so

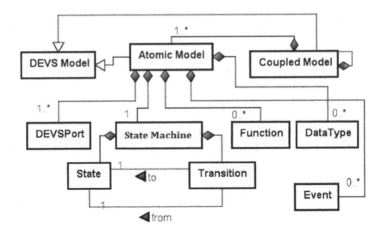

Fig. 1. DEVS metamodel adapted from [30]

complex that it should be broken down into other constituent parts, it can also be represented as a Coupled Model since there is a recursive relation within the Coupled Model entity.

The term "discrete" in DEVS is exactly a counterpoint to the idea of continuous, i.e., in DEVS, simulation time is split into discrete portions (seconds, milliseconds, or any equivalent metric that should meet the real-world time), while continuous time is adopted in other simulation formalisms such as Systems Dynamics.

3.2 Fraunhofer FERAL

FERAL is a solution from Fraunhofer IESE for the development and evaluation of architectural concepts [39]. FERAL is a simulation framework with different building blocks, which enable integrating complex, heterogeneous devices into a test scenario and systematically checking properties in a protected virtual space with the help of digital twins. In the automotive sector, this can be, for example, the correct functioning of a pedestrian detection system or the error-free interaction of two functions from different manufacturers. Another example is the braking process of a car, which is nowadays supported by a large number of assistance systems, such as ABS or ESP. With cyber-physical systems, i.e., communicating embedded systems that can self-adapt to their environment and learn new tasks, the challenges for systems engineers are growing. This leads to entirely new challenges regarding the architecture of these systems. In the absence of empirical data, the only means to evaluate new architectural concepts is to build real prototypes. The selection of the best concepts requires the realization of very many prototypes. This causes very high costs and long development cycles.

To support challenges like these, Fraunhofer FERAL provides customizable simulation models of contemporary technologies like wired communication networks, including variants representing different abstraction levels. These features allow for the continuous evaluation of significant quality of service aspects like throughput, loss rate, and end-to-end delay regarding the interaction of components communicating via a data exchange infrastructure. Through a REST API implementation offered by Fraunhofer FERAL, remote clients are enabled to store simulation configurations on servers, perform simulation runs based on stored configurations, and retrieve evaluation results such as validation goal properties and simulation logs. The configuration of simulation scenarios builds upon a sequence of key-value pairs stored in configuration property files. The permutations of simulation component-specific property values, in turn, allow for systematic trials of alternative simulation scenarios to evaluate different requirements. When calling the simulation service for a specific simulation configuration, dedicated builder modules instantiate models for any referenced simulation component with corresponding property values. These model instances are then used in a simulation scenario that is further parameterized by configuration properties for the simulation setup like run-time duration and result output settings. In simulation execution, the simulation components representing the network details and applications running atop corresponding devices produce their simulation results. Depending on the validation goals and the requirements defined in terms of measurable metrics and value boundaries within the configuration files, watcher components are activated to keep track of any statistics of interest during simulation execution. Each simulation run produces a tailored result data set, including a full system console log; these are time-stamped and persisted to be retrievable and reproducible for traceability.

3.3   Other Simulation Technologies

Other technologies are also available for supporting simulation in industrial scenarios. Some are general-purpose and follow other paradigms apart from the instances brought here until now, and some are rather domain-specific. Important general-purpose technologies to be mentioned are MATLAB/Simulink [35], NetLogo [57], and JADE [7].

MATLAB/Simulink is a general-purpose simulation formalism for dynamic systems analysis broadly used in industry [35]. MATLAB is code-based, while Simulink is graphical. Simulink provides a graphical editor and solvers for modeling and simulating dynamic systems. Simulink integrates with MATLAB, which allows it to incorporate MATLAB code. Simulink was developed by MathWorks and is widely used in control theory and digital signal processing for multidomain design and simulation.

NetLogo and JADE are agent-based simulation modeling technologies [7,57]. In that paradigm, the simulation specification is based on the concept of agent, an entity with behavior that can interact with other agents and react/act on the surrounding environment. NetLogo offers a development environment and a respective formalism that enables to specify individual behavior for each agent. Once the agents' behavior is modeled, NetLogo environment enables to vary the values assigned to variables and predict the consequences of the emergent result derived from the interaction between agents. It offers a visual approach to predicting the consequences of a modeled emergent behavior. NetLogo is commonly used to simulate swarms, such as robot swarms, bird swarms, and other swarms types. In turn, JADE is a Java-based application framework for agent-based simulation, i.e., it fosters reuse by offering abstract structures and functionalities that can be extended to model the agents. A simulation execution engine is also provided to run the simulation, and results can be analyzed. JADE is commonly used in agent-based corporative applications, such as planning and distributing vehicles for maintenance in the power network of an urban space [32]. In that case, each vehicle is modeled as a geographically distributed agent. The distribution of vehicles in the geographic area is simulated to predict the travel time in the event of a power failure and the costs involved. That type of simulation enables optimizing service time and reducing maintenance time and costs by positioning the vehicles in strategic locations based on historical data.

4   Experience Report

Over the years, the authors involved in this work have invested efforts in several initiatives to adopt simulation in smart ecosystems' life cycle. This section reports our experience with M&S in different domains for multiple purposes.

4.1   Brazilian Cases

We have adopted simulation techniques in several research projects. Particularly, our motivations were (i) to predict systems properties still at design time, (ii) to exercise different architecture arrangements that a smart ecosystem could assume at run-time and their impact over the behavior being delivered and the quality attributes, (iii) to predict costs involved in the acquisition of constituents to form a smart ecosystem, and (iv) to assess software-intensive applications in critical domains, particularly the critical infrastructure involved.

Advances in research were needed [31,45]. Firstly, we created ASAS, an approach for the automatic generation of simulation models by a model transformation and smart ecosystems architectural evaluation [31]. ASAS enables the prediction of architectural arrangements that leverage systems operation and supports the evaluation of pre-determined quality attributes. For ASAS, we created a model-driven transformer specified in XTend to automatically produce DEVS simulation code from architectural models specified in SosADL [29]. The DEVS code was produced in DEVS Natural Language and deployed in the MS4Me[1] environment, a 1-year free license simulator for DEVS.

To make the entire infrastructure operational, we needed to propose a means for the automatic generation of artificial entities in the simulation to feed it with data; otherwise, the simulation dynamics would be driven by clicks, which would make it infeasible. The Stimuli-SoS approach was created to automatically derive

---

[1] http://www.ms4systems.com/pages/ms4me.php.

artificial stimuli from the SosADL models to imitate the surrounding environment, continuously delivering stimuli for the simulation [27]. Another important advance was Dynamic-SoS, an approach to also automatically generate an artificial entity for the simulation model named as Dynamic Reconfiguration Controller (DRC), an entity that made it possible to change the smart ecosystem architectural arrangement at simulation run-time, which supported us to predict the impact of such changes on the overall ecosystem behavior, structure, and quality properties [45]. The DRC enabled us to exercise the dynamic architecture, an essential property of smart ecosystems. Dynamic-SoS and Stimuli-SoS were incorporated into the ASAS approach.

ASAS infrastructure was used to model and simulate smart ecosystems in three critical domains: flood monitoring, space system, and smart building. The first case was a Flood Monitoring Smart Ecosystem (FMSE) in the city of São Carlos, Brazil. That FMSE refers to a set of independent systems with no central authority to monitor rivers that cross urban areas (where floods can occur and pose great danger in rainy seasons, potentially damaging property, threatening lives, and spreading diseases). It notifies possible emergency situations to residents, business owners, pedestrians, drivers near the flooding area, and governmental entities and emergency systems. Moreover, FMSE is intended to be part of a larger ecosystem composed of wireless river sensors, telecommunication gateways, unmanned aerial vehicles (UAVs), vehicular ad hoc networks (VANETs), meteorological centers, fire and rescue services, hospital centers, police departments, short message service centers, and social networks. Such an ecosystem involves the National Center for Natural Disaster Monitoring, which monitors 1,000 cities with 4,700 sensors, including 300 hydrological sensors and 4,400 rain gauges. This ecosystem is deployed over the river; in particular, its sensors are spread on the riverbank's edges, and data is transmitted to gateways. Drones fly over the river and communicate flood threat alerts. People walking close to the river can also communicate the water level increases through mobile apps. For FMSE, we achieve the number of 112 different constituents being simulated.

The second scenario was the Brazilian Space System, i.e., a smart ecosystem composed of constituents in ground and space that accomplish missions, such as telecommunication, global position (GPS), weather forecast, Earth and space observation, meteorology, resource monitoring, and military observation. In collaboration with INPE (National Institute for Space Research) in Brazil, we acquired data from the Brazilian satellites to feed the simulation and predict the impact of adding more satellites to the Brazilian Space System [28]. The general mission of such a space system was data collection. Several types of data collection included the water and deforestation index. This system was designed to undertake two missions: (i) capturing pictures (monitor) of the Amazon region and (ii) distributing environmental data collected by Data Collection Platforms (DCP).

We conducted requirements elicitation meetings with an expert from INPE to model the software architecture of this ecosystem. The expert helped us understand the smart ecosystem structure, its main constituents, and how they interoperate to achieve the expected results. A small-scale smart ecosystem was modeled with one mission to be accomplished. After conducting this pilot study, we planned to generate and execute two other simulations. The space system was composed of one data center, one command and control (C2) center, and one ground station. We designed the architecture in SosADL with an initial set of 126 DCP and one satellite, representing the architecture involving some Brazilian states. The architecture consisted of one data center, a C2 center, a ground station, a satellite, and 126 DPC (distributed in three Brazilian states, namely São Paulo, Minas Gerais, and Rio de Janeiro) (130 constituents, apart from mediators). DCP are located inland or in water (rivers or ocean). The simulation was executed, and DCP from the other four Brazilian states (Paraná, Goiás, Mato Grosso, and Amazonas) were dynamically included until 307 platforms (a total of 311 constituents). To use realistic data, we selected one-year data for each DCP platform. Such data referred to the 75 DCP stations in São Paulo state, 51 stations in Minas Gerais, and 12 in Rio de Janeiro, which totaled 138 DCP stations. The simulation lasted 1,676 min (approximately 27 h) and took 2–3 core processors.

The third scenario was a smart building [26]. This ecosystem provides essential services to residents and visitors of a building, such as energy savings, light control by sensors, and fire alarms. This ecosystem was composed of three other ecosystems: fire system (composed of sensors, alarms, and sprinklers), lighting system (composed of sensors and lamps), and room (composed of sensors, air conditioners, and alarms). It also had a smart building control unity (SBCU), which manages all constituent systems in the building. In that study, we evaluated the quality attribute functional suitability and predicted constituents acquisition costs for different architectural arrangements that the ecosystem could assume at run-time. Our results can support acquisition managers in the decision making-process, trading-off acquisition costs and quality.

In total, using the ASAS approach, we successfully (and automatically) generated more than one million LOC of DEVS simulation code and successfully simulated more than 130 h of smart ecosystems architectures.

After those cases, other studies were conducted in other domains: smart parking [15] and autonomous cars [56]. The former, as well as another study [42], focused on investigating the availability quality attribute and how architectural changes at run-time could impact it. The latter focused on exploring how to architecturally equip systems to enable them to exhibit operational independence to allow them, if required and desired, to join smart ecosystems as constituents.

4.2 Continuous Simulations for Industry 4.0

Industry 4.0 (hereafter I4.0) is a software revolution aiming at end-to-end digitalization and the flexibilization of industrial manufacturing and supply chains [40]. I4.0 deals with computer-based automation of industrial production shop floors, to achieve full vertical and horizontal integration of production processes and products [58]. The diversity of manufacturing sectors and the crosscutting technologies involved (e.g., IoT, robotics, simulation, and DevOps) require significant integration efforts based on a plethora of industry standards and the combination of software platforms and technologies [17]. In this light, automating the production requires creating flexible ways to adapt smart factories [52] to varying demands and achieve higher productivity. Therefore, the emergence of "on-demand" customized products requires Reconfigurable Manufacturing Machines (RMS) [47] that interoperate to dynamically meet the requirements and offer continuous process monitoring. Also, as smart factories are driven by digital data, adapting factories to new products requires interoperability of all the elements' data models.

Today, I4.0 systems require stringent and accurate monitoring techniques that employ continuous supervision of both run-time and development time quality properties to ensure the ability of I4.0 systems to quickly respond to continuous changes in product requirements, and to enable mass-customization of small lot sizes instead of long-term mass production of pre-defined assets [17]. Such systems stand in contrast to traditional production systems, in which quality is evaluated at infrequent milestones.

The implementation strategy of I4.0 systems relies on the notion of service oriented architectures [55] and digital twins [51]. Digital twins are executable virtual models updated dynamically by being connected to their physical counterparts using sensors [6]. Key goals of digital twins in I4.0 based systems are: (i) reducing the downtime of physical production plants by enabling practices like monitoring production quality of service (QoS); (ii) enabling the analysis of deployment and scheduling strategies in the virtualizations of physical production machines, production pieces, and processes [22]; and (iii) accurately analyzing the associated run-time and development-time properties like performance, interoperability, fault tolerance, security, reconfiguration and portability [2].

It has been discussed how important it is to continuously evaluate these quality aspects with the high confidence offered by simulation-based techniques, to expose the limits of the current design (e.g., cases where peaks of production capabilities are required, or where failures occur) [5,55]. In this case the notion of exploratory scenarios is suitable for describing situations that approach the limits of the system, where we may need to check performance and availability properties while the system is running, or where we want to explore unsafe states. These types of scenarios can serve as a basis to motivate scenarios that specify concrete challenges stressing the quality of I4.0 systems at run-time.

In the case of simulating digital twins in the context of Industry 4.0, simulating complex digital twin structures to evaluate whether the modifications on the plant will meet production Quality of Services expectations is fundamental to improve the efficiency and confidence of selecting a replacement for a faulty component and to properly reschedule/reassign tasks of a faulty component to a spare. More specifically, this is about verifying whether specific functional and quality attribute properties such as production rate-the number of goods that are produced in a specific time period-and the degree of compliance of the production to industrial policies and metrics will still be achieved. In the context of industry 4.0, Fraunhofer IESE have been using Fraunhofer FERAL to perform continuous quality evaluation by means of simulations considering the information made available by systems in the different automation layers.

5 Challenges and Research Agenda

After presenting an overview and advances in the area of smart ecosystems simulation, this section aims to name the pain, exposing the challenges that remain in regards to the adoption of simulation in the life cycle of software architecture design and production for smart ecosystems. We also provide a research agenda based on the challenges we still face aiming to drive efforts of the international research community to foster the adoption of simulation in the Smart Ecosystems engineering life cycle.

5.1 Difficulties and Challenges of M&S in Smart Ecosystems

Over the years, we have acquired experience on how M&S fits the life cycle of different types of software-intensive systems. Similarly, despite the benefits provided, we also suffered from the barriers, difficulties, and challenges posed by their adoption. Given that, we list below the main difficulties we have faced in our projects so that the community can be aware of them when adopting simulation. Nevertheless, we also mention how we overcame/solved these problems in our projects besides pointing out, in the next section, some challenges that remain and that can be used as a research agenda to guide the community in the forthcoming years.

Sense of Community and Training. In the past three years, we have organized the Workshop on Modeling and Simulation of Software-intensive Systems (MSSiS[2]). Despite the success and adherence of the public to the event, we still notice that the M&S community, particularly in Brazil, is still scarce. In general, it is not clear to the Software Engineering community the contexts in which M&S techniques are required and can offer benefits. Then, one of our challenges is about a sense of community and training and to provide the academic and industrial professionals with technical knowledge and abilities to use M&S in a diversity of contexts and, particularly, for prototyping and analyzing systems at design time in critical domains. Other countries can have the same scenario, but it must be investigated.

Quality Assessment via Simulation. Particularly in the context of smart ecosystems, we have used M&S to evaluate specific quality attributes at design time, such as functional suitability [26], Availability [15], reconfigurability [45] and even operational independence as a quality attribute [56]. We have investigated the quality model for smart ecosystems [54] and investigated how quality attributes have been addressed in that context, as well [8]. Each quality attribute required us to develop specific strategies of representation and analysis in the simulation model, such as the creation of artificial entities to support the analysis, observation of the simulation dynamics, or analysis of the output log. Hence, we observe that dealing with a larger set of quality attributes being prioritized in a large-scale project can be significantly onerous and require research on how

---

[2] https://ww2.inf.ufg.br/mssis/en/index.html.

to precisely represent and analyze each relevant quality attribute for that system and its respective domain. Then, further research is needed to generate and catalog techniques to precisely represent each relevant quality attribute that an ecosystem should satisfy, besides investigating how to co-exist all these underpinning specification details in the final simulation model.

Trust and Reliability in the Simulation Model and its Results. One recurrent question for those who use M&S (or any type of model) is "How do I know that the model is precise enough so that I can trust the results being delivered?". This has been a philosophical question since software engineers started to invest in models. We are aware that the absence of modeling activities in systems development often brings negative impacts on it. Models are a type of abstraction, i.e., details necessarily and intentionally are suppressed to represent only the relevant aspects of that system of interest. This difficulty is the same regard other types of models. At first glance, we advocate that a simulation model is precise enough if it covers all (or the majority of) the relevant aspects needed to draw conclusions about that system. Hence, the first advice is to involve a stakeholder highly skilled in modeling in the development team. With his/her experience, s/he can help on the level of details the simulation model should exhibit to be minimally reliable about its results. As a classical and already well-succeeded agile practice, a peer review would also be welcome. Nevertheless, in M&S community, they have adopted a solution called Multiresolution Modeling (MRM) [60]), i.e., they prescribe the adoption of multiple and complementary models (similar to the architectural views of Kruchten [38]) besides a concept of multiple instances sizes to analyze the problem. They advocate that MRM is essential for exploratory analysis of the design spaces of complex and adaptive systems as smart ecosystems because it is neither cognitively nor computationally possible to keep track of all relevant variables and causal relationships [60]. Their concept is close to the induction principle from computer science: we test for a small instance and some larger instances and assume, by induction, that larger frames are also feasible, varying the resolution with which the simulation model is observed and modeled. In practice, this would correspond to modeling a smart ecosystem with two constituent systems, another one with three constituents, another with ten, another with a hundred, and then analytically predict how it could behave for larger instances, which could help on the assurance of the reliability of the simulation model and how close it is to the real-world counterpart being represented. A last desirable characteristic to assure simulation model trustworthiness leads to the next challenge.

Status Quo of Simulation in the Software Loop and the Presence of Professionals of that Specific Domain. Currently, the basic process that we follow to incorporate simulation models in our projects (and when we say "we", we claim that this can mean software engineering teams in general, or, at least, the two teams from Brazil and Germany involved in this work): Step 1 - Understanding the problem, Step 2 - A mapping between problem and space solution, Step 3 - A system specification, Step 4 - Design of the simulation model by mapping the system specification into the simulation formalism basic concepts, Step

5 - Simulation execution, observation, and logging, Step 6 - Analysis of results, and Step 7 - Smart ecosystem development itself. Actually, when we designed the Brazilian space system to be simulated, we luckily could count on an expert in space systems, i.e., a Ph.D. student from the INPE that was in an internship in our lab at that time. He fed us with all the needed expertise that allowed us to precisely model that system. Moreover, he also acted as an evaluator for the quality and reliability of our simulation model. Then, we believe that the presence of an expert in the domain for which the simulation is being specified is essential for assuring the trustworthiness of the model being developed (in the context of a software system development or not). Another possible solution could be the joint adoption of domain-specific simulators, like those mentioned in Sect. 3.3.

Cost of Simulating. Another issue about M&S regards its cost from a diversity of perspectives, including the man-hour cost to specify the model and the execution costs. The former issue is another recurrent concern when we deal with modeling at large. Modeling has a cost, but not modeling can be even more expensive. Simulation modeling still requires the presence of a professional with simulation expertise, who can be roughly expensive and/or rare due to the first challenge we raised (lack of training among the developers). However, for critical domains where failures can lead to significant losses, the cost involved in hiring a simulation expert is undoubtedly lower than the consequences of an eventual failure due to a non-exhaustive design time evaluation or testing. The latter issue regards the needed infrastructure to support a large-scale simulation execution. In prior work, we already raised this issue in the light of our experience [31]. We recalled that, in our studies, some of the simulations had only a couple of hundreds of constituents (around 300) and took more than 30 h to simulate using powerful processors. We then foresaw that, for simulating smart ecosystems such as the forthcoming smart cities, if we consider the population of New York city or São Paulo and the number of cell phones, autonomous cars, smart buildings, houses, and hospitals, with different granularities that could potentially compose that ecosystem, the simulation could reach about potentially reaching 50 million constituents. Currently, we do not have computational processing power or simulation techniques to tame such complexity. As stated before, techniques such as the MRM should be adopted to avoid such a high cost, framing different subparts of that larger system and abstracting parts to represent them interacting as black boxes. Co-simulation, as mentioned in the Background, could also be used for that purpose. However, co-simulation itself is also a significant challenge, and we discuss it as follows.

Co-simulation. In Sect. 4.2, we witnessed real cases of industrial adoption of simulation in large companies, like John Deere and Airbus. Those companies have their simulators or use general-purpose ones, such as MATLAB/Simulink, to specify simulation models and perform their analyses. However, those companies have required researchers to extrapolate the simulation of a single type of system (such as a mechanical or electrical system) towards holistically integrating them into other artifacts and obtain a cohesive simulation that includes several aspects of several domains, such as the combination of simulations of the mechanical, electrical, hydraulic, aerodynamic, hardware, software, people, and environmental parts of the same system (as an aircraft), and how these parts interplay, i.e., integrating various simulators to perform together as a composite simulation, which has been termed as co-simulation. As stated by Zeigler et al. [60], this task involves weaving the time series behavior and data exchanges accurately since a failure on it could yield inaccurate simulation results. Equipping companies with a holistic solution that covers all these aspects is certainly still a challenge. Digital twins are perhaps an embrionary solution in that direction, but a significant research effort is still required.

5.2   Research Agenda

We highlight the challenges themselves can also be considered as part of the research agenda since some of them are still not entirely solved. However, we want to shed light on some specific and important research paths for the forthcoming years.

Co-simulation of Constituents of Smart Ecosystems. We have observed that smart industrial ecosystems are composed of a high diversity of types of constituent systems. For instance, if we could use Omninet[3] to simulate networks and integrate it with Canoe (from the company Vector), we could obtain a certification program based on simulation models since Canoe[4] is a certified tool and can deliver ISO certification. However, interoperating simulators is not trivial; besides, combining tools from different domains, developed in various technologies, potentially using different measurement systems and variables, and dealing with heterogeneous concerns is undoubtedly more challenging. Then, a relevant research avenue is the establishment of co-simulation approaches among simulators used to simulate components of a given smart ecosystem.

Simulation, Co-simulation, and Continuous Engineering. Continuous engineering (CE) has emerged because of the need for a more holistic approach to dealing with rapid changes within an ecosystem that depends on software-based systems [18]. These practices have been successfully implemented in the development of traditional information systems. Players from the automotive sector like Tesla and BMW have reported the successful adoption of CE practices in developing critical embedded systems [1]. Indeed, we have observed the adoption of these practices in several industry sectors, but mainly regarding the software artifacts. The big challenge in the industry is how to integrate artifacts from other disciplines in a CE-centered process. For instance, artifacts produced by mechanical and production engineers are of great value to boost the added value resulting from the adoption of CE practices. Still, they are not usually done because of the lack of tooling integration and, mainly, the lack of the right

---

[3] https://omnetpp.org/.

[4] https://www.vector.com/int/en/products/products-a-z/software/canoe/simulation/.

motivation to pursue this path. This holistic set of artifacts would enable more complete simulations, which would result in a more accurate evaluation. The convincing arguments should emerge through the improvement of architecture drivers centered related to competition, finance, and time-to-market aspects. There is still a lack of methodologies and techniques to properly consider artifacts from multiple disciplines in a CE-based process.

Testing with Simulation. Another possible research avenue regards the adoption of simulation models for testing software. We are already aware that due to trends, such as Behavior-Driven Development (BDD) and Test-Driven Development (TDD), testing activities have been part of the entire system development life cycle. Since we prescribe the adoption of simulation still at design time, it could certainly support an early testing activity with the simulated system. Using Stimuli-SoS and the concept of experimental frame brought from the M&S community can frame a diversity of testing case samples and use simulators as the underlying platform to execute those tests. Although we already have well-established technologies for unit test cases, such as JUnit, we are unaware of testing infrastructures for smart ecosystems architectures. Moreover, from the results of a recent systematic mapping [43], we are already aware that (i) simulation is recommended as a relevant technique to test smart ecosystems, but (ii) testing smart ecosystems is still a challenge, mainly because of the scalability of it (the difficulties in testing a large number of interactions among constituents) and the high degree of uncertainty brought by those systems, both because of the stimuli that can come from the surrounding environment (and the impossibility of predicting all of them) and the need to fully test realistic situations, such as the constituents joining or leaving the ecosystem at run-time and the interactions with the real-world environment itself. Dynamic-SoS can be one of the possible solutions for benchmarking several different architectural arrangements that a smart ecosystem can assume at run-time. However, novel testing techniques are still required to cope with all the issues raised.

6   Final Remarks

With the increasing complexity of software-intensive systems, assuring the quality of these systems has become hard, while the evaluation of software architectures, in particular, architectures of large, complex systems like smart ecosystems, seems to be a way that could contribute to the quality assurance. Meanwhile, simulation has proved its value and has provided various benefits for traditional systems evaluation, but it has not been widely experimented with and adopted by the community of smart ecosystems. In short, this work intends to contribute with insights that could open new research directions to mature the field of smart ecosystem simulation.

Acknowledgments. This work was financed by CNPq (Grant No.: 313245/2021-5, 133436/2020-9), and FAPESP (Grant No.: 2015/24144-7).

References

1. Antonino, P.O., et al.: Enabling continuous software engineering for embedded systems architectures with virtual prototypes. In: Cuesta, C.E., Garlan, D., Pérez, J. (eds.) Software Architecture, pp. 115–130 (2018)
2. Antonino, P.O., Schnicke, F., Zhang, Z., Kuhn, T.: Blueprints for architecture drivers and architecture solutions for industry 4.0 shopfloor applications. In: 13th European Conference on Software Architecture (ECSA), vol. 2, pp. 261–268 (2019)
3. Banks, J.: Introduction to simulation. In: 31st Winter Simulation Conference (WSC), vol. 1, pp. 7–13 (2000)
4. Barcio, B., Ramaswamy, S., Macfadzean, R., Barber, K.: Object-oriented analysis, modeling, and simulation of a notional air defense system. Simulation **66**(1), 5–21 (1996)
5. Bass, L., Clements, P., Kazman, R.: Software Architecture in Practice. SEI Series in Software Engineering, 4 edn. (2021)
6. Bauer, T., Antonino, P., Kuhn, T.: Towards architecting digital twin-pervaded systems. In: IEEE/ACM 7th International Workshop on Software Engineering for Systems-of-Systems (SESoS) and 13th Workshop on Distributed Software Development, Software Ecosystems and Systems-of-Systems (WDES), pp. 66–69 (2019)
7. Bellifemine, F., Poggi, A., Rimassa, G.: Developing multi-agent systems with JADE. In: Castelfranchi, C., Lespérance, Y. (eds.) ATAL 2000. LNCS (LNAI), vol. 1986, pp. 89–103. Springer, Heidelberg (2001). https://doi.org/10.1007/3-540-44631-1_7
8. Bianchi, T., Santos, D.S., Felizardo, K.R.: Quality attributes of systems-of-systems: a systematic literature review. In: 3rd IEEE/ACM International Workshop on Software Engineering for Systems-of-Systems, pp. 23–30 (2015)
9. Blas, M.J.: An analysis model to evaluate web applications quality using a discrete-event simulation approach. In: 50th Winter Simulation Conference (WSC), pp. 4648–4649 (2017)
10. Bogado, V., Gonnet, S., Leone, H.: Modeling and simulation of software architecture in discrete event system specification for quality evaluation. Simulation **90**(3), 290–319 (2014)
11. Cadavid, H., Andrikopoulos, V., Avgeriou, P.: Architecting systems of systems: a tertiary study. Inf. Softw. Technol. **118**(1), 106202 (2020)
12. Cavalcante, E., Quilbeuf, J., Traonouez, L., Oquendo, F., Batista, T., Legay, A.: Statistical model checking of dynamic software architectures. In: 10th European Conference on Software Architecture (ECSA), pp. 185–200 (2016)
13. Combemale, B., DeAntoni, J., Baudry, B., France, R.B., Jézéquel, J.M., Gray, J.: Globalizing modeling languages. Computer **47**(6), 68–71 (2014)
14. Dahmann, J.S., Jr., G.R., Lane, J.A.: Systems engineering for capabilities. CrossTalk. J. J. Defense. Softw. Eng. **21**(11), 4–9 (2008)
15. Delécolle, A., Lima, R., Graciano Neto, V., Buisson, J.: Architectural strategy to enhance the availability quality attribute in system-of-systems architectures: a case study. In: IEEE 15th International Conference of System of Systems Engineering (SoSE), pp. 93–98 (2020)
16. Dobrica, L., Niemele, E.: A survey on software architecture analysis methods. IEEE Trans. Softw. Eng. **28**(7), 638–653 (2002)
17. Federal Ministry of Education and Research, Germany: Industrie 4.0 platform (2011)

18. Fitzgerald, B., Stol, K.J.: Continuous software engineering: a roadmap and agenda. J. Syst. Softw. **123**, 176–189 (2017)

19. França, B., Travassos, G.: Are we prepared for simulation based studies in software engineering yet? CLEI. Electron. J. **16**(1), 9 (2013)

20. de França, B.B.N., Ali, N.B.: The role of simulation-based studies in software engineering research. In: Contemporary Empirical Methods in Software Engineering, pp. 263–287. Springer, Cham (2020). https://doi.org/10.1007/978-3-030-32489-6_10

21. France, R., Ghosh, S., Dinh-Trong, T., Solberg, A.: Model-driven development using UML 2.0: Promises and pitfalls. Computer **39**(2), 59–66 (2006)

22. Fuller, A., Fan, Z., Day, C., Barlow, C.: Digital twin: enabling technologies, challenges and open research. IEEE Access **8**(1), 108952–108971 (2020)

23. Gomes, C., Thule, C., Broman, D., Larsen, P.G., Vangheluwe, H.: Co-simulation: a survey. ACM Comput. Surv. **51**(3), 1–33 (2018)

24. Goncalves, M., Cavalcante, E., Batista, T., Oquendo, F., Nakagawa, E.Y.: Towards a conceptual model for software-intensive system-of-systems. In: IEEE International Conference on Systems, Man, and Cybernetics (SMC 2014), pp. 1605–1610 (2014)

25. Graciano Neto, V.V., Manzano, W., Antonino, P.O., Nakagawa, E.Y.: Simulation of software architectures of smart ecosystems: theory and practice. In: 15th European Conference on Software Architecture (ECSA 2021), pp. 1–4 (2021)

26. Graciano Neto, V., et al.: SOB (Save Our Budget) - a simulation-based method for prediction of acquisition costs of constituents of a system-of-systems. iSys - Braz. J. Inf. Syst. **12**(4), 6–35 (2019)

27. Graciano Neto, V., Paes, C., Garcés, L., Guessi, M., Oquendo, F., Nakagawa, E.Y.: Stimuli-SoS: a model-based approach to derive stimuli generators in simulations of software architectures of systems-of-systems. J. Braz. Comput. Soc. **23**(1), 13:1–13:22 (2017)

28. Graciano Neto, V., Paes, C., Rohling, A., Manzano, W., Nakagawa, E.Y.: Modeling & simulation of software architectures of systems-of-systems: an industrial report on the Brazilian space system. In: SpringSim, pp. 1–12 (2019)

29. Graciano Neto, V.V.: A simulation-driven model-based approach for designing software intensive systems-of-systems architectures. Université de Bretagne Sud; Universidade de São Paulo, Theses (2018)

30. Graciano Neto, V.V., et al.: ASAS: an approach to support simulation of smart systems. In: 51st Hawaii International Conference on System Sciences (HICSS), pp. 5777–5786 (2018)

31. Graciano Neto, V.V., Manzano, W., Kassab, M., Nakagawa, E.Y.: Model-based engineering & simulation of software-intensive systems-of-systems: Experience report and lessons learned. In: 12th European Conference on Software Architecture (ECSA). ECSA 2018 (2018)

32. Graciano Neto, V.V., Teles, R.M., Ivamoto, M., Mello, L.H.S., De Carvalho, C.L.: Um sistema de apoio à decisão baseado em agentes para tratamento de ocorrências no setor elétrico. Rev. Inform. Teór. Apl. **17**(2), 1–15 (2010)

33. Gray, J., Rumpe, B.: Models in simulation. Softw. Syst. Model. **15**(3), 605–607 (2016). https://doi.org/10.1007/s10270-016-0544-y

34. Guessi, M., Graciano Neto, V.V., Bianchi, T., Felizardo, K.R., Oquendo, F., Nakagawa, E.Y.: A systematic literature review on the description of software architectures for systems of systems. In: 30th Symposium On Applied Computing (SAC 2015), pp. 1433–1440 (2015)

35. Higham, D.J., Higham, N.J.: MATLAB Guide (2000)
36. INCOSE: The Guide to the Systems Engineering Body of Knowledge (SEBoK) (2016)
37. ISO: ISO/IEC/IEEE 42010:2011(E) (Revision of ISO/IEC 42010:2007 and IEEE Std 1471-2000) (2011)
38. Kruchten, P.: The 4+1 view model of architecture. IEEE Softw. **12**(6), 42–50 (1995)
39. Kuhr, T., Forster, T., Braun, T., Gotzhein, R.: Feral - framework for simulator coupling on requirements and architecture level. In: ACM/IEEE 11th International Conference on Formal Methods and Models for Codesign (MEMOCODE), pp. 11–22 (2013)
40. Lasi, H., Fettke, P., Kemper, H.G., Feld, T., Hoffmann, M.: Industry 4.0. Bus. Inf. Syst. Eng. **6**(4), 239–242 (2014). https://doi.org/10.1007/s12599-014-0334-4
41. Lebtag, B.G., Teixeira, P.G., Santos, R.P., Viana, D., Graciano Neto, V.V.: Strategies to evolve exm notations extracted from a survey with software engineering professionals perspective. J. Softw. Eng. Res. Dev. **9**(1), 17:1–17:24 (2022)
42. Lima, R., Kassab, M., Neto, V.: Discussing the availability quality attribute in systems-of-systems architectures based on a simulation experiment, pp. 416–421 (2021)
43. Lopes, V.C., et al.: A systematic mapping study on software testing for systems-of-systems. In: Proceedings of the 5th Brazilian Symposium on Systematic and Automated Software Testing, pp. 88–97. SAST 2020, Association for Computing Machinery, New York, NY, USA (2020). https://doi.org/10.1145/3425174.3425216
44. Maier, M.: Architecting principles for systems-of-systems. Syst. Eng. **1**(4), 267–284 (1998)
45. Manzano, W., Graciano Neto, V., Nakagawa, E.Y.: Dynamic-SoS: an approach for the simulation of systems-of-systems dynamic architectures. Comput. J. **63**(5), 709–731 (2020)
46. Mellor, S.J., Balcer, M., Jacobson, I.: Executable UML: a foundation for model-driven architecture (2002)
47. Morgan, J., Halton, M., Qiao, Y., Breslin, J.G.: Industry 4.0 smart reconfigurable manufacturing machines. J. Manuf. Syst. **59**, 481–506 (2021)
48. Nakagawa, E.Y., Goncalves, M., Guessi, M., Oliveira, L., Oquendo, F.: The state of the art and future perspectives in systems of systems software architectures. In: 1st International Workshop on Software Engineering for Systems-of-Systems (SESoS), pp. 13–20 (2013)
49. Nielsen, C.B., Larsen, P.G., Fitzgerald, J., Woodcock, J., Peleska, J.: Systems of systems engineering: basic concepts, model-based techniques, and research directions. ACM Comput. Surv. **48**(2), 18:1–18:41 (2015)
50. Oquendo, F.: Software architecture challenges and emerging research in software-intensive systems-of-systems. In: 10th European Conference on Software Architecture (ECSA), pp. 3–21 (2016)
51. Piroumian, V.: Digital twins: universal interoperability for the digital age. Computer **54**(01), 61–69 (2021)
52. Radziwon, A., Bilberg, A., Bogers, M., Madsen, E.S.: The smart factory: exploring adaptive and flexible manufacturing solutions. Proc. Eng. **69**, 1184–1190 (2014)
53. Santos, D.S., Oliveira, B.R.N., Kazman, R., Nakagawa, E.Y.: Evaluation of systems-of-systems software architectures: state of the art and future perspectives. ACM Comput. Surv. (2022)

54. Santos, D.S., Oliveira, B.R.N., Duran, A., Nakagawa, E.Y.: Reporting an experience on the establishment of a quality model for systems-of-systems. In: The 27th International Conference on Software Engineering and Knowledge Engineering (SEKE 2015), pp. 304–309 (2015)

55. Schnicke, F., Kuhn, T., Antonino, P.O.: Enabling industry 4.0 service-oriented architecture through digital twins. In: Muccini, H., et al. (eds.) ECSA 2020. CCIS, vol. 1269, pp. 490–503. Springer, Cham (2020). https://doi.org/10.1007/978-3-030-59155-7_35

56. Teixeira, P.G., et al.: Constituent system design: a software architecture approach. In: IEEE International Conference on Software Architecture Companion (ICSA-C), pp. 218–225 (2020)

57. Tisue, S., Wilensky, U.: Netlogo: a simple environment for modeling complexity. In: In International Conference on Complex Systems, pp. 16–21 (2004)

58. Ustundag, Alp, Cevikcan, Emre: Industry 4.0: Managing The Digital Transformation. SSAM, 1st edn. Springer, Cham (2018). https://doi.org/10.1007/978-3-319-57870-5

59. Zeigler, B., Sarjoughian, H.S., Duboz, R., Souli, J.C.: Guide to Modeling and Simulation of Systems of Systems. Springer Briefs in Computer Science, 1st edn. Springer, London (2012). https://doi.org/10.1007/978-1-4471-4570-7

60. Zeigler, B.P., Mittal, S., Traore, M.K.: MBSE with/out simulation: State of the art and way forward. Systems 6(4), 40 (2018)

Author Index